Pro PowerShell for
Database Developers

Bryan Cafferky

Apress®

Pro PowerShell for Database Developers

ISBN-13 (pbk): 978-1-4842-0542-6

ISBN-13 (electronic): 978-1-4842-0541-9

Trademarked names, logos, and images may appear in this book. Rather than use a trademark symbol with every occurrence of a trademarked name, logo, or image we use the names, logos, and images only in an editorial fashion and to the benefit of the trademark owner, with no intention of infringement of the trademark.

The use in this publication of trade names, trademarks, service marks, and similar terms, even if they are not identified as such, is not to be taken as an expression of opinion as to whether or not they are subject to proprietary rights.

While the advice and information in this book are believed to be true and accurate at the date of publication, neither the authors nor the editors nor the publisher can accept any legal responsibility for any errors or omissions that may be made. The publisher makes no warranty, express or implied, with respect to the material contained herein.

Managing Director: Welmoed Spahr
Lead Editor: Jonathan Gennick
Technical Reviewer: Jason Horner and Mike Robbins
Editorial Board: Steve Anglin, Mark Beckner, Gary Cornell, Louise Corrigan, Jim DeWolf,
     Jonathan Gennick, Robert Hutchinson, Michelle Lowman, James Markham, Susan McDermott,
     Matthew Moodie, Jeffrey Pepper, Douglas Pundick, Ben Renow-Clarke, Gwenan Spearing,
     Matt Wade, Steve Weiss
Coordinating Editor: Jill Balzano
Copy Editor: April Rondeau
Compositor: SPi Global
Indexer: SPi Global
Artist: SPi Global
Cover Designer: Anna Ishchenko

Distributed to the book trade worldwide by Springer Science+Business Media New York, 233 Spring Street, 6th Floor, New York, NY 10013. Phone 1-800-SPRINGER, fax (201) 348-4505, e-mail orders-ny@springer-sbm.com, or visit www.springer.com. Apress Media, LLC is a California LLC and the sole member (owner) is Springer Science + Business Media Finance Inc (SSBM Finance Inc). SSBM Finance Inc is a Delaware corporation.

For information on translations, please e-mail rights@apress.com, or visit www.apress.com.

Apress and friends of ED books may be purchased in bulk for academic, corporate, or promotional use. eBook versions and licenses are also available for most titles. For more information, reference our Special Bulk Sales–eBook Licensing web page at www.apress.com/bulk-sales.

Any source code or other supplementary material referenced by the author in this text is available to readers at www.apress.com/. For detailed information about how to locate your book's source code, go to www.apress.com/source-code/.

Dedicated to my mother, Virginia Cafferky, who passed in 2013.
She was an example of how to live life fully, and her compassion knew no bounds.
Virginia was a librarian who loved learning and the written word,
so it is fitting that my first book be dedicated to her. Thanks Mom!

"Education is not the filling of a pail, but the lighting of a fire."

—W. B. Yeats

Contents at a Glance

Contents

About the Author

Bryan Cafferky, of BPC Global Solutions LLC, is an independent business intelligence consultant with decades of experience in information technology focused on the Microsoft stack. He is the founder and leader of the SQL PASS chapter known as The Rhode Island Microsoft Business Intelligence User Group. Bryan has spoken on a number of subjects at various PASS chapters, Code Camps, and SQL Saturdays. He has worked in banking, insurance, Internet/ecommerce, utilities, and health care. Bryan holds an undergraduate degree in Computer Information Systems from Bryant University and a Masters in Business Administration from Bentley University. Nothing makes Bryan happier than to learn and pass the knowledge on to others. You can contact Bryan at bryancafferky@outlook.com and on LinkedIn at https://www.linkedin.com/in/bryancafferky. You can join his PASS Chapter at http://www.meetup.com/The-RI-Microsoft-BIUG/. See his blog at www.sql-fy.com.

About the Technical Reviewer

Mike F Robbins is a Microsoft MVP on Windows PowerShell and a SAPIEN Technologies MVP. He is a coauthor of *Windows PowerShell TFM*, 4th Edition, and is a contributing author of a chapter in the *PowerShell Deep Dives* book. Mike has written guest blog articles for the Hey, Scripting Guy! Blog, *PowerShell Magazine*, and PowerShell.org. He is the winner of the advanced category in the 2013 PowerShell Scripting Games. Mike is also the leader and cofounder of the Mississippi PowerShell User Group. He blogs at mikefrobbins.com and can be found on twitter @mikefrobbins.

Acknowledgments

Over the course of writing this book, my father jokingly said that I could not have written the book without him. He is more right than he guessed. He is a source of encouragement, a good friend, and a great father. My mother chose well. Thanks, Dad.

Perhaps the person who sacrificed the most for this book is my life partner, Paul, who has shown nothing but complete support, faith, and patience throughout the process. Pretending to be riveted when I read my chapters out loud, his encouragement and enthusiasm were invaluable.

Most parents hope to inspire their children. However, I am humbled by the drive, determination, intelligence, and accomplishments of my daughters, Patricia and Virginia. They inspired me to pursue the challenge of writing this book and they set an example of commitment and hard work.

Thank you to Jonathan Gennick, the editor who was open to my suggested book and worked diligently with me to define its structure and content. I appreciate your patience for a fledging author learning his way. Thank you to Grant Fritchey for recommending me to Jonathan. Thanks to Jill Balzano for all your help keeping things on track. Finally, a big thank you to the entire Apress team for making this book a reality.

Thanks to Robert Cain of Pragmatic Works for his wonderful "Introduction to PowerShell" presentation that started me on my journey, and for recommending Mike Robbins as a technical reviewer for the book.

A big thanks to the technical reviewers, Jason Horner and Mike Robbins, who saved me from myself with their excellent ideas and suggestions. A special thanks to Mike for being true to the PowerShell community and convincing me to adhere to its generally accepted practices—most of them, at least.

Thank you to the PowerShell community and all the talented people who freely give so much time to help others learn and use PowerShell. Stars like Lee Holmes, Don Jones, Ed Wilson—the Scripting Guy, and Jeffrey Hicks have provided an astounding amount of excellent information on using PowerShell and are household names to any PowerShell user, including this one. A big thanks to SQL PASS and the SQL Server community. I am amazed at how knowledgeable, generous, and patient so many volunteers are in helping others learn and grow. Among those who have helped me and who truly exhibit the spirit of PASS are Matt Batalon, John Minor (MVP), and Steve Simon (MVP). Thanks to Microsoft for supporting the user community so extensively and, of course, for developing and improving PowerShell and SQL Server.

Introduction

My introduction to PowerShell came from a webinar presented by Pragmatic Works' consultant and Microsoft MVP, Robert Cain. I was amazed by PowerShell but did not have an immediate application for it. Then, I started on a contract to migrate a client from a cloud architecture to a hybrid of cloud and on-premises SQL Server. The ETL tool was not SQL Server Integration Services, and it had a number of limitations. We needed to load external files, which required a good deal of pre-processing. For example, we needed to decrypt the files and unzip them. In some cases, we needed to add a header row with column names. Multiple files had to be consolidated into one file before loading. After processing, the files had to be archived. The client had already started coding these tasks as legacy-style batch files. The deadlines were tight, and the client did not want any delays. As I reviewed the batch files, with their cryptic coding, I knew investing in this outdated technology was the wrong way to go. I convinced them to let me rewrite the scripts in PowerShell.

It was a challenge to learn a new language from scratch while developing a solution with frequent deliverables, but it turned out to be the right decision. The final solution was scalable, extensible, and reusable. Most important, my passion for PowerShell started.

Before long, I started doing PowerShell presentations at PASS chapter meetings, Code Camps, and SQL Saturdays. The more I learned about PowerShell, the more excited I became. However, I found it difficult to find books or blogs that did anything but Windows Administration tasks. I used bits and pieces of these to cobble together what I needed. I was surprised that no one had written a book that covered application or database development. Professional colleagues agreed this was lacking, which kept many from adopting PowerShell. Maybe I could step up and fill in the gap?

A colleague from my FM Global days, Grant Fritchey, had written several successful books on SQL Server, so I asked him if he would refer me to a publisher. Grant recommended me to Jonathan Gennick at Apress, which eventually led to this book. This is a labor of love. I worked hard to make the examples complex and real world enough to be useful. This poses a challenge when making the scripts work in any environment without change, but I did my best. PowerShell was originally intended to be a Windows Administration tool, and many will adamantly insist that is all it should be used for. However, I have found PowerShell to be as capable as any language, but richer in features and far less verbose. I don't recommend abandoning C# or VB.NET, but I do think there are applications where PowerShell is a better choice. In the end, PowerShell is another tool in your belt.

Why This Book?

This is the book I wish 0'dI had when I started learning PowerShell. Once I got beyond the preliminaries and the "Hello World" scripts, I found a dearth of material to go further. I searched the Internet for examples of advanced scripting, but rarely found more than a few lines, and even that was focused on Windows Administration. There are many PowerShell books available, but I found these to also be focused on administration tasks. A few books covered using PowerShell to create utilities to aid in development, but I could not find any that presented PowerShell as a development language or discussed advanced programming. For example, there are many blogs on how to retrieve data from SQL Server, but what about manipulating the data and writing it back? Professional applications need to isolate items that can change, such as server names, folder names, and credentials, so they can be easily reconfigured from one environment to the next. But I could not find any books or blogs on this subject. I found short explanations on how to create function libraries called modules, but none that explained how to include logic that controlled how the module loaded. While I found some simple examples of creating custom PowerShell objects, I could not find any that included methods that could accept parameters. This book covers all these things and more!

A challenge to learning PowerShell is that there is so much hype that no one wants to point out its bugs and limitations. Even the online Microsoft documentation sometimes omits what a command or parameter cannot do. An example this is the documentation on PowerShell transactions. The documentation leads you to think this feature is far more powerful than it is. Another potential challenge, especially to database professionals, is what PowerShell calls `nulls`. I found this to be particularly confusing and included a detailed discussion about it in the book. By reading this book, you can save many hours searching the Internet to resolve issues and questions.

Whether or not you agree that PowerShell should be used for application development, I think the language must be treated as such in order to truly see its capabilities and limitations. To summarize, the purpose of this book is to present PowerShell as a development platform and demonstrate many techniques toward this end.

Who Is This Book For?

This book is for the professional who wants to go beyond the basics and master PowerShell development. It is not intended as a reference or as a beginner guide, although it does include some background and an introduction to the basics. The ideal reader has some experience in a programming language and its related constructs, such as variables, loops, conditional expressions, etc. It helps to have a degree of comfort reading code. While most of the examples focus on data-orientated tasks, the techniques are universally applicable to professional development. Application developers and database developers will probably get the most out of this book, but anyone willing to learn and develop their PowerShell programming skills will benefit.

How to Read This Book

This book starts with the basics and develops more-advanced concepts with each chapter. It is recommended that the reader start at the beginning and read the chapters sequentially. The scripts tend to build on each other as the book progresses and often reference prior chapters. This is necessary to lay the groundwork for the truly advanced topics such as using PowerShell for ETL and developing workflows. I find the best way to learn a language is with examples. With that in mind, the approach used here is to provide a complete listing first and then walk through it a few lines at a time and explain exactly how it works.

System Requirements

The code in this book was developed and tested using:

- PowerShell 4.0

- Windows 7 SP1.

- SQL Server 2012

- Adventure Works 2008 (or later should work with those examples)

- Office 2013

- Internet Explorer 11

- PostgreSQL 9.3

About the Files...

You can download example files for this book from the Apress.com catalog page at:

`http://www.apress.com/9781484205426`

Look for the tab or link labeled Source Code/Downloads. The examples will be in a .zip archive. Download that archive. Unzip it. Begin at the readme file.

Note: Formatting of the code listings in the book was a challenge, because PowerShell does not allow a statement to continue onto another line without a special continuation character. As much as possible, these line continuation characters were added so the book matches the script files, but in some cases the line in the book may wrap. If you see a difference, the script file is the correct one.

■ ■ ■

## CHAPTER 1

PowerShell Basics

In this chapter we will discuss what PowerShell is and do a quick review of its history. We'll describe the two PowerShell environments, which are the Command Line Interface (CLI) and the Integrated Script Environment (ISE). The PowerShell CLI is used for the immediate execution of commands entered at a prompt. The ISE is the PowerShell development environment and is intended for the creation and debugging of scripts. By default, PowerShell will not allow scripts to be executed. Therefore, we will discuss how to enable scripting. Then we will discuss using the ISE to write scripts. We'll review how we can customize the ISE settings to fit our needs. Then we'll run a script with a bug in it to see how PowerShell displays error messages.

What Is PowerShell?

If you have ever used Linux or any command-line-based operating system, then you have interacted with the system by entering commands at a prompt something like this one:

```
C:\
```

Likely, you sometimes stacked a bunch of commands together and stored them in a file where they could be executed as a script. In the same way, PowerShell is a command interface to Windows, and commands can be stored in a file and then executed as script.

For those who have only used Graphical User Interface (GUI) based operating systems, a little history is in order. Before Windows, the desktop operating system was called DOS (Disk Operating System), and you had to interact with the computer via a command prompt. For example, entering dir would cause the system to display the list of files in the current folder. Needless to say, when Microsoft released Windows people were happy to leave the command line behind and click their way to happiness. In those days, the environment was simple, so doing everything, even systems administration, via a GUI was fine. But the world has changed, and now there are many resources to manage: Active Directory, Internet Information Services, SharePoint, SQL Server, Outlook, and the list goes on. As a result, doing administration by clicking and dragging is not very effective. Imagine that you need to reassign permissions on a thousand users by clicking on each one and navigating a series of GUI screens. Suddenly, the ability to create and execute command scripts is appealing. Technically, Windows always had the command line (CMD.EXE), but this feature was based on the ancient DOS technology. The commands are cryptic, and it is difficult to write and maintain complex scripts.

Microsoft saw the need for an effective scripting tool a long time ago, and their first product in this area was called Windows Script Host in 1998. However, this tool fell short of the job, and in 2006 Microsoft came out with PowerShell 1.0. It has gone through many enhancements, and currently the latest production version is 4.0 with 5.0 in prerelease.

Why Is PowerShell Important?

At first glance, we might think, so what? What's the big deal about another scripting language? The answer is that PowerShell is a lot more than just a Windows version of Linux scripting. First, it is very extensible, thus allowing users and Microsoft to add functionality very quickly. Second, assuming we install the associated modules, PowerShell can easily connect to and manage virtually any resource available to Windows, which includes SQL Server, Active Directory, IIS, SharePoint, the file system, and so forth, as shown in Figure 1-1. Third, PowerShell is completely object based, meaning all variables are objects—as is anything returned by a PowerShell command. Not only that, but PowerShell seamlessly enables us to use the latest .NET framework and COM object libraries. Technically, PowerShell is not object oriented, because it does not support creating classes or inheritance, nor does it support polymorphism. However, I will cover these limitations and discuss some effective workarounds. Note: PowerShell 5.0 is adding these features.

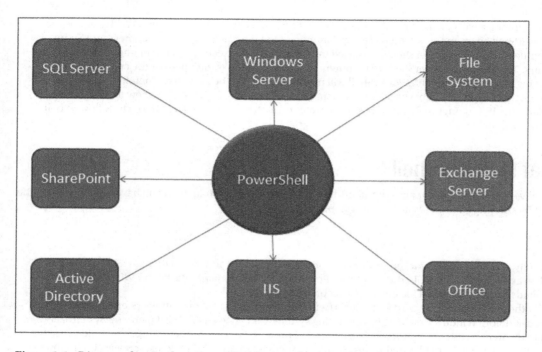

Figure 1-1. *Diagram showing how PowerShell fits into the Windows Environment*

PowerShell is architected to execute scripts either locally or remotely, provided the remote machines have been configured for remote execution. This means that we can run a script on one machine that executes scripts on any number of remote machines. Imagine deploying an upgrade to a hundred SQL Servers simultaneously or building a number of virtual machines. If you ever wondered how a large and complex environment like Azure is administered, PowerShell is the answer. PowerShell provides a high degree of scalability. Figure 1-2 shows that PowerShell can query remote machines, restart computers, and invoke commands on remote machines—all from a single PowerShell session. No wonder it is the main tool for system administrators.

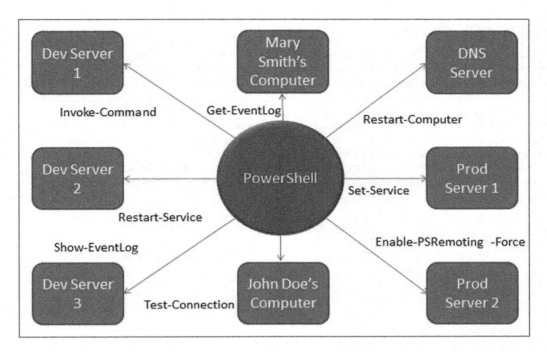

Figure 1-2. *Diagram showing that PowerShell can execute commands both locally and remotely*

History of PowerShell Versions

PowerShell was first released in 2006 and is now on version 4.0 with 5.0 in prerelease. Each release of PowerShell typically corresponds to a .NET framework version, as PowerShell is integrated with the .NET framework. Table 1-1 provides a review of each PowerShell version.

Table 1-1. *PowerShell Version History*

Version	Release Year	Description
1.0	2006	Initial release
2.0	2008	Many revisions and extensions, including support for remote execution, background execution, modules, ability to write cmdlets, and the addition of the Integrated Scripting Environment (ISE)
3.0	2011	Added new cmdlets and support for scheduled jobs, intellisense in the ISE, and delegation of tasks
4.0	2014	Addition of desired state configuration to support deployment and management of configuration data for systems, save help, and enhanced debugging; default execution policy changed to RemoteSigned
5.0	2015	Added ability to create classes with support for inheritance, Windows Management Framework 5.0 (WMF5) and extension of desired state configuration, an advanced set of features to support the automated installation of software packages.

Starting PowerShell

We can run PowerShell in two modes: the Command Line Interface (CLI) or the Integrated Scripting Environment (ISE). The CLI is a command mode in which you enter one command line at a time to be processed. It is interactive and meant as an alternative to the Windows Graphical User Interface (GUI) to get work done. If you have used the Windows command prompt, know that the PowerShell CLI is a much more powerful alternative. The PowerShell ISE, however, is a development studio for writing PowerShell code. It is provided so you can store a series of commands—called a *script*—to be executed as a program. While the CLI is focused on one-time tasks, i.e., get in, copy a file, and get out, the ISE is focused on writing a series of statements that will need to be executed repeatedly.

To start in either mode, click on the Windows Start menu, then select All Programs ➤ Accessories ➤ Windows PowerShell. Depending on your computer, you may see several versions of PowerShell, as shown in Figure 1-3.

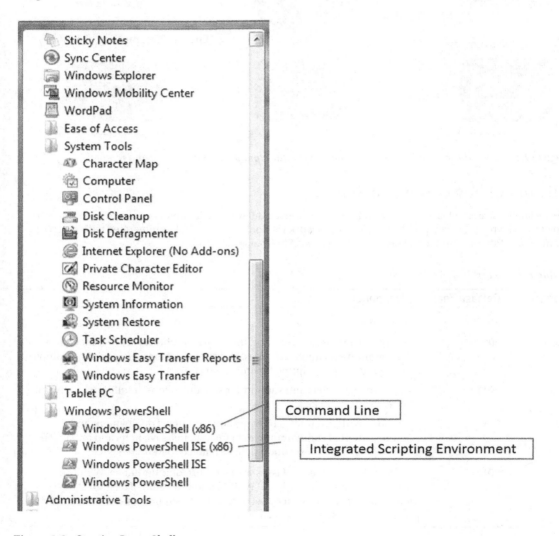

Figure 1-3. Starting PowerShell

The programs with (x86) next to them are 32-bit versions, while the programs without the (x86) are 64-bit versions. If your computer is 64 bit, you probably want to use the 64-bit versions, which, in theory, should run faster. However, if the PowerShell code requires it, you may need to use the 32-bit version. A good example of this is when you need to use 32-bit drivers. If you only see the (x86) versions, then you have a 32-bit machine.

The Command Line Interface (CLI)

To start the CLI, click on the program Windows PowerShell, or if your machine is 32 bit, click Windows PowerShell (x86). You will see a screen similar to that shown in Figure 1-4. This is the command line interface, because it only accepts one command line at a time. Note: It is possible to stack statements on a line by separating each with a semicolon which is the statement terminator.

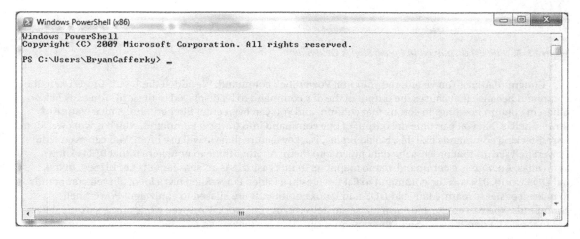

Figure 1-4. *The 32-bit PowerShell Command Line Interface (CLI)*

Using the CLI, enter your first PowerShell command. Enter the line below and you should see the result similar to that shown in Figure 1-5.

```
DIR | Out-Gridview
```

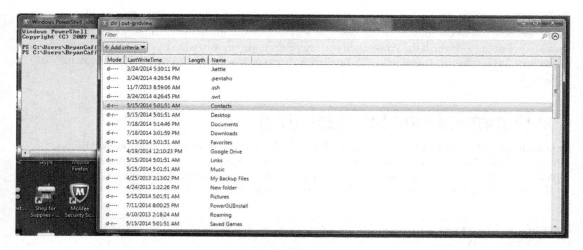

Figure 1-5. *File list displayed in PowerShell's Gridview*

Congratulations! You've entered your first PowerShell command. We added the | Out-Gridview to the command because that causes the output of the dir command to be displayed in the grid. You can click on different column headings to sort by that column, and you can even enter filter criteria. A nice feature of PowerShell is that you can pipe the output of one command into the next command, which is what was done here. Stacking commands like this, called *piping*, is a key feature that we will use often. You can even write PowerShell scripts that process the data piped into them. Another thing to note here is that DIR is known as an *alias*. An *alias* is a command-name mapping. In this case dir is an alias for Get-ChildItem. In the old DOS world, DIR was the command to list the files in a folder. PowerShell has a lot of aliased commands to make it easier to learn. Many old DOS and Linux commands are aliased to equivalent PowerShell commands. You can create your own aliases to help you in your work. However, while aliases are great for use in the CLI, I don't recommend their use in scripts that are to be used by others because it is not obvious what they mean.

There are two commands that are particularly useful to PowerShell newcomers, which are Get-Command and Get-Help. Let's see how they work.

Enter the following:

```
Get-Command
```

You will get a list of all the PowerShell commands. You can filter on the command name using wild cards, as shown below:

```
Get-Command *win*
```

This will display a list of all commands with the string "win" in the name.

If you want to know more about a specific command, such as Write-Host, you can enter:

```
Get-Help Write-Host
```

And you will get a screen full of information about the command, similar to Figure 1-6.

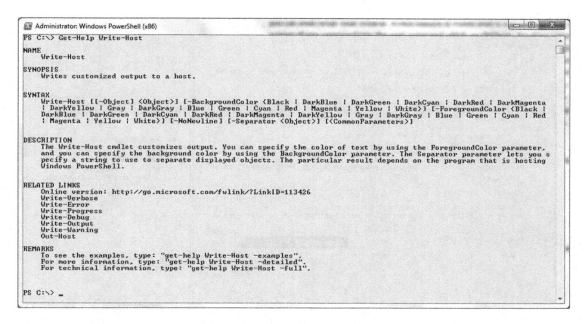

Figure 1-6. *The PowerShell console showing output of Get-Help*

Later, we will discuss how we can get PowerShell to display similar information about our scripts via the Get-Help command.

The CLI is very useful in working in the Windows environment, but let's shift gears and focus on developing scripts using the Integrated Scripting Environment (ISE). To exit the CLI, just close the CLI window.

The Integrated Scripting Environment (ISE)

Start the PowerShell ISE by clicking on the Windows Start menu ➤ All Programs ➤ Accessories ➤ Windows PowerShell ISE (or Windows PowerShell ISE (x86) if you are running a 32-bit machine). You should see a screen similar to that shown in Figure 1-7 less the code in the script editor window.

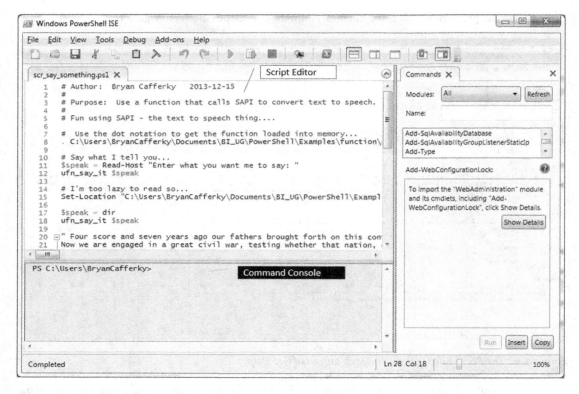

Figure 1-7. *The PowerShell Integrated Scripting Environment (ISE)*

If you have a 64-bit machine, you may think you should always just run the 64-bit version of PowerShell, i.e., the one not suffixed with x86. However, there are times when you MUST use the 32-bit version, such as when you need to use 32-bit drivers as required by Microsoft Office products such as Access. If you have trouble getting a script to run under one version, try running it under the other version.

Enabling Scripting

By default, PowerShell will not let you run scripts at all. Note: The Microsoft documentation says the exception to this is Windows Server 2012 R2 which defaults to allow local scripting. You can enable scripting by using the Set-Execution-Policy command. However, to do this you need to start PowerShell as an administrator. You can start the PowerShell CLI as administrator by clicking the Start Menu ➤ All Programs ➤ Accessories ➤ Windows PowerShell and right mouse-clicking on either Windows PowerShell or Windows PowerShell (x86), whichever applies to your machine, and selecting *Run as administrator* as shown in Figure 1-8.

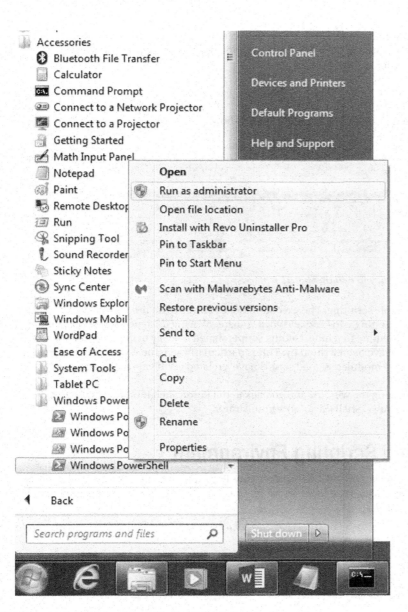

Figure 1-8. *Starting PowerShell as an administrator*

The PowerShell CLI takes one command line at a time. You want to enable scripting so you can execute lists of commands that are stored in files. To enable scripting, you need to use the command Set-ExecutionPolicy, as shown here:

Set-ExecutionPolicy RemoteSigned

When you enter this statement, you should be prompted, as shown in Figure 1-9:

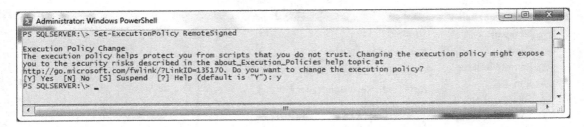

Figure 1-9. *Setting the execution policy to RemoteSigned*

Enter 'Y' at the prompt to enable scripting. The execution policy controls the modes in which PowerShell scripting is allowed. By setting it to RemoteSigned you are allowing unsigned scripts to be executed locally only, i.e., not by a remote machine. Getting scripts signed is a way of guaranteeing the script was written by who it is claimed to have been written by. This is particularly an issue if you bring in scripts from the outside, such as third-party modules. Signed scripts have a related certificate that guarantees the code has not been tampered with.

Exit the PowerShell CLI by closing the window and go back to the PowerShell ISE. Now that scripting is enabled you don't need to run the PowerShell ISE as an administrator.

Using the Integrated Scripting Environment

If it is not running, start the ISE. See Figure 1-3 for help. Enter your PowerShell script into the script pane as shown in Figure 1-10. The toolbar provides easy access to some common functions, such as the green arrow that will execute the script when clicked.

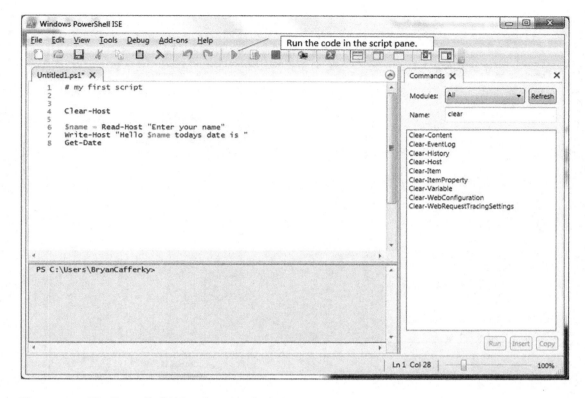

Figure 1-10. *The PowerShell ISE — Running the script*

Now let's write your first script. In the script pane, enter the script shown in Figure 1-10 and click on the green arrow which will run the script. Notice that the gray box in the toolbar turned red, as shown in Figure 1-11.

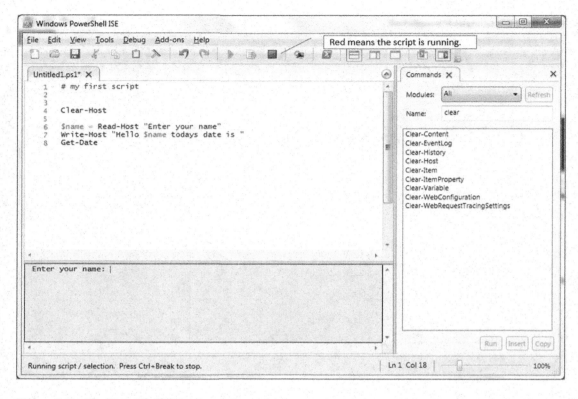

Figure 1-11. *The PowerShell ISE —A running script*

The red box indicates that the script is running. Remember this, because sometimes you may not realize your script is still executing when you are testing it.

Enter your name when prompted in the command pane. You should see a message come back greeting you and telling you the current date and time, as shown in Figure 1-12.

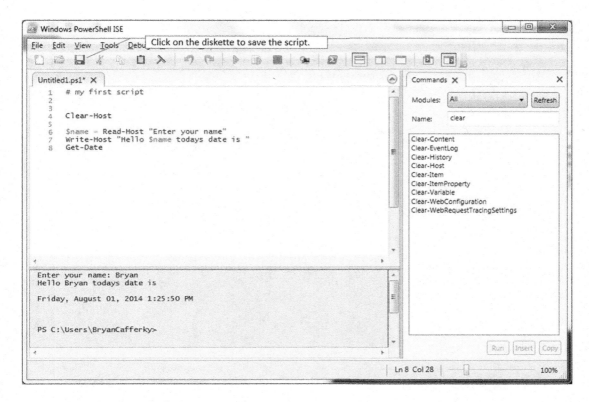

Figure 1-12. *The PowerShell ISE —Saving the script*

Congratulations! You've written your first PowerShell script! Now to save it, click on the diskette icon in the toolbar. This might be a good time to create a subfolder named WindowsPowerShell in your Documents folder if you don't already have one. WindowsPowerShell is the default place PowerShell looks for a profile script, which is a special script we will discuss later.

Let's look at the ISE screen more closely. The toolbar provides easy access to the most commonly used ISE functions. Note: Hovering the mouse over an icon will cause a short description to appear. Figure 1-13 shows what the tollbar buttons do. The toolbar is handy, but most toolbar buttons have equivalent menu bar item options as well. Some actions can also be performed using function keys.

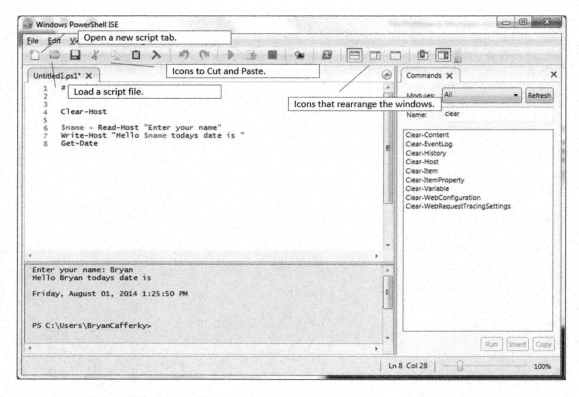

Figure 1-13. *The PowerShell ISE — Running the script*

Notice the tab on the right in Figure 1-14 labeled *Commands*. If you don't see it, select the View menu and select "Show Command Add-on." This feature is especially useful to newcomers because it provides a simple wizard-like tool to write PowerShell statements. For example, click in the Name text box and type `Get-C` as shown in Figure 1-14. Notice that the list filters down to commands that start with those letters. Now double click on `Get-ChildItem`, and the tab displays the possible parameters. Fill in some values and click the Insert button. The command is written to the Command pane, where you can execute it or copy and paste it into the Script Pane. This is a fun way to explore PowerShell commands.

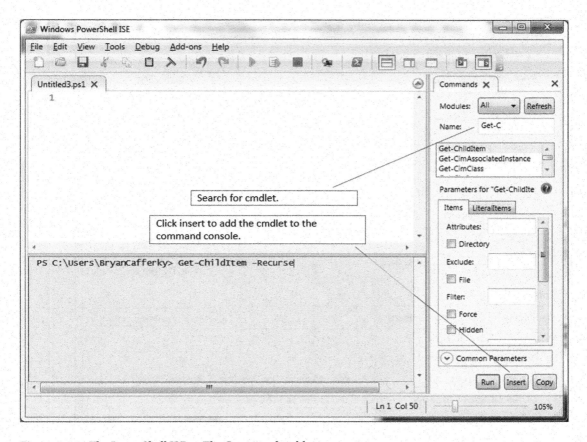

Figure 1-14. *The PowerShell ISE — The Commands add-on*

Most of the menus and options follow standard Windows conventions and are easy to learn. The File menu has options to load and save files. The Edit menu has typical editing options like Find and Replace. The View menu has some features you may not be used to including ones that will move the ISE panes around. I like the configuration above, but there are a number of possibilities. Clicking on the Tools menu bar and selecting *Options...* will display the Options screen as shown in Figure 1-15. Here you can set the ISE options to fit your preferences.

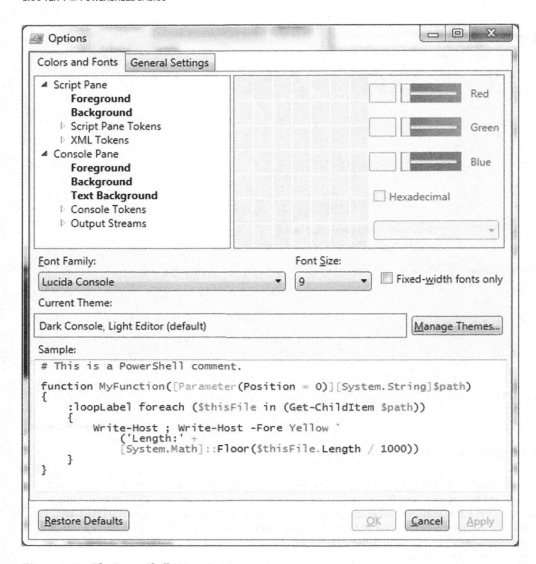

Figure 1-15. *The PowerShell ISE — Options*

Encountering Script Errors

Let's enter another script, but one with a bug. First, click the leftmost icon in the toolbar that looks like a page. Then enter the script shown in Figure 1-16.

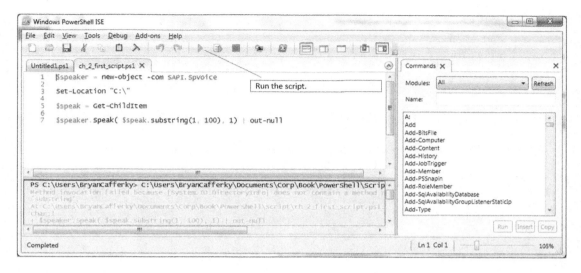

Figure 1-16. *The PowerShell ISE—Writing a script*

After entering the code in the script window, click on the green arrow to run it. Notice, you get red error messages in the command window. What went wrong? When the variable $speak was assigned a value, the variable type was not defined. You can declare the variable type or let it default to object. However, if you take the default type, you don't get the handy string methods like substring. The line causing the error is copied below.

```
$speaker.Speak( $speak.substring(1, 100), 1) | out-null
```

This line fails because $speak is not a string. Let's change the $speak variable to be a string. To do this we need to modify the line that assigns a value to $speak as shown here:

```
[string] $speak  = Get-ChildItem
```

Now click on the green arrow (or press F5), and this time you should hear your computer read the contents of the root directory of your C: drive. Note: To run just highlighted code, you would press F8.

Now save the script by clicking on the diskette icon in the toolbar. I like to save scripts like this in a subfolder named Scripts. This makes it easy to remember where I put it. As with other types of code, it is a good practice to put PowerShell scripts under source-code control and back up the files frequently.

Summary

In this chapter we discussed what PowerShell is and reviewed its history. We described the two modes of using PowerShell—i.e., the Command Line Interface (CLI) and the Integrated Script Environment (ISE). The PowerShell CLI is used for the immediate execution of commands entered at a prompt. The ISE is the PowerShell script development environment for PowerShell. By default, PowerShell will not allow scripts to be executed. We discussed how to enable scripting. Then we used the ISE to write our first script. We discussed how we can customize the ISE settings to fit our needs. Finally, we reviewed a script with an error and showed how to correct the error.

CHAPTER 2

■ ■ ■

The PowerShell Language

In this chapter, we will introduce the PowerShell language. We will start by considering some of the challenges faced when learning PowerShell, which can be discouraging. Then we will review a simple script so as to get a feel for the language. From there we will discuss comparison and mathematical operators and logical operands. PowerShell commands are called cmdlets, pronounced *command-lets*. We'll discuss Microsoft's cmdlet naming conventions, then review of some of the most prominent cmdlets. After this, we'll discuss how to use variables and go over the supported data types. PowerShell has advanced support for string manipulation, and we will review some of these features, including regular expressions, which are used for string matching, and here strings, which allow long string values that include special characters. Then we'll discuss PowerShell's control flow statements that support conditional code execution and various looping constructs. We will close the chapter by reviewing PowerShell's support for arrays and a special object called a hash table. Hash tables are arrays of key/value pairs ideal for code translations, such as a state abbreviation code for the state name. By the end of this chapter, you will have a basic grasp of the PowerShell language.

Challenges to Learning PowerShell

There are a number of challenges to learning PowerShell that can discourage beginners. First, there is the architecture of PowerShell as a scripting language; to use it, we need to learn to think differently than we would in languages like C#. For example, piping data from one command to the next is ubiquitous in PowerShell but is not something C# supports. Second, there is a competing legacy shell, CMD.Exe, which, though limited in its use, still has loyal users who resist changing to PowerShell. Third, PowerShell started as a Windows administration tool and therefore most examples available focus on Windows administration. Getting examples of typical development scenarios is difficult. Fourth, because PowerShell is so versatile, there are many ways to accomplish a given task, and this can be overwhelming to a beginner.

Thinking Differently

If you are used to programming languages like T-SQL, C#, or VB.Net, PowerShell's architecture takes some getting used to. For example, piping the output of one command into another, which is fundamental to PowerShell, is not something inherently supported by most languages. Rather, you would loop through a collection and process each item. In PowerShell you can usually avoid the work of setting up loops and individually accessing object properties. To really leverage PowerShell, you need to integrate piping into your thinking. Similarly, as a database developer, you may tend to think of variables as distinct data types, like strings and integers. After all, T-SQL variables are simple data types. PowerShell variables are always objects, which you need to bear in mind when you code. Otherwise, you could end up doing a lot more work than is needed. For example, say you want to read a text file and write out the lines that contain the string "stuff" to another file. There are a few ways to do this. Let's review two of them to contrast the different methods. First, let's set up the text file as shown in Listing 2-1.

Listing 2-1. Creating a text file

```
Set-Location $env:USERPROFILE

@"
This is just a file
stuff1
stuff2
lastline
"@ > "$env:USERPROFILE\file1.txt"
```

The first line in Listing 2-1 sets the current folder to the user's default. The second line uses a PowerShell feature called a here string to create the file. We will discuss what here strings are later, but for now just know this will create a text file with exactly what is in the quotes. Note: The following two code examples require the default location be set to $env:USERPROFILE.

One way we can perform the task is to read the text file and write out lines that contain the string "stuff" to another file, as shown in Listing 2-2.

Listing 2-2. Writing output to a file using StreamWriter

```
Set-Location $env:USERPROFILE
$streamin = new-object System.IO.StreamReader("file1.txt")
$streamout = new-object System.IO.StreamWriter("file2.txt", 'Append')

[string] $inline = $streamin.ReadLine()

Do
{
   if ($inline.Contains("stuff") )
     {
        $inline
        $streamout.WriteLine($inline)
     }
     $inline=$streamin.ReadLine()
  } Until ($streamin.EndOfStream)

$streamout.Close()
$streamin.Close()
```

This example is intentionally complex so as to show how difficult you can make your work. We could simply pipe everything to the Add-Content cmdlet as shown here:

```
Get-Content file1.txt | Where-Object { $_.Contains("stuff") } | Add-Content file2.txt
```

This statement uses the cmdlet Get-Content to load the file, pipes this into the Where-Object cmdlet that extracts lines with the word "stuff" and pipes that into Add-Content, which adds the lines to file2.txt. The lesson here is to leverage what PowerShell does best; it is worth your time searching to find an efficient method to do the work.

Again, compared to other languages you may have used, PowerShell's syntax is very different. For example, languages like VB and C# do not allow variables to start with a $, but in PowerShell all variables start with a $. In the old BASIC programming days, a variable ending with a $ meant it was a string. Comparison operators in many languages use standard mathematical syntax, i.e., > for greater than, < for less than, = for equal, etc. PowerShell uses a dash, followed by several letters for operators, i.e., -gt for greater than, -lt for less than, -eq for equals. Logical operands are –and and -or. And to make the adjustment to PowerShell even more awkward, comparisons must be enclosed in parentheses. Finally, even calling functions is different than what you may be used to. Functions and cmdlets are called without parentheses, and parameters are separated by spaces. Let's look at the PowerShell Syntax versus T-SQL and C#.

Declaring a variable...

```
PowerShell:    $myvar = "value"
C#:            string myvar = "value";
T-SQL:         declare @myvar varchar(50) = "value";
```

If condition...

```
PowerShell:    if ($myvar -eq "value") -and ($myothervar = "value") { .. some code ..}
C#:            if (myvar   == "value" and mothervar == "value") {...some code...}
T-SQL          IF @myvar = 'value' and @myothervar = 'value'  BEGIN  ...some code...
               END
```

Making a function call...

```
PowerShell:    ufn_myfunction parm1 parm2
C#:            ufn_myfunciton(parm1, parm2);
T-SQL
  Scalar       select dbo.ufn_myfunction(@parm1, @parm2);
  Table Valued  select * from dbo.ufn_myfunction(@parm1, @parm2);
```

Just Got to Get the Job Done

One of the main reasons I put off learning PowerShell was the pressure to get the job done as soon as possible. When I mentioned learning and using PowerShell, the typical response would be that there was not time, so we should do the task the tried and proven way, such as using old command batch files. The truth is that there is never a good time to slow down development by learning and applying new tools. However, how can anything ever improve if you don't take the time to do so? In my case, I was developing a new, complex ETL process with a tool other than SQL Server Integration Services (*SSIS*). It required loading a number of flat files in various formats. The ETL tool had a number of limitations. For example, all flat files must have column headings, and you must assign a single fixed file name for the ETL to reference. I needed to merge multiple files into one file and insert column headings at the top of the merged file. I also needed to decrypt and unzip the files coming in and move them to an archive folder after processing. My client was comfortable with the old DOS-style command files and had already developed some to handle these tasks. When I considered developing dozens of batch command files with the archaic syntax, limitations, and lack of reusability, I knew that was heading in the wrong direction. I sold the client on PowerShell. In retrospect, it was a great decision, because I left behind a clean library of reusable functions, thus making the ETL process more maintainable and extensible. I relate this story to you to encourage you to sell management and maybe even yourself on learning and using PowerShell.

Getting Good Examples

One of the challenges I found in learning PowerShell was the lack of examples targeted to development or ETL tasks. Since PowerShell was initially created to support Windows administration, most books, blogs, and online articles are about administrative tasks. This is starting to change, and I hope this book is a big help in that direction. More and more writing about using PowerShell for development is being published. I am convinced PowerShell is too useful to stay limited to Windows administration tasks and that developers will need to learn it.

The Paradox of Power

Ironically one of the things that makes PowerShell a challenge to master is that it is so incredibly flexible, extensible, and integrated into the Windows environment that it's easy to get overwhelmed by all the things you can do and various ways you can code it. No matter how well I think I have mastered PowerShell, I am humbled by just searching the Internet for some new applications of the language. Each release of Windows, .Net, SQL Server, SharePoint, and other Microsoft applications is quickly integrated into PowerShell. My advice is to take your time learning and focus on basic tasks you need to get done in your job.

The PowerShell Language

In this section we will discuss the PowerShell language. We'll start by reviewing a simple script in order to provide an overview of the language components and syntax. Then we will review the elements of the language, starting with comparison and mathematical operators and logical operands. We'll discuss PowerShell commands and how to use them. This will be followed by a discussion of variables and variable types. Because PowerShell's support for strings is so extensive, we will review strings and string manipulation in great detail. Then we will discuss reading and writing to flat files. After this, we'll discuss the control flow statements, which include conditional and looping constructs. An interesting feature of PowerShell is its built-in support for storing scripts in variables know as script blocks. We will discuss this useful feature in detail. PowerShell has excellent support for variable arrays, and we'll review how to make use of these features, including the special array type called a hash table, which has built-in support to look up values based on a key.

A Brief Introduction Using a Script

Now that we've considered the challenges to learning PowerShell, let's start to look at the language itself. I find the best way to learn a language is to jump right in and look at the code in a small program. This shows the syntax and also provides a sense of context on how various elements are used together. So let's take a look at Listing 2-3. It's a long script, but don't worry. We're going to discuss how it works in detail.

Listing 2-3. This script uses the Windows speech API to speak

```
<# Author:  Bryan Cafferky      Date:  2013-11-29
   Purpose:  Speaks the input...
   Fun using SAPI - the text to speech thing....
#>

# Variable declarations...
$speaker = new-object -com SAPI.SpVoice  # PowerShell defaults variables to objects

[string]$saythis = ""    # Note: declare the type as string to have the string methods available

[string] $option = "x"

while ($option.toUpper() -ne "S")
```

```
{
# --> Open Brace defines the start of a code block.
   $option = read-host "Enter d for read directory, i for say input, s to stop"

   if ($option -eq "d")
   {
     $saythis = Get-ChildItem
     $saythis = $saythis.substring(1, 50)
   }
   elseif ($option -eq "i") {
         $saythis = read-host "What would you like me to say?"
       }
   else {
         $saythis = "Stopping the program."
       }

   $speaker.Speak($saythis, 1) | out-null    # We are piping the return value to null
}                                            # --> Closing Brace defines the end of a code block.
```

This script in Listing 2-3 creates an instance of a Windows Speech Application Interface (SAPI) object and stores it in the variable $speaker. It then prompts you with a message "Enter d for read directory, i for say input, s to stop" to enter an option. If you enter 'I', you are prompted for what you want SAPI to say and then SAPI says it. If you enter a 'd', a partial list of the current directory contents, i.e., the first one hundred characters, is read. A while loop will cause the script to keep looping back until the user enters an 's' or 'S'. When you enter an 's' or 'S', the script will say "Stopping the program" and stop. This short program covers a lot of elements in the PowerShell language. I encourage you to look at the code closely to see what you can figure out about the language. How is it different from other languages you have used?

Let's review the code more closely to discover more about the PowerShell language. You can see comments in the program lines copied below. Multi-line comments start with <# and end with #>, and a single-line comment starts with #. Comments are very important for documenting what the code does.

So a comment block is coded as shown below.

```
<# Author:  Bryan Cafferky      Date:  2013-11-29
   Purpose:  Speaks the input...
  Fun using SAPI - the text to speech thing....
#>
```

And a single-line comment is coded with a # character as shown below.

```
# Variable declarations...
```

Of course, you can include a single-line comment on the same line as a statement...

```
{                                           # --> Open Brace defines the start of a
                                                    code block.
```

Let's look closer at the variables...

```
$speaker = New-Object -com SAPI.SpVoice
[string]$saythis = ""
[string]$option = "x"
```

Variables start with a $. Notice that $speaker does not have a type preceding it as the other two variables do. When you state a type in braces, such as [string], you are telling PowerShell to treat the variable as a string and to only allow string values to be stored there. It also makes the methods and properties of a string class available to the variable, which is why we can use the substring method later on. If no type is specified when you create a variable, PowerShell creates the variable as an object. You can create variables on the fly just by storing something in it; for instance, $myvar = Get-ChildItem would automatically create the $myvar variable and store the list of file properties in the current folder in it. Let's look again at $speaker:

```
$speaker = new-object -com SAPI.SpVoice
```

This line creates an instance of the COM object SAPI.SpVoice, which enables speech. PowerShell makes it very easy to create instances of COM and .Net objects. Notice that we did not have to add a reference or namespace prior to referencing the object. Many of the Windows object libraries are known to PowerShell without you having to do anything. All PowerShell variables are objects and provide a rich set of methods and properties. Avoid doing things the hard way and don't write unnecessary code to do something already provided by the object.

Next we have a loop, copied below. A loop will repeat some block of code until it reaches an end condition.

```
while ($option.toUpper() -ne "S")
{
```

This statement says to start a loop—beginning with the following open brace and ending with the matching closing brace—that will not end until the variable $option = "s" or "S". Wait a minute, it doesn't say that! Actually, rather than have to test for an upper case and lower case value, we use the built-in string function ToUpper() to convert the value to upper case before testing it. Notice that the condition is in parentheses. Although this format may be unfamiliar to you, if you omit them, the code will fail. Finally, notice the operand -ne. In T-SQL and many other languages, this would be coded as <>, but operands in PowerShell all start with a dash followed by letters. This may take some time to get used to. If you are getting a syntax error, check to make sure your operands are coded correctly. Not only are comparison operands coded this way, but so too are the logical operands—but more on that later.

```
$option = read-host "Enter d for read directory, i for say input, s to stop"
```

This line prompts the user with the message "Enter d for read directory, i for say input, s to stop" and waits for a reply to be entered. Once the user hits Enter, the response is stored in the variable $option:

```
if ($option -eq "d")
  {
    $saythis = Get-ChildItem
    $saythis = $saythis.substring(1, 50)
  }
  elseif ($option -eq "i") {
        $saythis = read-host "What would you like me to say?"
  }
  else {
        $saythis = "Stopping the program."
    }
```

The above if block does most of the work. It tests the value of $option, and if it is equal to "d", executes the immediately following statements found between the { and the }. If $option is not equal to "d", the code checks for a value of "i" and, if true, executes the immediately following statements found between the { and the }. Finally, if it reaches the else statement, the other two tests were false and it executes the statements after the else statement found between the { and the }. There are some PowerShell nuances to get used to here. First, the parentheses around the condition are required, and you will get errors if you omit them. Second, the conditional operand is not the usual = sign we might see in other languages. Finally, the braces to make off script blocks is similar to C#. Be careful when in your code that you line them up so you know you have a closing brace for each open brace. The result of this if block is that the variable $saythis is assigned a value.

```
$speaker.Speak($saythis, 1) | out-null   # We are piping the return value to null
```

This statement uses the Speak method of the object $speaker to read the string $saythis out loud. The parameter, 1, is the voice and | out-null absorbs the return of the method, much like a void statement in C#. This is done fairly often in PowerShell.

We can't be complete without our program's ending brace, copied below.

```
}
```

Operators and Operands

PowerShell comparison operators can be a bit difficult to get used to because they are not the usual mathematical operators most languages use. Instead they look like parameters with a dash prefix followed by the operand name. Logical operands are more intuitive, i.e., and, not, and !, but these also must be prefixed with a dash. Fortunately, mathematical operations use the traditional operators.

Comparison operators are used to compare values such as if A equals B. PowerShell has a comprehensive set of comparison operators. By default all operands are case insensitive. To make an operand case sensitive, prefix it with a c. The complete list of comparison operators is shown in Table 2-1.

Table 2-1. *PowerShell Comparison Operators*

Case Insensitive	Case Sensitive	Description	Case Insensitive Example
-eq	-ceq	Test for equal values.	$s -eq "test"
-ne	-cne	Test for non-equal values.	$s -ne "test"
-ge	-cge	Test for greater than or equal value.	$s -ge 5
-gt	-cgt	Test for greater than value.	$s -gt 5
-lt	-clt	Test for less than value.	$s -lt 5
-le	-cle	Test for less than or equal to value.	$s le 5
-like	-clike	Test for pattern in value.	$s -like "smith*"
-notlike	-cnotlike	Test for pattern not being in a value.	$s -notlike "smith*"
-match	-cmatch	Test for pattern using a Regular Expression.	"Megacorp" -match "corp"
-notmatch	-cnotmatch	Test for no match of a pattern using a Regular Expression.	"Megacorp" -notmatch "corp"
-replace	-creplace	Replace a set of characters with another set of characters.	$s -replace "old", "new"
-contains	-ccontains	Test if a array contains an item.	"a","b" -contains "b"
-notcontains	-cnotcontains	Test if a string does not contain a character or set of characters.	"a","b" -notcontains "b"

Logical operands connect expressions and are also prefixed with a dash. Table 2-2 shows PowerShell's logical operands with examples.

Table 2-2. *PowerShell Logical Operands*

Case Insensitive	Description	Example	Result
-and	Logical and	(5 -eq 5) -and (5 -eq 6)	false
-or	Logical or	(5 -eq 5) -or (5 -eq 6)	true
-not	Logical not	(5 - eq 5) -and -not (5 -eq 6)	true
!	Logical not	(5 - eq 5) -and !(5 -eq 6)	true

Fortunately, mathematical operators are the same as used in most languages. Table 2-3 lists the operators with a description and coding example.

Table 2-3. *PowerShell Mathamatical Operators*

Operator	Description	Example
=	Assigns a value to a variable.	$x = 5
+	Adds two values or append strings.	$x = 1 + 5
+=	Increments a variable or appends a string 'r to a string variable.	$x+=5
-	Subtracts two values.	$x = 5 - 1
-=	Decrements a variable.	$x-=5
/	Performs division on a number.	$x = 6/2
/=	Divide a variable.	$x /= 3
%	Performs division and returns the remainder.	$x = (3/10)
%=	Perform division on a variable, returning the remainder to the variable.	$x %= 3

Cmdlets

The heart of PowerShell is made up of a vast array of commands called cmdlets, pronounced *Command-lets*. We can identify command-lets by their naming, i.e., a verb and a noun separated by a dash. Taken from Listing 2-3, cmdlets are highlighted in bold on the lines below.

New-Object returns an object of the type specified, i.e., COM in this case.

```
$speaker = New-Object -com SAPI.SpVoice
```

Get-ChildItem returns the list of items in the current directory.

```
$saythis = Get-ChildItem
```

Read-Host prompts the user for input, which is stored in the variable $saythis.

```
$saythis = Read-Host "What would you like me to say?"
```

There are many command-lets, and more are added with each PowerShell release. You can even write your own command-lets. Naming follows a convention, which helps the developer get an idea of what a command-let does. Command-lets that get values start with Get, while command-lets that set a value start with Set. Here is a list of some common command-let prefixes and their meanings. For a complete list, see http://msdn.microsoft.com/en-us/library/ms714428%28v=vs.85%29.aspx

Table 2-4. *Cmdlet Verb Prefixes*

Cmdlet Verb Prefix	Meaning/Example Cmdlet
Add	Adds something on to an object. Add-Content adds to a file.
Clear	Clears out an object. Clear-Content empties a file.
Copy	Copies an item. Copy-Content copies data.
Export	Reformat or extract data. Export-CSV outputs the data in CSV format.
Format	Formats output. Format-Table formats the output as a table.
Import	Loads something into memory. Import-CSV reads in a file in CSV format.
Move	Moves something from a source to a target. Move-Item moves an item such as a file.
New	Creates an instance of an object. New-Object creates a new object instance.
Out	Outputs data. Out-GridView writes data to a windows grid.
Read	Takes input. Read-Host takes input from the keyboard.
Remove	Removes an item. Remove-Item deletes an object, such as a file.
Rename	Renames something. Rename-Item renames an object, such as a file.
Write	Outputs data. Write-Host outputs to the console.

Variables

In my work I find that most of the time my variables are either an object or a string. However, PowerShell supports a number of data types. In reality, all PowerShell variables are objects. However, by casting these objects to a type, PowerShell will treat the variable consistently with that type and expose properties and methods that are useful for the type. Table 2-5 provides a list of PowerShell variable types supported, with a description and example.

Table 2-5. *PowerShell Data Types*

Type	Description	Example Declaration
string	A string of Unicode characters.	`[string] $mvar = "somestring"`
char	A single Unicode character.	`[char] $myvar = "A"`
datetme	A datetime stamp.	`[datetime] $myvar = Get-Date`
single	Single-precision floating decimal point number.	`[single] $myvar = 12.234`
double	Double-precision floating decimal point number.	`[double] $myvar = 123.5676`
Int	32-bit integer.	`[int] $myvar = 10`
wmi	Windows Management Instrumentation instance or collection.	`[wmi] $myvar = GetWMI-Object Win32_Bios`
adsi	Active Directory Services object.	`[adsi]$myvar = [ADSI]"WinNT:// BRYANCAFFERKYPC/BryanCafferky,user"`
wmiclass	Windows Management Instrumentation Class.	`[wmiclass] $my1 = [wmiclass]'win32_ service'`
boolean	True or False.	`[boolean] $myvar = $true`

Cmdlet Output

If a cmdlet returns a value, you can either capture the output of it to a variable or push it through the pipe into another cmdlet. Values returned are objects, which means you can access the properties and methods through the variable. For example, the code below will get information about the current folder, store it in $myvar, which is then piped into Get-Member, which will list all the properties and methods available to $myvar.

```
$myvar = Get-ChildItem
$myvar | Get-Member
```

Now that we have the object loaded, we can do a lot of things with it. $myvar will display the properties of the folder in a list in the format shown below. Note: The values will be for whatever you have the current path point set at.

```
    Directory: C:\Users\BryanCafferky


Mode                LastWriteTime     Length Name
----                -------------     ------ ----
d-r--         8/15/2014   12:06 PM            Contacts
d-r--         8/15/2014   12:06 PM            Desktop
d-r--          9/3/2014    3:10 PM            Documents
d-r--          9/1/2014    6:38 PM            Downloads
d-r--         8/15/2014   12:06 PM            Favorites
d-r--         8/15/2014   12:06 PM            Links
d-r--         8/15/2014   12:06 PM            Music
d----         4/25/2013    2:13 PM            My Backup Files
d----         4/24/2013    1:32 PM            New folder
d-r--          9/3/2014    2:45 PM            Pictures
```

We can filter rows in $myvar using the Where-Object cmdlet.

```
$myvar | Where-Object  {$_.name -like "d*"}
```

The statement above will list just the lines that have a name that start with the letter 'd'.

```
   Directory: C:\Users\BryanCafferky


Mode              LastWriteTime     Length Name
----              -------------     ------ ----
d-r--        8/15/2014  12:06 PM           Desktop
d-r--         9/3/2014   3:10 PM           Documents
d-r--         9/1/2014   6:38 PM           Downloads
-a---         1/9/2014   9:13 AM         7 db.txt
```

You can also select just the properties you want and have them appear in the order you specify.

```
$myvar | Select-Object -Property Name, LastWriteTime


Name                                LastWriteTime
----                                -------------
Contacts                            8/15/2014 12:06:54 PM
Desktop                             8/15/2014 12:06:54 PM
Documents                           9/3/2014 3:10:54 PM
Downloads                           9/1/2014 6:38:20 PM
Favorites                           8/15/2014 12:06:54 PM
Links                               8/15/2014 12:06:54 PM
Music                               8/15/2014 12:06:54 PM
My Backup Files                     4/25/2013 2:13:02 PM
New folder                          4/24/2013 1:32:26 PM
Pictures                            9/3/2014 2:45:39 PM
```

These are just some examples. Let your imagination go wild as you play with variables that hold cmdlet return values. The possibilities are endless.

Strings

PowerShell's support for strings sets it above most languages. First, we have the basic string support that we would expect; i.e., we can create string variables and manipulate them. However, there is a special string type called a *here string* that is designed to store exactly what you assign it; formatting, line feeds, special characters, and all. Additionally, the string object type exposes a number of useful methods for searching, comparing, and manipulation. Some languages support a feature called *regular expressions*. Regular expressions are a standardized, powerful string pattern-matching and manipulation language. PowerShell supports regular expressions, and we will discuss how to apply this technology later.

Basic Strings

When you want to write out strings, you can enclose the value in double quotes or in single quotes. There is a big difference between what you choose. When you use double quotes, PowerShell will replace any variables or expressions in the string before it is output. See the examples below.

```
$myvar = get-date

Write-host "The date and time is $myvar `t more stuff."
```

Displays the output below.

```
The date and time is 08/09/2014 14:27:25        more stuff.
```

The variable is replaced with its value and `t is replaced with a tab.
If we code this with single quotes as shown below:

```
Write-host 'The date and time is $myvar `t more stuff.'
```

We get the output below.

```
The date and time is $myvar `t more stuff.
```

Single quotes tell PowerShell to write exactly what is in the quotes. The `t is called an *espace sequence*. That is a character that controls formatting. Some common escape characters are:

```
`b     Alert/beep
`n     New line
`r     Carriage return
`r`n   Carriage reurn and line feed, which is often used for writing to files
```

Sometimes you need a single quote to be output, and the string is already encased in single quotes. To tell PowerShell this you double the character, i.e., use two single quotes to output one single quote, as follows:

```
write-host 'This has ''single quotes''.'
```

This will display the output below.

```
This has 'single quotes'.
```

If the string is enclosed in double quotes and you need to include a double quote, put two double quotes in the string:

```
write-host "This has ""double quotes"" "
```

Writes the output below to the console.

```
This has "double quotes"
```

If we are enclosing the string in double quotes, we can just use single quotes within the string and it will be output correctly. Similarly, if our string is enclosed in single quotes and we need to include a double quote, we can include double quotes within the string and it will be output correctly. This is because the overall string quote delimiter we use is different than the quote character we want to include in the string. The examples below shows how this works.

```
write-host "This has 'single quotes'."
```

Writes the output below to the console.

```
This has 'single quotes'.
```

```
write-host 'This has "double quotes". '
```

Writes the output below to the console.

```
This has "double quotes".
```

Here Strings

Sometimes we need to assign a value to a string that has multiple lines, embedded single and double quotes, and various special characters. Doing this in C# or T-SQL or most languages is a pain, and you have to build the string by concatenating pieces. PowerShell has a special way to handle this called a here string. Let's look of using here strings in Listing 2-4.

Listing 2-4. Using here strings

```
$myvar = "Bryan"

$myherestring = @"
" Four score and $ *

Seven years... ,,, ~` ' ago

$myvar

!
"
"@

Write-Host $myherestring
```

The above script displays the output shown below.

```
" Four score and $ *

Seven years... ,,, ~` ' ago

Bryan

!
"
```

A here string is marked by the beginning and ending @ with the value in quotes. You can enter anything you want just as you want it to be retained, with carriage returns and special characters. Not only that, but embedded variables will still be expanded for you, as we can see above where $myvar is replaced with the value "Bryan". Here strings are very useful, indeed.

String Manipulation

As a database developer I often need to do some pretty hairy string manipulation. T-SQL is limited in this area, but PowerShell is the best tool for string manipulation I've ever used. Let's start with the typical things you might need to do. The comment above each statement explains what the method does. Listing 2-5 shows some examples of string manipulation.

Listing 2-5. Manipulating strings

```
[string] $mystring = "  This is a nifty nifty string. "

# Get a part of the string.
Write-Host $mystring.Substring(0,5)

# Get the length of the string.
Write-Host $mystring.Length

# Comparing...
Write-Host $mystring.CompareTo("This is a nifty nifty string.")   # 0 = a match and
-1 = no match.
Write-Host $mystring.Equals("This is a nifty string.")        # returns True or False

# Search for set of characters in the string.
Write-Host $mystring.Contains("nifty") # returns True or False

# Does the string end with the characters passed into the method?
Write-Host $mystring.EndsWith(".")    # returns True or False

# insert the set of characters in the second parameter starting at the position specified in
the first parameter.
Write-Host $mystring.Insert(5, "was ")

# Convert to Upper Case
Write-Host $mystring.ToUpper()

# Convert to Lower Case
Write-Host $mystring.ToLower()

# Strip off beginning and trailing spaces.
Write-Host $mystring.Trim()

# Replace occurences of the set of characters specified in the first parameter with the set
in the second parameter.
Write-Host $mystring.Replace("nifty", "swell")
```

Regular Expressions

Something lacking in T-SQL but available in PowerShell is built-in support of regular expressions. If you have never used regular expressions, you're in for a treat, because they support amazingly flexible pattern matching on strings.

To test if a string has only digits, you would code something like statements below:

```
$var1 = "4017771234"
$var1 -match "^[0-9]+$"   # Returns true as there are only digits.
$var2 = "401B7771234"
$var2 -match "^[0-9]+$"  # Returns false as there is a non-digit, B, in the string.
```

Regular expressions are powerful, but that power comes with complexity; regular expressions are practically a language in itself. I found the free website below that has, among other useful things, a searchable regular expression library. You can just search for the expression that fits your needs and copy it.

```
http://www.regxlib.com/?AspxAutoDetectCookieSupport=1
```

On that site, contributor Steven Smith supplied a number of useful expressions, a few of which I would like to share:

This expression tests for a phone number being in the U.S. format:

```
"333-444-5555" -match "^[2-9]\d{2}-\d{3}-\d{4}$"   # Returns True
```

This expression tests for a string matching the U.S. 5- or 9-digit zip code format:

```
"12345-1234" -match "^\d{5}$|^\d{5}-\d{4}$"   # Returns True.
```

This expression tests for string in date format MM/DD/YYYY:

```
"01/01/2014" -match "^\d{1,2}\/\d{1,2}\/\d{4}$"    # Returns True
```

```
"01/15/14" -match "^\d{1,2}\/\d{1,2}\/\d{4}$"    # Returns False
```

Editing Strings Using Regular Expressions

We can use regular expressions with the replace operator to edit strings. Some examples of this are below. The comment to the right of each example gives the result.

Replaces all occurrences of the letter e with the letter b.

```
"ppowershell" -replace 'e', 'b'  # Result is 'ppowbrshbll'
```

Replaces the letter p with the letter b only if p is the first character.

```
"ppowershell" -replace '^p', 'b' # Result is 'bpowershell'
```

Replaces the letter l with the letter b only if l is the last character.

```
"ppowershell" -replace 'l$', 'b' #. Outputs ppowershelb
```

Files

Reading in and writing to flat files is so simple in PowerShell that you may do what I did when I started, which is do a lot more work than necessary. Let's do some things with files to give you a sense of how simple it is. First let's create a text file to play with, as shown in Listing 2-6.

Listing 2-6. Creating a file for testing

```
# Create a file...
"this is a test file created for demostration purposes" > infilepsbook.txt

$myfile = Get-Content infilepsbook.txt

$myfile
```

The first line above creates a new file and inserts the quoted string into it, as the single carrot, >, is a piping symbol that tells PowerShell to create a new file or overwrite a file if one is there already. Then we use the Get-Content cmdlet to load the file into the variable $myfile. That's all you need in order to do anything you want to load a flat file into a variable.

If you enter a period just after $myfile, you will get a list of methods and properties available. Right off the bat, you have a lot of things you can do.

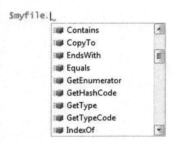

Figure 2-1. *Intellisense showing a variable's methods and properties*

I encourage you to play with the properties and methods to see what you can do. Search the Internet for examples of how people are using them.

Let's make a copy of our file.

```
$myfile > outfilepsbook.txt
```

How about concatenating these files?

```
Get-Content infilepsbook.txt > newfilepsbook.txt
Get-Content outfilepsbook.txt >> newfilepsbook.txt
Get-Content newfilepsbook.txt
```

We use Get-Content to load the file's data and then redirect it to newfilepsbook.txt. Notice that the second line uses >>. Using >> causes the data to be appended to existing file contents. Another way to do this is:

```
Add-Content newfilepsbook.txt (Get-Content outfilepsbook.txt)
```

The parentheses cause Get-Content to load outfilepsbook.txt before trying to add it to newfilepsbook.

Control Flow

In this section, we will discuss PowerShell's control flow statements, which include condition expressions and looping constructs. As expected, we have the traditional If/Else support, but we also have more concise ways of performing such conditional executions, such as by using the Switch statement. Looping constructs include a number of ways to conditionally iterate over a block of code, and we'll cover these in detail. The following link provides some nice coverage of PowerShell loops:

http://powershell.com/cs/blogs/ebookv2/archive/2012/03/15/chapter-8-loops.aspx

If/Elseif/Else

The if conditional tests for a condition, and if it is true, executes the block of code following the if. Consider this example:

```
if (test-path C:\Users\) {
   write-host "The path exists."
   }
else {
   write-host "The path does not exist."
   }
```

The statement above uses the Test-Path cmdlet to verify the path C:\Users\ exists. If it does, true is returned and the first code block executes. If the path does not exist, false is returned and the else code block executes. The braces define the beginning and end of the code block.

For more complex conditions, we can include the elseif statement to add other conditions to test for. Listing 2-7 shows an example of this.

Listing 2-7. Using If/ElseIf

```
$datetime = Get-Date
$answer = Read-Host "Enter t for time, d for date or b for both"

if ($answer -eq 't') {
   Write-Host "The time is " $datetime.ToShortTimeString()
   }
elseif ($answer -eq "d") {
  Write-Host "The date is " $datetime.ToShortDateString()
   }
else {
  Write-Host "The date and time is $datetime"
}
```

The first statement in Listing 2-7 gets the current date/time and stores it in variable $datetime. An interesting thing in the above example is that usually you can incorporate variables into a string implicitly just by inserting the variable name. However, with the object method datetime.ToShortDateString() and $datetime.ToShortTimeString() this does not work, as you get a value like "08/09/2014 08:01:01. ToShortDateString()". By rewording the Write-Host statement to close the quoted string and have the object method call separated by a space, we get the desired result. Note how many different ways the same thing can be coded.

Switch

The Switch statement provides an efficient way to test for multiple conditions with minimal code. It starts with evaluating an expression followed by each possible result and related code to be executed.

```
$datetime = Get-Date
switch (Read-Host "Enter t for time, d for date or b for both")
{
"t"      {write-host "The time is " $datetime.ToShortTimeString()}
"d"      {write-host "The date is " $datetime.ToShortDateString()}
"b"      {write-host "The date and time is $datetime"}
default  {write-host "The date and time is $datetime"}
}
```

The value entered is compared to several possible values. If a match is found, the code in between the braces will execute. Notice how compact and readable this is compared to the equivalent If statement example earlier. We even made it more concise by including the Read-Host prompt within the switch expression. The default condition will execute if none of the prior conditions are met.

This next example demonstrates how the switch statement works using the test expression with multiple True value results. Unlike if statements, switch statements continue running when True value matches are found. So it is possible that more than one code block will be executed. The results shows that test expressions that equal 10 will run:

```
switch (10)
{
  (1 + 9) {Write-Host "Congratulations, you applied addition correctly"}
  (1 + 10) {Write-Host "This script block better not run"}
  (11 - 1) {Write-Host "Congratulations, you found the difference correctly"}
  (1 - 11) {Write-Host "This script block better not run"}
}
```

When a condition is met in the switch statement, the switch statement is not exited after running the associated condition code. Rather, PowerShell continues to evaluate the other conditions, and if another condition is met, executes the associated code. In the first example, this cannot happen, but consider any case in which multiple conditions can be met, but you want the switch statement to exit once a condition has been met. This can be accomplished by adding the break statement, as shown in the example below.

```
$salesamount = 1000.00

switch ($salesamount)
{
{$_ -ge 1000}    {write-host "Awesome sales."; break}
{$_ -ge 100}     {write-host "Good sales."; break}
{$_ -lt 100}     {write-host "Poor sales."; break}
default          {write-host "Bad value"}
}
```

You may be wondering what $_ means. It is a special name PowerShell gives to the current object being processed. In the case above, $_ -ge 1000, means $salesamount –ge 1000.

For Loop

The For loop is a simple looping construct that iterates a code block a certain number of times, which is determined by comparing a counter value to a termination value and incrementing the counter value with each iteration.

```
for ($counter = 1; $counter -le 5; $counter++)
{
    Write-Host "Counter is $counter"
}
```

This code initializes the variable $counter to 1 and will execute the code in braces while $counter is less than or equal to 5. On each loop execution, $counter is incremented by 1.

For Each

The foreach loop differs from the For loop in that it iterates over an object collection, and since virtually everything in PowerShell is an object, this looping construct is very handy.

```
$objectarray = (0..3)

foreach ($number in $objectarray) {
Write-Host "Counter value is $number"
}
```

In the code above, the first line creates an array, $objectarray, consisting of integers with values 0, 1, 2, and 3. The foreach statement iterates once for each element in $objectarray.

An interesting thing about the foreach loop is that it can be coded in a very compressed manner. For example, the above code could be written as follows

```
(0..3) |% {
Write-Host "Counter value is $_"
}
```

Notice the piping | symbol followed by %, which is a placeholder for an object instance. So (0..3) implicitly creates a four-element array of integers and then pipes it into the code block that follows.

While

While and Do Until loops are very similar, but apply the test condition a little differently. The While loop will interact as long as the test condition is true. The Do Until loop will iterate until the test condition is true. Let's look at Listing 2-8, which demonstrates how to use the While loop.

Listing 2-8. Using the while loop

```
$datetime = Get-Date
$answer = "x"

While ($answer -ne "e")
{
    $answer = Read-Host "Enter d for date, t for time or e to exit"
    if ($answer -eq "t")
        {
        write-host "The time is " $datetime.ToShortTimeString()
        }
     elseif ($answer -eq "d")
        {
        write-host "The date is " $datetime.ToShortDateString()
        }
}
```

Listing 2-8 shows a good example of when you might choose to use a While loop. The first line initializes $datetime as the current timestamp. Then $answer is initialized to "x". The loop will keep repeating until the user decides to end it by entering "e" when prompted by the Read-Host cmdlet. If "t" is entered, the time is displayed. If "d" is entered, the date will display. The While and Do Until loops can provide more flexibility than the For loop we saw earlier can. Now let's look at an example of using a Do Until Loop, as shown in Listing 2-9.

Listing 2-9. Using the Do Until loop

```
$datetime = Get-Date
$answer = "e"

Do
{
    $answer = Read-Host "Enter d for date, t for time or e to exit"
    if ($answer -eq "t")
        {
        write-host "The time is " $datetime.ToShortTimeString()
        }
     elseif ($answer -eq "d")
        {
        write-host "The date is " $datetime.ToShortDateString()
        }
}
until ($answer -eq "e")
```

As you can see, there is not a big difference between the While loop and the Do Until loop. What we use is a matter of preference. However, there are a couple of differences that may matter when deciding which to use. One difference is that the condition is tested before the code block is executed with the While loop, but after the code has been executed with the Do Until block. In the example above, although $answer is assigned a value of "e" prior to the loop, the loop still executes at least once. If $answer is assigned a value of "e" prior to the While loop, the code in the loop would never execute. Another difference is that test condition operands are reversed; i.e., the While loop is executed while a condition is true, but the Do Until loop is executed until the condition is true. These differences can affect the way you need to organize your code.

Script Blocks

An interesting feature of PowerShell is that you can store scripts in variables and then execute the code by referencing the variable. This provides a simple form of reusability. For example, suppose you have a block of code you need to execute several times in a script. You could just copy the code multiple times, but then you would need to modify each copy if any changes are needed. It also would make the code harder to read. This is where reusability comes in. Later, I will cover more sophisticated ways to maximize code reusability, but script blocks offer the simplest way to get some of the benefits.

Imagine you have the following code:

```
$message = "Hi"
$title = "Title"
$type = 1

[System.Windows.Forms.MessageBox]::Show($message , $title,  $type)
```

And you want to display message boxes from different places in your script. After all, it is a useful bit of code. However, the syntax [System.Windows.Forms.MessageBox]::Show($message, $title, $type) is not very easy to remember, and it would be possible to mess up the format. What if we could code this statement in such a way as to make it easy to call wherever we need it? Listing 2-10 shows an example of how to do this.

Listing 2-10. Using a script block with parameters

```
$MsgBox = {param([string] $message, [string] $title, [string] $type)  $OFS=','; [System.
Windows.Forms.MessageBox]::Show($message , $title,  $type) }

Invoke-Command $MsgBox -ArgumentList "First Message", "Title", "1"

Invoke-Command $MsgBox -ArgumentList "Second Message", "Title", "1"

Invoke-Command $MsgBox -ArgumentList "Third Message", "Title", "1"
```

The code in Listing 2-10 creates a variable, $MsgBox, and stores the PowerShell script to display a message box in it. Once that is done, the script can be called as many times as we like. Best of all, we can pass parameters to the script so we can change the message, title, and message-box type with each call. Bear in mind, the script can be much longer and more complex, but the concept still applies. If the code for parameters is not clear to you, don't worry. I'll be covering that in detail later.

Arrays

Arrays are one of the most useful constructs in programming, and PowerShell has the best support for arrays of any language I've used. What I mean by this is that in most languages the syntax and amount of code required to effectively use arrays is significant, but in PowerShell arrays are easy to create and use. Actually, PowerShell is designed around arrays and often returns values that are arrays either of simple types or objects. For example, consider the following code:

```
$FileList = Get-ChildItem
$FileList.Count
```

$FileList contains an array returned from Get-ChildIte, which is confirmed by the Count property—i.e., the number of elements in the array. You access an element in the array by specifying the array name followed by the element number in brackets, as shown below. Notice that array numbering starts at zero by default.

```
$FileList[0]
```

In other languages, we tend to think of arrays in terms of two types, which are simple arrays and object collections. An array of integers is a simple array, whereas an array of Windows controls is a collection. However, this distinction is not relevant in PowerShell, as all variables are objects. Let's look at Listing 2-11, which shows some examples of creating arrays.

Listing 2-11. Using arrays

```
# Create an array of integers...
$array = (1,2,3,4,5)
foreach ($item in $array) {write-Host $item}

# Create an array of strings..
$array = ("Mary","Joe","Tom","Harry","Lisa")
foreach ($item in $array) {write-Host $item}
```

In Listing 2-11, notice that we can easily load the array by listing the elements separated by commas. In fact, because of the format of the value initialization, PowerShell automatically creates an array. Bear in mind that each element in the array has a number of methods and properties that can be leveraged. The ISE's intellisense makes this particularly clear, as shown in Figure 2-2.

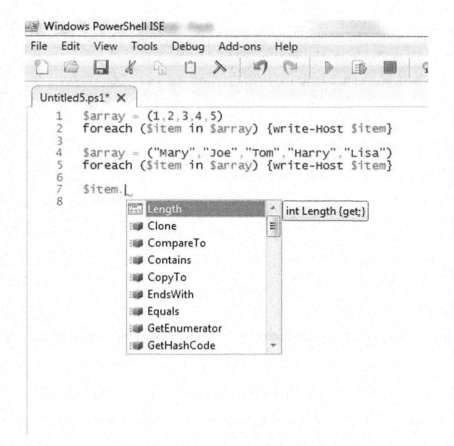

Figure 2-2. *Intellisense in the PowerShell ISE*

Associative Arrays

As a database developer, using lookup tables to get values related to a key is very common. In PowerShell, we can use associative arrays known as hash tables to do something similar. Suppose we want to translate the state abbreviation into the state name. We can do this easily, as this code demonstrates:

```
$States = @{"ME" = "Maine"; "VT" = "Vermont"; "NH" = "New Hampshire"; "MA" =
"Massachusetts"; "RI" = "Rhode Island"; "CT" = "Connecticut" }
```

The @{ characters designate a hash table is being created. We used just the New England states to keep the example short. The key is the value on the left side of the equal sign and the value returned is on the right side. In a real scenario you might load the list from a SQL Server table or flat file.

To look up the name for a state code, enter:

```
$States["RI"]   # Returns the name of the state, i.e., Rhode Island
```

The hash table object has methods that allow you to add, change, and delete rows similar to a SQL Server table. Examples of these operations are shown below.

```
# Add a new row...
$States["NY"] = "New York"

# See the list...
$States

#Remove a row...
$States.Remove("NY")

# Clear the table...
$States.Clear()

# Test for the existence of a key...
$States.ContainsKey("ME")
```

Hash tables are a feature you will probably use a lot in development work. It can be used any time we need a simple code translation.

Summary

This chapter introduced the PowerShell language. We began by discussing some of the challenges to learning PowerShell. Then we reviewed a script in detail to get a sense of the language. From there we discussed comparison, as well as mathematical operators and logical operands. Then we discussed PowerShell commands, called cmdlets (pronounced *command-lets*). We started with a discussion of Microsoft's cmdlet naming conventions followed by a review of some of the most prominent cmdlets. After this, we explained how to use variables and reviewed the supported data types. PowerShell has advanced string manipulation features, and we reviewed some these, including regular expressions used for string matching, and here strings, which support long string values that include special characters. Then we discussed PowerShell's control flow statements, conditional code execution, and various looping constructs. We closed the chapter by reviewing PowerShell's support for arrays and a special object called a hash table. Hash tables are arrays of key/value pairs ideal for code translations.

CHAPTER 3

■ ■ ■

Advanced Programming

So far, we have just scratched the surface of what PowerShell can do—many books stop there. This can leave the reader with the impression that PowerShell is fairly limited as a development platform. This chapter will dispel that notion by discussing a wide variety of advanced programming techniques. We'll start by discussing the use of parameters to support code reusability. This leads into a discussion of the `CmdletBinding` attribute, which causes PowerShell to add a number of powerful features to the code, including parameter validation, parameter sets, and support for PowerShell's common parameters. We will then get into a discussion on creating functions so as to maximize reusability. From there we will move on to a discussion of creating custom objects in PowerShell complete with properties and methods. The value of custom objects will be demonstrated by creating a custom object to support ETL. To fully leverage PowerShell we need to understand how to use the pipeline. We will discuss how to write functions that do this with the special process blocks `begin`, `process`, and `end`. PowerShell's built-in support for customizing output is limited, so we will discuss how we can create highly customized output by using a function that generates HTML. Windows has built-in support for application automation. We will review an example of leveraging this to load an Excel spreadsheet with data from SQL Server. Although we can use the SQLPS module to access SQL Server, this adds unnecessary overhead, so we will show how we can write code to directly query SQL Server tables using the .Net library. There are times when we need to know when something happens to files on the network. For example, when a file is created, we may need to run an ETL job to load it. We will discuss trapping such events in order to execute custom code using the .Net `FileSystemWatcher` object. Hopefully, by the time you finish this chapter you will be convinced of the wide-ranging capabilities of PowerShell.

Passing Parameters

The key to code reusability is the ability to pass in values that modify the code's behavior. If a piece of code displays a window but all the properties of the window are assigned as constants, this is known as hard coding, and the related code can only be used to do a very specific task. When a block of code can be called and values passed to it that customize its process, the code can be reused to fill different needs at different times.

Values passed to a block of code are called *parameters*, and most programming languages, including C#, VB.Net, and T-SQL, support parameters. PowerShell not only supports parameters, but it also has a number of advanced features that enhance their implementation and use.

When we think of using parameters, we might tend to think of code organized into functions. Functions are blocks of code given a name and possibly a set of parameters, but the function only executes when it is called. If you run the function definition without any code outside the function to call it, the function is simply created in memory. If you've written stored procedures before, know that it's similar to that. Running the code that defines the stored procedure just creates the stored procedure object and saves it to the database catalog. To execute it, you need to use the T-SQL EXEC statement. Sometimes we just want to run a series of commands without going to the trouble of creating a function. We can think of this code as fall-through code, i.e., execution starts at the first line and just falls through, executing each line. Consider the code below that will display the Windows file-selection dialog shown in Figure 3-1.

```
[System.Reflection.Assembly]::LoadWithPartialName("System.windows.forms") | Out-Null

$OpenFileDialog = New-Object System.Windows.Forms.OpenFileDialog
$OpenFileDialog.initialDirectory = "C:\"
$OpenFileDialog.filter = "All files (*.*)| *.*"
$OpenFileDialog.ShowDialog() | Out-Null
$OpenFileDialog.filename
```

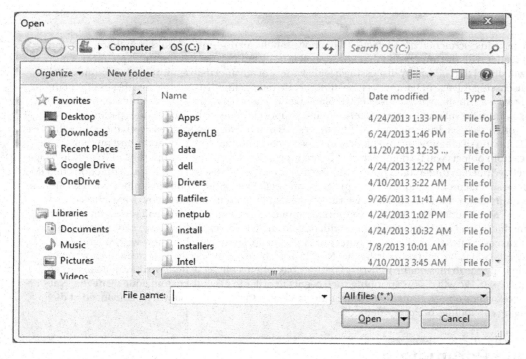

Figure 3-1. *The Open File dialog*

Note: Windows has a number of pre-built, ready-to-use dialogs called Common Dialogs that we can easily use from PowerShell. These include the Open File, Save File, Font Selection, and Color Chooser dialogs.

Displaying a file-selection dialog is a useful thing, but the code to do it is difficult to remember—and do we really want to have to cut and paste a block of code like that every time we need it? Let's rewrite this as a script that takes parameters. Parameters are passed via the $args array, which is automatically created by PowerShell. Consider the following code:

```
[System.Reflection.Assembly]::LoadWithPartialName("System.windows.forms") | Out-Null

$OpenFileDialog = New-Object System.Windows.Forms.OpenFileDialog
$OpenFileDialog.initialDirectory = $args[0]
$OpenFileDialog.filter = $args[1]
$OpenFileDialog.ShowDialog() | Out-Null
$OpenFileDialog.filename
```

This is the crudest yet simplest way to code for script parameters. $args is an automatically generated array that contains anything after the name of the script on the command line. Because the script now expects parameters, we need to save the script and call it. There is a script in the book's code files called scr_openfiledlg.ps1. Please copy it to your Documents folder and then call it with the lines below.

```
set-location ($env:HOMEDRIVE + $env:HOMEPATH + "\Documents\")

./scr_openfiledlg.ps1 "C:\" "All files (*.*)| *.*"
```

Note: This can be done from the ISE or from the CLI.

The first line above sets the current folder location to the current user's Documents folder. The second line calls the script we saved. Now we have a bit of reusable code. However, we can improve upon this by naming the parameters, as shown below.

```
Param(
  [string]$initdir,
  [string]$filter
 )

[System.Reflection.Assembly]::LoadWithPartialName("System.windows.forms") | Out-Null

$OpenFileDialog = New-Object System.Windows.Forms.OpenFileDialog
$OpenFileDialog.initialDirectory = $initdir
$OpenFileDialog.filter = $filter
$OpenFileDialog.ShowDialog() | Out-Null
$OpenFileDialog.filename
```

The above version of the script is called scr_openfiledlg_with_parms.ps1 in the book's code files. Please copy it to your Documents folder and call it with the lines below.

```
set-location ($env:HOMEDRIVE + $env:HOMEPATH + "\Documents\")
./scr_openfiledlg_with_parms.ps1 "C:\" "All files (*.*)| *.*"
```

In this code, notice that the values passed get mapped to the parameters based on the order of the values passed. We can also explicitly map the values to the parameters as shown below.

```
set-location ($env:HOMEDRIVE + $env:HOMEPATH + "\Documents\")
./scr_openfiledlg_with_parms.ps1  -filter "All files (*.*)| *.*"  -initdir "C:\"
```

Calling code using named parameters improves readability and can help you to avoid encountering bugs. It also helps to insulate you from changes to the code if the parameter order changes.

Among some useful features related to parameters, PowerShell supports parameter validation. It is implemented using the CmdletBinding statement, as shown below.

```
[CmdletBinding()]
Param(
  [Parameter(Mandatory=$True,Position=1)]
  [string]$initdir,

  [Parameter(Mandatory=$True,Position=2)]
  [string]$filter
)
```

```
[System.Reflection.Assembly]::LoadWithPartialName("System.windows.forms") | Out-Null

$OpenFileDialog = New-Object System.Windows.Forms.OpenFileDialog
$OpenFileDialog.initialDirectory = $initdir
$OpenFileDialog.filter = $filter
$OpenFileDialog.ShowDialog() | Out-Null
$OpenFileDialog.filename
```

By changing the parameter declaration to include CmdletBinding, we have made the parameters required via the Mandatory property. A nice aspect of this is that if we forget to pass a parameter, we will be prompted for it. We need to be careful about this if we are running the script in batch mode, however, such as from SQL Agent. CmdletBinding also enables the use of built-in common parameters such as Debug and Verbose, which allow the display or suppression of the output of Write-Debug and Write-Verbose statements. Write-Debug is intended to allow you to print informational messages during code testing and debugging. Write-Verbose is useful for display of extra information when desired. Let's take a look at how they are used in the following code:

```
[CmdletBinding()]
Param(
    [Parameter(Mandatory=$True,Position=1)]
    [string]$initdir,

    [Parameter(Mandatory=$True,Position=2)]
    [string]$filter
)
"VerbosePreference is $VerbosePreference"
"DebugPreference is $DebugPreference"

Write-Verbose "The initial directory is: $initdir"
Write-Debug   "The filter is:  $filter"

[System.Reflection.Assembly]::LoadWithPartialName("System.windows.forms") | Out-Null

$OpenFileDialog = New-Object System.Windows.Forms.OpenFileDialog
$OpenFileDialog.initialDirectory = $initdir
$OpenFileDialog.filter = $filter
$OpenFileDialog.ShowDialog() | Out-Null
$OpenFileDialog.filename
```

What PowerShell does when it sees Write-Verbose and Write-Debug cmdlets depends on the value assigned to $VerbosePreference and $DebugPreference variables respectively. These are predefined preference variables we can set to tell how PowerShell it should proceed after executing the Write-Verbose or Write-Debug statements. We can set them to Stop, which halts execution of the script, SilentlyContinue, which suppresses the message and continues with the line after the message, Continue which displays the message and continues with the next line, and Inquire, which prompts the user for the action they want to take. If we call the script with the Verbose switch, the $VerbosePreference variable is overridden with Continue and the Write-Verbose message is displayed. If we call the script with the Debug switch, the $DebugPreference variable is overridden with Inquire and we are prompted on what we want to do. The first two lines of the script above display the value of the preference variables. The default values for both preference variables is SilentlyContinue. Full documentation on PowerShell's preference variables is available at the link below.

http://technet.microsoft.com/en-us/library/hh847796.aspx

Please copy the script scr_openfiledlg_with_parms_andswitches.ps1 from the code accompanying the book to your documents folder. We can execute it and get the Write-Verbose message to display by including the Verbose switch parameter as shown below.

```
set-location ($env:HOMEDRIVE + $env:HOMEPATH + "\Documents\")
./scr_openfiledlg_with_parms_andswitches "C:\" "All files (*.*)| *.*" -Verbose
```

If we include the Debug switch as shown below, we are prompted on what action we want to take when the Write-Debug statement is encountered.

```
./scr_openfiledlg_with_parms_andswitches "C:\" "All files (*.*)| *.*" -Debug
```

Not only do we get the built-in Verbose and Debug switches, but we can also create switches of our own to use to control how our code will execute. The Open File dialog supports multiple-file selection if the MultiSelect property is set to True. Let's add a switch called Multifile to the script that, if passed, will enable the selection of multiple files. If not passed, the dialog will only allow one to be selected as before:

```
[CmdletBinding()]
Param(
  [Parameter(Mandatory=$True,Position=1)]
    [string]$initdir,

    [Parameter(Mandatory=$True,Position=2)]
    [string]$filter,

    [switch]$multifile
)

[System.Reflection.Assembly]::LoadWithPartialName("System.windows.forms") | Out-Null

$OpenFileDialog = New-Object System.Windows.Forms.OpenFileDialog
$OpenFileDialog.initialDirectory = $initdir
$OpenFileDialog.filter = $filter

If ($multifile) {
  $OpenFileDialog.Multiselect = $true
}

$OpenFileDialog.ShowDialog() | Out-Null
$OpenFileDialog.filename
```

A nice feature of switches is that they are optional. Suppose this script was used by hundreds of other scripts and we needed to add an option like this. The switch provides an elegant way to do so without breaking any existing calls to the script.

Functions

The reusability supported by fall-through scripts is impressive, but the real power comes when we structure our code as functions. Everything we've learned so far about scripts applies to functions, except that if we run the code of a function, it will only define the function in memory without executing. We need code outside the function to actually execute the function. Functions can call other functions—i.e., can be nested. From a coding standpoint there are only a couple of changes needed to turn the above script into a function. Listing 3-1 shows the code as a function.

Listing 3-1. Function to call Windows Open File dialog

```
function Invoke-UdfOpenFileDialog{
[CmdletBinding()]
Param(
   [Parameter(Mandatory=$True,Position=0)]
   [string]$initdir,

   [Parameter(Mandatory=$True,Position=1)]
   [string]$filter,

   [switch]$multifile
)

   [System.Reflection.Assembly]::LoadWithPartialName("System.windows.forms") | Out-Null

   $OpenFileDialog = New-Object System.Windows.Forms.OpenFileDialog
   $OpenFileDialog.initialDirectory = $initdir
   $OpenFileDialog.filter = $filter

   If ($multifile)
   {
     $OpenFileDialog.Multiselect = $true
   }

   $OpenFileDialog.ShowDialog() | Out-Null
   $OpenFileDialog.filename
}

# Example calling the function...
Invoke-UdfOpenFileDialog "C:\" "All files (*.*)| *.*"  -multifile
```

All that we did to the code above was to add the word function followed by the name we want to give the function. This was followed by an open brace, {. We marked the end of the function with an end brace, }. If we want to call functions with parameters being passed based on position, we can add the order attribute to the Parameter properties. The last line—Invoke-UdfOpenFileDialog"C:\" "All files (*.*)| *.*" -multifile —is not part of the function. We need it to call the function. It's a good idea to include a sample call at the end of a function to help in testing it and to help others understand how to call it. Just remember to comment out the call when you are done testing.

Functions are all about reusability, but if others don't understand how to use your function, it will probably not get used. Remember how PowerShell provides Get-Help to display detailed information on any built-in cmdlet? Well, we can add the documentation to our functions and make it accessible to Get-Help. It is called *comment-based help*, which means that you can add comments to your code with special tags known to PowerShell, and Get-Help will pull them out and display them on demand. Let's look at the function we saw earlier with comment-based help added in Listing 3-2.

Listing 3-2. Function to call Windows Open File dialog with comment-based help

```
function Invoke-UdfOpenFileDialog{
<#
.SYNOPSIS
    Opens a Windows Open File Common Dialog.
.DESCRIPTION
    Use this function when you need to provide a selection of files to open.
.NOTES
    Author: Bryan Cafferky, BPC Global Solutions, LLC

.PARAMETER initdir
The directory to be displayed when the dialog opens.

.PARAMETER title
This is the title to be put in the window title bar.

.PARAMETER filter
The file filter you want applied, such as *.csv in the format 'All files (*.*)| *.*' .

.PARAMETER multifile
Switch that is passed enables multiple files to be selected.

.LINK
    Place link here.
.EXAMPLE
    Invoke-UdfOpenFileDialog "C:\" "All files (*.*)| *.*"  -multifile
.EXAMPLE
    Invoke-UdfOpenFileDialog "C:\" "All files (*.*)| *.*"
#>

[CmdletBinding()]
Param(
  [Parameter(Mandatory=$True,Position=0)]
  [string]$initdir,

  [Parameter(Mandatory=$True,Position=1)]
  [string]$filter,

  [switch]$multifile
)
```

```
[System.Reflection.Assembly]::LoadWithPartialName("System.windows.forms") | Out-Null
$OpenFileDialog = New-Object System.Windows.Forms.OpenFileDialog
$OpenFileDialog.initialDirectory = $initdir
$OpenFileDialog.filter = $filter

If ($multifile)
{
  $OpenFileDialog.Multiselect = $true
}

$OpenFileDialog.ShowDialog() | Out-Null
$OpenFileDialog.filename

}
```

The statement below will call Get-Help for our function.

```
Get-Help  Invoke-UdfOpenFileDialog-full
```

Get-Help displays the comments from the function. A partial Listing of the output is shown below.

```
NAME
    Invoke-UdfOpenFileDialog

SYNOPSIS
    Opens a Windows Open File Common Dialog.

SYNTAX
    Invoke-UdfOpenFileDialog[-initdir] <String> [-filter] <String> [-multifile]
[<CommonParameters>]

DESCRIPTION
    Use this function when you need to provide a selection of files to open.

PARAMETERS
    -initdir <String>
        The directory to be displayed when the dialog opens.

        Required?                 true
        Position?                 1
        Default value
        Accept pipeline input?    false
        Accept wildcard characters? false
```

Professional features like this are critical to separating a simple scripting language from a professional development language.

There are a lot of reserved documentation tags. See this link for full coverage:

```
http://technet.microsoft.com/en-us/library/hh847834.aspx
```

It's All about Objects

As we've seen, PowerShell is object based, so it makes sense that we can create our own custom objects with properties and methods. If you are used to an object-orientated programming language like C#, be aware that the way you accomplish this in PowerShell is different. There is no support for creating classes, nor are there any statements for having source code inherit methods and properties from other source code. However, PowerShell does recognize the .Net hierarchy of objects you create and exposes their methods and properties. PowerShell provides us with an object type called psobject that is like a template to which we can add properties and methods.

Since this is a book about using PowerShell for database development, let's create a useful example of a common task—looking up values based on a key. In this case, the example creates a state object that allows us to translate the state code into the state name and the state name into the state code. It also has a Show method that will display the state data in a grid view. The nice thing about this is that once we have the function written, we can just call it when we need it. Let's look at Listing 3-3.

Listing 3-3. Function New-UdfStateObject to look up state codes

```
function New-UdfStateObject
{
 [CmdletBinding()]
        param (
               [ref]$stateobject
            )

    $instates = Import-CSV -PATH `
               (($env:HOMEDRIVE + $env:HOMEPATH + "\Documents\") + "state_table.csv")

    # Properties...

     $stateobject.value  | Add-Member -MemberType noteproperty `
                                      -Name statedata `
                                      -Value $instates `
                                      -Passthru

    [hashtable] $stateht = @{}
    foreach ($item in $instates) {$stateht[$item.abbreviation] = $item.name}

    $stateobject.value  | Add-Member -MemberType noteproperty `
                                     -Name Code `
                                     -Value $stateht `
                                     -Passthru

    [hashtable] $statenameht = @{}
    foreach ($item in $instates) {$statenameht[$item.name] = $item.abbreviation}

    $stateobject.value  | Add-Member -MemberType noteproperty `
                                     -Name Name `
                                     -Value $statenameht `
                                     -Passthru
```

```
    #  Methods...

    $bshowdata = @'

     $this.statedata | Out-GridView

'@

    $sshowdata = [scriptblock]::create($bshowdata)

    $stateobject.value | Add-Member -MemberType scriptmethod `
                                    -Name Show `
                                    -Value $sshowdata `
                                    -Passthru
}
```

Let's look at the parameter-binding code from Listing 3-3, copied here:

```
[CmdletBinding()]
param (
    [ref]$stateobject
)
```

New-UdfStateObject declares a parameter named $stateobject that is a type REF, which is a reference to the object. This allows the code to modify the object passed in—i.e., we can add properties and methods to it. When we call this function, we will pass in a psobject, and the function will add useful properties and methods to it.

The first thing the function does is load the state data from a csv file. Thank you to Dave Ross, a Boston-area web developer, for his free state data at http://statetable.com/. Please go to this site and download the file to your Documents folder as state_table.csv. The code below, from New-UdfStateObject, loads this data and adds it as a property to our object, $stateobject:

```
$instates = Import-CSV -PATH `
            (($env:HOMEDRIVE + $env:HOMEPATH + "\Documents\") + "state_table.csv")

$stateobject.value  | Add-Member      -MemberType noteproperty `
                                      -Name statedata `
                                      -Value $instates `
                                      -Passthru
```

In Listing 3-3, we use the built-in cmdlet Import-CSV to load the CSV file into a format that we can directly add as an object property. This is not a hash table, but rather is a collection of rows with each column name exposed as a property. We can add methods that can use this property to do things like display the data in a grid, which we do in the Show method. Hash tables are great, but they are limited to two columns. By loading the entire set of rows into a property, we can pull out any columns we need later.

To modify the object passed into the function, the code must set the referenced object's Value property. This is important as you cannot directly update the object; i.e., $stateobject.value = 1 will assign a value of 1 to the object. The cmdlet Add-Member is used to add a new property named statedata to the referenced object and assigns the imported CSV data to the property. The Passthru switch tells PowerShell to pipe this property to cmdlets that support piping. We must pipe the psobject variable that was passed in as a parameter into the Add-Member cmdlet to add properties or methods. Note the tick marks, `, which are used as a line continuation to keep the code readable.

The function adds two additional properties that themselves are objects—i.e., hash tables. By adding these hash tables to a psobject, we can use the hash table properties as methods that allow us to look up a value from a key. We have state names and state codes, so we add the hash table property twice, reversing the name and code on each. This lets us look up the name for a code or the code for a name.

Here is how we load the first hash table...

```
[hashtable] $stateht = @{}
foreach ($item in $instates) {$stateht[$item.abbreviation] = $item.name}

$stateobject.value | Add-Member -MemberType noteproperty `
                                -Name Code `
                                -Value $stateht `
                                -Passthru
```

Above, we create an empty hash table type with the statement 'hashtable] $stateht = @{}'. Then we loop through each row in the state data collection using the foreach statement. $item will contain the specific row on each iteration, so we use that to get the abbreviation and name and assign them respectively to the key and value properties of the hash table. By syntax convention, what is on the left side is the key and what is on the right side is the value; i.e., what will be returned is based on the key given—format is $key = $value.

Let's look at how we attach a script to a psobject shown below.

```
$bshowdata = @'

 $this.statedata | Out-GridView

'@

$sshowdata = [scriptblock]::create($bshowdata)

$stateobject.value | Add-Member -MemberType scriptmethod `
                                -Name Show `
                                -Value $sshowdata `
                                -Passthru
```

In New-UdfStateObject, the code block is assigned to variable $bshowdata. Then we cast $bshowdata to a script:block type because that is what the MemberType scriptmethod expects. A script method is really just another property, but it contains code that can be executed. $stateobject.value is piped into the Add-Member cmdlet, where the scriptmethod MemberType named Show is added.

Once we have executed the function in Listing 3-3 to define it in memory, we can use it with the lines below.

```
[psobject] $states1 = New-Object psobject
New-UdfStateObject ([ref]$states1)
```

The first line above creates a new psobject variable named $states1. Then we call the function New-UdfStateObject, passing a reference to $states1. The function will add the properties and method to $states1.

After running the above statements, enter the statement below:

```
$states1.Code["RI"]
```

You should get the following output:

```
PS C:\Windows\system32> $states1.Code["RI"]
Rhode Island

$states1.Name["Vermont"]
```

Which displays the abbreviation for the state as shown below.

```
VT
```

To demonstrate that we can add methods to the object, we added a `scriptproperty` that displays the state data in a grid via `Out-GridView`. Enter the following statement to see how this works:

```
$states1.Show()
```

We get the data presented in a grid, as shown in Figure 3-2.

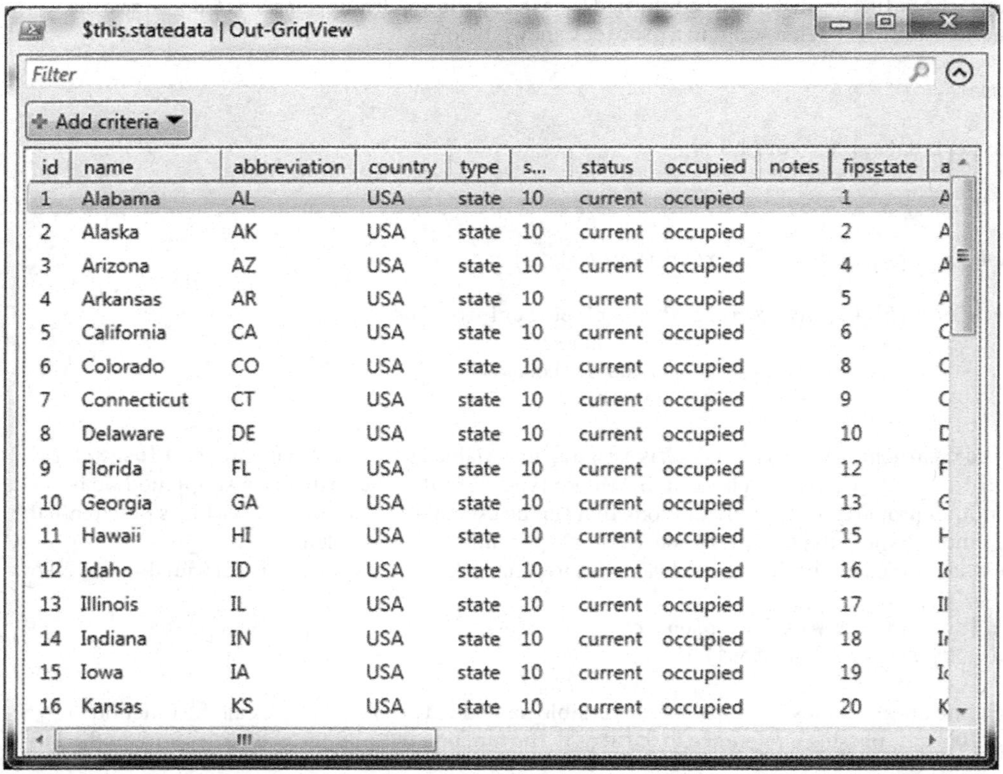

Figure 3-2. *Using Out-GridView from a function*

A Real-World Use of PowerShell Objects for ETL

Since the goal of this book is to provide real-world examples, I want to present a fairly extensive function that really shows you how to get a bang out of the psobject. This is coded as a function so it can easily be called wherever it is needed. In my ETL work I find I often have to do look ups related to geographic data—i.e., look up a territory for a region, convert currency, and so on. The function creates a psobject with the following properties and methods:

Properties

> Territory – a collection of sales territories

> Currency – list of currency codes and names

> CurrencyConversion – conversion rate by currency

Methods

> GetCountryForTerritory – returns the country a territory is in

> ConvertCurrency – converts amount passed from US dollars to the currency specified

Listing 3-4 shows the code. It is a long listing, but we will go over it in detail after you have reviewed it. Note: You must have the SQLPS module installed for the code to work. This installs automatically when SQL Server client tools are installed. For information on installing the SQLPS module, see the link below.

https://msdn.microsoft.com/en-us/library/hh231683.aspx

Listing 3-4. Function New-UdfGeoObject supports code translations

```
function New-UdfGeoObject ()
{
 [CmdletBinding()]
       param (
              [ref]$geoobject
          )

 #  Check if the SQL module is loaded and, if not, load it.
    if(-not(Get-Module -name "sqlps"))
       {
              Import-Module "sqlps"
       }

  set-location SQLSERVER:\SQL\BryanCafferkyPC\DEFAULT\Databases\Adventureworks\Tables

  # Load Territory

  $territoryrs = Invoke-Sqlcmd -Query "SELECT distinct [Name],[CountryRegionCode] FROM
  [AdventureWorks].[Sales].[SalesTerritory];" -QueryTimeout 3

  $territoryhash = @{}
  foreach ($item in $territoryrs) {$territoryhash[$item.Name] = $item.CountryRegionCode}
```

```
$geoobject.value | Add-Member -MemberType noteproperty `
                        -Name Territory `
                        -Value $territoryhash

#  Load Currency

$currencyrs = Invoke-Sqlcmd -Query "SELECT [CurrencyCode], [Name] FROM [AdventureWorks].
[Sales].[Currency];" -QueryTimeout 3

$currencyhash = @{}
foreach ($item in $currencyrs) {$currencyhash[$item.CurrencyCode] = $item.Name}


$geoobject.value | Add-Member -MemberType noteproperty `
                        -Name Currency `
                        -Value $currencyhash

# Load CurrencyConversion

$sql = "SELECT [FromCurrencyCode], [ToCurrencyCode],[AverageRate], [EndOfDayRate],
cast([CurrencyRateDate] as date) as CurrencyRateDate
        FROM [AdventureWorks].[Sales].[CurrencyRate]
        where [CurrencyRateDate] = (select max([CurrencyRateDate]) from
        [AdventureWorks].[Sales].[CurrencyRate]);"

$convrate = @{}

$convrate = Invoke-Sqlcmd -Query $sql -QueryTimeout 3

$geoobject.value | Add-Member -MemberType noteproperty `
                        -Name CurrencyConversion `
                        -Value $convrate

#  Define Methods...

#  Territory - Look Up Country

$bterritorytocountry = @'
param([string] $territory)

RETURN $this.Territory["$territory"]
'@


$sterritorytocountry = [scriptblock]::create($bterritorytocountry)

$geoobject.value | Add-Member        -MemberType scriptmethod `
                                     -Name GetCountryForTerritory `
                                     -Value $sterritorytocountry `
                                     -Passthru
```

```
$convertcurrency = @'
param([string] $targetcurrency,[decimal] $amount)

    $row = $this.CurrencyConversion | where-object {$_["ToCurrencyCode"] -eq
    "$targetcurrency" }
    $result = $row["AverageRate"] * $amount
    RETURN $result
'@

    $sconvertcurrency = [scriptblock]::create($convertcurrency)

    $geoobject.value | Add-Member -MemberType scriptmethod `
                            -Name ConvertCurrency `
                            -Value $sconvertcurrency `
                            -Passthru
}
```

The function in Listing 3-4 is similar to New-UdfStateObject we saw earlier, but this one adds a little complexity to show how much can be done using the psobject.

Loading the SQLPS module can take a couple of minutes, so to avoid reloading it with every execution of the function during testing, we can tell PowerShell to load it only if it is not loaded already by using this code:

```
if(-not(Get-Module -name "sqlps"))
{
    Import-Module "sqlps"
}
```

The SQLPS module provides easy access to SQL Server functionality. We will talk about this module in detail later, but to understand the code above, we need to review the SQL Server–related code. Consider this statement:

```
Set-Location SQLSERVER:\SQL\BryanCafferkyPC\DEFAULT\Databases\Adventureworks\Tables
```

PowerShell provides an abstraction that allows us to navigate SQL Server like we do a file system. The Set-Location cmdlet sets your context to where you specify. Note: The setting above must be modified to fit your environment and you must have the AdventureWorks database installed. The format of the cmdlet is:

```
set-location SQLSERVER:\SQL\[Machine Name]\[Instance]\Databases\[DatabaseName]\[ObjectType]
```

Where:

[MachineName]	=	The server name.
[Instance]	=	The SQL Server Instance Name, if there is more than one
[DatabaseName]	=	The database you want to access
[ObjectType]	=	The type of object you want to access, i.e., tables, views, etc.

Once the context is set, we can run multiple SQL queries, and they will all use that context, as the statement that follows does:

```
$territoryrs = Invoke-Sqlcmd -Query "SELECT distinct [Name],[CountryRegionCode] FROM
[AdventureWorks].[Sales].[SalesTerritory];" -QueryTimeout 3
```

The statement above submits the SQL statement we pass in the Query parameter and returns the results to $territoryrs. The results are in a format that can easily be used by PowerShell. For example, we could pipe the results to Out-GridView or to a file.

To get a quick sense of what this psobject offers, let's review Listing 3-5, which exercises its features. You will need to run Listing 3-4 which defines the function New-UdfGeoObject before running the code in Listing 3-5. Reminder: The function uses the SQLPS module so that module must be installed to run the code in Listing 3-5.

Listing 3-5. Example of using the geo object

```
# Create the geo object...
[psobject]$mygeo = New-Object PSObject
New-UdfGeoObject ([ref]$mygeo)

#  Since this is a hash table, let's look up a territory by country...
Write-Host "`r`nTranslate Territory directly from Global Object not fully Qualified..."
$mygeo.Territory["Southeast"]

Write-Host "`r`nTranslate Territory using a custom method..."
$mygeo.GetCountryForTerritory("Southeast")

write-host "`r`nCurrency Keys..."
write-host $mygeo.currency.Keys

Write-Host "`r`nCurrency Values..."
write-host $mygeo.currency.Values

Write-Host "`r`nTranslate currency code to currency name..."
$mygeo.currency["FRF"]

Write-Host "`r`nLook up currency conversion row for USD to Japanese Yen..."
$mygeo.CurrencyConversion  | where-object {$_["ToCurrencyCode"] -eq "JPY" }

Write-Host "`r`nConvert currency from USD to Japanese Yen..."
$mygeo.ConvertCurrency("JPY", 150.00)
```

Listing 3-5 starts by creating a new psobject variable to hold the geo object. We then call New-UdfGeoObject, passing the variable by reference, i.e., using the REF type. Passing by reference allows the function to modify the object passed in. Notice the escape characters in the Write-Host statements above—"`r`n". These send commands to the formatter; the `r is a carriage return and `n is a line feed. Embedding them like this gives us a quick way to get extra spacing rather than adding extra Write-Host statements.

Using objects as containers for methods and properties is powerful, but we can also extend the objects. In C#, classes can inherit other classes thereby gaining the methods and properties of those classes. However, that is done at the source-code level, and as of version 4.0, PowerShell does not support inheritance or the ability to define classes. *Note: PowerShell 5.0 will implement support for inheritance and the creation of classes.* Instead it is object based, and we can achieve much of the same functionality using objects. For example, we just created a useful geo object. Let's extend that object by adding more properties and methods using the function created in Listing 3-6.

Listing 3-6. Extending the geo object with the function New-UdfZipCodeObject.

```
function New-UdfZipCodeObject{

[CmdletBinding()]
      param (
             [ref]$zipobject
           )

   #  Load Zip Codes

   $zipcodes = Import-CSV `
                 ($env:HOMEDRIVE + $env:HOMEPATH + "\Documents\" + "free-zipcode-database.csv")


    $zipobject.value | Add-Member -MemberType noteproperty `
                            -Name ZipCodeData `
                            -Value $zipcodes

  #  Find Zip Codes...

    $bgetdataforzip = @'
    param([string] $zip)

    RETURN $this.ZipCodeData | where-object {$_.Zipcode -eq "$zip" }
'@

    $sgetdataforzip = [scriptblock]::create($bgetdataforzip)

    $zipobject.value | Add-Member -MemberType scriptmethod `
                            -Name GetZipDetails `
                            -Value $sgetdataforzip `
                            -Passthru
}
```

We call this function passing in the geo object we created earlier. Therefore, you must run Listings 3-4 and 3-5 before you run the code below. The idea is that we are extending the previously created object.

```
New-UdfZipCodeObject([ref]$mygeo)
```

Note that we do not declare the $mygeo object variable because it already exists. We pass it into the function to add zip code functionality, using the REF type again so the function can extend the object.

Let's test the features added using the following code:

```
Write-Host "`r`nVerify a Zip Code is valid..."
$mygeo.ZipCodeData.Zipcode.Contains("02886")

Write-Host "`r`nGet the details for a zip code..."
$mygeo.GetZipDetails("02886")

Write-Host "`r`nGet the city or cities for a zip..."
$mygeo.GetZipDetails("02886").City
```

Creating custom objects in PowerShell using psobject may seem unintuitive at first. The REF type creates a wrapper around the object that it uses to access it. The way to modify the object is to assign values to the Value property. The REF type is an object is its own right, but its purpose is to allow you to access the object it references. This is to avoid the risk that code might corrupt the object.

Remember the Pipeline

PowerShell is designed around a concept called the pipeline; i.e., the output of one command becomes the input to the next. Many cmdlets support this, which is why you can do so much with so few lines of code. To really leverage PowerShell, you need to know how to use the pipeline in your code. It really is easy to do, and if you come from a development background, it should seem fairly intuitive. For example, if you were to write a SQL stored procedure that used a cursor to read a table and step through each row, then you have the concept of programming for the pipeline already. In the stored procedure you would 1) have a start block of code that opens the cursor and perhaps gets the first row; 2) have a loop to process the rows; and 3) have an ending block that closes the cursor and cleans up after itself. In PowerShell, writing a function to process a pipeline consists of the same basic parts, which are listed here:

Begin	Runs only once upon initial call of the function and does not have access to the pipeline.
Process	Runs once for each item in the pipeline. This is where you process the pipeline.
End	Runs only after the pipeline has been processed. Good place to clean things up.

Extract, Transform and Load (*ETL*) work is all about sources, transformations, and destinations, and you can think of the pipeline as the equivalent of a *SQL Server Integration Services* (SSIS) data flow. A difference, however, is that unlike SSIS, the pipeline is seamlessly integrated into the program flow.

Listing 3-7 is a simple example of a function that processes the pipeline.

Listing 3-7. A function that processes the pipeline

```
function Invoke-UdfPipeProcess( [Parameter(ValueFromPipeline=$True)]$mypipe = "default")

{

    begin {
            Write-Host "Getting ready to process the pipe. `r`n"
        }
```

```
process {  Write-Host "Processing : $mypipe"
          }

end {Write-Host "`r`nWhew!  That was a lot of work." }

}

# Code to call the function...
Set-Location  ($env:HOMEDRIVE + $env:HOMEPATH + "\Documents\")
Get-ChildItem | Invoke-UdfPipeProcess
```

Let's look at the function declaration in Listing 3-7. The key thing is the ValueFromPipeline attribute. This tells PowerShell to expect this parameter through the pipeline. The begin block is just going to print a message once before the pipeline gets passed. Then the process will print out the items in the pipeline, in this case a list of file names. Finally, the end block prints a message after the pipeline has been processed. The output on my machine is shown below.

```
Getting ready to process the pipe.

Processing : Program Files
Processing : Program Files (x86)
Processing : SQL Server 2008 R2
Processing : Temp
Processing : Users
Processing : Windows
Processing : header.txt
Processing : set_config.bat

Whew!  That was a lot of work.

PS C:\>
```

Pipelining Example: SQL Server Deployment

A common problem in database development is managing the database deployment process—i.e., maintaining the scripts to create and alter the database objects and establishing a process to easily deploy these objects and run the scripts. In one place I worked, they developed a custom in-house application called a kit manager to do this. The SQLPS module allows us to easily execute SQL scripts, so I thought an example of a function that uses the pipeline to process SQL scripts would be a great way to explain this topic. Let's start by reviewing the steps involved.

Steps:

Begin	Connect to the target server and database. Write out log file header rows.
Process	Run each script file passed in the pipeline and write a row to the log file.
End	Clean things up and write ending log row entries.

Listing 3-8 shows a function that implements these steps to run all the scripts passed in the pipeline.

61

Listing 3-8. A function, Invoke-UdfSQLScript, that uses the pipeline to execute SQL scripts

```
function Invoke-UdfSQLScript
([string] $p_server, [string] $p_dbname, [string] $logpath)

{

 begin
 {
   if(-not(Get-Module -name "sqlps")) { Import-Module "sqlps" }

   set-location "SQLSERVER:\SQL\$p_server\DEFAULT\Databases\$p_dbname\"
   write-host $p_server $p_dbname
   "Deployment Log:  Server: $p_server Target Datbase: $p_dbname Date/Time: " `
   + (Get-Date)  + "`r`n" > $logpath
   # > means create/overwrite and >> means append.
 }

 process
 {
  Try
   {
     $filepath = $_.fullname   # grab this so we can write it out in the Catch block.
     $script = Get-Content  $_.fullname      # Load the script into a variable.
     write-host $filepath
     Invoke-Sqlcmd -Query  "$script ;" -QueryTimeout 3
     "Script: $filepath successfully processed. " >> $logpath
   }
   Catch
   {
     write-host "Error processing script: $filepath . Deployment aborted."
     Continue
   }
  }

 end
  {
    "`r`nEnd of Deployment Log:  Server: $p_server Target Datbase: $p_dbname Finished
    Date/Time: " + (Get-Date)  + "`r`n" >> $logpath
  }
}

# Lines to call the function. Passing paramters positionally...

$datapath = $env:HOMEDRIVE + $env:HOMEPATH + "\Documents\"
$scriptpath = $datapath
$logpath    = $datapath + "deploy1_log.txt"
Get-ChildItem -Path $scriptpath | Invoke-UdfSQLScript "(local)" "AdventureWorks" $logpath
```

When we run the code above to call the function `Invoke-UdfSQLScript`, we should see lines similar to the output below.

```
(local) AdventureWorks
C:\Users\BryanCafferky\Documents\create_table_1.sql
WARNING: Using provider context. Server = (local), Database = AdventureWorks.
```

The script `create_table_1.sql` was provided with the book files and should be copied to your Documents folder prior to running the code. Make sure there are no other files with an extension of `.sql` in your Documents folder as this function will attempt to execute them. This script was executed by the function `Invoke-UdfSQLScript`. The function will execute any files in the Documents folder with the `sql` file extension so if you have any SQL scripts already in Documents, they will execute also. You may see `Verbose` and `Debug` messages display depending on the setting of the PowerShell `$DebugPreference` variable. Preference variables will be discussed in Chapter 8.

In Listing 3-8, we create `$datapath` to hold the path to our files using the environment variables `$env:HomeDrive` and `$env:HomePath`, which always point to the current user's home drive and path, i.e., `C:\user1\`. Then we just concatenate the `Documents` folder to this. This is to make it easier to run the sample. In reviewing Listing 3-8, notice that functions can get the pipeline as a parameter while still supporting non-pipeline parameters. This is important because we may need to provide information to the function on how we want the pipeline processed. In this case, the server name, database name, and log file path are passed as regular parameters. Notice that we do not declare the pipeline as a parameter. You *can* do that, but in this case, the pipeline is passed to the function automatically. This is why we use the default name `$_` to access items in the pipeline. In general, it is better to declare the pipeline as a parameter, as it makes the function's intention clearer. See the code below.

```
function Invoke-UdfSQLScript
([string] $p_server, [string] $p_dbname, [string] $logpath)
```

The `begin` block is for initialization purposes as it only gets called once, before the pipeline is passed to the function. This means the `begin` block cannot access the pipeline. However, the non-pipeline parameters are available to the `begin` block. Above, the `begin` block is used to load SQLPS, if needed, and to point SQLPS to the server and database that we want the scripts to target. We also write out the header rows of our log file. Writing lines to a file is so simple that it can be overlooked. To write a line to a file, use one greater than sign, `>`, to replace the contents of the file or create it if it does not exist. To append a line to a file, use two greater than signs together, `>>`. Let's look at the begin code block below.

```
begin
{
    if(-not(Get-Module -name "sqlps")) { Import-Module "sqlps" }

    set-location "SQLSERVER:\SQL\$p_server\DEFAULT\Databases\$p_dbname\"
    write-host $p_server $p_dbname
    "Deployment Log:  Server: $p_server Target Datbase: $p_dbname Date/Time: " `
    + (Get-Date)  + "`r`n" > $logpath
    # > means create/overwrite and >> means append.

}
```

The process block is the engine of the function—i.e., it processes each item in the pipeline. So, how did we get away with not declaring the pipeline as a parameter? PowerShell automatically tracks the current item in the pipeline with a name of $_. Note: The entire pipeline is available via the default pipeline object variable $input.

```
process
{
Try
  {
     $filepath = $_.fullname    # grab this so we can write it out in the Catch block.
     $script = Get-Content  $_.fullname        # Load the script into a variable.
     write-host $filepath

     Invoke-SQLcmd -Query  "$script ;" -QueryTimeout 3
     "Script: $filepath successfully processed. " >> $logpath
  }
     Catch
     {
       write-host "Error processing script: $filepath . Deployment aborted."
       Continue
     }

}
```

When we pipe the output of Get-ChildItem as we do above, we get a number of attributes. Notice how we use the Fullname property of $_ to get the full path with file name for each script. Why are we storing the file path in the $filepath variable? As the Catch block cannot access the pipeline, we store the file path in a variable so we can display it if an error occurs. After each script has executed, we write a line to the log file.

We could write this function using the Invoke-SQLCmd parameter InputFile to directly execute the script from the file. However, if an error occurs, the error messages are written to the console and cannot be captured. There is the option to suppress error messages by passing the parameter OutputSQLErrors $false, but then the Catch block would not be fired and the error would go unnoticed. Using the Query parameter allows us to trap an error if one occurs. Now let's look at the end block below.

```
end
{
     "`r`nEnd of Deployment Log:  Server: $p_server Target Datbase: $p_dbname
     Finished Date/Time: " + (Get-Date)  + "`r`n" >> $logpath }
}
```

The end block is simple. This is where we wrap things up. There is a nice discussion of pipeline processing at this link:

https://www.simple-talk.com/dotnet/.net-tools/down-the-rabbit-hole--a-study-in-powershell-pipelines,-functions,-and-parameters/

Formatting Output

Out-GridView offers a nice presentation and user experience for out-of-the-box output viewing, but there are times when that will not suit our needs. For example, we may want to email the output. A handy cmdlet, ConvertTo-HTML, converts the output to HTML that we can then display.

Let's display the state_table.csv file we downloaded. Displaying output in HTML format is not a one-line command, because there is no built-in Out-HTML cmdlet. However, with a few lines, we can do it with the code here:

```
# First, we need to clear the SQL Provider by setting the
# location to a system folder...
Set-Location ($env:HOMEDRIVE + $env:HOMEPATH + "\Documents\")

# Now we can run our code...
$datapath = $env:HOMEDRIVE + $env:HOMEPATH + "\Documents\"
$instates = Import-CSV ($datapath + "state_table.csv")
$instates | ConvertTo-HTML | Out-File MyBasicReport.HTML
Invoke-Item  MyBasicReport.HTML
```

Providers like the one created by the SQLPS module can interfere with other PowerShell code. To reset the provider context back to the file system, the first line above uses Set-Location to change the current location to the user's Documents folder. The line after that sets $datapath to the user's Documents folder. Then, we use Import-CSV to load the file into the variable $instates. The path parameter to the Import-CSV cmdlet is enclosed in parentheses to force PowerShell to resolve the value before passing it to the cmdlet. The line below converts the data in $instates to HTML and saves to file MyBasicReport.html.

```
$instates | ConvertTo-HTML | Out-File MyBasicReport.html
```

We need the next line to get the files displayed:

```
Invoke-Item  MyBasicReport.HTML
```

Invoke-Item can execute a command or open a file, if the file type is registered on the machine—i.e., it displays the file with the program associated for the file type. This is very useful, as we can use it with Office documents and any other file types your machine knows about. In this case, it will use the default browser to display the HTML file, which should look something like Figure 3-3.

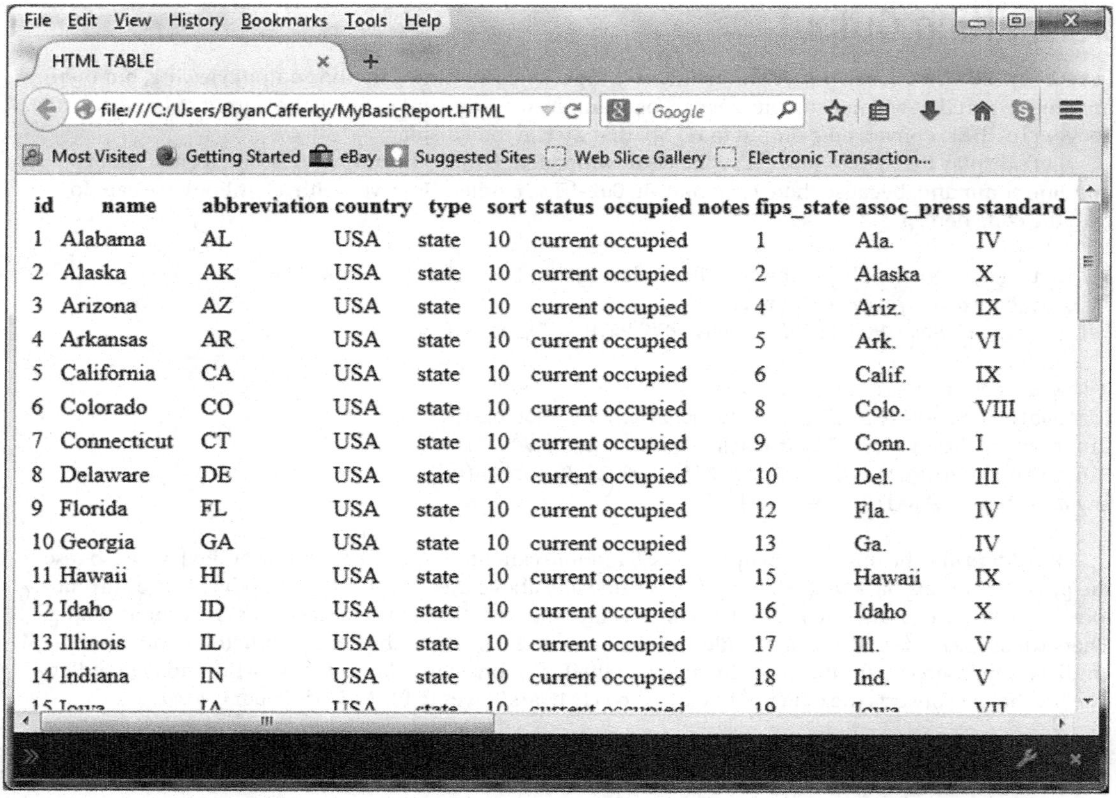

id	name	abbreviation	country	type	sort	status	occupied	notes	fips_state	assoc_press	standard_
1	Alabama	AL	USA	state	10	current	occupied		1	Ala.	IV
2	Alaska	AK	USA	state	10	current	occupied		2	Alaska	X
3	Arizona	AZ	USA	state	10	current	occupied		4	Ariz.	IX
4	Arkansas	AR	USA	state	10	current	occupied		5	Ark.	VI
5	California	CA	USA	state	10	current	occupied		6	Calif.	IX
6	Colorado	CO	USA	state	10	current	occupied		8	Colo.	VIII
7	Connecticut	CT	USA	state	10	current	occupied		9	Conn.	I
8	Delaware	DE	USA	state	10	current	occupied		10	Del.	III
9	Florida	FL	USA	state	10	current	occupied		12	Fla.	IV
10	Georgia	GA	USA	state	10	current	occupied		13	Ga.	IV
11	Hawaii	HI	USA	state	10	current	occupied		15	Hawaii	IX
12	Idaho	ID	USA	state	10	current	occupied		16	Idaho	X
13	Illinois	IL	USA	state	10	current	occupied		17	Ill.	V
14	Indiana	IN	USA	state	10	current	occupied		18	Ind.	V

Figure 3-3. *Presenting output in HTML*

It seems a bit cluttered, so let's eliminate columns we don't need via the `Select-Object` cmdlet, shown below in bold.

```
$instates = Import-CSV ($datapath + "state_table.csv")
$instates | Select-Object -Property name, abbreviation, country, census_region_name |
ConvertTo-HTML | Out-File MyBasicReport.HTML
Invoke-Item  MyBasicReport.HTML
```

This code pipes the data through the `Select-Object` cmdlet, which allows us to pick the properties we want to keep in the pipeline using the `Property` parameter. Now we will just get the columns we asked for, as shown in Figure 3-4.

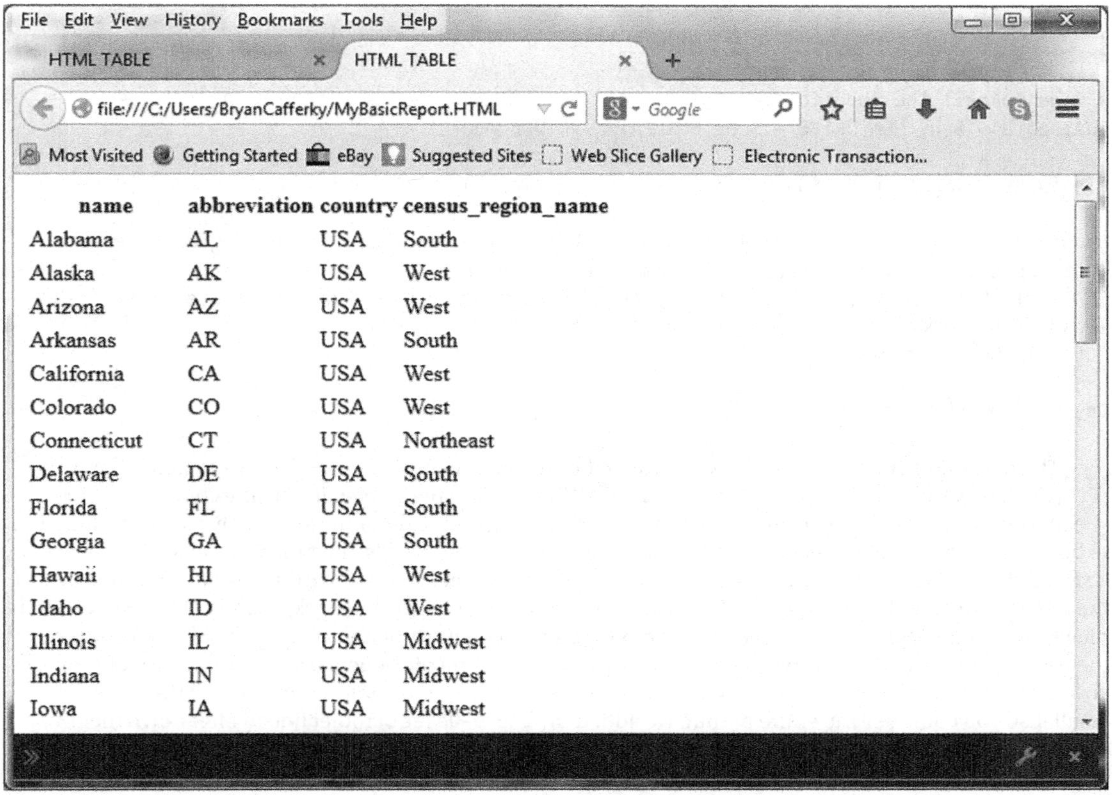

Figure 3-4. *HTML output of selected columns*

We can add more enhancements to the output. The ConvertTo-HTML supports some parameters that allow us to customize the format. Rather than do this as a one-time, hard-coded script, let's do this with a reusable function, as shown in Listing 3-9.

Listing 3-9. A function, Out-UdfHTML, that converts output to HTML

```
function Out-UdfHTML ([string] $p_headingbackcolor, [switch] $AlternateRows)
{
  if ($AlternateRows) {$tr_alt = "TR:Nth-Child(Even) {Background-Color: #dddddd;}"}

  $format = @"
<style>
TABLE {border-width: 1px;border-style: solid;border-color: black;border-collapse:
collapse;}
TH {border-width: 1px;padding: 3px;border-style: solid;border-color: black;
background-color:
$p_headingbackcolor;}
$tr_alt
TD {border-width: 1px;padding: 3px;border-style: solid;border-color: black;}
</style>
"@
```

```
  RETURN $format
}

# Code to call the function...
$datapath = $env:HOMEDRIVE + $env:HOMEPATH + "\Documents\"

$instates = Import-CSV ($datapath + "state_table.csv")

$instates | Select-Object -Property name, abbreviation, country, census_region_name |
where-object -Property census_region_name -eq "Northeast" |
ConvertTo-HTML -Head (Out-UdfHTML "lightblue" -AlternateRows) -Pre "<h1>State List</h1>"
-Post ("<h1>As of " + (Get-Date) + "</h1>") |
Out-File MyReport.HTML

Invoke-Item  MyReport.HTML
```

The new thing in the code above is the use of the custom function Out-UdfHTML to set some custom HTML styles, which are then passed to ConvertTo-HTML's -Head parameter. In the line ConvertTo-HTML -Head (Out-UdfHTML "lightblue"), the function call is enclosed in parentheses, which causes the function to be executed before being passed as the Head parameter. In other words, the function call itself is treated as a string, since that is what it passes back. There are two parameters to Out-UdfHTML; the background color of the table heading and a switch to get the table rows to alternately toggle the background color, which adds a nice effect. To turn this feature off, we would omit the switch on the function call. The small tweak of adding the function call to define and pass custom styling produces some big benefits. So as to be complete in my coverage of ConvertTo-HTML, we added the Pre and Post options. In the interest of keeping the screen shot smaller so you could see the entire output, we added the Where-Object cmdlet line to filter down the rows. The output now should look like Figure 3-5.

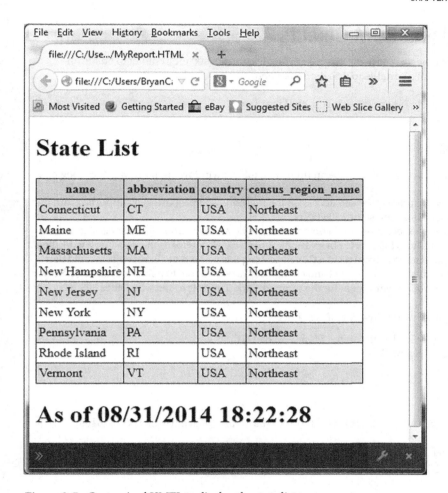

Figure 3-5. *Customized HMTL to display the state list*

In the interest of simplicity, the options that the function Out-UdfHTML supports are limited. However, more parameters can easily be added—for example, to allow the table row's toggle background color to be customizable. Note: The HTML color values can be set using names, a hexadecimal value, or by setting the three properties' RGB; for instance, RGB (255, 0, 255). For coverage of this, see the link: http://www.w3schools.com/cssref/pr_background-color.asp

The use of HTML for PowerShell output was inspired by the links that follow:

https://technet.microsoft.com/en-us/library/ff730936.aspx
https://www.penflip.com/powershellorg/creating-html-reports-in-powershell/blob/master/building-the-html.txt

Creating and Using COM Objects

Creating instances of COM objects is easy in PowerShell. Just use the New-Object cmdlet to create an instance of the object and point a variable to it as demonstrated:

```
$ie = New-Object -ComObject InternetExplorer.Application
$ie.visible = $true
$ie.silent = $true
$ie.Navigate( "www.google.com" )
```

When we run the code above, we should see an Internet Explorer window open up with the Google page displayed.

Once we have the object reference, we can access all the methods and properties it supports. From here we can navigate to sites, enter data, and so on, all via code.

Office applications such as Excel expose COM objects that can be accessed from PowerShell. The code in Listing 3-10 stores query results from SQL Server in a variable, opens Excel, and loads the data into a worksheet. Then we call the export method to write the data to a CSV file. Doing this without the Excel object would be a lot more work. Note: You must have Excel installed and change the Set-Location to point to a valid SQL Server AdventureWorks database for your environment for the script to work. This was tested with Office 365.

Listing 3-10. Loading an Excel worksheet from a SQL query

```
#  Check if the SQL module is loaded and, if not, load it.
if(-not(Get-Module -name "sqlps"))
{
   Import-Module "sqlps"
}

set-location SQLSERVER:\SQL\BryanCafferkyPC\DEFAULT\Databases\Adventureworks\Tables

$territoryrs = Invoke-Sqlcmd -Query "SELECT [StateProvinceID],[TaxType],[TaxRate],[Name]
FROM [AdventureWorks].[Sales].[SalesTaxRate];" -QueryTimeout 3

$excel = New-Object -ComObject Excel.Application

$excel.Visible = $true  # Show us what's happening

$workbook = $excel.Workbooks.Add()  # Create a new worksheet

$sheet = $workbook.ActiveSheet # and make it the active worksheet.

$counter = 0

# Load the worksheet
foreach ($item in $territoryrs) {

    $counter++

    $sheet.cells.Item($counter,1) = $item.StateProvinceID
    $sheet.cells.Item($counter,2) = $item.TaxType
```

```
        $sheet.cells.Item($counter,3) = $item.TaxRate
        $sheet.cells.Item($counter,4) = $item.Name
}

#  Exporting Excel data is as easy as...
$sheet.SaveAs("taxrates.csv", 6)
```

Suppose we wanted to use Word to print address labels using addresses in our SQL Server database. We can use the Office Word application object to do this, as shown in Listing 3-11. Note: You must have Word installed on the machine for the code to work.

Listing 3-11. Automating Word in a PowerShell script

```
Import-Module "sqlps"

$word = New-Object -ComObject Word.Application
$doc = $word.Documents.Add()

$stores = Invoke-Sqlcmd -Query "select top 10 * from
[AdventureWorks].Sales.vStoreWithAddresses;" -QueryTimeout 3

$outdoc = ""

foreach ($item in $stores) {
    $outdoc = $outdoc + $item.Name + "`r`n"
    $outdoc = $outdoc + $item.AddressLine1 + "`r`n"
    $outdoc = $outdoc + $item.City + ", " + $item.StateProvinceName + " " + $item.PostalCode
    + "`r`n"
    $outdoc = $outdoc + "`f"  # Does a page break
}

$outtext = $doc.Content.Paragraphs.Add()
$outtext.Range.Text = $outdoc
$word.visible = $true
```

This code is simplified to keep it concise, but the principles are all there. We are getting the data from SQL Server and loading it into a new Word document. We are using the escape sequences tab (`` `t ``), line feed (`` `n ``), and form feed for a page break (`` `f ``). The point here is that we can easily leverage Office applications like Excel, Word, Access, and PowerPoint.

Creating and Using .Net Objects

Accessing COM objects is easy. Creating and using .Net objects is even easier. This is because PowerShell is integrated with the .Net framework, so much so that each release of the .Net framework usually comes with a new version of PowerShell.

Since a key thing in database development is accessing databases, let's try a different way to get to SQL Server. After all, we may not always have the SQLPS module installed. Let's use the .Net library directly, as shown in Listing 3-12.

Listing 3-12. Querying SQL Server using the .Net library

```
$conn = New-Object System.Data.SqlClient.SqlConnection ("Server=(local);
DataBase=AdventureWorks;Integrated Security=SSPI")
$conn.Open()  | out-null

$cmd = new-Object System.Data.SqlClient.SqlCommand("select top 10 FirstName, LastName from
Person.Person", $conn)

$rdr = $cmd.ExecuteReader()

While($rdr.Read()){
    Write-Host "Name: " $rdr['FirstName'] $rdr['LastName']
}

$conn.Close()
$rdr.Close()
```

The nice thing about the code in Listing 3-12 is that it should always work and it has less overhead than the SQLPS module. Since we don't want a COM object, we omit the COM parameter and request a specific .Net object, i.e., System.Data.SqlClient.SqlConnection. When actually using this code, a good idea would be to create a function with parameters for the server and database name. Note: Although the line below wraps, it must be all on one line.

```
$conn = new-Object System.Data.SqlClient.
SqlConnection("Server=(local);DataBase=AdventureWorks;Integrated Security=SSPI")
```

This code creates the connection object, which is our hook into the database. We open the connection with this statement:

```
$conn.Open()  | out-null
```

This line opens the database connection, but to do something with it, we need to create a command object, as shown here:

```
$cmd = new-Object `
System.Data.SqlClient.SqlCommand("select top 10 FirstName, LastName from Person.Person",
$conn)
```

Above, we pass the query string in as the first parameter and the connection object as the second, and we get the command object returned. We could do any type of SQL command including calling stored procedures with parameters, which we will cover later. The line below will execute the query using ExecuteReader.

```
$rdr = $cmd.ExecuteReader()
```

The line above calls the command object ExecuteReader method, which runs the query and returns a reader object. We can use the Read method to get the query results, as shown here:

```
While($rdr.Read())
{
    Write-Host "Name: " $rdr['FirstName'] $rdr['LastName']
}
```

The While loop above iterates over the results returned by the ExecuteReader writing the first and last name columns to the console. The loop automatically ends after all the rows have been processed. Then we just close things up with these statements:

```
$conn.Close()
$rdr.Close()
```

Remember to close your connection and reader objects. Holding database connections indefinitely ties up valuable resources.

Waiting for a File

Sometimes we need to take an action when an event occurs, such as a new file arriving on the server. There is a .Net object we can use to do this called the File System Watcher. To use it, we register a subscription to the event we want monitored and specify the code to execute when the event occurs. In the interest of making the examples reusable, the code in Listing 3-13 is formatted as a function.

Listing 3-13. Function Register-UdfFileCreateEvent to trap file events

```
function Register-UdfFileCreateEvent([string] $source, [string] $filter)
{
   try
   {
     Write-Host "Watching $source for new files..."

     $fsw = New-Object IO.FileSystemWatcher $source, $filter -Property
     @{IncludeSubdirectories = $false; NotifyFilter = [IO.NotifyFilters]'FileName,
     LastWrite'}

     Register-ObjectEvent $fsw Created -SourceIdentifier FileCreated -Action {
     write-host "Your file has arrived."   }

   }
   catch
   {
     "Error registering file create event."
   }
}

$datapath = $env:HOMEDRIVE + $env:HOMEPATH + "\Documents\"
Register-UdfFileCreateEvent $datapath "*.txt"
```

The Try/Catch command used in Listing 3-13 is a nice feature supported by PowerShell. PowerShell will try to execute the statements between the braces after the Try statement. If it fails, the statements in the Catch block are executed. This is an elegant way to trap errors. The line copied below creates a FileSystemWatcher object.

```
$fsw = New-Object IO.FileSystemWatcher $source, $filter -Property @{IncludeSubdirectories =
$false; NotifyFilter = [IO.NotifyFilters]'FileName, LastWrite'}
```

The statement above creates a `FileSystemWatcher` object where $source is the folder to be monitored and $filter is the file pattern to be looked for. In this case, we want to fire the event for any file ending in .txt. Subdirectories will not be monitored due to the parameter IncludeSubdirectories = $false. Then we need to register the event we want to monitor, which the following code does:

```
Register-ObjectEvent $fsw Created -SourceIdentifier FileCreated -Action {
    write-host "Your file has arrived."   }
```

The line above is subscribing to the `FileCreated` event, and the code enclosed in braces after the `Action` parameter is the code that will be executed when the event occurs; i.e., the line "Your file has arrived." will be displayed.

We are pushing the work of waiting for the file to arrive to Windows. We can also subscribe to `FileDeleted` and `FileChanged` events. However, you can only subscribe to one type of `FileWatcher` event at a time—i.e., once you've subscribed to the `FileCreated` event, you cannot add another subscription to that event. To remove a subscription from an event, we use the `Unregister-Event` cmdlet, passing to the event type as shown here:

```
Unregister-Event FileDeleted
Unregister-Event FileCreated
Unregister-Event FileChanged
```

Summary

The goal of this chapter is to demonstrate the wide-ranging capabilities of PowerShell as a development platform. To this end, we discussed a wide variety of advanced programming techniques. We started by discussing the use of parameters to support code reusability. This led to a discussion of the `CmdletBinding` attribute, which causes PowerShell to add a number of powerful features to our code, including parameter validation, parameter sets, and support for PowerShell's common parameters. Since maximum reusability can only be accomplished with functions, we discussed how to develop functions using examples. From here we moved on to a discussion of creating custom objects in PowerShell complete with properties and methods. To fully leverage PowerShell, we need to understand how to use the pipeline. We discussed how to write functions that employ the special code blocks `begin`, `process`, and `end` to use the pipeline. Then we discussed how we can create highly customized output using a function that generates HTML. Windows has built-in support for application automation, so we reviewed an example of leveraging this to load an Excel spreadsheet with data from SQL Server and an example of Word automation. Although we can use the SQLPS module to access SQL Server, this adds unnecessary overhead, so we demonstrated how we can write code to directly query SQL Server tables using the .Net library. There are times when we need to know when something happens to files on the network. For example, when a file is created, we may need to run an ETL job to load it. We discussed trapping such events to execute custom code using the .Net `FileSystemWatcher` object. Hopefully, the limitless capabilities of PowerShell as a development language have been successfully demonstrated.

CHAPTER 4

■ ■ ■

Writing Scripts

This chapter focuses on PowerShell features critical to developing professional code. We will start by discussing the `Set-StrictMode` cmdlet that protects us from uninitialized variables, incorrect method calls, and invalid property references. Then we'll discuss how to gracefully handle errors raised when your scripts execute. Error handling leads us into a discussion of common cmdlet parameters, so called, because all the built-in cmdlets support them. Then we introduce the PowerShell Integrated Script Environment's debugging features. Since PowerShell has excellent support for event-driven programming, we proceed with a discussion of implementing Windows forms and events to provide a GUI for our scripts. Building on this, we show how events can be used with other .NET objects. Then we discuss PowerShell's implementation of transaction support via a set of special cmdlets. This is an important section, as PowerShell transactions are not what we might expect. Finally, we will briefly discuss the PowerShell ISE options; what they do, and how to use them. It is easy to overlook these features, but they can make development easier.

Strict Mode

PowerShell is very loose about enforcing variable initialization, property name references, and call formats. This can cause bugs that are difficult to track down. The `Set-StrictMode` cmdlet was added in version 2.0 to help with this. By default, strict mode is off, but you can turn it on with the `Set-StrictMode` cmdlet. You need to pass the `Version` parameter to tell PowerShell the level of enforcement you want.

To get the benefits of strict mode with the fewest rule enforcements, `-Version 1` is passed, i.e., `Set-StrictMode -Version 1`.

To get stronger enforcement, you want to pass `-Version 2`, i.e., `Set-StrictMode -Version 2`.

To get the strictest enforcement available, you would enter `Set-StrictMode -Version Latest`. The PowerShell documentation states that using `-Version Latest` will automatically give you the strictest rules available, even in future PowerShell releases. In other words, if Microsoft adds a new Version parameter value of 3, using `Latest` would automatically upgrade the enforcement to that level. Be careful if you use this, because it may mean that scripts that had been working suddenly break when you upgrade to a new release of PowerShell.

So, what do these `Version` values actually mean? The table that follows documents the specific rules enforced by each version.

Table 4-1. *Strict Mode Version Valid Values and Their Effect*

1.0	Variables referenced must be initialized except for references within strings.
2.0	All variables must be initialized.
	Will not allow references to non-existent properties of an object.
	Will not allow function calls that use the calling syntax of a method.
	Will not allow a variable without a name such as (${}).
Latest	Uses the strictest rules available with the idea that stronger versions will be added.

It would be nice if one of the versions forced variable types to be declared, as undeclared variables can also cause bugs. As a best practice, it is a good idea to set strict mode on in new scripts you write and try to declare variable types as much as possible. I hesitate to say *always*, because sometimes it can take a bit of trial and error to determine what object type is returned from a cmdlet.

■ **Note** An alternative to using Set-StrictMode is to use the Set-PSDebug cmdlet, but that approach affects all PowerShell scopes, whereas the Set-StrictMode just affects the current execution scope.

Error Handling

PowerShell supports error handling with the Try/Catch block for specific statements and the Trap statement as a general error handler. Error information is stored in the PowerShell $Error object. To control how we want PowerShell's built-in cmdlets to handle errors, we use the ErrorAction parameter and the $ErrorActionPreference variable.

Using the Try/Catch Block

Errors can be trapped in scripts by using the Try/Catch block. This can be combined with the cmdlet ErrorAction parameter to control how errors are processed. PowerShell provides information about the error to the Catch block via the current object variable $_ and the $Error automatic variable. There are two types of errors; terminating and non-terminating. As the name implies, terminating errors will cause the program to stop. The good news is that terminating errors are easily trapped and handled. Non-terminating errors cannot be trapped by default and are usually generated by cmdlets. However, you can use the ErrorAction cmdlet parameter to tell PowerShell to treat non-terminating errors as if they were terminating errors, i.e., by passing ErrorAction Stop. Then the Catch block can handle the error. What follows is a script that will search a given folder for files that match a filename pattern, merge the file contents, and write out the merged file. It will also add the original filename to each line. This is a script I developed because the ETL tool I was using had to be mapped to a single input file. So why add the original filename to each line? Since the plan is to load the merged file into a SQL Server table, having the originating filename will help us track down the source of bad data. Let's take a look at Listing 4-1.

Listing 4-1. Merging files and using the Try/Catch block

```
set-location ($env:HOMEDRIVE + $env:HOMEPATH + "\Documents\")

# Let's use Here strings to create our input files...

@"
Joe Jones|22 Main Street|Boston|MA|12345
Mary Smith|33 Mockingbird Lane|Providence|RI|02886
"@ > outfileex1.txt

@"
Tom Jones|11 Ellison Stree|Newton|MA|12345
Ellen Harris|12 Warick Aveneu|Warwick|RI|02885
"@ > outfileex2.txt

# We could make these parameters, but we'll just use variables so the code stands alone...
$sourcepath =  "c:" + $env:HOMEPATH + "\Documents"
$filter = "outfileex*.txt"

$filelist = Get-ChildItem -Path $sourcepath  -filter $filter

$targetpathfile =  "c:" + $env:HOMEPATH + "\Documents\outmergedex.txt"

try
{
 Remove-Item $targetpathfile -ErrorAction Stop
 }
catch
{
    "Error removing prior files."
     Write-Host $_.Exception.Message
}
finally
{
    Write-Host "Done removing file if it existed."
    "out files merged at " + (Get-Date) | out-file outmerge.log -append
}

foreach ($file in $filelist)
 {
     "Merging file $file..."
     $fc = Get-Content $file
     foreach ($line in $fc)  {$line + "|" + $file.name >> $targetpathfile  }
 }
```

Look at the Try/Catch block in listing 4-1. Remove-Item will try to delete the specified file, but since the file is not there, an error is generated. Our ErrorAction parameter is Stop, so we are forcing a terminating error, which means the code in the Catch block will execute and display the error message. The Finally block is always executed, so it is a good place to put clean-up code or things you always want done, such as logging. The foreach block is looping through each file in the list and loading the file contents into the variable $fc using the Get-Content cmdlet. Then the script loops through each line in the file, appends the file name, and writes the line out to the path specified in $targetpathfile. Remember: >> means to append to the filename that follows.

Sometimes it is useful to handle some types of errors differently than other errors. Some errors may be anticipated while others require intervention. The script in Listing 4-2 uses the Get-Process cmdlet to demonstrate how to handle one error type differently than others.

Listing 4-2. Using Catch to trap different types of errors

```
Try
{
    Get-Process -Id 255 -ErrorAction Stop
}
Catch [Microsoft.PowerShell.Commands.ProcessCommandException]
{
    write-host "The process id was not found." -ForegroundColor Red
}
Catch
{
  "Error: $Error" >> errorlog.txt
}
Finally
{
  "Process complete."
}
```

In this example, Get-Process tries to access process ID 255, which does not exist, so an error is thrown. Since the ErrorAction is Stop, the Catch blocks will be executed. The first Catch block tests for whether the error name is [Microsoft.PowerShell.Commands.ProcessCommandException] and will only execute if the name matches. The second Catch block processes any error. However, if the specific Catch block executes, the second general handler will not. So, how do you know what the error name is for a given error? If you can trigger the error, you can get the name with the following statement:

```
$error[0].Exception.GetType().FullName
```

Note: You can list multiple error names on the catch line to handle a list of error types the same way.

The Trap Statement

The Trap statement lets us define a default error handler, i.e., one that catches any errors not otherwise caught. While the Try/Catch block traps errors on specific statements, the Trap statement will catch any unhandled errors for the entire script. Consider the following code:

```
$Error.Clear()

trap { "Error Occurred: $Error." }
Get-Content "nosuchfile" -ErrorAction Stop

"The script continues..."
```

CHAPTER 4 ■ WRITING SCRIPTS

In the first line in the script, `$Error.Clear()` clears out any prior errors so the script is re-runnable. Having clean-up code at the top of scripts like this can really help when testing. The `trap` line defines a block of code between the braces to be executed on any terminating error. In this case, the file "nosuchfile" does not exist so error messages will be displayed. Since by default, after the `trap` block has executed, the script continues to run so the message "The script continues" will be written to the console. You can override this behavior and have the script stop by adding the break keyword. The code that follows shows the previous script but with the break statement in the `trap` block. Notice that the line "The script does not continue" is not written to the console:

```
trap { "Error Occurred: $Error."; break }
Get-Content "nosuchfile" -ErrorAction Stop

"The script does not continue..."
```

The `trap` statement has a bug that can cause some havoc if you are not aware of it. You cannot replace a `trap` statement block that was previously defined. Once set, any more `trap` statements are ignored. Listing 4-3 provides an example to illustrate this.

Listing 4-3. Demonstrates a trap cannot be replaced

```
trap { "Error Occurred: $Error." }
Get-Content "nosuchfile" -ErrorAction Stop

"The script continues..."

trap { "Another Error Occurred: $Error."; Break }

Get-Content "nosuchfile" -ErrorAction Stop

"This line will still execute"
```

The console output is shown here:

```
Error Occurred: Cannot find a process with the name "255". Verify the process name and call
the cmdlet again..
Get-Process : Cannot find a process with the name "255". Verify the process name and call
the cmdlet again.At
C:\Users\BryanCafferky\Documents\GitHub\Source\PowerShell\Book\Chapter04\ch04_script8_error_
trap_statement.ps1:5 char:1
+ Get-Process 255 -ErrorAction Stop
+ ~~~~~~~~~~~~~~~~~~~~~~~~~~~~~~~~~~~
    + CategoryInfo          : ObjectNotFound: (255:String) [Get-Process],
                              ProcessCommandException
    + FullyQualifiedErrorId : NoProcessFoundForGivenName,Microsoft.PowerShell.Commands.
                              GetProcessCommand

The script continues...
Error Occurred: Cannot find a process with the name "255". Verify the process name and call
the cmdlet again. Cannot find a process with the name "255
". Verify the process name and call the cmdlet again..
Get-Process : Cannot find a process with the name "255". Verify the process name and call
the cmdlet again.At
```

```
C:\Users\BryanCafferky\Documents\GitHub\Source\PowerShell\Book\Chapter04\ch04_script8_error_
trap_statement.ps1:11 char:1
+ Get-Process 255 -ErrorAction Stop
+ ~~~~~~~~~~~~~~~~~~~~~~~~~~~~~~~~~~~
    + CategoryInfo          : ObjectNotFound: (255:String) [Get-Process],
                              ProcessCommandException
    + FullyQualifiedErrorId : NoProcessFoundForGivenName,Microsoft.PowerShell.Commands.
                              GetProcessCommand

This line will still execute
```

In listing 4-3, the first trap statement displays the error, and since it does not have a break statement, the script will continue, which is proven because the line "The script continues..." is displayed. Then a new trap is defined, and this one has the break statement. In spite of this, we can see that the old trap code was executed, as the message "Another Error Occurred" is not displayed and "This line will still execute" is displayed. There may be times when you want to modify the behavior of a trap block, but you can't do it directly. Instead, you can set variables that the trap block uses to modify its behavior. The code in Listing 4-4 uses this approach.

Listing 4-4. Workaround to replace a trap

```
[boolean] $stopscript = $false

trap { "Error Occurred: $Error."; If ($stopscript -eq $true) {break}  }
Get-Process 255 -ErrorAction Stop

"The script continues..."
$stopscript = $true

Get-Process 255 -ErrorAction Stop

"This line will NOT execute"
```

In this code, the trap block conditionally executes a break statement depending on the value of the variable $stopscript.

Using Try/Catch and the Trap Statement Together

Let's look at how to use the Try/Catch block together with a Trap statement to complement each other. Let's do this while solving a real-world problem. Sometimes database object names like table names and column names are changed. Subsequently, all the code that uses them needs to be updated with the new names.

For example, I once had a client decide to rename all the primary key columns in a source database. I needed a way to update the stored procedures that referenced these columns with the new names. I solved the problem by creating an old-to-new name mapping file in csv format, which was used to automate the updates.

To demonstrate, let's simplify the solution to just update one script. So you can set this up and test it, the code uses Adventure Works. First, let's create a copy of the table HumanResources.Department called HumanResources.CompanyUnit and then insert all the rows from HumanResources.Department to the new table. Use listing 4-5 to create the table. Note: You will need a copy of the AdventureWorks database to run the Insert statement. I used the SQL Server 2008 R2 version of AdventureWorks but the Insert should be compatible with later versions.

Listing 4-5. Creating the CompanyUnit table

```
CREATE TABLE [HumanResources].[CompanyUnit](
        [UnitID] [smallint]  NOT NULL,
        [UnitName] [dbo].[Name] NOT NULL,
        [UnitGroupName] [dbo].[Name] NOT NULL,
        [UpdateDate] [datetime] NOT NULL,
 CONSTRAINT [PK_DepartmentNew_UnitID] PRIMARY KEY CLUSTERED
(
        [UnitID] ASC
) )
Go

insert into  [HumanResources].[CompanyUnit]
select * from [HumanResources].[Department]
go
```

The original table will serve as the table we are migrating from and the new table will serve as the table we are migrating to. The SQL script that follows will serve as a legacy script that we will rewrite using our PowerShell script. Note: This script is a data file in the files accompanying the book and should be copied to your Documents folder.

```
USE AdventureWorks
GO

SELECT [DepartmentID]
     ,[Name]
     ,[GroupName]
     ,[ModifiedDate]
  FROM [HumanResources].[Department];

SELECT distinct DepartmentID
     ,[Name]
  FROM [HumanResources].[Department];

SELECT DepartmentID, [Name], GroupName, ModifiedDate
  FROM [HumanResources].[Department];
```

The text file named columnmapping.csv will serve as the driver to the remapping process. This file accompanies the book and should be copied to your Documents folder.

```
SourceColumn,TargetColumn
DepartmentID,UnitID
[Name],[UnitName]
GroupName,UnitGroupName
ModifiedDate,UpdateDate
```

The file has just two columns, SourceColumn and TargetColumn, which are the source column name and new column name, respectively. Having column names as the first row will make it easier to use this file with the Import-CSV cmdlet.

Let's look at Listing 4-6, which shows the script that rewrites the SQL code.

Listing 4-6. Script to modify SQL scripts

```
$sourcepath = $env:HOMEDRIVE + $env:HOMEPATH + "\Documents\"

# Let's trap any errors...
trap { "Error Occurred: $Error." >> ($sourcepath + "errorlog.txt") }

$file = Get-Content ($sourcepath + "script.sql") -ErrorAction Stop

$file = $file.replace('[HumanResources].[Department]', '[HumanResources].[CompanyUnit]');

# Load the column Mappings...
$incolumnemapping = Import-CSV ($sourcepath + "columnmapping.csv")

foreach ($item in $incolumnemapping) { $file = $file.replace(($item.SourceColumn), ($item.
TargetColumn) ) }

Try
{
    $file > ($sourcepath + "script_revised.sql")
    "File script.sql has been processed."

}
Catch
{
    "Error Writing file Occurred: $Error." >> ($sourcepath + "errorlog.txt")
}
Finally
{
    "Mapping process executed on " + (Get-Date) + "." >> ($sourcepath + "executionlog.txt")
}
```

Let's step through this code to see how it works.

```
$sourcepath = $env:HOMEDRIVE + $env:HOMEPATH + "\Documents\"
```

To make the script runnable on any machine, the last line in the script sets the folder path to the logged-on user's Documents folder. The script will look for all files there.

We want a general error handler in case something fails, which the following line will take care of:

```
trap { "Error Occurred: $Error." >> ($sourcepath + "errorlog.txt") }
```

If an error occurs, the previous line will log the error message to errorlog.txt.

Now that we have a general error handler, we can start the real work. We will start by loading the script file into variable $file using the Get-Content cmdlet as shown:

```
$file = Get-Content ($sourcepath + "script.sql")
```

Since $sourcepath and `script.sql` need to be concatenated before the Get-Content uses it as a file path, the concatenation is enclosed in parentheses, which means it will be done prior to the Get-Content operation.

Let's look at the first remapping line of code:

```
$file = $file.replace('[HumanResources].[Department]', '[HumanResources].[CompanyUnit]');
```

This line just replaces all occurrences of the old table name with the new table name. I hard coded this to keep things simple. We need to assign the result to $file or the replace result will not be retained. We are using the replace method of the string object to do the replacement, but we could have used the replace operator instead. We are using the replace method because it does not support regular expressions whereas the replace operator does. In some cases we will want to use regular expressions, but since the input file has the special regular expression characters of periods and braces we do not want them used here. In fact, if you use the replace operator, you will get some odd results.

To load the column mappings, we can use the Import-CSV cmdlet as shown here:

```
$incolumnmapping = Import-CSV ($sourcepath + "columnmapping.csv")
```

We can now loop through each row of $incolumnmapping and use the SourceColumn and TargetColumn to replace each SourceColumn with the TargetColumn value. The code that follows does this:

```
foreach ($item in $incolumnmapping) { $file = $file.replace(($item.SourceColumn),
($item.TargetColumn) ) }
```

Finally, we want to write the new version of the script out to a file while handling any errors raised rather than use the default error handler we created with the Trap statement. Here we use the Try/Catch/Finally block as shown:

```
Try
{
    $file >  ($sourcepath + "script_revised.sql")
}
Catch
{
    "Error Writing file Occurred: $Error." >> ($sourcepath + "errorlog.txt")
}
Finally
{
    "Mapping process executed on " + (Get-Date) + "." >> ($sourcepath + "executionlog.txt")
}
```

Let's review this code. The code in the braces after the Try statement will execute. If an error is raised, the code between the Catch block braces will execute, which logs a message along with the error message provided by the $Error automatic variable. We are piping the $file variable into a file using the > operator to tell PowerShell to overwrite the file. We use >> when we want to append the data to the file, as in the case of logging errors.

In practice, you will probably need to update many stored procedures. You can use the SQLPS module to automatically write out all the stored procedures to text files, as the code in Listing 4-7 does.

Listing 4-7. Scripting out stored procedures

```
Import-Module "sqlps" -DisableNameChecking

$outpath =  $env:HOMEDRIVE + $env:HOMEPATH + "\Documents\storedprocedures.sql"

# Let's clear out the output file first.
"" > $outpath

# Set where you are in SQL Server...
set-location SQLSERVER:\SQL\BryanCafferkyPC\DEFAULT\Databases\Adventureworks\
StoredProcedures

foreach ($Item in Get-ChildItem)
{
    $Item.Schema + "_" + $Item.Name
    $Item.Script() | Out-File -Filepath $outpath -append
}
```

Here, the script starts by importing the SQLPS module so we can use its cmdlets. Then we create the variable $outpath to store the output file path. Note: This should work on any machine.

It's a good idea to clear out any contents that might be in the output file from a prior run, which we can do with this statement:

```
"" > $outpath
```

Here we are just writing an empty string to $outpath using the > operator, which overwrites the file contents with the empty string.

The SQLPS module lets us navigate SQL Server as if it were a file system. We can use Set-Location to place us in the virtual folder where the AdventureWorks stored procedures are located by using the statement that follows:

```
set-location SQLSERVER:\SQL\BryanCafferkyPC\DEFAULT\Databases\Adventureworks\
StoredProcedures
```

Since we can treat SQL Server like a file system, we can loop through the stored procedures as it they were files with this code:

```
foreach ($Item in Get-ChildItem)
{
    $Item.Schema + "_" + $Item.Name
    $Item.Script() | Out-File -Filepath $outpath -append
}
```

The foreach statement will loop through each stored procedure and save it in the $Item variable. We use $Item to write to the console the procedures schema and procedure name, separated by an underscore. The Script method will extract the code of the SQL object, i.e., the stored procedure code in this case. By piping this into the Out-File cmdlet with a FilePath of $outfile and using the append parameter, the stored procedure code is written to our output file. Note: In this example, we are writing all the code to one output file, but you can easily modify the script to write out separate files for each procedure by using the $Item.Schema and $Item.Name to build a unique output filename for each object.

As useful as this is, it may take some playing with to get reliable results. For example, if the word Department were to be replaced with a new value, it would change Department, DepartmentID, and DepartmentName. When the SQL code is auto-generated from the database, as we did earlier, it places braces around columns and table names, which can help, as we could replace [Department] and it would then update only the values required. It is well worth the time to automate these kinds of tasks. Once we have, we can modify the script to fit similar situations. As Mr. Scott on the old *Star Trek* series would say, "How do you think I got the reputation as a miracle worker?"

Setting the $ErrorActionPreference Preference Variable

The PowerShell variable $ErrorActionPreference controls how PowerShell will handle non-terminating errors for all cmdlet calls where the ErrorActionPreference parameter is not passed. The table that follows shows the possible values for $ErrorActionPreference and its effect.

Table 4-2. *ErrorActionPreference Values*

Continue	Shows the error message but continues running the script. It will not be trapped by an error handler as it does not raise an error. The error message is added to the $Error automatic variable.
Ignore	Suppresses error messages and continues running the script. It does not add the error to the $Error automatic variable.
Inquire	Shows the error message and prompts the user for the action to take. Choice may affect how the $Error variable is set.
SilentlyContinue	Suppresses error messages and continues running the script.
Stop	Displays error message and stops running the script.
Suspend	Only used to suspend Windows PowerShell workflows.

Using the $Error Variable and the ErrorAction Parameter

The $Error variable is an object and, except for when ErrorActionPreference is set to Ignore, will get populated with the error message. To prove this, let's try the script in listing 4-8. Play with it in the ISE to see how $Error is handled. Notice that the line that passes ErrorAction Ignore does not display an error message. The first two lines in listing 4-8 just clean things up. Clear-Host erases the console and the Set-Location is just used to clear out the SQL Server provider context which may be set from prior code.

Listing 4-8. Exploring ErrorAction

```
Clear-Host

Set-Location ($env:HOMEDRIVE + $env:HOMEPATH + "\Documents")
$Error.Clear()
Get-Content "nonfile" -ErrorAction Continue
"Continue: $Error "

$Error.Clear()
Get-Content "nonfile" -ErrorAction Ignore      # Error message is not set.
"Ignore: $Error "
```

```
$Error.Clear()
Get-Content "nonfile" -ErrorAction Inquire
"Inquire: $Error "

$Error.Clear()
Get-Content "nonfile" -ErrorAction SilentlyContinue
"SilentlyContinue: $Error "

$Error.Clear()
Get-Content "nonfile" -ErrorAction Stop
"Stop: $Error "

#  Suspend is only available for workflows.
$Error.Clear()
Get-Content "nonfile" -ErrorAction Suspend
"Suspend: $Error "
```

A nice feature of cmdlets is that they let us store error messages in a variable we specify via the ErrorVariable parameter. We can have the message overwrite previous values in the variable or have it append the messages. Let's look at the same code in Listing 4-9 to see how this works.

Listing 4-9. Storing the ErrorVariable

```
for($i=1; $i -le 2; $i++) {
Get-Process -Id 255 -ErrorAction SilentlyContinue -ErrorVariable hold
"Loop Iteration: $i"
}
write-host "`r`nError Variable contains..."
$hold
```

The script output is as follows:

```
Loop Iteration: 1
Loop Iteration: 2

Error Variable contains...
Get-Process : Cannot find a process with the process identifier 255.At
C:\Users\BryanCafferky\Documents\GitHub\Source\PowerShell\Book\Chapter04\ch04_script2_error_
variable.ps1:2 char:1
+ Get-Process -Id 255 -ErrorAction SilentlyContinue -ErrorVariable hold
+ ~~~~~~~~~~~~~~~~~~~~~~~~~~~~~~~~~~~~~~~~~~~~~~~~~~~~~~~~~~~~~~~~~~~~~~~~~
    + CategoryInfo          : ObjectNotFound: (255:Int32) [Get-Process],
                              ProcessCommandException
    + FullyQualifiedErrorId : NoProcessFoundForGivenId,Microsoft.PowerShell.Commands.
                              GetProcessCommand
```

The script in Listing 4-9 loops two times trying to execute Get-Process, passing an invalid process ID and thereby generating an error. The ErrorAction of SilentlyContinue tells PowerShell to store the message but not to display it. The ErrorVariable parameter is followed by the name of the variable where the message is to be stored. Notice that the $ is not included in the variable name. Each iteration replaces the variable with the error message, so at the end there is only the last message in the variable. If you want to append the error message to the variable, prefix the variable name with +. Listing 4-10 is the same code but with that small change.

Listing 4-10. Appending to the variable that stores ErrorVariable

```
for($i=1; $i -le 2; $i++) {
Get-Process -Id 255 -ErrorAction SilentlyContinue -ErrorVariable +hold
"Loop Iteration: $i"
}
write-host "`r`nError Variable contains..."
$hold
```

The script output is as follows:

```
Loop Iteration: 1
Loop Iteration: 2

Error Variable contains...
Get-Process : Cannot find a process with the process identifier 255.At
C:\Users\BryanCafferky\Documents\GitHub\Source\PowerShell\Book\Chapter04\ch04_script3_error_
variable2.ps1:4 char:1
+ Get-Process -Id 255 -ErrorAction SilentlyContinue -ErrorVariable +hold
+ ~~~~~~~~~~~~~~~~~~~~~~~~~~~~~~~~~~~~~~~~~~~~~~~~~~~~~~~~~~~~~~~~~~~~~~~~~
    + CategoryInfo          : ObjectNotFound: (255:Int32) [Get-Process],
                              ProcessCommandException
    + FullyQualifiedErrorId : NoProcessFoundForGivenId,Microsoft.PowerShell.Commands.
                              GetProcessCommand

Get-Process : Cannot find a process with the process identifier 255.At
C:\Users\BryanCafferky\Documents\GitHub\Source\PowerShell\Book\Chapter04\ch04_script3_error_
variable2.ps1:4 char:1
+ Get-Process -Id 255 -ErrorAction SilentlyContinue -ErrorVariable +hold
+ ~~~~~~~~~~~~~~~~~~~~~~~~~~~~~~~~~~~~~~~~~~~~~~~~~~~~~~~~~~~~~~~~~~~~~~~~~
    + CategoryInfo          : ObjectNotFound: (255:Int32) [Get-Process],
                              ProcessCommandException
    + FullyQualifiedErrorId : NoProcessFoundForGivenId,Microsoft.PowerShell.Commands.
                              GetProcessCommand
```

Being able to store error messages in our variables is useful if we want to process different types of error messages from different parts of a script.

The variable that collects multiple error messages is an array, and we can access an individual item using array notation, i.e., use $hold[0] to get the first item.

More on the $Error Variable

In addition to holding the error message, $Error is an object with a number of methods and properties. To get an idea of what these are, enter the following statement:

```
$error | Get-Member
```

And you should see output in the console similar to what follows:

```
Name                   MemberType      Definition
----                   ----------      ----------
Equals                 Method          bool Equals(System.Object obj)
GetHashCode            Method          int GetHashCode()
GetObjectData          Method          void GetObjectData(System....
GetType                Method          type GetType()
ToString               Method          string ToString()
CategoryInfo           Property        System.Management.Automation.ErrorCategory...
ErrorDetails           Property        System.Management.Automation.ErrorDetails
                                       ErrorDetails...
Exception              Property        System.Exception Exception {get;}
FullyQualifiedErrorId  Property        string FullyQualifiedErrorId {get;}
InvocationInfo         Property        System.Management.Automation.InvocationInfo
                                       Invocat...
PipelineIterationInfo  Property        System.Collections.ObjectModel.
                                       ReadOnlyCollection[int]...
ScriptStackTrace       Property        string ScriptStackTrace {get;}
TargetObject           Property        System.Object TargetObject {get;}
PSMessageDetails       ScriptProperty  System.Object PSMessageDetails
                                       {get=& { Set-StrictMod..
```

■ **Note** `$Error.Count` will return the number of errors stored in the `$Error` object. `$Error.InvocationInfo` will return details about what caused the error.

Common cmdlet Parameters

`ErrorAction` is called a common cmdlet parameter because it is implemented in all cmdlets. Table 4-3 documents the other common parameters and how to use them.

Table 4-3. *Common cmdlet Paramters*

Parameter	Description	Example
Debug	Causes `Write-Debug` messages to print in custom code. You must have a cmdlet parameter binding in your code for this to work.	`Invoke-Something –Debug`
ErrorAction	Overrides the default `$ErrorActionPreference` variable to tell PowerShell how to handle non-terminating errors.	`Get-Content "stuff" – ErrorAction Stop`
ErrorVariable	If an error occurs, causes the error message to be stored in the specified variable in addition to `$Error`. Prefix with a + to have the output appended to variable contents.	`Get-Content "stuff" – ErrorVariable +v`
OutVariable	Stores the output of the command to the specified variable and displays it. Prefix with a + to have the output appended to variable contents.	`Get-Content "stuff" – OutVariable v`
OutBuffer	Specifies the number of items to accumulate in the pipeline before they are sent through the pipeline. If not specified, objects are sent as they are generated.	`Get-ChildItem -OutBuffer 15 | Where-Object -Property Name -like "t*"`
PipelineVariable	Stores the value of the current pipeline item to a variable.	`Get-ChildItem -OutVariable v`
Verbose	Causes extra informational messages to display for built-in PowerShell cmdlets and `Write-Verbose` messages to print in custom code. You must have a cmdlet parameter binding in your code for this to work.	`Invoke-Something -Verbose`
WarningAction	Controls how PowerShell should respond to warnings generated from the command. Valid values are `Continue`, `Inquire`, `SilentlyContinue`, and `Stop`.	`Get-Content -WarningAction Stop`
WarningVariable	Stores any warning messages generated by the command in the specified variable. Prefix with a + to have the output appended to variable contents.	`Get-Content - WarningVariable +v`
WhatIf	Will display a message about the effect of the command instead of executing the command. This parameter is only supported by cmdlets that can potentially do damage.	`Stop-Process 340 -WhatIf`
Confirm	Prompts for a confirmation before executing the command. This parameter is only supported by cmdlets that can potentially do damage.	`Stop-Process 340 -Confirm`

Debugging

PowerShell has some great debugging features, but the editor itself provides such nice visibility into the script variables that I find I rarely need the full debugging tools. Consider the following simple script:

```
$sourcepath =  $env:HOMEDRIVE + $env:HOMEPATH + "\Documents\state_table.csv"

$CheckFile = Import-CSV $sourcepath
```

After running the script in the ISE, the variables are loaded with values. Simply highlight the variable and click on the Execute Selected toolbar button as shown in Figure 4-1.

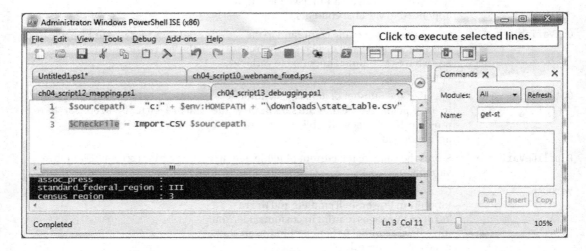

Figure 4-1. *Showing how to execute only selected lines in the PowerShell ISE*

Intellisense helps you find properties and methods on objects. By entering a period after an object name, the intellisense menu pops up, as shown in Figure 4-2. The Count property contains the number of lines in the variable.

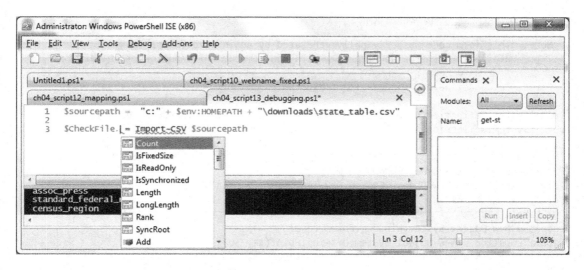

Figure 4-2. *Using intellisense in the PowerShell ISE*

I do most of my debugging by playing with selected lines of code and viewing the value of variables. Because of this, and because there are a lot of great references available on using the advanced debugging facilities of PowerShell, we will not go into it in detail here. A good reference on debugging and other subjects is available at this link:

```
http://gegeek.com/documents/eBooks/Windows%20Powershell%203.0%20First%20Steps.pdf
```

Events and Script Blocks: The Perfect Marriage

In this section, we will discuss how PowerShell supports events and how you can leverage this in your code. The best place to start this discussion is with Windows' form objects and events. PowerShell scripts can create Windows forms and then connect code to when an event—such as a button click—occurs. By first explaining how that works, we will leverage that knowledge to explain how you can use the same concepts on other .NET objects.

Using Windows Events

We've seen script blocks, and we know that Windows traps events, but PowerShell puts these together in way that greatly extends the functionality of event trapping. We can register for events we want trapped and assign code to be executed when the event occurs. It's surprisingly simple, yet powerful. A good way to demonstrate this is to walk through a simple script that displays a Windows form. Review Listing 4-11. Note: The window may appear in the background. If so, hovering the mouse over the PowerShell icon in the taskbar should bring it up.

Listing 4-11. Displaying a Windows form

```
# Note:  This form code was originally generated by AdminScriptEditor 4.0
#               available for free at http://www.itninja.com/community/admin-script-editor

# First, let's define our Windows form objects...

[void][System.Reflection.Assembly]::LoadWithPartialName("System.Windows.Forms")
[void][System.Reflection.Assembly]::LoadWithPartialName("System.Drawing")

#~~< Form1 >~~~~~~~~~~~~~~~~~~~~~~~~~~~~~~~~~~~~~~~~~~~~~~~~~~~~~~~~~~~~~~~~~~~
$Form1 = New-Object System.Windows.Forms.Form
$Form1.ClientSize = New-Object System.Drawing.Size(167, 148)
$Form1.Text = "Form1"
#~~< Label1 >~~~~~~~~~~~~~~~~~~~~~~~~~~~~~~~~~~~~~~~~~~~~~~~~~~~~~~~~~~~~~~~~~~
$Label1 = New-Object System.Windows.Forms.Label
$Label1.Location = New-Object System.Drawing.Point(41, 50)
$Label1.Size = New-Object System.Drawing.Size(100, 23)
$Label1.TabIndex = 1
$Label1.Text = "Start"
#~~< Button1 >~~~~~~~~~~~~~~~~~~~~~~~~~~~~~~~~~~~~~~~~~~~~~~~~~~~~~~~~~~~~~~~~~
$Button1 = New-Object System.Windows.Forms.Button
$Button1.Location = New-Object System.Drawing.Point(41, 87)
$Button1.Size = New-Object System.Drawing.Size(75, 23)
$Button1.TabIndex = 0
$Button1.Text = "Button1"
$Button1.UseVisualStyleBackColor = $true

# Second, add the controls to the form...
$Form1.Controls.Add($Label1)     # Add the label to the form.
$Form1.Controls.Add($Button1)    # Add the button to the form.

# Third, the function to handle the button click...
function DaButtonWasClicked( $object ){
  $Label1.Text = "Button Clicked";
}

# Fourth, hook up the button-click event to the function that will execute...
$Button1.add_Click({DaButtonWasClicked($Button1)})

# Fifth, declare the function to open the form and start the event trapping...
function Main{
        [System.Windows.Forms.Application]::EnableVisualStyles()
        [System.Windows.Forms.Application]::Run($Form1)
}

# Finally, call the function Main to open the Windows form...
Main # This call must remain below all other event functions
```

A nice thing about PowerShell is that we can create a Windows form application completely within the language—i.e., no extra add-on to deploy. However, as we can see from the script, it takes a lot of lines of code to create the form objects. Thankfully there are tools out there to help. I found a free comprehensive PowerShell development tool called Admin Script Editor 4.0, available at the link: http://www.itninja.com/community/admin-script-editor, which supports designing Windows forms. While I was happy to get such a useful tool for free, it is unfortunate that the company that developed it has gone out of business. Therefore, there will not be any updates to it. Nonetheless, it is full featured and includes excellent support for developing Windows form–based applications in PowerShell. Eventually, I found I needed a full powered development environment that supported Windows forms and other advanced features. So I purchased Sapien's PowerShell Studio, which I have been very happy with. It's like Visual Studio for PowerShell. You can learn more about this product at the link: https://www.sapien.com/software/powershell_studio.

Let's review the code. Note: I commented the code sections so it is easier to follow what is happening.

```
#  First, let's define our Windows form objects...
[void][System.Reflection.Assembly]::LoadWithPartialName("System.Windows.Forms")
[void][System.Reflection.Assembly]::LoadWithPartialName("System.Drawing")

#~~< Form1 >~~~~~~~~~~~~~~~~~~~~~~~~~~~~~~~~~~~~~~~~~~~~~~~~~~~~~~~~~~~~~~~~~~~
$Form1 = New-Object System.Windows.Forms.Form
$Form1.ClientSize = New-Object System.Drawing.Size(167, 148)
$Form1.Text = "Form1"
#~~< Label1 >~~~~~~~~~~~~~~~~~~~~~~~~~~~~~~~~~~~~~~~~~~~~~~~~~~~~~~~~~~~~~~~~~~
$Label1 = New-Object System.Windows.Forms.Label
$Label1.Location = New-Object System.Drawing.Point(41, 50)
$Label1.Size = New-Object System.Drawing.Size(100, 23)
$Label1.TabIndex = 1
$Label1.Text = "Start"
#~~< Button1 >~~~~~~~~~~~~~~~~~~~~~~~~~~~~~~~~~~~~~~~~~~~~~~~~~~~~~~~~~~~~~~~~~
$Button1 = New-Object System.Windows.Forms.Button
$Button1.Location = New-Object System.Drawing.Point(41, 87)
$Button1.Size = New-Object System.Drawing.Size(75, 23)
$Button1.TabIndex = 0
$Button1.Text = "Button1"
$Button1.UseVisualStyleBackColor = $true
```

Notice how PowerShell easily creates the required .NET objects and calls their methods. The first thing the script does is create references to the Windows form object libraries via the lines here:

```
#  First, let's define our Windows form objects...
[void][System.Reflection.Assembly]::LoadWithPartialName("System.Windows.Forms")
[void][System.Reflection.Assembly]::LoadWithPartialName("System.Drawing")
```

Most of the time you don't need to explicitly define namespaces in PowerShell, but in the case of the Windows form libraries, you do. Once we have the namespaces defined we can create the form objects as shown here:

```
#~~< Form1 >~~~~~~~~~~~~~~~~~~~~~~~~~~~~~~~~~~~~~~~~~~~~~~~~~~~~~~~~~~~~~~~~~~~~~~~~~~~~~~~~~~
$Form1 = New-Object System.Windows.Forms.Form
$Form1.ClientSize = New-Object System.Drawing.Size(167, 148)
$Form1.Text = "Form1"
#~~< Label1 >~~~~~~~~~~~~~~~~~~~~~~~~~~~~~~~~~~~~~~~~~~~~~~~~~~~~~~~~~~~~~~~~~~~~~~~~~~~~~~~~~
$Label1 = New-Object System.Windows.Forms.Label
$Label1.Location = New-Object System.Drawing.Point(41, 50)
$Label1.Size = New-Object System.Drawing.Size(100, 23)
$Label1.TabIndex = 1
$Label1.Text = "Start"
#~~< Button1 >~~~~~~~~~~~~~~~~~~~~~~~~~~~~~~~~~~~~~~~~~~~~~~~~~~~~~~~~~~~~~~~~~~~~~~~~~~~~~~~~
$Button1 = New-Object System.Windows.Forms.Button
$Button1.Location = New-Object System.Drawing.Point(41, 87)
$Button1.Size = New-Object System.Drawing.Size(75, 23)
$Button1.TabIndex = 0
$Button1.Text = "Button1"
$Button1.UseVisualStyleBackColor = $true
```

In the code above, we use New-Object to create the required form objects, i.e., the form, the label, and the button. Notice that after the object is defined, we can set the properties that control how it will be displayed. The text property is the caption that will be displayed for the object.

Now let's look at how the form objects are added to the form with the code here:

```
# Second, add the controls to the form...
$Form1.Controls.Add($Label1)    # Add the label to the form.
$Form1.Controls.Add($Button1)   # Add the button to the form.
```

The question comes to mind, where did these object names come from? The answer is that they came from the form editor when we created the form. The editor creates default names, but we can change them if we want to. I kept the default names to keep this simple. Figure 4-3 shows how the form looks in the editor. Since the button is selected, you can see its properties, including the text property, which is the display value, and the name property, which is the name of the object. Since the form editor will generate PowerShell code, it turns these names into variables by prefixing them with a $. If you review the code, you will see how each object was created as a variable in the script.

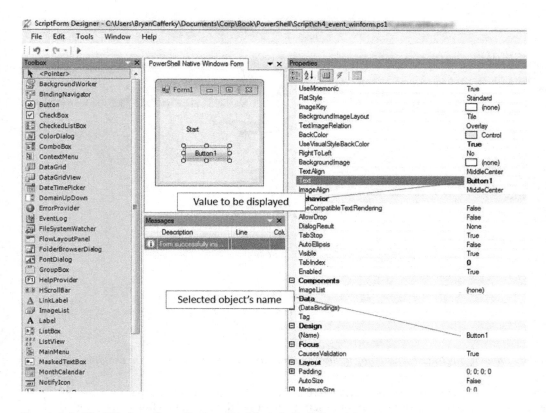

Figure 4-3. *The Windows Form Designer in AdminScriptEditor 4.0*

We can see that the form editor generated the related PowerShell code as standard .NET Windows calls storing the objects in PowerShell variables named using the object name we assigned in the editor.

The form editor lets us define event handlers when we click on the lightning bolt icon of the properties window. Figure 4-4 shows an event handler being defined for the button-click event.

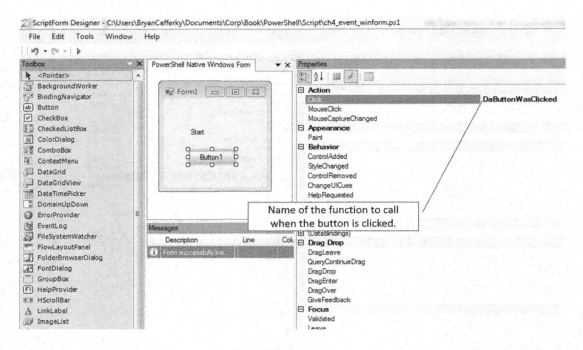

Figure 4-4. *Showing the Click event setting in the AdminScriptEditor 4.0 Windows Form Desginer*

Notice that the `Click` event property is `DaButtonWasClicked`. What does that mean? We are saying that when the user clicks on the button, a script block executes that calls a function named `DaButtonWasClicked`. A script block is just an inline script. Script blocks can be anonymous, i.e., unnamed, or can be assigned to a variable. The form editor does not let us actually enter the code to execute, but it will create the inline script that calls the function we specify. Then, we need to go into the script and add the function code as shown here:

```
# Third, the function to handle the button click...
function DaButtonWasClicked( $object ){
  $Label1.Text = "Button Clicked";
}
```

But how does the script block get connected to the event? PowerShell lets us connect code to an event with the object's add event method; i.e., `add_someevent` where `someevent` is the event name we want to hook the code to. `Click` is an event defined to Windows, so PowerShell understands we are linking the code to the `Click` event. Since we execute the add method on the `$Button1` object variable, it connects the event code to the button's click event. The line that follows connects the function `$DaButtonWasClicked` to `$Button`'s click event:

```
# Fourth, hook up the button-click event to the function that will execute...
$Button1.add_Click({DaButtonWasClicked($Button1)})
```

The code between the braces is the anonymous script block, i.e., `{DaButtonWasClicked($Button1)}`. We can see that our function will be called, passing the button object variable to it. Notice, the function definition accepts an object parameter. This allows the function access to the button's methods and properties.

We have the objects defined and code linked to the button's clicked event. Now we need the statements to open the form and get things going. The form editor wrote the code to do that for us. First, it created a function to create the objects and show the form. Then, it added a statement at the end of the overall script to call that function. The code is shown here:

```
# Fifth, declare the function to open the form and start the event trapping...
function Main{
        [System.Windows.Forms.Application]::EnableVisualStyles()
        [System.Windows.Forms.Application]::Run($Form1)
}


# Finally, call the function Main to open the Windows form...
Main # This call must remain below all other event functions
```

The Main function first enables the visual elements of the application with the EnableVisualStyles method. The line following calls the Run method, passing the form object variable we created, $Form1, thereby opening the form. Since these two lines are defined in the function named Main, the last line of the script calls that function.

Using .NET Object Events

Similar to the way Windows events can call PowerShell code, we can subscribe to .NET object events and supply code that we want executed when the event fires. A common ETL requirement is to load external flat files into SQL Server tables when the files arrive. The problem is, how do we know when files arrive? One way to run code when a new file is created in a specific folder is to use the built-in .NET object FileSystemWatcher. Three events are supported by FileSystemWatcher: file created, file deleted, and file changed. The coding to register for an event is similar to what we have already seen, except for the event name. Let's look at Listing 4-12, which shows an example of calling a function that registers for a file-create event.

Listing 4-12. Trapping the file-create event

```
function Register-UdfFileCreateEvent([string] $source, [string] $filter)
{
   try
   {
     Write-Host "Watching $source for new files..."
     $filesystemwatcher = New-Object IO.FileSystemWatcher $source,
     $filter -Property @{IncludeSubdirectories = $false; NotifyFilter = [IO.
     NotifyFilters]'FileName, LastWrite'}
     Register-ObjectEvent $filesystemwatcher Created -SourceIdentifier FileCreated -Action {
     write-host "Your file has arrived. The filename is " $Event.SourceEventArgs.Name "."
}
   }
   catch
   {
     "Error registering file create event."
   }
}

Register-UdfFileCreateEvent ($env:HOMEDRIVE + $env:HOMEPATH + "\Documents\") "*.txt"
```

In the code in listing 4-12, we start by defining a function named `Register-UdfFileCreateEvent` that takes a folder path as the first parameter and a file pattern filter as the second parameter. After displaying an informational message, we create the variable $filesystemwatcher using the New-Object cmdlet as an instance of the IO.FileSystemWatcher .NET object. The IO.FileSystemWatcher object requires that we pass the path to the folder we want monitored, which is why we pass $source. We pass $filter to limit the files being watched to just the files that match the filename pattern. We use the Property parameter to set some preferences, such as not including subdirectories, i.e., @{IncludeSubdirectories = $false. The statement 'NotifyFilter = [IO.NotifyFilters]'FileName, LastWrite' is asking to watch for changes to the FileName and LastWrite properties.

Let's look at the line that tells Windows to monitor the event:

```
Register-ObjectEvent $filesystemwatcher Created -SourceIdentifier FileCreated -Action {
    write-host "Your file has arrived. The filename is " $Event.SourceEventArgs.Name "."
}
```

The RegisterObjectEvent cmdlet is used to assign the code we want executed when the FileCreated event is fired. The Action parameter defines the code block that will be executed—i.e., the code that is contained between the braces, {}. In the example, we just display a message that the file has arrived with the name of the file.

The line that runs all this is the one here:

```
Register-UdfFileCreateEvent ($env:HOMEDRIVE + $env:HOMEPATH + "\Documents\") "*.txt"
```

This line calls the function Register-UdfFileCreateEvent, passing the folder to be monitored as the first parameter and the filename pattern filter as the second; i.e., only filenames that meet the filter pattern will cause our code to execute. When we run this, we get the following output:

```
Watching C:\Users\BryanCafferky\Documents\ for new files...

Id  Name          PSJobTypeName       State       HasMoreData    Location    Command
--  ----          -------------       -----       -----------    --------    -------
9   FileCreated                       NotStarted  False                      ...
```

To test this script, we use Notepad to create and save a new text file that meets the filter criteria. The console output should confirm the file-creation event code is firing, as shown here:

```
Your file has arrived. The file name is  testit.txt .
Your file has arrived. The file name is  testit.txt .
```

We are not seeing double. There is a bug in the FileSystemWatcher object that causes it to fire multiple times if the program that created the file performs multiple file system actions. For more details on this, see this link:

```
http://stackoverflow.com/questions/1764809/filesystemwatcher-changed-event-is-raised-twice
```

Nonetheless, this is still a useful function, and if you are monitoring an FTP folder or something similar, we may not see this happen. To trap file deletion or file changed, use event names `FileDeleted` and `FileChanged` respectively. One drawback of using PowerShell to trap events is that if the script stops running, the event will no longer fire your code. You can get around this by making the script a service and installing it on the server. Although the PowerShell ISE does not support compiling scripts, which is a required step in registering a program as a service. Both the Admin Script Editor and PowerShell Studio do support code compilation. Another free and popular PowerShell tool is PowerGUI, available at: `http://en.community.dell.com/techcenter/powergui`. This product has a *Compile Script into Service* option. See the link: `https://technet.microsoft.com/en-us/library/Hh849830%28v=wps.630%29.aspx` for information on registering a service using the `New-Service` cmdlet.

Using PowerShell Transactions

The PowerShell documentation covers a feature called `Transactions` that on the surface sounds great. The idea is that we can make all kinds of changes to the environment and then roll them back as if they never happened. First, we'll briefly review the overall concept. Then, we will discuss a real-world script that automates a Windows application and includes the use of transactions. Finally, we will discuss why the transaction support in the example does not work and the limitations of PowerShell transactions.

Conceptual Overview

As a database developer you can understand and appreciate SQL Server's support for transactions. The ability to define a set of updates that must all be successfully committed or rolled back is critical to complex database updates. So when we see that PowerShell supports transactions, we are intrigued. Imagine—we could delete files, move folders, update data, encrypt and unzip and perform any number of other actions, and if something went wrong we could just roll it back. The documentation seems to support that conclusion, but I could not find any examples of using transactions other than code that updated the Window's registry. Let's cover how transactions are supposed to work. First, transactions are supported by the cmdlets `Start-Transaction`, `Complete-Transaction`, and `Undo-Transaction`. Similar to database transactions, the overall flow would be something like in the following pseudo-code:

```
Start-Transaction
Some PowerShell statements that change things.
IF all updates were successful
        Complete-Transaction
Else
        Undo-Transaction
```

The program starts by creating a transaction context using the `Start-Transaction` cmdlet. A transaction context simply means a transaction has begun and subsequent statements may enroll themselves to be included in the transaction. By enrollment, I mean that all the updates in the transaction are either committed together or rolled back. The script makes changes to the environment under the transaction context and at the end, if everything was successful, the work is committed, meaning it is made permanent. The `Complete-Transaction` cmdlet commits the changes. If there was a problem, the script has the option of cancelling the changes, i.e., rolling them back, with the `Undo-Transaction` cmdlet. The idea is that some types of changes need to all happen together or the data is left in a corrupt state. For example, if a customer order header were committed to the database but the order detail were lost, the data for that order would not be in a valid state.

An Example of How Transactions Should Work

Now that we have the basics, let's discuss a scenario in which you might use this functionality. The state table object we saw earlier uses a file downloaded from a website, so it is reasonable to assume the data may change and need to be updated. We have a script that will download a new file and replace the old file with it. However, it is possible something could go wrong and the new file would not be complete. To handle this the script wraps the file copy operation in a transaction and checks the new file to see if there are at least 50 rows in it, and if not, rolls back the update using Undo-Transaction. Since we are covering transactions, we'll include some other useful ideas in the example too. The website does not just let us simply connect and download the file. Instead, there are a series of menus to navigate that determine the specifics of the data we want. So the example uses application automation, in which PowerShell clicks on links and enters data into the Internet Explorer session automatically, as shown in Listing 4-13.

■ **Note**   Please be patient when you run the script as it may take a moment to load Internet Explorer.

Listing 4-13. A script using transactions

```
Import-Module WASP

$url = "http://statetable.com/"

get-process -name iexplore -ErrorAction SilentlyContinue | Stop-Process -Force -ErrorAction
SilentlyContinue
$ie = New-Object -comobject InternetExplorer.Application
$ie.visible = $true
$ie.silent = $true
$ie.Navigate( $url )

while( $ie.busy){Start-Sleep 1}
Select-Window "iexplore" | Set-WindowActive

$btn=$ie.Document.getElementById("USA")
$btn.Click()

while( $ie.busy){Start-Sleep 1}
$btn=$ie.Document.getElementById("major")
$btn.Click()

while( $ie.busy){Start-Sleep 1}
$btn=$ie.Document.getElementById("true")
$btn.Click()

while( $ie.busy){Start-Sleep 1}
$btn=$ie.Document.getElementById("current")
$btn.Click()

while( $ie.busy){Start-Sleep 1}
$btn = $ie.Document.getElementsByTagName('A') | Where-Object {$_.innerText -eq 'Do not
include the US Minor Outlying Islands '}
$btn.Click()
```

```
while( $ie.busy){Start-Sleep 1}
$btn=$ie.Document.getElementById("csv")
$btn.Click()

start-sleep 8
while( $ie.busy){Start-Sleep 1}
Select-Window iexplore | Set-WindowActive | Send-Keys "%S"

Start-Transaction -RollbackPreference TerminatingError

$sourcepath = $env:HOMEDRIVE + $env:HOMEPATH + "\downloads\state_table.csv"
$targetpath = $env:HOMEDRIVE + $env:HOMEPATH + "\Documents\state_table.csv"

Copy-Item $sourcepath $targetpath  -UseTransaction

$CheckFile = Import-CSV $targetpath

If ($CheckFile.Count -lt 50) { Write-host "Error"; Undo-Transaction } else { "Transaction
Committed" ; Complete-Transaction }
```

Let's review the code above step by step. The first statement, copied here, imports a module that greatly aids us in our task:

```
Import-Module WASP
```

We will cover modules in detail later. Modules extend PowerShell's functionality by adding cmdlets. There are many free modules available for download, and typically a module adds extra support for a specific type of functionality. For example, SQLPS adds SQL Server connectivity. The module being loaded above, WASP, adds some powerful Windows application interaction functionality. Unless you have already downloaded WASP, you will need to do so. You can download it from http://wasp.codeplex.com/. After you download it, extract the file WASP.dll and copy it to a folder where PowerShell looks for modules. To determine where that is, enter the following into PowerShell:

```
$env:PSModulePath
```

We should see a list of folder paths separated by semicolons. This environment variable holds the places PowerShell will look for modules. Pick one of the folders, ideally one under your documents folder, and create a new folder named WASP in it. Then paste the unzipped WASP.dll in that folder. A module must have its own folder. We should be able to import the module now.

■ **Note** A shortcut to the precedincg process is to create a folder named WindowsPowerShell in your Documents folder, create a folder named Modules under it, and add the WASP module folder and DLL there. That WASP module folder is the PowerShell default location for user modules.

Now we can look at the application automation code. If you have trouble running the code, it may be that IE is not giving your script the HTML source for the web page. If so, you should be able to resolve this by running PowerShell as administrator:

```
Get-Process -name iexplore -ErrorAction SilentlyContinue | Stop-Process -Force -ErrorAction
SilentlyContinue
$ie = New-Object -comobject InternetExplorer.Application
$ie.visible = $true
$ie.silent = $true
$ie.Navigate( $url )
```

The Get-Process is piping any running instances of Internet Explorer that are running into the Stop-Process cmdlet so that when we create a new instance it will be the only one. Then, we create a new instance of Internet Explorer and load the reference to it into the variable $ie. Using the $ie variable, we set the visible property to $true so the window will show. Setting it to $false will make the window invisible. The silent property is to reduce messages. Then we just use the Navigate method to go to the URL stored in the variable $url. The code below activates IE.

```
while( $ie.busy){Start-Sleep 1}
Select-Window "iexplore" | Set-WindowActive
```

These statements above wait for IE to finish bringing up the page and then set the focus to that screen. Now we need to navigate through the web page to get the data, which we do with the following code:

```
$btn=$ie.Document.getElementById("USA")
$btn.Click()

while( $ie.busy){Start-Sleep 1}
$btn=$ie.Document.getElementById("major")
$btn.Click()

while( $ie.busy){Start-Sleep 1}
$btn=$ie.Document.getElementById("current")
$btn.Click()
```

The web page source code is available to the $ie object, and we can navigate around the web page by using the document object model. The first line searches the document for an element with the ID = "USA" and stores the reference in $btn. Then we can use the $btn click method to click the link. The while statement is just giving IE time to complete the action before continuing. The statement following the wait locates the link with the ID = "major" followed by a statement that clicks that. The same thing is done for the "current" link. What happens if the element you need does not have a unique ID? The code that follows shows a way to handle that:

```
$btn = $ie.Document.getElementsByTagName('A') | Where-Object {$_.innerText -eq 'Do not
include the US Minor Outlying Islands '}
$btn.Click()
```

Due to different browser settings, the behavior when a file is downloaded may be slightly different. On my browser, a pop-up dialog appears at the bottom of the screen with various options. If your browser behaves differently, you may need to play with the line of code here to get the script to work for you:

```
Select-Window iexplore | Set-WindowActive | Send-Keys "%S"
```

Send-Keys triggers key strokes to the window. The '%' is used to represent the Alt key, i.e., Alt + S is being pressed. You can play with these if the script does not work right at this point.

Here we find the elements with a TagName = "A" and then pipe them into a Where-Object cmdlet, which filters on the element with the innerText = 'Do not include the US Minor Outlying Islands'. An important point here is that sometimes more than one element meets the initial criteria, so remember that you can pipe the results into a Where-Object cmdlet and filter on specific attributes of the collection returned. The challenge in IE automation is getting to the element you need.

Finally, we get to the transaction, as shown here:

```
Start-Transaction -RollbackPreference TerminatingError

$sourcepath =  "c:" + $env:HOMEPATH + "\downloads\state_table.csv"
$targetpath =  "c:" + $env:HOMEPATH + "\Documents\state_table.csv"

Copy-Item $sourcepath $targetpath  -UseTransaction

$CheckFile = Import-CSV $targetpath

If ($CheckFile.Count -lt 50) { Write-host "Error"; Undo-Transaction } else { "Transaction
Committed" ; Complete-Transaction }
```

Start-Transaction kicks off the transaction; it has an interesting parameter RollbackPreference, which tells PowerShell under what error conditions, if any, the transaction should automatically be rolled back. Then we just set the source and destination path variables. The Copy-Item cmdlet call includes the UseTransaction parameter, which we use to tell PowerShell we want this action included in the transaction. Then we load the newly copied file into $CheckFile. Finally, we test that the new file has at least 50 rows, and if it does not we roll back the transaction using the Undo-Transaction cmdlet. Otherwise, we commit the transaction using the Complete-Transaction cmdlet.

Why Doesn't It Work?

PowerShell transactions sound good, but there is one problem: They don't work! Instead, PowerShell complains 'The provider does not support transactions. Perform the operation again without the -UseTransaction parameter.' You might think you are doing something wrong. After all, the documentation clearly shows UseTransaction as a valid parameter not only for Copy-Item but for many cmdlets. It turns out that the only context in which transactions are supported is in making changes to the Windows registry. This is not mentioned anywhere in the standard Microsoft documentation, but I confirmed it on some blogs and in conferring with others. Although Microsoft may decide to expand on transaction functionality, it seems unlikely since it was added in version 2.0 with no subsequent enhancements. The bottom line is that if you need to edit registry settings, you may want to use transactions. Otherwise, there's not much here of value to a developer. Try running the statement that follows as another way to verify this:

```
Get-Psprovider | where {$_.Capabilities -like "*transactions*"}
```

Sure enough, only the registry will come back as supported.

I focused a lot on this to save you wasted time trying to use PowerShell transactions. Database developers might be attracted to them because they are used to SQL Server transactions and the ability to commit and rollback changes. The problem is not so much the limited implementation as the lack of documentation on these limitations.

However, we can code in a way that precludes the need for transactions. For example, the previous transaction related code can be rewritten as shown below which would provide the same benefit without the need for transactions. Even on SQL Server, you need to consider the overhead and potential locking issues explicit transactions can generate.

```
$CheckFile = Import-CSV $sourcepath

If ($CheckFile.Count -lt 50) { Write-host "Error"; Undo-Transaction } else
{ "Transaction Committed" ; Copy-Item $sourcepath $targetpath  }
```

We just check the downloaded file before we copy over the file we use for our application.

■ **Warning!**   The only context in which transactions are supported is in making changes to the Windows registry.

Setting the Integrated Script Editor (ISE) Options

The ISE provides a number of options that control the behavior of the editor, and we can access these settings by selecting Tools from the drop-down menu and then selecting Options, as shown in Figure 4-5. It is worth taking the time to become familiar with these options, as we can access a number of time-saving features by selecting the right settings.

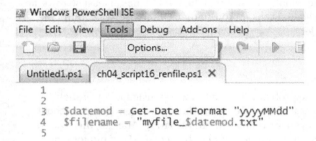

Figure 4-5. *Accessing the PowerShell ISE Tools options menu*

The first tab, shown in Figure 4-6, Colors and Fonts, lets us control the ISE color. Select the General tab to view the scripting settings as shown in Figure 4-6.

Figure 4-6. *The PowerShell ISE tool options General Settings panel*

Let's review what the options in Figure 4-6 do.

Show Outlining in the Script Pane enables the ability to hide blocks of code to make it easier to view large scripts. Figure 4-7 shows these feature enabled and the function's code hidden.

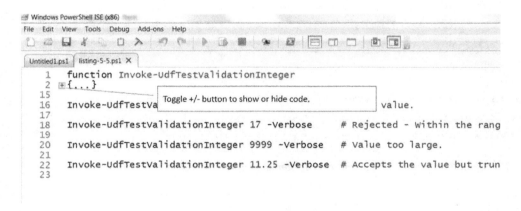

Figure 4-7. *The Script Editor in outline mode with function code hidden*

Clicking on the + will expand the code as shown in Figure 4-8.

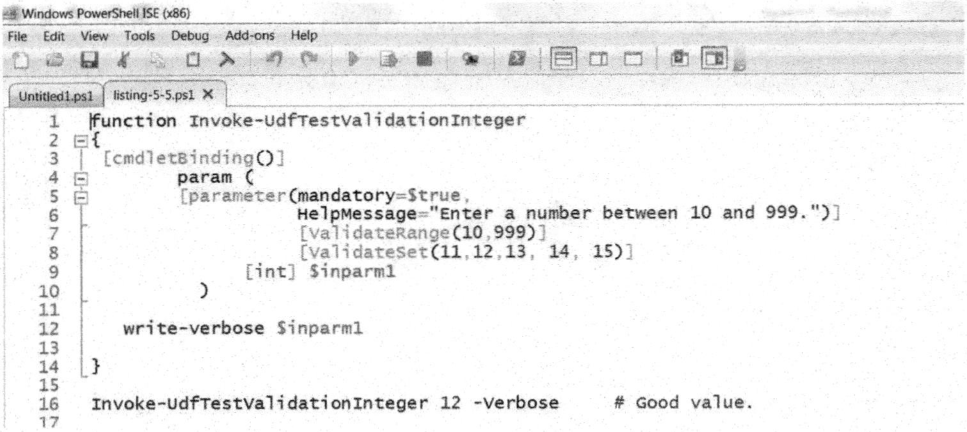

Figure 4-8. *The Script Edttor in outline mode with function code expande*

Show line numbers in the script pane will display line numbers in the left margin of the script when checked. When unchecked, line numbers are suppressed, as shown in Figure 4-9.

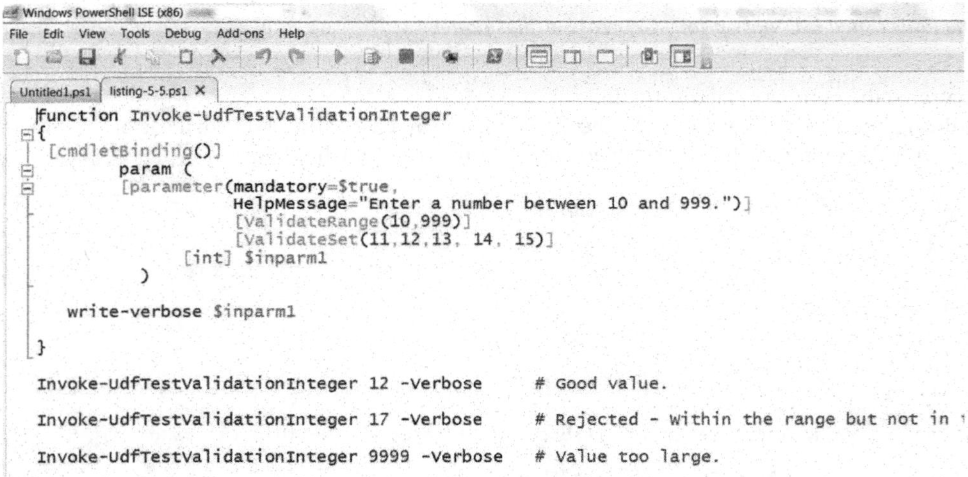

Figure 4-9. *The Script Editor with the line numbers option unchecked*

Warn me when I edit duplicate files is a feature to protect you from yourself. When enabled, if you open the same script in two different ISE tabs, you will be warned.

Prompt to save scripts before running them is another safety feature; after you make changes to a script that you have not saved, you will be prompted to do so when you try to run the script.

The **Script Pane position** drop-down combo box lets you control the placement of the script pane.

Show Intellisense in the Console Pane enables intellisense in the console window, which is very helpful in testing and development as you can try out cmdlets interactively. When enabled, you can get intellisense in the console, as shown in Figure 4-10.

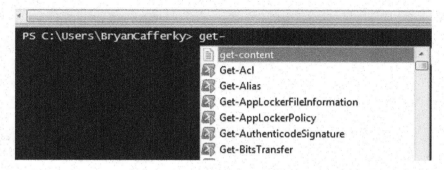

Figure 4-10. *The ISE's Console Pane with intellisense enabled for the console pane*

Enter selects Intellisense items in the Console Pane relates to intellisense being enabled in the Console Pane.

Show Intellisense in the Script Pane enables intellisense in the script window, which is very helpful in testing and development.

Enter selects Intellisense items in the Script Pane relates to intellisense being enabled in the script pane. If enabled, when intellisense pops up with a help list, pressing Enter on a selected item will copy it to the script at the current line.

Intellisense timeout in seconds sets the amount of time PowerShell will allow the ISE to load the required intellisense help. If it takes longer, no intellisense is provided, which can happen as the ISE has to look up the required information. If you have this problem, just increase the time allowed.

Use local help content instead of online content will get help information stored on your machine rather than getting it over the Internet.

Show the toolbar will display the ISE toolbar when checked.

Use default snippets enables the ability to bring up and insert a default set of snippets. Snippets are code fragments that you can insert into your scripts and that provide a starting point for some coding. The delivered snippets provide a skeleton set of code for many statements and cmdlets. If this feature is checked, you can bring up available snippets by right mouse clicking in the script pane and selecting snippets, as shown in Figure 4-11. You can also access snippets from the File drop-down menu.

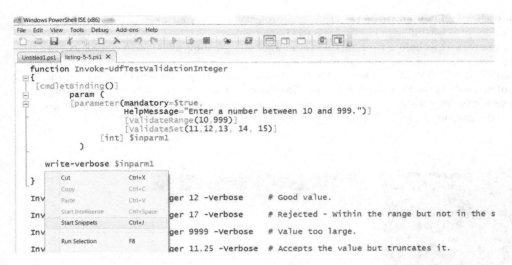

Figure 4-11. *Right mouse click in the script pane and select Start Snippets to bring up a pop up list of default snippets*

To select the desired snippet, select it from the scrolling snippet menu and press Enter, as shown in Figure 4-12.

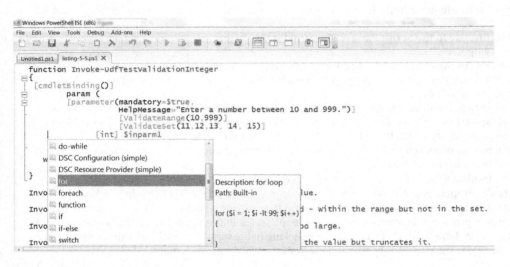

Figure 4-12. *The snippet selection menu*

AutoSave interval for scripts in minutes sets the amount of time the ISE waits after a change to save the code.

Number of recent files to show controls how many files are listed is the File drop-down menu.

Summary

We started the chapter by learning how to use `Set-StrictMode` to enforce coding rules that help avoid uninitialized variables, incorrect method calls, and invalid property references. Using `Set-StrictMode` during development can help avoid difficult-to-debug errors. Then, we had a detailed discussion on how to handle errors that get raised in scripts. This was followed by a review of the common cmdlet parameters, so called because all built-in cmdlets support them. From there, we touched briefly on PowerShell's debugging features. Then, we delved into how PowerShell can implement Windows forms to provide a GUI for our applications. This led into a discussion on how you can leverage .NET object events. We discussed PowerShell transactions and how they may not be as useful as we would have hoped. Finally, we discussed the PowerShell ISE options and how to use them.

CHAPTER 5

■ ■ ■

Writing Reusable Code

This chapter will cover how to use PowerShell to write the most robust reusable code possible. To do this, we will discuss how to use CmdletBinding in our functions. There are two types of CmdletBinding attributes: general attributes and parameter-specific attributes. The general attributes control how the overall function behaves. The parameter-specific attributes give us control over each parameter, including value validation. When a parameter is not provided, a default value is given. PowerShell defaults may not be what you expect, so we'll cover what they are and how to handle them. We'll also review how to define default values for parameters. Object-orientated languages support function overloading, which allows the same function name to be used with different types of parameters. We'll discuss how to simulate this using parameter sets, and we'll cover how to combine the pipeline with passed parameters to maximize the power and flexibility of your functions. Finally, in this age of globalization, we often need to support multiple languages, so we'll discuss how multiple language support can be implemented easily with special PowerShell features.

CmdletBinding Arguments

The use of the CmdletBinding attribute is so powerful that Microsoft documentation calls functions that employ it *advanced functions*. But don't let that scare you. Using the CmdletBinding is simple and makes your code much easier to use, test, and maintain. Although there are many attributes available with CmdletBinding, we don't have to include any of them to get the benefits of advanced functions. Let's look at a simple example below that uses CmdletBinding with no attributes.

```
function Write-UdfMessages
{
  [CmdletBinding()]
  param ()

  Write-Host    "This is a regular message."
  Write-Verbose "This is a verbose message."
  Write-Debug   "This is a debug message."

}

Write-UdfMessages -Verbose
Write-UdfMessages -Debug
```

The function uses minimal code to apply `CmdletBinding`, i.e. the `CmdletBinding` attribute followed by the param keyword. Just by adding those two lines, our function will support all the PowerShell common parameters including Verbose and Debug. When the Verbose parameter is passed, our function will display message output by the `Write-Verbose` statement. When the Debug parameter is passed, our function will display message output by `Write-Debug`, and then prompt us for the action we want to take. Without the `CmdletBinding` attribute, the Verbose and Debug parameters will be ignored along with the `Write-Verbose` and `Write-Debug` statements. Run the code. You should see the following output:

```
This is a regular message.
This is a regular message.
VERBOSE: This is a verbose message.
This is a regular message.
DEBUG: This is a debug message.
```

The real power of `CmdletBinding` comes with the numerous attributes it supports that allow us to customize how our functions should behave. Much of the additional functionality is automatically provided by PowerShell. Let's review the `CmdletBinding` attributes and how to use them starting with `SupportsShouldProcess`.

SupportsShouldProcess

The `SupportsShouldProcess` attribute adds support for the `Confirm` parameter which prompts the user for confirmation before performing a potentially risky action like deleting a file. It also adds support for the `WhatIf` parameter that lets you run a command and have it tell you what it will do without actually doing it. Many built-in cmdlets use this attribute, so let's take a look at one to see how this works:

```
"test" > myfile.txt    # Creates a text file.

Remove-Item myfile.txt -Confirm
```

Here we create a file with the line `"test" > myfile.txt`. Then, when we execute the `Remove-Item` cmdlet with the `Confirm` parameter, we are prompted on whether we want to perform the operation or not. Running the command from the ISE, we get the dialog box shown in Figure 5-1.

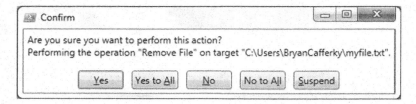

Figure 5-1. *The cmdlet confirmation dialog box*

We can also run the cmdlet, passing the `WhatIf` parameter to see what would happen if we ran the command. For example, the line below will perform the `Remove-Item` cmdlet with the `WhatIf` parameter:

```
Remove-Item myfile.txt -Whatif
```

When we run this command, we get a message like the one here, but the file is not deleted:

```
What if: Performing the operation "Remove File" on target "C:\Users\BryanCafferky\myfile.txt".
```

We can add support for the Whatif and Confirm parameters to our functions by adding the SupportsShouldProcess attribute. Let's look at the function in Listing 5-1 to see how the SupportsShouldProcess attribute works.

Listing 5-1. Function using the SupportShouldProcess attribute

```
function Invoke-UdfFileAction {
[CmdletBinding(SupportsShouldProcess=$true)]
        param (
                [Parameter(Mandatory = $true, Position = 0, ParameterSetName = "delete")]
                [switch]$dodelete,
                [Parameter(Mandatory = $true, Position = 1, ParameterSetName = "delete")]
                [string]$filetodelete,
                [Parameter(Mandatory = $true, Position = 0, ParameterSetName = "copy")]
                [switch]$docopy,
                [Parameter(Mandatory = $true, Position = 1, ParameterSetName = "copy")]
                [string]$filefrom,
                [Parameter(Mandatory = $true, Position = 2, ParameterSetName = "copy")]
                [string]$fileto
                )

if ($dodelete)
    {
      try
      {
          Remove-Item $filetodelete -ErrorAction Stop
          write-host "Deleted $filetodelete ."
      }
      catch
      {
          "Error:  Problem deleting old file."
      }
    }

if ($docopy)
    {
      try
      {
          Copy-Item $filefrom $fileto -ErrorAction Stop
          write-host "File $filefrom copied to $fileto."
      }
      catch
      {
          "Error:  Problem copying file."
      }
    }

}
```

Let's create a file to test the function using the following statement:

```
"somestuff" > somedata.txt    # Creates a file.
```

Now let's call the function using the Whatif parameter.

```
Invoke-UdfFileAction -dodelete 'somedata.txt' -Whatif
```

This function call would normally delete the text file because we passed the dodelete switch. However, because we included the Whatif parameter, the file is not deleted. Instead we see these messages:

```
What if: Performing the operation "Remove File" on target "C:\Users\BryanCafferky\somedata.txt".
Deleted somedata.txt .
```

Let's call the function again to copy a file:

```
"somestuff" > copydata.txt
Invoke-UdfFileAction -docopy 'copydata.txt' 'newcopy.txt' -Whatif
```

This code calls the function passing the –docopy switch, but since we passed the –whatif parameter, we see messages telling us what would be copied, with no copy operation actually being performed.

We will get the output seen here:

```
What if: Performing the operation "Copy File" on target "Item: C:\Users\BryanCafferky\
copydata.txt Destination: C:\Users\BryanCafferky\newcopy.txt".
File copydata.txt copied to newcopy.txt.
```

We can also use the Confirm parameter to be prompted before the action is taken. Since ETL processes are usually performed in batch, be careful to remove these parameters after testing.

HelpURI

The HelpURI attribute lets you specify a web link where help information can be found. The function in Listing 5-2 shows how it is used.

Listing 5-2. Usingthe HelpURI attribute

```
function Invoke-UdfHelp
{
[CmdletBinding(HelpURI="http://www.microsoft.com/en-us/default.aspx")]
        param (
                )

  Write-Host "Just to show the HelpURI attribute."
}
```

If we request help with the online switch parameter as shown below, the page specified in the HelpURI attribute is displayed in the default browser:

```
Get-Help -Online Invoke-UdfHelp
```

This help link is just to demonstrate how to use the HelpURI attribute. It is Microsoft's website.

SupportsPaging

The SupportsPaging attribute is used by built-in cmdlets to add some paging support. For example, the Get-Content command leverages this attribute to allow us to get portions of a file. Let's look at some examples.

This command will display the last ten lines of a file:

```
Get-Content somedata.txt  -Tail 10
```

This command displays the first ten lines of a file:

```
Get-Content somedata.txt  -Head 10
```

For a large file, we can speed up the display of data by using ReadCount to tell PowerShell to break up the pipeline into blocks of rows indicated by the ReadCount parameter. Let's look at an example:

```
Get-Content somedata.txt -ReadCount 1000
```

This statement will stream the file through the pipeline into blocks of 1,000 rows.

As an ETL developer, the obvious use in custom functions for the SupportsPaging attribute would be to control the reading of files. However, as just seen, the Get-Content cmdlet already provides a great deal of flexibility.

Validating Parameters

There are a number of parameter attributes that support validating that the parameter values meet criteria you specify. To understand what they are and how to use them, we'll discuss validation by data type.

Validating a String

There are a number of validation attributes to ensure that string parameters comply with our requirements. It is common in flat files to have strings storing dollar amounts that must be loaded. The function in Listing 5-3 requires a value be passed with a minimum length of 5 and a maximum length of 15 and that it consists of numbers followed by a decimal point and two digits, i.e., is a monetary amount.

Listing 5-3. Validating monetary amounts

```
function Invoke-UdfTestValidationMoney
{
 [CmdletBinding()]
        param (
        [parameter(mandatory=$true,
                  HelpMessage="Enter a number with two decimal places.")]
                  [ValidateLength(5,15)]
                  [ValidatePattern("^-?\d*\.\d{2}$")]
              [string] $inparm1
        )

   Write-Verbose $inparm1
}
```

In this code, the Mandatory attribute will force the caller to pass a value. ValidateLength requires a minimum length of 5 and a maximum of 15. Note: This includes the decimal point. The ValidatePattern uses a regular expression to make sure the value is a number with two decimal places.

Let's look at some calls to this function:

```
Invoke-UdfTestValidationMoney "123.22" -Verbose  # Good value.

Invoke-UdfTestValidationMoney "1.1" -Verbose  # Not enough digits after the decimal.

Invoke-UdfTestValidationMoney "12345678912345.25" -Verbose # String is too long.
```

The first call is good and the number passes validation. The second fails the format validation because it has only one digit after the decimal. The third call fails because it is passing a number that is greater than 15 characters in length.

Another option for validating strings is to restrict the accepted values to a list using the ValidationSet attribute, as shown in Listing 5-4.

Listing 5-4. Validating against a set

```
function Invoke-UdfTestValidationNEState
{
 [CmdletBinding()]
        param (
        [parameter(mandatory=$true,
                HelpMessage="Enter a New England state code .")]
                [ValidateSet("ME","NH","VT", "MA", "RI", "CT")]
            [string] $newenglandstates
        )

   write-verbose $newenglandstates
}
```

The ValidateSet attribute allows us to restrict the allowed values to the list we specify. In this case, we only want New England state codes.

Here are some examples of calling this function:

```
Invoke-UdfTestValidationNEState "RI" -Verbose   # Passes - RI is in the validation list.

Invoke-UdfTestValidationNEState "NY" -Verbose   # Fails - NY is not in the validation list
```

The first call succeeds because "RI" is in the validation set but the second call fails because "NY" is not in the validation set.

Validating a Number

To validate an integer, we can use the ValidateRange and ValidateSet. Let's look at the code in Listing 5-5.

Listing 5-5. Validating an integer

```
function Invoke-UdfTestValidationInteger
{
 [CmdletBinding()]
        param (
        [parameter(mandatory=$true,
                  HelpMessage="Enter a number between 10 and 999.")]
                  [ValidateRange(10,999)]
                  [ValidateSet(11,12,13, 14, 15)]
              [int] $inparm1
          )

   write-verbose $inparm1
}
```

The ValidateRange restricts the value to be between 10 and 999 inclusive. The ValidateSet attribute limits the values to those specified in the parentheses, i.e., 11, 12, 13, 14, or 15. Note that even though a value may pass the ValidateRange attribute, it may fail the ValidateSet attribute. Validating decimal numbers is similar to validating integers, except you can include decimal numbers in the ValidateRange and ValidationSet attributes.

Here are some examples of calling this function with various values:

```
Invoke-UdfTestValidationInteger 12 -Verbose      # Good value.

Invoke-UdfTestValidationInteger 17 -Verbose       # Rejected - Within the range but not in the set.

Invoke-UdfTestValidationInteger 9999 -Verbose     # Value too large.

Invoke-UdfTestValidationInteger 11.25 -Verbose  # Accepts the value but truncates it.
```

The first call is successful. The second is rejected because 17 is not in the validation set. The third call passes a value that exceeds the range. The fourth call shows that you need to be careful. You might think that a decimal value would be rejected since it is not an integer, but instead the decimal is just truncated without warning.

Validating an Array

You can still use all the validation attributes we've seen so far to validate individual elements of the array, but we have another useful attribute, ValidateCount, that sets the minimum and maximum number of array elements the array may have. In the example in Listing 5-6, the function has a parameter that is an array of Social Security numbers.

Listing 5-6. Validating an array

```
function Invoke-UdfTestValidationArray
{
 [CmdletBinding()]
        param (
        [parameter(mandatory=$true,
                  HelpMessage="Enter a string value.")]
                  [ValidateLength(9,11)]
```

```
                [ValidatePattern("^\d{3}-?\d{2}-?\d{4}$")]  # Pattern for SSN
                [ValidateCount(1,3)]
            [string[]] $inparm1
        )

    foreach ($item in $inparm1) {
    write-verbose $item
    }
}
```

Notice that we use the attribute ValidateCount, which takes the minimum number of elements as the first parameter and the maximum number of elements as the second parameter. If zero elements are passed or more than three elements are passed, the value will fail validation. Notice also that we still have ValidateLength and ValidatePattern attributes. These are applied to individual array elements. The following code will call this function with various values:

```
Write-Host "Good parameters..."
Invoke-UdfTestValidationArray @("123445678","999-12-1234") -Verbose  # Passes validation
write-host ""

Write-host "Bad parameters, Invalid format..."
Invoke-UdfTestValidationArray @("1234456789","999-12-123488") -Verbose # Fails validation -
first element does not match pattern.
write-host ""

Write-host "Bad parameters, Too many elements in the array..."
Invoke-UdfTestValidationArray @("123445678","999-12-1234","123-22-8888","999121234")
-Verbose
```

The first call above passes validation. It has the correct number of elements, each element is an acceptable length, and each element matches the validation pattern for a Social Security number. The second and third calls fail.

Using the ValidateScript Attribute

One of the most powerful validation attributes is ValidateScript as it allows us to call custom code to perform the validation. The final result returned must be a Boolean value, i.e., $true or $false. To give you an idea of just how useful this can be, let's consider an ETL-orientated application. We need to load a file, and as part of the process we want to validate the function parameters being passed to our load function. The two function parameters are a folder path and a state code. We want to confirm the path is valid—i.e., actually exists—and we want to make sure the state code is validated against a SQL Server table of state codes. To present the ideas clearly, the code that follows is focused on the validation without actually loading anything.

Before we validate the state code, we'll need to load them into an array. Technically, we could just validate each code by running a select query against SQL Server, but that would not be scalable. The goal here is to show you a practical example. Let's look at the code in Listing 5-7, which loads the state codes into an array.

Listing 5-7. Getting values from a table

```
#  Load the state code array
function Get-udfStatesFromDatabase
{
 [CmdletBinding()]
        param (
            )

$conn = new-object System.Data.SqlClient.SqlConnection("Data Source=(local);Integrated
Security=SSPI;Initial Catalog=AdventureWorks");
$conn.Open()

$command = $conn.CreateCommand()

$command.CommandText = "SELECT cast(StateProvinceCode as varchar(2)) as StateProvinceCode
FROM [AdventureWorks].[Person].[StateProvince] where CountryRegionCode = 'US';"

$SqlAdapter = New-Object System.Data.SqlClient.SqlDataAdapter
$SqlAdapter.SelectCommand = $command
$DataSet = New-Object System.Data.DataSet
$SqlAdapter.Fill($DataSet)

Return $DataSet.Tables[0]

$conn.Close()
}
```

Notice that the function in Listing 5-7 does not take any parameters. Rather, we want to load an array of state codes and pass it back to the calling code. The first thing we'll need to do is open a SQL Server connection, which the code that follows does:

```
$conn = new-object System.Data.SqlClient.SqlConnection("Data Source=(local);Integrated
Security=SSPI;Initial Catalog=Development");
$conn.Open()
```

Notice: We are not using the SQLPS module. We're going directly to the SQL Client API. This saves us the overhead of loading the SQLPS module. The first line creates a connection object pointing to a database named AdventureWorks on the local server instance. Then we just call the Open method of the connection object.

Next, we need to define the SQL command to be executed, which this code does:

```
$command = $conn.CreateCommand()

$command.CommandText = "SELECT cast(StateProvinceCode as varchar(2)) as StateProvinceCode
FROM [AdventureWorks].[Person].[StateProvince] where CountryRegionCode = 'US';"
```

The first line creates a SQL command object. The second line assigns the SQL statement to be executed but does not run it.

Commands that do not return data are simpler to code for, but as we *do* need to return data, we will use the following code:

```
$SqlAdapter = New-Object System.Data.SqlClient.SqlDataAdapter
$SqlAdapter.SelectCommand = $command
$DataSet = New-Object System.Data.DataSet
$SqlAdapter.Fill($DataSet)
```

The first line creates a SQLDataAdapter object. Then we assign the command object to the SQL Data Adapter's SelectCommand property. To hold the retrieved data, we create a data-set object with the statement $DataSet = New-Object System.Data.DataSet. Finally, we load the data set, $DataSet, with the query results, i.e., $SqlAdapter.Fill($DataSet).

Now that the results are in $DataSet, we can pass it back to the calling code with this statement:

```
Return $DataSet.Tables[0]
```

DataSet objects can hold multiple result sets, so the results are stored in a collection called Tables. Since we only ran a single select statement, we just need the first item in that collection, i.e., subscript 0. Finally, we close the connection object with the statement $conn.Close().

The code to call the above function is shown below.

```
$global:statelistglobal = Get-udfStatesFromDatabase #  Loads the state codes into variable
$global:statelistglobal
```

We need to have the state code array available to the validation script in our function shown in Listing 5-8. We could create a new state table array each time we call the function with the validate script, but that is very inefficient. Instead, we create a globally accessible array variable before we call the function with the validation script. Prefixing the variable name with $global: gives it a global scope, which means it is accessible to the entire PowerShell session. Note: It is not available to other PowerShell sessions.

The function that will validate the state code is shown in Listing 5-8.

Listing 5-8. Validating the state code

```
function Invoke-UdfValidateStateCode ([string] $statecode)
{
    $result = $false

    foreach ($states in $global:statelistglobal)
    {
        if ($states.StateProvinceCode -eq  $statecode)
        {
            $result = $true  }
    }

    Return $result
}
```

The code in Listing 5-7 must be executed prior to running the code in Listing 5-8. This is so the variable $global:statelistglobal is available. The function Invoke-UdfValidateStateCode takes only the state code as a parameter. We'll use a Boolean variable to hold the result, i.e. $true if the state code is in the list and $false if it is not. We initialize the $result to $false and then use foreach to loop through the StateProvinceCode values to see if any match the $statecode value passed into the function. If a match is found, $result is set to $true. If all items in the global array $global:statelistglobal are compared and no match is found, $result remains $false. The last line just returns $result.

The previous functions in Listings 5-7 and 5-8 laid the groundwork for our validation function, which is presented in Listing 5-9. You must run the other listings before running Listing 5-9.

Listing 5-9. Testing the validations

```
function Invoke-UdfTestValidation
{
 [CmdletBinding()]
       param (
       [              parameter(mandatory=$true, HelpMessage="Enter a folder path .")]
                      [ValidateScript({ Test-Path $_ -PathType Container })]
                      [string] $folder,
                      [parameter(mandatory=$true, HelpMessage="Enter a New England state code.")]
                      [ValidateScript({ Invoke-UdfValidateStateCode $_ })]
                      [string] $statecode

       )
   write-verbose $statecode
}
```

This function accepts two parameters: $folder, which is the path to a folder where a file resides, and $statecode, which is a two-character state code. Let's look at the ValidateScript attribute for the $folder parameter:

```
[ValidateScript({ Test-Path $_ -PathType Container })]
```

The script enclosed in the braces within the parentheses will execute with every function call. In this case, we have an in-stream code block that executes. $_ references the value being passed to the $folder parameter. We can use this to test its value. The Test-Path statement is verifying that the path actually exists.

As powerful as an in-stream script is, the real power comes when we call an external function, which is what we do to validate the state code. Let's look at the ValidateScript attribute for $statecode:

```
[ValidateScript({ Invoke-UdfValidateStateCode $_ })]
```

The function Invoke-UdfValidateStateCode is the function defined previously in the script. The ValidateScript is calling that function and passing the parameter $statecode to it via the $_ variable. If the state code is not in the state code array, the parameter will be rejected.

Listing 5-10 provides some examples of how to call our function. The comment on each line explains the expected output.

Listing 5-10. Running the validations. Note: You must run Listings 5-7, 5-8, and 5-9 prior to this to load the functions

```
$global:statelistglobal = Get-udfStatesFromDatabase # To load the global statelist

$rootfolder = $env:HOMEDRIVE + $env:HOMEPATH + "\Documents\"

Invoke-UdfTestValidation $rootfolder 'MA'  # Passes - good path and state code

Invoke-UdfTestValidation $rootfolder 'XX'  # Fails - Invalid state code

Invoke-UdfTestValidation "c:\xyzdir" 'RI'  # Fails - Invalid path
```

Default Parameter Values

What happens if An optional parameter is not passed to a function? What value will the parameter get assigned? The answer is that it depends. The function can specify a default value for the parameter. Default parameter values can also be set in the $PSDefaultParameterValues preference variable. If no default value is defined, a default value indicating no value is assigned.

Specifying a Default Parameter Value

As a best practice, it is good to provide default parameter values when possible. Fortunately, setting a default value for a parameter is easy. Just add the equal sign and the value after the parameter name, i.e., $myparm = 'somevalue'. The function in Listing 5-11 has defaults set for the most common parameter data types.

Listing 5-11. Setting default parameter values

```
function Invoke-UdfTestDefaultParameters
{
 [CmdletBinding()]
       param (
           [string]    $p_string = 'DefaultString',
           [int]       $p_int    = 99,
           [decimal]   $p_dec    = 999.99,
           [datetime]  $p_date   = (Get-Date),
           [bool]      $p_bool   = $True,
           [array]     $p_array  = @(1,2,3),
           [hashtable] $p_hash   = @{'US' = 'United States'; 'UK' = 'United Kingdom'}
           )
  "String is : $p_string"
  "Int is: $p_int"
  "Decimal is: $p_dec"
  "DateTime is  $p_date"
  "Boolean is: $p_bool"
  "Array is: $p_array"
  "Hashtable is: "
  $p_hash
}
```

Let's call the function with the following statement:

```
Invoke-UdfTestDefaultParameters
```

We should see output similar to these lines:

```
String is : DefaultString
Int is: 99
Decimal is: 999.99
DateTime is  12/04/2014 13:40:55
Boolean is: True
Array is: 1 2 3
Hashtable is:

Name                       Value
----                       -----
US                         United States
UK                         United Kingdom
```

Using $PSDefaultParameterValues

Suppose we have a parameter such as a server name that will always be the same value. We want a way to set this parameter with a default value so it does not need to be specified on every function call. This is where $PSDefaultParameterValues comes in. The PowerShell built-in variable $PSDefaultParameterValues is a hash table of key/value pairs that define default values to be used when a parameter that matches the key value is missing from a function call. This is useful as it can provide a good way to support multiple configurations. For example, we can specify one set of values for the Development environment, another for QA, and another for Production. Also, by setting the value as a default it only has to be maintained in one place. For example, if the development SQL Server name changes, we just have to change the name in the default setting.

Since $PSDefaultParameterValues is a hash table, we can make changes to it using standard hash table commands. The format of adding a new default to this variable is shown here:

```
$PSDefaultParameterValues.Add("cmdlet:Parameter Name","Parameter Value")
```

The Add method will insert an entry into $PSDefaultParameterValues. The first parameter is the key, and in the examples we just looked at, we want all cmdlets and functions to use these defaults so the first part is a wildcard, followed by a colon and the parameter name. The second parameter is the default value.

If we only want the default to apply to a specific cmdlet, we can specify the cmdlet as the first part of the key parameter as shown here:

```
$PSDefaultParameterValues.Add("Send-MailMessage:SmtpServer","smtp.live.com")
```

We could use a partial wildcard as show here:

```
$PSDefaultParameterValues.Add("Send*:SmtpServer","smtp.live.com")
```

This statement sets the parameter default only for cmdlets that start with "Send".

Code Using $PSDefaultParameterValues

In the previous examples, we wanted the parameter specified to use the default value for all cmdlets and functions. Each environment could have a different set of values. To see how this might be used in practice, let's look at the function in Listing 5-12, which queries a SQL Server database.

Listing 5-12. Running a SQL Query

```
$PSDefaultParameterValues.Add("*:sqlserver","(local)")
$PSDefaultParameterValues.Add("*:sqldatabase","AdventureWorks")

function Invoke-UdfSQLQuery
{
[CmdletBinding()]
        param (
                [string] $sqlserver        ,    # SQL Server
                [string] $sqldatabase      ,    # SQL Server Database.
                [string] $sqlquery              # SQL Query
          )

  $conn = new-object System.Data.SqlClient.SqlConnection("Data Source=$sqlserver;Integrated
  Security=SSPI;Initial Catalog=$sqldatabase");

  $command = new-object system.data.sqlclient.sqlcommand($sqlquery,$conn)

  $conn.Open()

  $adapter = New-Object System.Data.sqlclient.sqlDataAdapter $command
  $dataset = New-Object System.Data.DataSet
  $adapter.Fill($dataset) | Out-Null

  RETURN $dataset.tables[0]

  $conn.Close()
}
```

Notice that before we call the function, we add default values for the parameters sqlserver and sqldatabase. Then to run a query, we just need to call the following function:

```
Invoke-UdfSQLQuery   -sqlquery 'select top 100 * from person.address'
```

Assuming $PSDefaultParameterValues has been loaded with the default parameter values, this call will work in any environment. Ideally we would want the default parameter values to load automatically so that there is no risk that they will not be set. This can be accomplished by adding the code that loads $PSDefaultParameterValues into the user's profile script. We'll cover how to do that in Chapter 8, "Customizing the PowerShell Environment."

To remove items from $PSDefaultParameterValues, just use the Remove method, as shown here:

```
$PSDefaultParameterValues.Remove("*:sqlserver")
```

A nice feature of $PSDefaultParameterValues is that we can disable the entire set of defaults without removing them. We can do this by adding a special key of Disabled as shown here:

```
$PSDefaultParameterValues.Add("Disabled", $true)
```

To reactivate parameter defaults, we can either remove it as follows:

```
$PSDefaultParameterValues.Remove("Disabled")
```

Or we can just set the value of Disabled to $false as shown here:

```
$PSDefaultParameterValues[Disabled]=$false
```

For more information on using $PSDefaultParameterValues, see this link:

```
http://technet.microsoft.com/en-us/library/hh847819.aspx
```

Default Parameter Values When No Default Is Specified

It is tempting to assume that if a parameter is passed to a function with no default value specified, the default value assigned will be NULL. However, this is not the case with PowerShell. The value assigned depends on the data type of the parameter. The easiest way to understand this is to see it. The function in Listing 5-13 evaluates each parameter passed to determine the default value assigned.

Listing 5-13. Testing for unassigned parameters

```
function Invoke-UdfTestParameter
{
 [CmdletBinding()]
        param (
            [string]    $p_string,
            [int]       $p_int,
            [decimal]   $p_dec,
            [datetime]  $p_date,
            [bool]      $p_bool,
            [array]     $p_array,
            [hashtable] $p_hash
            )

#  Test the string...
   Switch ($p_string)
      {
      $null      { "String is null"  }
      ""         { "String is empty" }
      default    { "String has a value: $p_string" }
      }

   Switch ($p_int)
      {
      $null      { "Int is null"  }
      0          { "Int is zero" }
      default    { "Int has a value: $p_int" }
      }
```

```
Switch ($p_dec)
 {
  $null      { "Decimal is null"  }
  0          { "Decimal is zero" }
  default    { "Decimal has a value: $p_dec" }
 }

Switch ($p_date)
 {
  $null      { "Date is null"  }
  0          { "Date is zero" }
  default    { "Date has a value: $p_date" }
 }

Switch ($p_bool)
 {
  $null      { "Boolean is null"  }
  $true      { "Boolean is True" }
  $false     { "Boolean is False" }
  default    { "Boolean has a value: $p_bool" }
 }

Switch ($p_array)
 {
  $null      { "Array is null"  }
  default    { "Array has a value: $p_array" }
 }

Switch ($p_hash)
 {
  $null      { "Hashtable is null"  }
  default    { "Hashtable has a value: $p_hash" }
 }

}
```

In this simple function we use the Switch statement to test the value of each parameter. On the left side is the test value that, if matched, will cause the code in the braces to the right to be executed. Let's call the function with no parameters with the command that follows:

```
Invoke-UdfTestParameter
```

The output to the console is shown here:

```
String is empty
Int is zero
Decimal is zero
Date is null
Boolean is False
Array is null
Hashtable is null
```

We can see from the output that only the datetime, array, and hashtable data types are assigned null. Strings default to an empty string. Numeric parameters are set to zero. Boolean parameters default to False. It is important to be aware of this behavior and write code accordingly. For example, if a function were writing sales values to a table and the amount parameter were omitted, zero might be written, erroneously indicating there were zero sales. When testing for a Boolean value, the function's user may not be aware that by omitting the parameter they are actually selecting the False value.

Distinguishing Parameter Default Values from Intended Values

The default values PowerShell assigns when no parameter value is passed can cause problems. For example, a function may need to know you intended to pass a zero to an amount parameter versus omitting the parameter or passing a null. The CmdletBinding supports a Mandatory attribute that forces the calling code to provide a value. However, that alone will not solve the issue. Let's look at the function in Listing 5-14, which uses the Mandatory attribute.

Listing 5-14. Using the mandatory attribute

```
function Invoke-UdfTestMandatoryParameter
{
 [CmdletBinding()]
        param (
            [Parameter(Mandatory = $true)]
            [string]    $p_string,
            [Parameter(Mandatory = $true)]
            [int]       $p_int,
            [Parameter(Mandatory = $true)]
            [bool]      $p_bool,
            [Parameter(Mandatory = $true)]
            [array]     $p_array,
            [Parameter(Mandatory = $true)]
            [hashtable] $p_hash
            )
  "String is : $p_string"
  "Int is: $p_int"
  "Boolean is: $p_bool"
  "Array is: $p_array"
  Write-Host "Hashtable is: "
  $p_hash
}
```

String Parameters

If we call the function in Listing 5-14 without any parameters, we will be prompted for each parameter value. For the string parameter, suppose we want to force the user to pass a value, but also want to allow the value to be a zero-length string. See the following:

```
Invoke-UdfTestMandatoryParameter -p_string ''
```

Since the string is the first parameter, we can omit the others for now. When we run the function call, the value is rejected because a zero-length string is not considered a value. Suppose we try to pass a null as the string parameter as shown here:

```
Invoke-UdfTestMandatoryParameter -p_string $null
```

We still get an error. What we want is to accept an empty string but reject null or having the parameter omitted from the call. We can do this by using the AllowEmptyString attribute as shown in **bold** in Listing 5-15.

Listing 5-15. Using AllowEmptyString

```
function Invoke-UdfTestMandatoryParameter2
{
 [CmdletBinding()]
       param (
          [Parameter(Mandatory = $true)]
          [AllowEmptyString()]
          [string]    $p_string,
          [Parameter(Mandatory = $true)]
          [int]       $p_int,
          [Parameter(Mandatory = $true)]
          [bool]      $p_bool,
          [Parameter(Mandatory = $true)]
          [array]     $p_array,
          [Parameter(Mandatory = $true)]
          [hashtable] $p_hash
             )
  "String is : $p_string"
  "Int is: $p_int"
  "Boolean is: $p_bool"
  "Array is: $p_array"
  Write-Host "Hashtable is: "
  $p_hash
}
```

By adding the AllowEmptyString attribute, we get the desired behavior. Let's try a few calls to test this:

```
Invoke-UdfTestMandatoryParameter2                      # Will be prompted for parameter values.

Invoke-UdfTestMandatoryParameter2 -p_string ''         # Parameter passes validation.

Invoke-UdfTestMandatoryParameter -p_string $null       # Parameter fails validation.
```

The first call causes PowerShell to prompt you for a value. The second call accepts the string value. The third call rejects the string value.

Numeric Parameters

What about numeric parameters? Ideally, we want to accept zero only if it is passed to the function. Omitting the parameter or passing a null should be rejected. Let's test calling our function while omitting the integer parameter as shown here:

```
Invoke-UdfTestMandatoryParameter2 -p_string ''
```

When we run this statement, we are prompted for a value for $p_int. Let's try again but pass a null to $p_int:

```
Invoke-UdfTestMandatoryParameter2 -p_string '' -p_int $null
```

PowerShell accepted the null value, so it prompts us for the next parameter, $p_bool. What we want is to require that a value for $p_int be passed and to not allow it to be null. However, a zero should be accepted. Unfortunately, if we pass $null to the $p_int parameter, it is translated into a zero before it gets validated. How can we distinguish an intentional zero versus a null? I found the answer to this question at the link here:

```
http://stackoverflow.com/questions/25459799/passing-null-to-a-mandatory-parameter-to-a-
function
```

The solution is ingenious in that by replacing the parameter data type int with the .NET equivalent, [System.Nullable[int]], that allows nulls, we can now accept zero and reject null values. Let's look at the revised function in Listing 5-16.

Listing 5-16. Testing for null integers

```
function Invoke-UdfTestMandatoryParameter2
{
 [CmdletBinding()]
        param (
            [Parameter(Mandatory = $true)]
            [AllowEmptyString()]
            [string]    $p_string,
            [Parameter(Mandatory = $true)]
            [ValidateNotNull()]
            [System.Nullable[int]]  $p_int,
            [Parameter(Mandatory = $true)]
            [bool]      $p_bool,
            [Parameter(Mandatory = $true)]
            [array]     $p_array,
            [Parameter(Mandatory = $true)]
            [hashtable] $p_hash
            )
  "String is : $p_string"
  "Int is: $p_int"
  "Boolean is: $p_bool"
  "Array is: $p_array"
  Write-Host "Hashtable is: "
  $p_hash
}
```

Now let's test the function by passing null for $p_int:

```
Invoke-UdfTestMandatoryParameter2 -p_string '' -p_int $null
```

As expected, the null value is rejected. Now let's try passing a zero into $p_int:

```
Invoke-UdfTestMandatoryParameter2 -p_string '' -p_int 0
```

The zero value is accepted, so we are prompted for $p_bool. Just press Control+Break to exit the prompt.

Boolean Parameters

Remember, PowerShell supports the [switch] type, which in many cases is better suited to a task than a Boolean parameter. Since the boolean type parameter defaults to false, how do we require the user to provide a value and still allow both true and false? In this case, PowerShell does not translate the default before doing the validation, so we can address this by simply adding the ValidateNotNull attribute, as shown in Listing 5-17.

Listing 5-17. Testing for null Boolean parameters

```
function Invoke-UdfTestMandatoryParameter3
{
 [CmdletBinding()]
      param (
          [Parameter(Mandatory = $true)]
          [AllowEmptyString()]
          [string]    $p_string,
          [Parameter(Mandatory = $true)]
          [ValidateNotNull()]
          [System.Nullable[int]]  $p_int,
          [Parameter(Mandatory = $true)]
          [ValidateNotNull()]
          [bool]       $p_bool,
          [Parameter(Mandatory = $true)]
          [array]      $p_array,
          [Parameter(Mandatory = $true)]
          [hashtable] $p_hash
          )
  "String is : $p_string"
  "Int is: $p_int"
  "Boolean is: $p_bool"
  "Array is: $p_array"
  Write-Host "Hashtable is: "
  $p_hash
}
```

Let's test the change with the two statements that follow:

```
Invoke-UdfTestMandatoryParameter3 -p_string '' -p_int 0 -p_bool $null     # Rejected

Invoke-UdfTestMandatoryParameter3 -p_string '' -p_int 0 -p_bool $false     # Accepted
```

The first statement is rejected due to the null $p_bool parameter. The second statement has the $p_bool parameter accepted, so we are prompted for the $p_array parameter.

130

Array Parameters

A common requirement for an array parameter would be to allow an empty array but require the parameter, and to not allow a null value. We can get this behavior by adding the AllowEmptyCollection attribute to the parameter. The code in Listing 5-18 has this modification.

Listing 5-18. Using AllowEmptyCollection

```
function Invoke-UdfTestMandatoryParameter3
{
 [CmdletBinding()]
       param (
           [Parameter(Mandatory = $true)]
           [AllowEmptyString()]
           [string]    $p_string,
           [Parameter(Mandatory = $true)]
           [ValidateNotNull()]
           [System.Nullable[int]]  $p_int,
           [Parameter(Mandatory = $true)]
           [ValidateNotNull()]
           [bool]      $p_bool,
           [Parameter(Mandatory = $true)]
           [AllowEmptyCollection()]
           [array]     $p_array,
           [Parameter(Mandatory = $true)]
           [hashtable] $p_hash
           )
  "String is : $p_string"
  "Int is: $p_int"
  "Boolean is: $p_bool"
  "Array is: $p_array"
  Write-Host "Hashtable is: "
  $p_hash
}
```

Let's test the function with the following statement:

```
Invoke-UdfTestMandatoryParameter3 -p_string '' -p_int 0 -p_bool $false -p_array $null
```

This statement will cause PowerShell to reject the $p_array parameter. Let's try the call with an empty array as shown here:

```
Invoke-UdfTestMandatoryParameter3 -p_string '' -p_int 0 -p_bool $false -p_array @()
```

PowerShell accepts the empty array from the statement.

Interestingly, hashtable parameters behave differently than arrays do. For the hashtable parameter in the previous function, a null value will be rejected without adding the [AllowEmptyCollection()] attribute but an empty hashtable is accepted. Let's test this with the statements that follow:

```
Invoke-UdfTestMandatoryParameter3 -p_string '' -p_int 0 -p_bool $false -p_array @()
-p_hash $null  # Rejected
Invoke-UdfTestMandatoryParameter3 -p_string '' -p_int 0 -p_bool $false -p_array @()
-p_hash @{}   # Accepted
```

Validating Parameters the Old-Fashioned Way

Sometimes, with so many advanced features, we forget that we can do things ourselves using the traditional approach. If the built-in CmdletBinding validation attributes do not fit your needs, you can write the validation code into the function itself, as shown in Listing 5-19.

Listing 5-19. Validating parameters in the function

```
function Invoke-UdfTestManualValidation
{
 [CmdletBinding()]
      param (
          [string]    $p_string,
          [System.Nullable[int]]  $p_int,
          [bool]      $p_bool,
          [array]     $p_array,
          [hashtable] $p_hash
          )

  if ($p_string.Length -eq 0) {  Write-Host -foregroundcolor Red 'Specify a string value
  please.';         return    }

  if ($p_int -le 0) {  Write-Host -foregroundcolor Red 'Specify an integer greater than zero
  please.';         return  }

  if ($p_array.Count -eq 0 ) {  Write-Host -foregroundcolor Red 'Specify an array with at
  least one element please.';    return  }

  if ($p_hash.Count -eq 0) {  Write-Host -foregroundcolor Red 'Specify a hashtable with at
  least one element please.';    return  }

  "String is : $p_string"
  "Int is: $p_int"
  "Boolean is: $p_bool"
  "Array is: $p_array"
  Write-Host "Hashtable is: "
  $p_hash
}
```

This function is simple but shows that you can write custom code to do any validations you need. It just tests the values of the parameters passed into the function. Note: The Return statement at the end of each code block exits the function. Play with calling the function with various values. The statement that follows passes the validations:

```
Invoke-UdfTestManualValidation -p_string 'x' -p_int 1 -p_array @(1) -p_hash @{"a"="Test"}
```

Using Parameter Sets

Object-orientated languages usually support a feature called *function overloading*. This feature allows multiple functions with the same name to be created with different sets of parameters. When the function is called, the correct function is determined based on the parameter data types passed. In this way, the function will behave differently depending on the parameters passed. For example, we might have a function called get_size that returns the size of the variable passed to it. If the parameter is a string, we get back the length in bytes. If the parameter passed is a number, we get the value of the number. If the object passed is an array, we get the number of elements in the array. The nice thing about this feature is that it simplifies using a function library. For example, regardless of what the data is, you always call the print-output function. If we had a separate print function for every type of object we needed to print, the library would become cumbersome to use. Technically, PowerShell does not support function overloading. However, it has a feature called Parameter Sets that can be used to accomplish the same thing.

When we declare the parameters to a function, we can group them with a name, i.e., ParameterSetName. When the function is called, PowerShell determines which parameter set to use based on the parameter data types passed to the function. Let's consider an example. Suppose we want to have a function that will add type parameters. If two integers are passed to it, they should be added together. If two strings are passed to it, they should be concatenated. If a datetime and integer are passed to it, the integer value should be added as days to the datetime. Let's look at the function in Listing 5-20.

Listing 5-20. Using parameter sets to similate function overloading

```
function Invoke-UdfAddValue
{
[CmdletBinding(SupportsShouldProcess=$false)]
        param (
                [Parameter(Mandatory = $true, Position = 0, ParameterSetName = "number")]
                [int]$number1,
                [Parameter(Mandatory = $true, Position = 1, ParameterSetName = "number")]
                [int]$number2,
                [Parameter(Mandatory = $true, Position = 0, ParameterSetName = "string")]
                [string]$string1,
                [Parameter(Mandatory = $true, Position = 1, ParameterSetName = "string")]
                [string]$string2,
                [Parameter(Mandatory = $true, Position = 0, ParameterSetName = "datetime")]
                [datetime]$datetime1,
                [Parameter(Mandatory = $true, Position = 1, ParameterSetName = "datetime")]
                [int]$days
                )

    Switch ($PScmdlet.ParameterSetName)
    {
    "number"    { "Added Value = " + ($number1 + $number2)   }
    "string"    { "Added Value = " + $string1 + $string2   }
    "datetime"  { "Added Value = " + $datetime1.AddDays($days)  }
    }
}
```

In Listing 5-20, we can see there are three parameter sets, i.e., with the `ParameterSetNames` of number, `string`, and `datetime`. Depending on the parameter set used, a different action will be performed by the function. Providing a single method that can work with different types of objects is known as *polymorphism*, a key feature of an object-orientated language. Notice that the `Position` attribute uses positions 0 and 1 for all the parameter sets. This allows us to call the function and pass the parameters by position. Depending on the data types we pass, PowerShell will select the corresponding parameter set. Let's run the statements that follow to test our function:

```
Invoke-UdfAddValue 1 2
Invoke-UdfAddValue "one" "two"
Invoke-UdfAddValue (Get-Date)  5
```

We get output like the following lines:

```
Added Value = 3
Added Value = onetwo
Added Value = 12/11/2014 19:02:39
```

The one requirement for this to work is that for each parameter set, there must be at least one parameter that is not in any other sets.

We can have a parameter that participates in more than one parameter set. We do this by having each parameter set's name specified. The function in Listing 5-21 has a third parameter that is in both parameter sets. Note: If no parameter set is specified, the parameter is in all parameter sets.

Listing 5-21. Example of a parameter that is in multiple parameter sets

```
function Invoke-UdfMuliParameterSet
{
[CmdletBinding()]
        param (
                [Parameter(Mandatory = $true, Position = 0, ParameterSetName = "set1")]
                [int]$int1,
                [Parameter(Mandatory = $true, Position = 0, ParameterSetName = "set2")]
                [string]$string2,
                [Parameter(Mandatory = $true, Position = 1, ParameterSetName = "set2")]
                [Parameter(ParameterSetName = "set1")]
                [string]$string3
                )

    Switch ($PScmdlet.ParameterSetName)
    {
    "set1"    { "You called with set1." }
    "set2"    { "You called with set2." }
    }
    "You Always pass '$string3' which has a value of $string3."
}
```

We call the function as follows:

```
Invoke-UdfMuliParameterSet "one" "two"
```

Since only parameter set `set2` has two string parameters, PowerShell selects that parameter set. `$string3` is in both parameter sets.

Sometimes it is not clear to PowerShell which parameter set to use based on the data types passed. To avoid having the call fail, we can define a default parameter set to be used. Consider this function:

```
function Invoke-UdfDefaultParameterSet
{
[CmdletBinding()]
        param (
              [Parameter(Mandatory = $true, Position = 0, ParameterSetName = "set1")]
              [string]$string1,
              [Parameter(Mandatory = $true, Position = 0, ParameterSetName = "set2")]
              [string]$string2
              )

    Switch ($PScmdlet.ParameterSetName)
    {
    "set1"    { "You called with set1." }
    "set2"    { "You called with set2." }
    }

}
```

In this function, we have two parameter sets with the same data type. Try running it as shown here:

```
Invoke-UdfDefaultParameterSet "test"
```

The call fails because PowerShell cannot determine which parameter set to use. Let's try revising the function to add a DefaultParameterseName attribute, as shown in Listing 5-22.

Listing 5-22. Assigning a default parameter set

```
function Invoke-UdfDefaultParameterSet
{
[CmdletBinding(DefaultParametersetName="set1")]
        param (
              [Parameter(Mandatory = $true, Position = 0, ParameterSetName = "set1")]
              [string]$string1,
              [Parameter(Mandatory = $true, Position = 0, ParameterSetName = "set2")]
              [string]$string2
              )

    Switch ($PScmdlet.ParameterSetName)
    {
    "set1"    { "You called with set1." }
    "set2"    { "You called with set2." }
    }

}

Invoke-UdfDefaultParameterSet "test"
```

When we call the function as shown above, we get the message "You called with set1."

Using Switch Parameters with Parameter Sets

A handy technique for leveraging multiple parameter sets is to combine them with switch parameters. By including a switch—which groups the parameters—the function is easy to read. The switch serves as a parameter PowerShell can use to identify the correct parameter set. As an example, the function that follows will perform one of two actions. If called with the –dodelete parameter, it will delete the file identified in the $filetodelete parameter. If called with the –docopy parameter, the function will copy the file name in $filefrom to the file name in $fileto. Since the switch parameters are in different parameter sets, PowerShell will not let you pass both of them, and if you pass one of them, the related parameters will be required. Let's look at Listing 5-23.

Listing 5-23. Using a switch parameter with parameter sets

```
function Invoke-UdfFileAction {
[CmdletBinding()]
        param (
                [Parameter(Mandatory = $true, Position = 0, ParameterSetName = "delete")]
                [switch]$dodelete,
                [Parameter(Mandatory = $true, Position = 1, ParameterSetName = "delete")]
                [string]$filetodelete,
                [Parameter(Mandatory = $true, Position = 0, ParameterSetName = "copy")]
                [switch]$docopy,
                [Parameter(Mandatory = $true, Position = 1, ParameterSetName = "copy")]
                [string]$filefrom,
                [Parameter(Mandatory = $true, Position = 2, ParameterSetName = "copy")]
                [string]$fileto
                )

if ($dodelete)
    {
    try
    {
        Remove-Item $filetodelete -ErrorAction Stop
        write-host "Deleted $filetodelete ."
    }
    catch
    {
        "Error:  Problem deleting old file."
    }
    }

if ($docopy)
    {
    try
    {
        Copy-Item $filefrom $fileto -ErrorAction Stop
        write-host "File $filefrom copied to $fileto."
    }
    catch
    {
        "Error:  Problem copying file."
    }
    }
}
```

The following code shows some examples of calling the function Invoke-UdfFileAction using the different parameter sets:

```
"somestuff" > somedata.txt

Invoke-UdfFileAction -dodelete 'somedata.txt'

"somestuff" > copydata.txt
Invoke-UdfFileAction -docopy 'copydata.txt' 'newcopy.txt'
```

In the function in Listing 5-23, we tested which switch was passed using the if statement, and since a switch is a Boolean, we just need to say if ($myswitch) to test the value. If the switch is not passed, its value is false. The Try statement catches any errors. Notice that we use the ErrorAction parameter on the Remove-Item and Copy-Item cmdlets to force an error if there is a problem—i.e., the Catch block will handle it. The technique of combining switch parameters with parameter sets provides a great way to build multi-purpose functions that are easy to use and maintain. Admittedly, this example puts two very different behaviors together into one function. This is just to make the point that parameter sets can make functions quite dynamic.

ValueFromPipeline and ValueFromPipelineByPropertyName Attributes

We saw earlier how to take data in from the pipeline. We can combine the pipeline with passed parameters to get even greater flexibility. By setting the parameter attribute ValueFromPipeline=$true, we flag a parameter as coming from the pipeline. The pipeline collection can contain any number of properties. PowerShell lets us map specific pipeline properties to a parameter with the ValueFromPipelineByPropertyName attribute. When we use this attribute, we need to make the parameter name match the property from the pipeline we want. To see how this works, we'll revise the Invoke-UdfFileAction function we saw earlier by having the copy action take file names from the pipeline. Let's look at the code in Listing 5-24.

Listing 5-24. Using ValueFromPipelineByPropertyName

```
function Invoke-UdfFileAction {
[CmdletBinding(SupportsShouldProcess=$true)]
    param (
        [Parameter(Mandatory = $true, Position = 0, ParameterSetName = "delete")]
        [switch]$dodelete,
        [Parameter(Mandatory = $true, Position = 1, ParameterSetName = "delete")]
        [string]$filetodelete,
        [Parameter(Mandatory = $true, Position = 0, ParameterSetName = "copy")]
        [switch]$docopy,
        [Parameter(Mandatory = $true,
                ValueFromPipelineByPropertyName=$True, ParameterSetName = "copy")]
        [string[]]$fullname,
        [Parameter(Mandatory = $true,
                ValueFromPipelineByPropertyName=$True, ParameterSetName = "copy")]
        [long[]]$length,
        [Parameter(Mandatory = $true, Position = 1, ParameterSetName = "copy")]
        [string]$destpath
        )
```

```
Begin
{
if ($dodelete)
    {
    try
        {
        Remove-Item $filetodelete -ErrorAction Stop
        write-host "Deleted $filetodelete ."
        }
    catch
        {
        "Error:  Problem deleting old file."
        }
    }
}

Process
{
if ($docopy)
    {
    try
        {
        foreach ($filename in $fullname)
        {
        Copy-Item $filename $destpath -ErrorAction Stop
        write-host "File $filename with length of $length copied to $destpath."
        }
        }
    catch
        {
        "Error:  Problem copying file."
        }
    }
}
}
```

The first thing to notice in the function is that the copy parameter set's file name property is called $fullname and now has the $ValueFromPipelineByName=$true. This tells PowerShell that 1) the value will be provided by the pipeline and 2) the property we want passed into this parameter is the FullName property. We also get the $length property from the pipeline, so we can display the length of each file as it is copied. This is included to show that you can pull multiple properties by name from the pipeline. Notice also that we now need to have separate code blocks in the function. By default, a function's code runs in the Begin block, so it does not need to be explicitly coded. However, now we need the Begin and the Process blocks. The Begin block will handle the Delete action, which does not use the pipeline. The Process block is used to copy each item in the pipeline.

The statements that follow will call our new function. Note: We're using the –Whatif parameter so that we can see what would happen without actually doing anything.

```
"somestuff" > somedata.txt

Invoke-UdfFileAction -dodelete 'somedata.txt' -whatif

Get-ChildItem *.txt | Invoke-UdfFileAction -docopy 'c:\users\BryanCafferky\hold\' -WhatIf
```

Don't forget that we can still call the function without using the pipeline. The statement here calls the function to copy a single file, passing the $fullname directly:

```
Invoke-UdfFileAction -docopy –length 0  -fullname 'c:\users\BryanCafferky\test.txt' `
'c:\users\BryanCafferky\hold\' –WhatIf
```

The length parameter does not make sense, since the user would have to look it up. In a case like this, it is easier just to pass a zero in. If you just want to take the whole pipe in, use the parameter attribute $ValueFromPipeline=$true. However, you will need to write code to pull out the properties you need, and the user could pass the function a pipe without the required property.

Internationalization with the Data Section

Nowadays, businesses are global and need to support multiple cultures and languages. PowerShell has a nice feature call the data section to support an easy implementation of multiple languages. The idea is to put all the strings that will be displayed into a separate file from the code. A separate file will store the string values in a specific language. Remember, PowerShell is used by Windows, so you can see this implemented on your computer. If you go to the folder C:\Windows\diagnostics\system\Power, you will see a folder with the default language for your machine. On my machine I see a folder named en-US. In this folder are a number of files, all with the file extension ".psd1". These files are PowerShell data section scripts. Let's take a look at one named RS_Balanced.psd1:

```
# Localized    11/20/2010 12:55 PM (GMT)    303:4.80.0411    RS_Balanced.psd1
ConvertFrom-StringData @'
###PSLOC
set_Balanced=Set active power plan to Balanced
Report_name_SetActiveSchemeGuid_result=The result of setting active scheme GUID
Report_name_ActiveSchemeGuid=Power Plan Adjustment
activeschemeguid_original=Original Plan
activeschemeguid_reset=New Plan
###PSLOC
'@
```

If this code looks familiar, that's because it is mostly a Here string. The ConvertFrom-StringData is a cmdlet that loads the key/value pairs defined in the string into a hash table. The file is loaded by the PowerShell script C:\Windows\diagnostics\system\Power\RS_Balanced.ps1. Let's look at the first few lines of that script to see how it works:

```
# Copyright © 2008, Microsoft Corporation. All rights reserved.

# Break on uncaught exceptions
trap {break}

. .\Powerconfig.ps1

#Localization Data
Import-LocalizedData localizationString

Write-DiagProgress -activity $localizationString.set_Balanced
```

The line that runs the Import-LocalizedData cmdlet is loading the data section from RS_Balances.psd1 into the hashtable variable $localizationString. When the statement 'Write-DiagProgress -activity $localizationString.set_Balanced' is executed, it will display the text associated with the key 'set_Balanced', which we can see in the data section is "Set active power plan to Balanced".

So, how did Windows know where to find the localization data section script? To determine the folder, Windows checked the default culture for the machine. Enter the following line at the PowerShell prompt:

```
$PSUICulture
```

On my machine this displays en-US. The first two characters identify the language as English. The two characters after the dash identify the country, i.e., dialect, as United States. The data section script is stored in a folder named en-US under the script that uses it. That explains how PowerShell knew where to find the file, but how did it know the name? Simple, the data section script has the same file name as the script that loads it, but with a psd1 extension instead of the script extension of ps1. If I were a user in Germany, my culture setting would probably be de-DE. The Windows installation would create a subdirectory with that name and store the German-language versions of the strings there. This allows the same PowerShell script to display the language appropriate to the machine.

One of the challenges to supporting a language is knowing the correct localization code to use for the folder name. The link that follows can help you with this:

```
http://msdn.microsoft.com/en-us/library/windows/desktop/dd318693(v=vs.85).aspx
```

To get a better idea of how we can use data sections in our own code, let's consider a simple demonstration. We want to display the day of the week in the language of the user. We'll assume we only need to support US English (en_US), Germany's German (de-DE) and Spain's Spanish (es-ES). Under the folder where our PowerShell script will run, we'll create the following folders: en-US, de-DE, and es-ES. Our script will be called translate.ps1, so in each of these folders we will create a data section called translate.psd1. Let's review the content of these files next. Listing 5-25 contains the US English version. Listing 5-26 has the Germany German translation. Listing 5-27 has the Spain Spanish translation.

Listing 5-25. En-US translation to be saved as translate.psd1 in the subfolder en-US

```
#  Folder: en-US
ConvertFrom-StringData @"
    Sunday=Sunday
    Monday=Monday
    Tuesday=Tuesday
    Wednesday=Wednesday
    Thursday=Thursday
    Friday=Friday
    Saturday=Saturday
"@
```

Listing 5-26. de-DE translation to be saved as translate.psd1 in the subfolder de-DE

```
# Folder:  de-DE
ConvertFrom-StringData @"
    Sunday=Sonntag;
    Monday=Montag;
    Tuesday=Deinstag;
    Wednesday=Mittwoch;
```

```
        Thursday=Donnerstag;
        Friday=Freitag;
        Saturday=Samstag
"@
```

Listing 5-27. es-ES translation to be saved as translate.psd1 in the subfolder es-ES

```
# Folder: es-ES
ConvertFrom-StringData @"
        Sunday=domingo
        Monday=lunes
        Tuesday=martes
        Wednesday=miércoles
        Thursday=jueves
        Friday=viernes
        Saturday=sábado
"@
```

We have three files—one to translate each language. We're using English as an anchor language to make this easier to follow. The key is always in English, but the translation will be whatever language is appropriate for the user. Note: If we need to support another language in the future, we would just need to add another subfolder with the appropriate localization name and then store the file translate.psd1 in it along with the required translation. Let's try the translations out with the script in Listing 5-28.

Listing 5-28. Translating to the default language

```
Import-LocalizedData -BindingVariable ds                    # Machine Default - English

$ds.Sunday
$ds.Monday
$ds.Tuesday
$ds.Wednesday
$ds.Thursday
$ds.Friday
$ds.Saturday
```

The output is shown below.

```
Sunday
Monday
Tuesday
Wednesday
Thursday
Friday
Saturday
```

The first line loads the data section using the Import-LocalizedData cmdlet. Again, since the data section script name is the same as the calling script, we do not need to supply the file name. The script will use the translation appropriate for your machine. On my machine, it will display English. Rather than change the default language on our machine to test the other translations, we supply the UICulture parameter to the Import-LocalizedData cmdlet, specifying the language we want. Let's try the German translation by passing the UICulture parameter de-DE, as shown in Listing 5-29.

Listing 5-29. Translating to the German language

```
Import-LocalizedData -BindingVariable ds -UICulture de-DE  # German

$ds.Sunday
$ds.Monday
$ds.Tuesday
$ds.Wednesday
$ds.Thursday
$ds.Friday
$ds.Saturday
```

Which produces the following output:

```
Sonntag
Montag
Deinstag
Mittwoch
Donnerstag
Freitag
Samstag
```

Finally, let's try the Spanish translation by passing the UICulture parameter es-ES, as shown in Listing 5-30.

Listing 5-30. Translating to the Spanish language

```
Import-LocalizedData -BindingVariable ds -UICulture es-ES  # Spanish

$ds.Sunday
$ds.Monday
$ds.Tuesday
$ds.Wednesday
$ds.Thursday
$ds.Friday
$ds.Saturday
```

The output for this is as follows:

```
domingo
lunes
martes
miércoles
jueves
viernes
sábado
```

This simple example shows how easy it is to add support for multiple languages. PowerShell lets you transparently leverage the localization configuration setting in Windows. Normally, we would not need to call the Import-LocalizedData with the language specified, because PowerShell would select the appropriate language for the machine on which the script is running. If there is any chance you will need to support multiple languages, it may be a good idea to separate your display strings into separate data section files so you can easily add more languages.

Summary

This chapter explained how to use PowerShell to write robust, reusable code. We discussed how to use `CmdletBinding` in our functions, with detailed discussions of using `CmdletBinding` general attributes and parameter-specific attributes. The general attributes control how the overall function behaves. The parameter-specific attributes give us control over each parameter, including value validation. Then we discussed what default values are given when a parameter is not passed to a function and how to handle them. We reviewed how to define default values for parameters. We discussed function overloading and how to simulate it using parameter sets. Then we discussed how to combine the pipeline with passed parameters to maximize the power and flexibility of our functions. Finally, we covered how to use PowerShell's unique features to implement multiple-language support in your code.

CHAPTER 6

■ ■ ■

Extending PowerShell

To load a single function for use in a script, we use the dot-sourcing method discussed previously. However, what if we have many related functions that we want to make available to our script? Do we need to dot source each function individually? Fortunately, the answer is no. PowerShell provides an elegant way to group a set of functions together into a module so they can be loaded in just one statement. We've already used this feature in previous examples, and now we're going to discuss how we can create our own modules. We will also cover how to merge multiple script files into a module by using a manifest. Modules can be written in PowerShell script or in .NET languages like C#. Modules are one of the great extensibility features of PowerShell, and you can find many free modules available for download. Some, such as the SQL Server Module, SQLPS, are written by Microsoft, and others by vendors or the Windows community. We'll discuss some of the popular modules available and how to use them.

The Four Types of Modules

There are four types of PowerShell modules: binary, script, dynamic, and manifest. Binary modules are modules written in a compiled .NET language like C#. Because binary modules can only be written in C# or VB .NET, we are not going to cover creating them as it is beyond the scope of this book. In PowerShell 1.0, all modules had to be written in a .NET language.

Dynamic modules are modules created within a script that are not saved. Rather, they just persist for the duration of the PowerShell session.

A manifest module is a module that includes a special file called a manifest that documents the module and supports the ability to include other modules and related files.

Script modules are the most important for our purposes because they are written in the PowerShell language. We will cover creating and using them in great detail. For more-detailed technical information about modules, see the following link: http://msdn.microsoft.com/en-us/library/dd878324%28v=vs.85%29.aspx.

Script Modules

To create a script module we need to save the source code of the functions in one script file, using the extension .psm1, and then store it in a folder where PowerShell looks for modules. Where would that be? We can find that out by looking at the environment variable $env:psmodulepath. Enter it on the console:

```
$env:psmodulepath.
```

On my machine, I get the following:

C:\Users\BryanCafferky\Documents\WindowsPowerShell\Modules;C:\Program Files\
WindowsPowerShell\Modules;C:\Windows\system32\WindowsPo
werShell\v1.0\Modules\;c:\Program Files (x86)\Microsoft SQL Server\110\Tools\PowerShell\
Modules\;C:\Users\BryanCafferky\Documents\P
owerShell\Modules\

The first folder, in bold, is the best place to put our custom modules. It is there for that purpose. By default PowerShell will look for modules under the current userListings Documents folder in WindowsPowerShell\Modules\. We don't want to mess around with anything under the Windows folder, as Microsoft maintains those. Let's assume we want to store the following script as a module:

```
# Simple module example

function Invoke-UdfAddNumber([int]$p_int1, [int]$p_int2)
{
     Return ($p_int1 + $p_int2)
}

function Invoke-UdfSubtractNumber([int]$p_int1, [int]$p_int2)
{
     Return ($p_int1 - $p_int2)
}
```

The module will be named umd_Simple. First, we need to create a folder named umd_Simple in our \Documents\WindowsPowerShell folder. If the folder does not have the same name as the module, PowerShell cannot find it. Then, we need to save the script in the umd_simple folder with the name umd_simple.psm1. Let's review the requirements of creating a module:

- It consists of a script file that contains one or more functions.
- It must be stored in a folder that is listed in $env:psmodulepath.
- The script must be stored in its own folder with the same name as the script file, less the extension.
- The script must be saved as the module name we want using the extension .psm1.

All these conditions must be met in order for PowerShell to be able to locate and use the module.

Now that we have the script umd_Simple.psm1 stored in our Documents folder under WindowsPowerShell\umd_simple, we can import the module with this statement:

```
Import-Module umd_Simple
```

With the module imported, let's try the functions as shown here:

```
Invoke-UdfAddNumber 1 4
Invoke-UdfSubtractNumber 4 1
```

We should get the following output:

```
5
3
```

It's that simple. This module is not very useful, but it demonstrates the process of creating and using modules.

■ **Note**   As a general rule, avoid putting spaces in any object names which includes folders and script names. It just makes things more complicated to deal with. Letters, numbers, and underscores are fine to use.

Microsoft wanted to make it as easy as possible for users to create script modules. In doing so, they automatically default some behaviors. For example, all functions are automatically visible to the script that imports the module, but variables of the module are not visible. Generally, that works pretty well. However, suppose we want to be able to access a module variable. An object-oriented programming best practice is to never let outside code directly access an object's variables. Instead, a Set function is provided to modify the variable's value, and a Get function is provided to retrieve the variable's value. This insulates the function from the outside world; i.e., external code cannot just assign any value, since the Set function can validate the data. Also, the internal implementation of the property may need to be changed over time, say from an int to a string, but the external interface, i.e., the Get and Set functions, can be maintained so that these changes do not affect external use of the properties.

Before we get into variations of modules, I want to introduce a more robust example. This module will load a sales tax rate table and a foreign currency conversion table. It exposes functions to set the path to the sales tax file; get the path to the sales tax file; get the tax rate for a given state; and get the currency conversion rate for a given foreign currency. The function to get the exchange rate uses parameter sets, so it can return either the number of units of the foreign currency to equal one US dollar or the number of US dollars to equal one foreign currency unit.

Let's review the code below.

```
<# Module Name:   umd_state.psm1

   Author:        Bryan Cafferky

   Purpose:       A module demostration.

#>
<#
   .SYNOPSIS
     Demonstrate the creation and use of a custom module written in PowerShell.

   .Description
         This module was created to demonstrate the use of custom PowerShell modules.

   .Notes
         Author:  Bryan Cafferky for Pro PowerShell Development.
         Version: 1.0

#>

[string]$script:salestaxfilepath = ($env:HomeDrive + $env:HOMEPATH + `
 "\Documents\StateSalesTaxRates.csv")

$inexchangerate = Import-CSV ($env:HomeDrive + $env:HOMEPATH + `
 "\Documents\currencyexchangerate.csv")
```

147

```powershell
[hashtable]$script:salestax = @{}

function Set-UdfSalesTaxFilepath {
        [CmdletBinding()]
        param (
            [Parameter(Mandatory = $true)]
            [ValidateScript({ Test-Path $_ })]
            [string]$p_taxfilepath
            )
        }
{
    $script:salestaxfilepath = $p_taxfilepath
}

function Get-UdfSalesTaxFilepath
{
    Write-Host $script:salestaxfilepath
}

function Invoke-UdfStateRateLoad
{

    $insalestax = Import-CSV $salestaxfilepath

    foreach ($item in $insalestax) {$script:salestax[$item.StateCode] = $item.SalesTaxRate}

}

function Get-UdfStateTaxRate
{
 [CmdletBinding()]
        param (
            [string]    $p_statecode
            )

    if ($script:salestax.Count -eq 0)
    {
        "Here"
        Invoke-UdfStateRateLoad
    }

    $script:salestax["$p_statecode"]

}

# Note:  Site: http://www.xe.com/currency/usd-us-dollar?r provided Currency Conversion
values.

$exchangerate = Import-CSV ($env:HomeDrive + $env:HOMEPATH + "\Documents\
currencyexchangerate.csv")
```

```
function Get-UdfExchangeRate
{
 [CmdletBinding()]
        param (
            [Parameter(Mandatory = $true, Position = 0)]
            [string]     $p_currencycd,
            [Parameter(Mandatory = $true, Position = 1)]
            [string]     $p_asofdate,
            [Parameter(Mandatory = $true, Position = 2, ParameterSetName = "unitsperusd")]
            [switch]     $UnitsPerUSD,
            [Parameter(Mandatory = $true, Position = 2, ParameterSetName = "usdperunits")]
            [switch]     $USDPerUnits,
            [Parameter(Mandatory = $true, Position = 2, ParameterSetName = "currencyname")]
            [switch]     $CurrencyName
            )

    foreach ($item in $exchangerate)
    {
        if ($item.CurrencyCD -eq $p_currencycd -and $item.AsOfDate -eq $p_asofdate)
        {
            if ($CurrencyName) { Return $item.CurrencyName  }
            if ($UnitsPerUSD)  { Return $item.UnitsPerUSD   }
            if ($USDPerUnits)  { Return $item.USDPerUnit    }
        }

    }
 }
```

There's a lot happening in this script, so we're going to walk through it slowly in order to understand everything it is doing. Note: The actual sales tax rates and conversion rates may not be accurate, so do not rely on them. The goal here is to provide a realistic example of how a script module might be used in database development.

In this code, I included both custom comments and PowerShell-supported comment tags to remind us that we should include these whenever possible. Remember, the comment tags are automatically provided to users when they request help. The first non-comment line declares a string variable, as shown here:

```
[string]$script:salestaxfilepath = $env:HomeDrive + $env:HOMEPATH + `
"\Documents\StateSalesTaxRates.csv"
```

This variable stores the location of a file be loaded. Remember, by default this variable is not visible to the script that imports the module. To avoid hard-coded file paths, we use the environment variables $env:HomeDrive and $env:HOMEPATH to get the path to the documents folder for the current user. This is approach is repeated elsewhere.

Then, we load an external CSV file into the variable $inexchangerate with the statement that follows:

```
$inexchangerate = Import-CSV $env:HomeDrive + $env:HOMEPATH + `
"\Documents\currencyexchangerate.csv"
```

We're going to load a state sales tax hashtable, so we declare it with the following line:

```
[hashtable]$script:salestax = @{}
```

This hashtable is empty but will be loaded by a function.

We want to allow the calling script to be able to change the sales tax file that gets loaded, but, as mentioned, it is not a good practice to give an external program access to a module variable. Instead, we create a special function to assign a value to the variable and another function to get the value of the variable. Let's look at the function that sets the variable's value:

```
function Set-UdfSalesTaxFilepath {
        [CmdletBinding()]
        param (
            [Parameter(Mandatory = $true)]
            [ValidateScript({ Test-Path $_ })]
            [string]$p_taxfilepath
            )
            }
{
    $script:salestaxfilepath = $p_taxfilepath
}
```

In this code, notice that we are using the CmdLetBinding ValidateScript feature to test the existence of the path being passed to the Set-UdfSalesTaxFilepath function. This is included to demonstrate how using a Set function can enhance the extensibility of the code. If the path exists, it is assigned to the module variable $script:salestaxfilepath.

To retrieve the value of the variable, the following function is provided:

```
function Get-UdfSalesTaxFilepath
{
    Return $script:salestaxfilepath
}
```

This code just returns the value of $script:salestaxfilepath. Although, in this case, it seems unnecessary to have a Get function, it is a good practice as requirements may change and the need to add additional logic is always a possibility.

Let's test these functions with the following code:

```
Import-Module umd_state

Set-UdfSalesTaxFilepath "c:\test\salestax.csvt"
Get-UdfSalesTaxFilepath
```

We need to import the module before we can use its function. The call to Set-UdfSalesTaxFilepath will fail, assuming the folder does not exist. The second line should display the default value assigned to $script:salestaxfilepath

To create this module, I thought a currency conversion function would be useful. I found the site: http://www.xe.com/currency/usd-us-dollar?r=, which provided some currency conversion values for a given date. I extracted that to a CSV file, which is loaded with the following statement:

```
$exchangerate = Import-CSV ($env:HomeDrive + $env:HOMEPATH + "\Documents\
currencyexchangerate.csv")
```

Unlike the sales tax function, we are not loading this into a hashtable. That's because there are several properties we need to get access to and hash tables only support a key/value pair. The following function uses the $exchangerate variable to return a selected property. Let's look at the following code:

```
function Get-UdfExchangeRate
{
[CmdletBinding()]
        param (
            [Parameter(Mandatory = $true, Position = 0)]
            [string]    $p_currencycd,
            [Parameter(Mandatory = $true, Position = 1)]
            [string]    $p_asofdate,
            [Parameter(Mandatory = $true, Position = 2, ParameterSetName = "unitsperusd")]
            [switch]    $UnitsPerUSD,
            [Parameter(Mandatory = $true, Position = 2, ParameterSetName = "usdperunits")]
            [switch]    $USDPerUnits,
            [Parameter(Mandatory = $true, Position = 2, ParameterSetName = "currencyname")]
            [switch]    $CurrencyName
            )

    foreach ($item in $exchangerate)
    {
        if ($item.CurrencyCD -eq $p_currencycd -and $item.AsOfDate -eq $p_asofdate)
        {
            if ($CurrencyName) { Return $item.CurrencyName  }
            if ($UnitsPerUSD)  { Return $item.UnitsPerUSD   }
            if ($USDPerUnits)  { Return $item.USDPerUnit    }
        }

    }
}
```

In this code, we use CmdLetBinding with parameter sets to provide the required functionality. All calls to Get-UdfExchangeRate must pass the country currency code and an as-of date—i.e., the date for the exchange rate. The third parameter must be one of three possible switches; UnitsPerUSD, USDPerUnits, CurrencyName. The switch that is passed determines what the function passes back. UnitsPerUSD is the number of units of the foreign currency required to equal the value of one US dollar. USDPerUnits is the number of US dollars required to equal one foreign currency unit. CurrencyName is the name of the currency for the currency code passed. By putting the switch parameter in the same position, making it mandatory, and assigning a separate parameter set name for each, we are requiring one switch to be passed, and only one switch. The foreach loop just cycles through each row in $exchangerates collection, and if a row has a CurrencyCD value and AsOfDate that match the parameters, a value will be returned depending on the switch passed.

Let's try the function out with the following code:

```
Get-UdfExchangeRate "GGP" '2014-12-22' -UnitsPerUSD
Get-UdfExchangeRate "GGP" '2014-12-22' -USDPerUnits
Get-UdfExchangeRate "GGP" '2014-12-22' –CurrencyName
```

A Warning about Variable Scopes

In the previous module, the functions to set and get a property value—i.e., Set-UdfSalesTaxFilepath and Get-UdfSalesTaxFilepath—respectively prefix the variable with the script scope, i.e., $script:salestaxfilepath. This is required due to a nuance about default variables scopes. A variable created in the module outside of a function gets a script-level scope, but a variable created in a function gets a local-function-level scope. If a function just reads a variable, it will use the script-level variable if there is no local-function-scoped variable of the same name. However, if the function assigns a value to a variable, it will create a local-function variable of that name, even if there is already one with a script-level scope (or a global one for that matter). This is called dynamic scoping and may be different than what you have seen in other programming languages. To illustrate, let's look at the following code:

```
$name = 'somevalue'                    # Creates the variable and assigns it to script scope

function Set-Name([string]$p_name)
{
        $name = $p_name                # Creates a new variable and assigns it to local-function scope
}

function Get-Name
{
        Write-Host $name     # Since no local variable $name exists, goes script-level
        variable.
}
```

This code is a very simple example of using Set and Get functions to assign a variable value. Let's test the code with the following statements:

```
Set-Name "test"
Get-Name
```

The call Get-Name returned "somevalue" instead of the value we set, i.e., "test." A small change to the code can correct this problem. Let's look at the revised code:

```
$name = 'somevalue'

function Set-Name([string]$p_name)
{
        $script:name = $p_name # Forces function to use the script level variable.
}

function Get-Name
{
        Write-Host $name
}
```

In this code, by simply prefixing the $name variable with the script scope, the Set function correctly assigns the value to the script-level variable. Test it with the following statements:

```
Set-Name "test"
Get-Name
```

Although you can just assign the scope when required, it is a better practice when using the Set and Get functions to assign and read module variables to always use the scope prefix. This makes the code easier to read and avoids bugs creeping into the module if changes are made.

Using a Module Like an Object

A nice feature of modules is that you can assign the loaded module to an object variable and then access the methods and properties using standard object notation. Let's look at the following code to see what I mean:

```
$mathobject = Import-Module umd_Simple -AsCustomObject

$mathobject.'Invoke-UdfAddNumber'(2, 3 )
```

The first line of code imports the module and uses the parameter –AsCustomObject, which causes PowerShell to return the module as an object that is assigned to $mathobject. Then the $mathobject's Invoke-UdfAddNumber method is called to add two numbers. PowerShell requires the function be enclosed in quotes because of the dash in the function name. Notice that when calling the method from an object variable we enclose the parameters in parentheses and separate them with a comma. It may not be obvious why you would want to use a module as an object. One reason is the readability of your code. In a long script, if you are importing many modules, it may not be clear where each function is coming from. The object notation makes it easy to see where the function resides. Another possible use is so that you can pass the module object to a function. An issue with PowerShell is that it does not support namespaces. A namespace is a tag used to group objects and methods much like a schema does for database objects. The same object or method name can exist in different namespaces. Prefixing the object or method with the namespace uniquely identifies the one you want. In PowerShell, if a function of the same name is defined in two different modules, there is no way to tell which one will get called. Calling the functions as methods of an object, as shown here, avoids these namespace collisions, i.e. the object variable acts like a namespace identifier.

Exporting Members

So far we have seen the default behavior that all functions are exposed to the script that imports it and all variables are not exposed. However, we can take direct control and specify which functions and variables to expose using the Export-ModuleMember cmdlet. Let's look at a simple example of this with the umd_Simple module we saw earlier:

```
# Simple module example

$somevar = 'Default Value'

function Invoke-UdfAddNumber([int]$p_int1, [int]$p_int2)
{
     Return ($p_int1 + $p_int2)
}

function Invoke-UdfSubtractNumber([int]$p_int1, [int]$p_int2)
{
     Return ($p_int1 - $p_int2)
}

Export-ModuleMember –function Invoke-UdfAddNumber
```

153

In this code, just by adding the line `Export-ModuleMember Invoke-UdfAddNumber`, we change the behavior to only allow external code to call the `Invoke-UdfAddNumber` function. There is a module variable added to help us see how this is affected. In this case, the module variable is still not available to external code. However, if we change the last line to the following code, the variable *will* be available to the client:

```
Export-ModuleMember -function Invoke-UdfAddNumber -variable somevar
```

Let's save this version of the script to umd_Simple.psm1 in the Windows PowerShell folder with the same name. With this change, we can run the following two statements:

```
$mathobject = Import-Module umd_Simple -AsCustomObject –Force  # Force will reload if
necessary.

$mathobject.'Invoke-UdfAddNumber'(2, 3)
$mathobject.somevar = 'test'
```

However, we get an error if we try the following statement:

```
$mathobject.'Invoke-UdfSubtractNumber'(5, 3)
```

As useful as modules are, there is one limitation with them that bothers me. We need to include the code to all the functions in one script. I think this is bad from a code-maintenance standpoint. First, let's assume we need to change a single function. Ideally, we would check out the source code to the single function, make our changes, test them, and check it back in for it to be deployed to production. If the function is in a module, we need to check out the script, which may contain hundreds of functions, then test, check in, and deploy the entire module. In the process, we may have inadvertently changed a function without realizing it. It's a good practice to have things modular so we can develop, test, and deploy units of work. Also, since there are many functions in a single module, there is a better chance another developer will need to make changes to the same module script at the same time. This leads to change-control issues. Even just locating the function code is more difficult. You have to load the entire module and search for the function you need.

The ideal solution to this would be to have the module dot source the function script files it needs. Then we get the discoverability of modules with the convenience of dot sourcing. The problem with dot sourcing within the module is that when the module loads, the current folder may not be the module's folder. We could hard code a path to where the function scripts are, but that would cause maintenance issues later. It turns out there is a PowerShell module variable $PSScripRoot that gets assigned a value when a module starts to load. By leveraging this variable, we can have the module script load individual function script files that are stored in the module folder. Let's look at the following module script:

```
<#
.Author
    Bryan Cafferky

.SYNOPSIS
    A simple module to demonstrate using dot sourcing to load the functions.

.DESCRIPTION
    When this module is imported, the functions are loaded using dot sourcing.

#>

. ($PSScriptRoot + "\Invoke-UdfAddNumber.ps1")

. ($PSScriptRoot + "\Invoke-UdfSubtractNumber.ps1")
```

In this script, we simply concatenate the variable $PSScriptRoot with the script file name that contains the function we want loaded. These functions are made available to the script that imported the module. Sample code to load and test this module can be seen here:

```
Import-Module umd_ModuleDotSource

Invoke-UdfAddNumber 1 2

Invoke-UdfSubtractNumber 5 1
```

To prove that the module is discoverable to PowerShell enter this command:

```
Get-Module -ListAvailable
```

You should see a list of modules, including umd_ModuleDotSource. Thus, we get the benefit of discoverability while being able to maintain our functions in separate script files.

Flexibility in Modules

When you read most of the books and documentation about modules, you get the sense that modules must be static and hold a bunch of functions. However, modules are scripts, which means they can execute code that customizes what and how things are loaded. To get an idea of what I mean, let's look at the code for the free open-source SQLPSCX module listed here:

```
#-------------------------------------------------------------------#
# SQLPSX.PSM1
# Author: Bernd, 05/18/2010
#
# Comment: Replaces Max version of the SQLPSX.psm1
#-------------------------------------------------------------------#

$PSXloadModules = @()
$PSXloadModules = "SQLmaint","SQLServer","Agent","Repl","SSIS","Showmbrs"
$PSXloadModules += "SQLParser","adolib"
if ($psIse) {
    $PSXloadModules += "SQLIse"
}

$oraAssembly = [System.Reflection.Assembly]::LoadWithPartialName("Oracle.DataAccess")
if ($oraAssembly) {
    $PSXloadModules += "OracleClient"
    if ($psIse) {
        $PSXloadModules += "OracleIse"
    }
}
else { Write-Host -BackgroundColor Black -ForegroundColor Yellow "No Oracle found" }

$PSXremoveModules = $PSXloadModules[($PSXloadModules.count)..0]
```

```
$mInfo = $MyInvocation.MyCommand.ScriptBlock.Module
$mInfo.OnRemove = {
    foreach($PSXmodule in $PSXremoveModules){
        if (gmo $PSXmodule)
        {
            Write-Host -BackgroundColor Black -ForegroundColor Yellow "Removing SQLPSX
            Module - $PSXModule"
            Remove-Module $PSXmodule
        }
    }

    Write-Host -BackgroundColor Black -ForegroundColor Yellow "$($MyInvocation.MyCommand.
    ScriptBlock.Module.name) removed on $(Get-Date)"
}

foreach($PSXmodule in $PSXloadModules){
 Write-Host -BackgroundColor Black -ForegroundColor Yellow "Loading SQLPSX Module -
 $PSXModule"
 Import-Module $PSXmodule -global
}
Write-Host -BackgroundColor Black -ForegroundColor Yellow "Loading SQLPSX Modules is Done!"
```

Looking at this code, we can see that the script loads multiple other modules. It also applies conditional logic to decide what to install. Consider the following lines from the module.

```
if ($psIse) {
    $PSXloadModules += "SQLIse"
}
```

In the code above, we can see that the module script loads a number of other modules. The switch $psIse is checked and if true, the module SQLIse is added to the list of modules to be loaded. The point is to remember that you have flexibility in how you code modules. The following lines check for the existence of the Oracle.DataAccess assembly, and if loads the OracleClient module was loaded and if the $psIse switch was passed, it loads the OracleIse module as well:

```
$oraAssembly = [System.Reflection.Assembly]::LoadWithPartialName("Oracle.DataAccess")
if ($oraAssembly) {
    $PSXloadModules += "OracleClient"
    if ($psIse) {
        $PSXloadModules += "OracleIse"
    }
}
else { Write-Host -BackgroundColor Black -ForegroundColor Yellow "No Oracle found" }
```

Since this module loads other modules, it has code to remove those modules when the SQLPSX module is unloaded. The code here does this:

```
$PSXremoveModules = $PSXloadModules[($PSXloadModules.count)..0]

$mInfo = $MyInvocation.MyCommand.ScriptBlock.Module
$mInfo.OnRemove = {
```

```
foreach($PSXmodule in $PSXremoveModules){
    if (gmo $PSXmodule)
    {
      Write-Host -BackgroundColor Black -ForegroundColor Yellow "Removing SQLPSX Module -
      $PSXModule"
      Remove-Module $PSXmodule
    }
}

Write-Host -BackgroundColor Black -ForegroundColor Yellow "$($MyInvocation.MyCommand.
ScriptBlock.Module.name) removed on $(Get-Date)"
}
```

In the first line of the code, the array variable $PSXremoveModules is being loaded from the list of loaded modules. The line after this uses $MyInvocation, a PowerShell variable that holds information about the currently executing script. The line $mInfo = $MyInvocation.MyCommand.ScriptBlock.Module is just getting the name of the module. The interesting thing is that this is used to attach code to the OnRemove vent of the module; i.e., if the user executes the Remove-Module cmdlet for this module, the code in the braces will execute. Let's look at the loop that executes:

```
foreach($PSXmodule in $PSXremoveModules){
    if (gmo $PSXmodule)
    {
      Write-Host -BackgroundColor Black -ForegroundColor Yellow "Removing SQLPSX Module -
      $PSXModule"
      Remove-Module $PSXmodule
    }
}
```

We can see that the code loops through the array of module names. The statement "if (gmo $PSXmodule)" is executing the Get-Module cmdlet for each module so that the code in the braces that removes the module will only execute for modules that are loaded. If you are wondering what "gmo" means, you are not alone. It is an alias for Get-Module. Avoid using aliases in your scripts. It is fine for interactive use in the CLI, but should be avoided in scripts that are to be used by multiple users. The point of this code review is to show you how flexible module scripts can be.

Making Our Module More Flexible

A concern that may arise with a module is that it takes a long time to load and consumes a lot of memory, i.e. PowerShell is loading many exported functions and variables. Suppose some of the functions are used very often, but others are rarely used. Why load the rarely used functions unless we need them? Let's revise the module we created earlier, umd_ModuleParms, that dot sourced its members, to include a switch parameter that tells the module to conditionally load the rarely used functions. Note: The module file for the book already has this change. Please review the code below.

```
param ( [switch]$IncludeExtended )

. ($PSScriptRoot + "\Invoke-UdfAddNumber.ps1")

. ($PSScriptRoot + "\Invoke-UdfSubtractNumber.ps1")
```

```
if ($IncludeExtended)
{
  Write-Host "Adding extended function: $PSScriptRoot\Invoke-UdfMultiplyNumber.ps1"
  . ($PSScriptRoot + "\Invoke-UdfMultiplyNumber.ps1")
}
```

The first line of code defines a switch parameter $IncludeExtended. Since it is a switch, it automatically gets assigned $false if it is not passed. Then the code dot sources the two functions Invoke-UdfAddNumber.ps1 and Invoke-UdfSubtractNumber.ps1. However, the function Invoke-UdfMultiplyNumber.ps1 is only loaded if the caller passed $true to the module. In other words, by default, Invoke-UdfMultiplyNumber.ps1 will not be loaded. Let's look at code that loads the module in Listing 6-1.

Listing 6-1. Loading a subset of module functions

```
Import-Module umd_ModuleParms -Force

Invoke-UdfAddNumber 1 2              # Returns 3

Invoke-UdfSubtractNumber 5 1        # Returns 4

Invoke-UdfMultiplyNumber 5 6       # Generates an error because the function is not loaded.

Get-Module umd_ModuleParms         # Confirms that the new function is not loaded.
```

When we execute the statements in Listing 6-1, we see that Invoke-UdfAddNumber and Invoke-UdfSubtractNumber work fine. However, the call to Invoke-UdfMultiplyNumber fails. Get-Module shows us the function Invoke-UdfMultiplyNumber was not imported. The Force parameter on Import-Module tells PowerShell to reload the module if it is already loaded. Note: To list all the functions in memory, we can enter Get-ChildItem function: which lists the function name and the module it was loaded from.

To import the module and pass a value to $IncludeExtended, we need to use the Import-Module ArgumentList parameter as shown in Listing 6-2.

Listing 6-2. Loading the optional module function

```
Import-Module umd_ModuleParms –Force -ArgumentList $true # Displays message new function loaded.

Invoke-UdfAddNumber 1 2              # Returns 3

Invoke-UdfSubtractNumber 5 1        # Returns 4

Invoke-UdfMultiplyNumber 5 6       # Returns 30

Get-Module umd_ModuleParms         # Confirms that the new function is loaded.
```

Listing 6-2 passes $true to the moduleListings ArgumentList parameter and Invoke-UdfMultiplyNumber is loaded. Now the call to Invoke-UdfMultiplyNumber succeeds. Get-Module confirms that Invoke-UdfMultiplyNumber is loaded. An interesting point is that internally the module named the parameter, i.e. $IncludeExtended, but when the module is loaded, we cannot pass the parameter by name. This makes sense since PowerShell does not know what parameters are defined for the module until it has been loaded. However, using meaningful parameter names in the module itself can make the code easier to understand. For a large module, customizing what gets loaded can save on resources. Alternatively, we could break functions up into separate modules.

Module Manifest

A module manifest is an optional file with a .psd1 extension that documents the module and how it is to be loaded—i.e., what files should be included. A manifest can be used for both binary and script modules. In its simplest usage, a manifest can provide basic information about the module, such as the author, copyright, description, and so forth. However, a manifest can also be used to nest modules and load custom .NET types and formats. When PowerShell executes the Import-Module cmdlet, it will look for a manifest to process before it looks for the module script. If there is none, it just loads the module. To make creating a manifest easier for developers, PowerShell provides the New-ModuleManifest cmdlet. Let's give it a try by entering the following command:

New-ModuleManifest

Because no parameters were specified, we are prompted for them. Most of the parameters will be written to the manifest file, but a few control the operation of the cmdlet. The parameters and their meanings are provided in Table 6-1.

***Table 6-1.** Module Manifest Parameters*

Parameter	Description	Example
Path	Path and file name of manifest file	C:\user1\modules\MyModule.psd1
AliasesToExport	List of aliases to be exported	Gtb,xyz
Author	Module author's name	Bryan Cafferky
ClrVersion	Required CLR version	4.0.30319
CmdletsToExport	List of cmdlets to be exported	Get-Something, Set-Something
CompanyName	Name of the company	BPC Global Solutions LLC
Copyright	Ownership copyright information	c BPC Global Solutions LLC All rights reserved.
DefaultCommandPrefix	To avoid potential name collisions, adds this prefix to exported functions and cmdlets	bryan
Description	Tells what the module does	Provides useful ETL functions
DotNetFrameworkVersion	.Net framework version required by this module.	
FileList	List of files to include	File1, file2
FormatsToProcess	Format files to process	@()
FunctionsToExport	Functions that are exported.	Get-Something, Set-Something
GUID	Unique module identifier. If not entered, PowerShell will generate one.	50cdb55f-5ab7-489f-9e94-4ec21ff51e59

(continued)

Table 6-1. (*continued*)

Parameter	Description	Example
HelpInfoURI	A link to where help information is located	http://www.somehelp.com
ModuleList	List of modules to be loaded	@()
ModuleVersion	Documents the module's version	1.0.0.0
NestedModules	Modules within modules	@()
PassThru	Use to pass the data to the pipe in addition to writing the output file	PassThru
PowerShellHostName	The PowerShell host name. If needed, this can be found in the variable $host.name.	Windows PowerShell ISE Host
PowerShellHostVersion	The minimum PowerShell host version required.	2.0
PowerShellVersion	The minimum PowerShell version required	2.0
PrivateData	This is any private data that needs to be passed to the root module.	System.IO.Compression.FileSystem
ProcessorArchitecture		IA64
RequiredAssemblies	List any required assemblies	@()
RequiredModules	Non-root modules to be imported	MyOtherModule.psm1
RootModule	The core module and possibly the only module	MyModule.psm1
ScriptsToProcess	A script to be executed in the caller's session state	Myprocess.ps1
TypesToProcess	Type files to process on module import	@()
VariablesToExport	Variables to export	*
Confirm	Tell PowerShell to confirm before creating the manifest	Confirm
WhatIf	Asks PowerShell to tell you what is would do without actually doing it, i.e., creating the manifest file	WhatIf

For more details on the module manifest, consult the following link:

http://msdn.microsoft.com/en-us/library/dd878337(v=vs.85).aspx

If there is a manifest, we can use Get-Module to retrieve this information. For example, for the open-source module WPK, we can run the following script to get information from the manifest:

```
Import-module WPK

$i = Get-Module WPK
```

```
$i.Author
$i.CompanyName
$i.Copyright
$i.Description
$i.guid
```

This will give the following output:

```
James Brundage
Microsoft
2009

The WPF Powershell Kit is a PowerShell module for making quick user interfaces using Windows
Presentation Foundation and Windows PowerShell

Guid
----
00000000-0000-0000-0000-000000000000
f23582a5-01e1-4519-856b-01b8d6997bc5
```

The WPK module is available as part of the IsePackV2 module download available at the link below. However, WPK may not remain compatible with new versions of PowerShell.

http://social.technet.microsoft.com/wiki/contents/articles/4308.popular-powershell-modules.aspx

Dynamic Modules

Temporary modules can be created by a script, used, and then discarded automatically when the script exits. These are called dynamic modules and are basically an extension of the script-block concept. As an example, Listing 6-3 has two functions: one that extracts only letters from a string and another that extracts only digits from a string.

Listing 6-3. An example of a dynamic module

```
# Example of a Dynamic Module...

$scrblock = {
function Get_UdfLetters([string]$p_instring)
  {
    Return ($p_instring -replace '[^A-Z ]','')
  }

function Get_UdfNumbers([string]$p_instring)
  {
    Return ($p_instring -replace '[^0-9]','')
  }

}

$mod = new-module -scriptblock $scrblock -AsCustomObject

$mod | Get-Member
```

```
                TypeName: System.Management.Automation.PSCustomObject
Name                    MemberType        Definition
----                    ----------        ----------
Equals                  Method            bool Equals(System.Object obj)
GetHashCode             Method            int GetHashCode()
GetType                 Method            type GetType()
ToString                Method            string ToString()
Get_UdfLetters          ScriptMethod      System.Object Get_UdfLetters();
Get_UdfNumbers          ScriptMethod      System.Object Get_UdfNumbers();
```

In Listing 6-3, we start by assigning two function definitions to a script-block variable $scrblock. Then we use the New-Module cmdlet to create a module in memory using the script block we defined. Notice the –AsCustomObject parameter. This tells PowerShell to pass back the module as a PowerShell object that is assigned to the variable $mod. Just to prove $mod is a valid module, we pipe $mod into Get-Member, which should show us the two functions we defined, as shown in the output above.

The nice thing about creating our dynamic module as a PowerShell custom object is that we can use object method-calling syntax to use its functions. Let's look at the following code:

```
$mod.Get_UdfLetters("mix of numbers 12499 and letters")
```

Displays the output below to the console.

```
mix of numbers  and letters
```

```
$mod.Get_UdfNumbers("mix of numbers 12499 and letters")
```

Displays the output below to the console.

```
12499
```

Notice that we are violating the cmdlet naming convention by separating the verb and noun with an underscore instead of a dash. This is because if we use a dash, PowerShell will require us to enclose the function name in quotes when we call it. Since this is just a temporary module, I think breaking the recommended naming convention is justified. In most cases, we would probably just want to create standard script modules. However, dynamic modules do offer some flexibility that may come in handy. Since the script block is just a variable, we could modify it on the fly, changing what the module does and how it works. Let's look at a revised version of the script in Listing 6-4 to see how this works:

Listing 6-4. Changing the script block definition dynamically

```
$option = Read-Host "Enter 'A' to Allow underscore or 'D' to disallow the underscore "

if ($option -ne 'A') {
$scrblock = {
function Get_UdfLetters([string]$p_instring)
  {
    Return ($p_instring -replace '[^A-Z ]','')
  }
```

```
function Get_UdfNumbers([string]$p_instring)
  {
    Return ($p_instring -replace '[^0-9]','')
  }

 }
}
else
{
$scrblock =
{
function Get_UdfLetters([string]$p_instring)
  {
    Return ($p_instring -replace '[^A-Z _]','')
  }

function Get_UdfNumbers([string]$p_instring)
  {
    Return ($p_instring -replace '[^0-9_]','')
  }
 }
}

$mod = new-module -scriptblock $scrblock -AsCustomObject

$mod.Get_UdfLetters("mix of numbers-_ 12499 and_ letters")

$mod.Get_UdfNumbers("mix of numbers-_ 12499 and_ letters")
```

When we run this script, we are prompted about whether we want to allow the underscore character to remain in the string parameter or not. If we enter "A", the script block is defined that allows the underscore to remain, but if we enter anything else, the script-block variable is assigned the code that removes underscores. This is a simple example, but there may be occasions when you need to dynamically change the module's code. It's just another tool in the toolbox.

Popular Free PowerShell Modules

Modules provide a way for PowerShell to be extended to include functionality not available in the base language. There are many free modules available, and it is worth familiarizing yourself with some of the more popular ones to see if they can help you. Some of these are documented at the following link:

http://social.technet.microsoft.com/wiki/contents/articles/4308.popular-powershell-modules.aspx

As useful as PowerShell community–developed modules are, there are drawbacks to using them. The biggest drawback is that they are developed for specific versions of PowerShell and the related .NET frameworks version. Thus, when you upgrade to a new version of PowerShell, you may break existing code that uses these modules. This can also cause an issue with deploying PowerShell code. For example, your code may work fine on your machine under Windows 7 using PowerShell 2.0 but fail on the target environment running PowerShell 4.0. Unfortunately, these version requirements are not always obvious on the module download sites. Besides the potential version problems, deployments become more complex, as you will need to install the required modules on the target environment. Exacerbating this problem is that some modules depend on other modules. For example, the module SQLIse depends on the modules SQLPSX and PowerShellPack to function. This can further complicate deployments.

OData PowerShell Explorer

OData is a new open data-sharing standard being advanced by Microsoft and OASIS, an international open standards consortium. The idea is to establish one flexible standard that can be applied to share data from anywhere. The OData PowerShell Explorer available at http://psodata.codeplex.com/ provides interesting insights into the capabilities of using PowerShell to access OData sources. PowerShell can also serve up data as an OData source. At this point I think the future of OData as a standard is uncertain, but I encourage you to play with the OData Explorer to get an idea of the potential

PowerShell Community Extensions (PSCX)

The PowerShell Community Extensions (PSCX) module adds a lot of useful cmdlets that extend PowerShell in many areas. When you follow the link to the download page, be sure to select the version appropriate to your version of PowerShell. Fortunately, this module has a release that supports PowerShell 4.0. You can find the version for PowerShell 3.0 and 4.0 and the help documentation about this module at http://pscx.codeplex.com/releases. The help file is named about_pscx.help.txt. Note: The link on the page Popular PowerShell Module's brings you to is the latest release. For the prior version, use https://pscx.codeplex.com/releases/view/98267.

A number of the PSCX cmdlets compress and decompress files into and from various formats. It also has some cmdlets to work with *Microsoft Message Queing*, MSMQ. Let's look at the following code to give a sense of some of the functionality this module provides.

```
"This is data in the clipboard." | Set-Clipboard

$myclipdata = Get-Clipboard

$myclipdata

Enable-OpenPowerShellHere      # Add Windows PowerShell open button to Windows Explorer.

"This is data." | Set-Clipboard

"some data" > mytestfile.txt

Set-ReadOnly mytestfile.txt     # Sets the ReadOnly attribute on so the file can only be read.

Set-Writable mytestfile.txt     # Turns off the Readonly attribute so the file can be modified.

Out-Speech "This is something"   # Uses Windows speech API.

# Zip all files with .txt extension into myzip.zip in current folder.
Write-Zip -Path *.txt -OutputPath 'myzip.zip'
```

An interesting set of cmdlets for database developers are the ones related to ADO.NET. These provide easy access to databases using .NET drivers. For SQL Server, we've previously seen code that directly accesses the .NET libraries to read data using ADO.NET. Let's look at the code that does this using the PSCX cmdlets:

```
# Reading from SQL Server...
Get-AdoConnection -Server "(local)"  -Database "AdventureWorks" `
                -ProviderName "System.Data.SQLClient"
$Provider="System.Data.SQLClient"
$ConnectionString="Data Source=.;Initial Catalog=AdventureWorks;Integrated Security=SSPI"
$Connection = Get-AdoConnection $Provider $ConnectionString
$Query = "SELECT top 10 * FROM person.person; select top 5 * from sales.customer;"

$mydata = Invoke-AdoCommand -ProviderName $Provider -Connection $Connection `
        -CommandText $Query -AsDataSet
$mydata.tables[0]  | Out-GridView
$mydata.tables[1]  | Out-GridView

$Connection.Close()
```

This code connects to the AdventureWorks database on the local machine and selects the top ten rows from person.person. It displays the result in a grid using Out-GridView. Notice that we first get a connection to the database with the statement $Connection = Get-AdoConnection $Provider $ConnectionString. $Connection holds the connection object that is used to execute the query in the statement $mydata = Invoke-AdoCommand -ProviderName $Provider -Connection $Connection -CommandText $Query -AsDataSet. The parameter –AsDataSet is critical for getting the data in a consumable format. We have two queries being executed. The result sets are stored in a collection named tables. Since $mydata is loaded with the query results, we can get the first resultset as $mydata.tables[0], which we pipe to Out-GridView, and the second result set as $mydata.tables[1], which is also piped to Out-GridView.

Accessing SQL Server is easy in the Windows world, as Microsoft provides many options. However, it can be more challenging to access other database products. PostgreSQL is a popular open source database, so let's look at how we would code statements that read from a PostgreSQL source. Note: If you need a good PostgreSQL ADO.NET driver for Windows, you can get one at http://www.devart.com/dotconnect/postgresql/download.html. They have a free Express edition, which is what I used for the example. You can also purchase a version with more-advanced functionality, such as support for Entity Frameworks. Now let's take a look at the code below.

```
# Reading from PostgreSQL...
$Provider="Devart.Data.PostgreSQL"
$ConnectionString="Data Source=localhost;Database=postgres;Initial
Schema=public;Port=5432;User ID=postgres;password=mypassword;Connection Lifetime=1000;"
$Connection = Get-AdoConnection $Provider $ConnectionString
$Query = "SELECT * FROM tmp_hold_log limit 10"

$mypgdata = Invoke-AdoCommand -ProviderName $Provider -Connection $Connection `
        -CommandText $Query -AsDataSet

$mypgdata.tables[0]  | Out-GridView

$Connection.Close()
```

The PostgreSQL code is not very different from the SQL Server version. The biggest difference is the connection string. Different .NET drivers support different options and names, so you need to find out what your driver supports. Integrated security is handy but is not typically supported by other database vendors, especially ones that do not run on Windows, so we need to specify a username and password. Note: We will talk about encrypting data in Chapter 9, which you may want to apply here. The SQL syntax for different databases varies, so we need to be careful not to use SQL Server syntax.

ShowUI

The ShowUI module offers an interesting option for adding a GUI to your PowerShell scripts. It provides a nice set of high-level PowerShell functions that make it easy to add visual elements like windows, buttons, text boxes, and so forth to your scripts. You can install ShowUI individually, or it can be installed as part of the module IsePackV2. Once installed, you can find some helpful examples in the folder named Examples in the ShowUI module folder. Unlike the other method of creating a GUI we've seen that uses a screen painter to generate the windows object code, ShowUI must be coded manually with location details specified via function parameters. This may be a good option for a simple GUI interface. Unfortunately, I found that ShowUI does not work with PowerShell 4.0, but does seem to work with 2.0. I hope the developers will bring this module up to date, but until they do, the usefulness of this module is limited.

SQL Server PowerShell Extensions

The SQL Server PowerShell Extensions, SQLPSX, is a free third-party set of modules that add SQL Server functionality as well as some support for Oracle. The cmdlets available are mostly administrative and probably are not ones you would include in the PowerShell code you deploy. However, they offer some nice features in working with SQL Server. Let's take a look at some examples:

```
Get-AgentJob "(local)" | Out-GridView
```

The statement above will get a list of SQL Agent jobs on the (local) server and display them in the grid view. Another example of using the SQLPSX modules can be seen below.

```
Get-SqlDatabase "(local)" AdventureWorks | Get-SqlTable -name 'person' -Schema person |
Get-SqlColumn | Select-Object -Property Name, DataType, Nullable | Out-GridView
```

This statement will get a database reference object, pipe it into the Get-Table cmdlet, which then gets a table reference object that is piped into the Get-SqlColumn cmdlet to get a list of columns in the table. This is piped into the Select-Object cmdlet, which pulls out the properties we want and then pipes that into the Out-Gridview for a nice readable display.

For documentation on the cmdlets available in this module, see the following URL:

```
http://files.powershellstation.com/SQLPSX/index.htm
```

In reading the help pages for SQLPSX, it is clear that the modules are intended mainly for database administration tasks like copying databases, moving SSIS packages, setting up replication, and things like that. The cmdlets I find most interesting are the Get cmdlets like the ones I demonstrated. However, some of these tasks can easily be done using the SQLPS module we've used throughout this book. For example, the code that follows will do the same thing as the first SQLPSX example:

```
Import-Module "sqlps" -DisableNameChecking
```

```
set-location SQLSERVER:\SQL\BryanCafferkyPC\DEFAULT\JobServer\Jobs
```

```
Get-ChildItem
```

One nice thing about this approach is that it sets the location context using the provider interface. This means that we only have to set the location once and subsequent commands will work in that context—i.e., SQL Agent jobs.

We can replace the example that gets column information with the following code that uses SQPPS:

```
Import-Module "sqlps" -DisableNameChecking

set-location SQLSERVER:\SQL\BryanCafferkyPC\DEFAULT\Databases\Adventureworks\Tables

$mytable = Get-ChildItem | Where-Object -Property Name -EQ 'Person'
$mytable.Columns | Select-Object -Property Name, DataType, Nullable | Out-GridView
```

The good thing about the SQLPS examples is that the SQLPS module is already installed on a machine that has SQL Server installed. I've also found that the SQLPS module tends to work pretty well across PowerShell versions. My recommendation is to use SQLPSX for daily administrative functions but to avoid deploying applications that depend on it. SQLPS is a better choice for that, or you can just use the SQL Client .NET library directly.

One thing to be aware of is that sometimes one module can cause problems with another module. For example, I found that if I imported the SQLPS module after I imported the SQLPSX module, the SQLPSX module did not work correctly. In fact, the SQLPS module can interfere with other modules as well. This is due to the provider interface. Using the Remove-Module cmdlet should correct the issue. However, you must set the location to a non–SQL Server context before PowerShell will let you unload the module. The statements below should do the trick.

```
set-location C:\Users      # Sets context to the File System provider.
Remove-Module SQLPS -Force # Unloads the module from memory.
```

SQLISE

SQLIse is a module that provides SQL Query Analyzer–like functionality within the PowerShell ISE. To use this module, you need to install ISEPackV2 and SQLPSX. As interesting as this is, I found it would not install under PowerShell 4.0, but I did get it to work under PowerShell 2.0—although the install did generate a lot of warning messages about running code from the Internet. This link provides some background on this module:

```
http://sev17.com/2010/03/09/sqlise-a-powershell-based-sql-server-query-tool/
```

SQLIse provides SQL Server Management Studio's Query Analyzer–like functionality right within the PowerShell ISE. It exposes itself as an add-on in the PowerShell ISE. Assuming you have everything installed correctly, you can start to use SQLIse by importing it with the command here:

```
Import-Module SQLIse
```

There's a lot of functionality here that can best be conveyed by looking at the SQLIse menu under Add-ons. Figure 6-1 shows that menu.

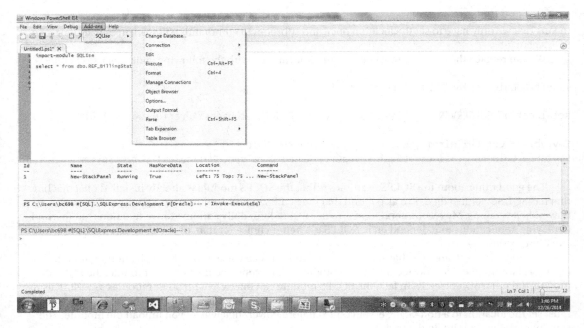

Figure 6-1. *Using the SQLIse Add-On*

Windows Automation Snap-In (WASP)

The Windows Automation Snap-In (WASP) is a useful module when you want to manipulate Windows applications as if you were a user interacting with the program. We've seen this used previously to automate navigating Internet Explorer to a website, going to a specific page, and downloading a file. It is a powerful functionality. However, such code tends to be a bit unstable because the application interface you are relying on can change. Let's look at a simple example of using WASP below.

```
Import-Module WASP

notepad.exe

start-sleep 3

Select-Window -ProcessName "notepad" | Send-Keys "This is an example of using WASP."
```

WASP was originally a PowerShell snap-in so for PowerShell versions earlier than 3.0, use the Add-PSSnapIn cmdlet to load it. The code above starts Notepad.exe, waits three seconds, sets the focus to the window running Notepad, and enters the text "This is an example of using WASP." WASP has a lot of features that are critical when you need to manipulate applications. However, many things can go wrong in this kind of application automation. In the code, for example, if you already had Notepad running when you ran the script, it would create a new instance of Notepad and would perhaps not write to the correct window. Nonetheless, this is a module that is good to be familiar with.

WASP is particularly useful for automating web access via *Internet Explorer*, IE. Let's look at the Listing 6-5 that starts Internet Explorer, navigates to Bing, and does a search for PowerShell WASP examples.

Listing 6-5. Using the WASP module

```
Import-Module WASP     # Use Import-Module starting with PowerShell 3.0

$url = "http://www.bing.com"

stop-process -processname iexplore*

$ie = New-Object -comobject InternetExplorer.Application
$ie.visible = $true
$ie.silent = $true
$ie.Navigate( $url )
start-sleep 2

Select-Window "iexplore" | Set-WindowActive

$txtArea=$ie.Document.getElementById("sb_form_q")

$txtArea.InnerText="PowerShell WASP Examples"
start-sleep 2
Select-Window "iexplore" | Set-WindowActive| Send-Keys "{ENTER}"
```

Listing 6-5 starts by importing the WASP module and assigning variable $url the link to Bing. The stop-process cmdlet is to end any Internet Explorer processes, so if you have any IE windows open, you may want to close them before running this code. Then the code below opens IE and navigates to the web page:

```
$ie = New-Object -comobject InternetExplorer.Application
$ie.visible = $true
$ie.silent = $true
$ie.Navigate( $url )
start-sleep 2
```

In the first line above, we are storing a reference to the Internet Explorer application in variable $ie. This makes it easy to assign properties like visible and silent and use its methods, such as navigate, which the script does to bring up the Bing page. Then the statement "start-sleep 2" pauses the script for 2 seconds to wait for the prior actions to complete. If the prior actions do not complete before we continue, any manipulation to the page such as keystrokes are lost. No errors are raised. The line below makes the IE window active and simulates pressing the enter key.

```
Select-Window "iexplore" | Set-WindowActive| Send-Keys "{ENTER}"
```

The next bit of code is interesting and important if we want to automate webpage access. This is where we enter something into the search textbox on the page. You might think that when the Bing page comes up, it will just automatically place the cursor in the search box. However, it does not, so to get the cursor there so we can enter some search terms, we use the statement seen here:

```
$txtArea=$ie.Document.getElementById("sb_form_q")
```

The method, GetElementByID will get us to the search text box, where we can use the following code to enter the search terms:

```
$txtArea.InnerText="PowerShell WASP Examples"
start-sleep 2
Select-Window "iexplore" | Set-WindowActive| Send-Keys "{ENTER}"
```

In the code above, we assign a value to InnerText which will enter text into the search text box. We need to give it time to complete this operation, so we use the start-sleep cmdlet. Then we need to simulate pressing the Enter key. But first, we need to make sure the focus is on the IE window, which we can do with the statements Select-Window "iexplore" | Set-WindowActive|. By piping this into the subsequent Send-Keys cmdlet, the cmdlet knows which windows to send the keystrokes to. Notice that to send the Enter key, we use "{ENTER}". This is a special name with which to tell send keys to send a named key rather than text. There are a number of these, which you can find in the documentation. For example, Send-Keys {TAB} will send a tab key.

You may be wondering how we can determine the control name for the search text box. A method we can use that often works is to use Internet Explorer to help us. First, we bring up the page that has the control we need to manipulate. Then we click on the control, in this case the search text box. Then we right mouse-click to bring up a list of possible actions, as shown in Figure 6-2.

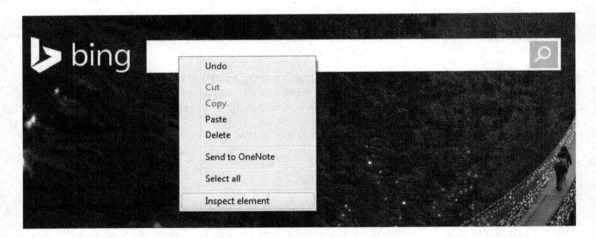

Figure 6-2. *Browser context menu showing the Inspect element option*

From the action menu, shown here, select Inspect Element. This will cause information about the selected element to display, as shown in Figure 6-3.

Figure 6-3. *Properties of a selected element*

The selected block is the element we want. We can see that the ID is "`sb_form_q`". Therefore, we can use the `GetElementByID("sb_form_q")` to position the script to this element. Admittedly, this can be a trial-and-error process, and as mentioned before, the element name could be changed without us knowing. These cautions aside, WASP provides some very powerful functionality.

Summary

This chapter covered extending PowerShell with modules. We discussed the four types of modules, which are script, manifest, binary, and dynamic. The most important of these is the script module because it is easy to implement, can be written in the PowerShell language, and provides an effective way to create reusable code. We discussed how to develop and deploy script modules. Then, we considered a weakness in script modules—i.e., all the functions must be stored in a single script file. We considered two approaches to solving this issue. We discussed what a module manifest is and how to create one. PowerShell supports the creation of temporary modules, called dynamic modules, within a script that can be created, used, and discarded. It is not always necessary to develop your own modules. We discussed a number of free open source modules that you can download and use in your applications.

■ ■ ■

## CHAPTER 7

Accessing SQL Server

We have seen some examples of executing queries against SQL Server. There are many ways to access a database, and it can hinder development to custom code each variation, as there are a number of questions to be resolved. What type of access method will be used: ADO.Net, OleDB, ODBC, or the native SQL Server driver? What type of authentication will be used: Windows Integrated Security, Logon ID and password, or a credential object? What database platform: On Premise SQL Server, SQL Azure, or a third-party database like MySQL or PostgreSQL? Why not write some functions to make this task easier? In this chapter, we will be carefully walking through a custom module that provides easy access to databases using ADO.Net.

About the Module

The module, umd_database, centers around a function that returns a custom database-connection object that is built on PowerShell's object template, PSObject. By setting the object's properties, we tell it how to execute SQL statements to the database. Using a method called RunSQL, we will run various queries. To run stored procedures that require output parameters, we can use the RunStoredProcedure method. Since an object is returned by the New-UdfConnection function, we can create as many database-connection object instances as we want. Each instance can be set for specific database-access properties. For example, one instance might point to a SQL Server database, another might point to an Azure SQL database, and yet another might point to a MySQL database. Once the connection attributes are set, we can run as many queries as we want by supplying the SQL. Beyond providing a useful module, the code will demonstrate many techniques that can be applied elsewhere. Using what we learned in the previous chapter, we copy the module umd_database to a folder named umd_database in a directory that is in $env:PSModulePath, such as \WindowsPowerShell\Modules\, under the current user's Documents folder. To run the examples that use SQL Server, we will need the Microsoft training database AdventureWorks installed. You can get it at http://msftdbprodsamples.codeplex.com/.

Using umd_database

Before we look at the module's code, let's take a look at how we can use the module. The idea is to review the module's interface to make it easier to understand how the code behind it works. Let's assume we want to run some queries against the SQL Server AdventureWorks database. We'll use the local instance and integrated security, so the connection is pretty simple. Since code using ADO.Net is so similar to code using ODBC, we will only review the ADO.Net-specific code in this chapter. However, you can also see in the module the ODBC-specific coding. Listing 7-1 shows the code to create and define the connection object. Note: You will need to change the property values to ones appropriate for your environment.

Listing 7-1. Using the umd_database module

```
Import-Module umd_database

[psobject] $myssint = New-Object psobject
New-UdfConnection ([ref]$myssint)

$myssint.ConnectionType = 'ADO'
$myssint.DatabaseType = 'SqlServer'
$myssint.Server = '(local)'
$myssint.DatabaseName = 'AdventureWorks'
$myssint.UseCredential = 'N'
$myssint.SetAuthenticationType('Integrated')
$myssint.AuthenticationType
```

In Listing 7-1, the first thing we do is import the umd_database module to load its functions. Then we create an instance of a PSObject named $myssint. Next, a statement calls New-UdfConnection to attach a number of properties and methods to the object we created. Note: The parameter $myssint is being passed as a [REF] type. As we saw previously, a REF is a reference to an object, i.e., we are passing our object to the function where it is modified. The lines that follow the function call set the properties of the object. First, we set the ConnectionType to ADO, meaning ADO.Net will be used. The DatabaseType is SQL Server. The server instance is '(local)'. Since we are using integrated security, we will not be using a credential object, which is a secure way to connect when user ID and password are being passed. We just set UseCredential = 'N'. Finally, we set the AuthenticationType to 'Integrated', i.e., integrated security. Notice that the authentication type is being set by a method rather than by our just assigning it a value. This is so the value can be validated. An invalid value will be rejected. With these properties set, we can generate the connection string using the BuildConnectionString method, as shown here:

```
$myssint.BuildConnectionString
```

If there is a problem creating the connection string, we will get the message 'Error - Connection string not found!'. Technically, we don't have to call the BuildConnectionString method, because it is called by the method that runs the SQL statement, but calling it confirms a valid connection string was created. We can view the object's ConnectionString property to verify it looks correct using the statement here:

```
$myssint.ConnectionString
```

We should see the following output:

```
Data Source=(local);Integrated Security=SSPI;Initial Catalog=AdventureWorks
```

Let's try running a query using our new connection object:

```
$myssint.RunSQL("SELECT top 20 * FROM [HumanResources].[EmployeeDepartmentHistory]", $true)
```

We use the object's RunSQL method to execute the query. The first parameter is the query. The second parameter indicates whether the query is a select statement—i.e., returns results. Queries that return results need to have code to retrieve. When we run the previous statement, we should see query results displayed to the console.

We can look at all the object's properties and their current values by entering the object name on a line, as follows:

```
$myssint
```

We should get the following output:

```
ConnectionType      : ADO
DatabaseType        : SqlServer
Server              : (local)
DatabaseName        : AdventureWorks
UseCredential       : N
UserID              :
Password            :
DSNName             : NotAssigned
Driver              : NotAssigned
ConnectionString    : Data Source=(local);Integrated Security=SSPI;Initial
                      Catalog=AdventureWorks
AuthenticationType  : Integrated
AuthenticationTypes : {Integrated, Logon, Credential, StoredCredential...}
```

Being able to display the object properties is very useful, especially for the connection string and authentication types. If there is a problem running the query, we can check the connection string. If we don't know what the valid values are for authentication types, the AuthenticationTypes property shows them. Notice UserID and Password are blank since they don't apply to integrated security.

Imagine we want to have another connection, but this time using a table in the SQL Azure cloud. Azure does not support integrated security or the credential object, so we'll use a login ID and password. We can code this as follows:

```
[psobject] $azure1 = New-Object psobject
New-UdfConnection ([ref]$azure1)
$azure1 | Get-Member

$azure1.ConnectionType = 'ADO'
$azure1.DatabaseType = 'Azure'
$azure1.Server = 'fxxxx.database.windows.net'
$azure1.DatabaseName = 'Development'
$azure1.UseCredential = 'N'
$azure1.UserID = 'myuserid'
$azure1.Password = "mypassword"

$azure1.SetAuthenticationType('Logon')
$azure1.BuildConnectionString()
```

With the connection properties set, we can run a query as follows:

```
$azure1.RunSQL("SELECT top 20 * FROM [HumanResources].[EmployeeDepartmentHistory]", $true)
```

Assuming you change the properties to fit your Azure database, you should see results displayed in the console.

Now that we have some connection objects, we can execute more queries, as follows:

```
$myssint.RunSQL("SELECT top 20 * FROM [HumanResources].[Department]", $true)

$azure1.RunSQL("SELECT top 20 * FROM [Person].[Person]", $true)
```

Each statement will return results. The connection is closed after getting the results, but the properties are retained so that we can keep running queries. The result data is not retained, so if we want to capture it, we need to assign it to a variable, as follows:

```
$myresults = $myssint.RunSQL("SELECT top 20 * FROM [HumanResources].[Department]", $true)
```

What if we want to run a query that does not return results? That's where the second parameter to the RunSQL method comes in. By setting it to $false, we are telling the method not to return results. For example, the following lines will execute an update statement using the first connection object we created:

```
$esql = "Update [AdventureWorks].[HumanResources].[CompanyUnit] set UnitName = 'NewSales2'
where UnitID = 3;"
$myssint.RunSQL($esql, $false)
```

Here we are assigning the SQL statement to $esql, which is passed to the RunSQL method.

How umd_database Works

The umd_database module consists of a set of functions and is designed so that it can easily be extended. As we can see from the examples that use the module, the core function, New-UdfConnection, is the one that returns the connection object to us. Because this function is so long, I'm not going to list all of it at once. However, you can see the entire function in the code accompanying this book, in the umd_database module script. Let's start with the following function header:

```
function New-UdfConnection
{

 [CmdletBinding()]
       param (
               [ref]$p_connection
               )
```

The first thing to notice in the function header is that the parameter is of type [REF], which means reference. The caller passes an object reference to the function. This gives the function the ability to make changes to the object passed, which is how the connection object is customized with properties and methods. Before calling the New-UdfConnection function, the calling code needs to create an instance of a PSObject and then pass a reference to it, as shown in the example code here:

```
[psobject] $myssint = New-Object psobject
New-UdfConnection ([ref]$myssint)
```

The function New-UdfConnection attaches properties and methods to the object passed in, as shown here:

```
# Connection Type...
$p_connection.value | Add-Member   -MemberType noteproperty `
                                   -Name ConnectionType `
                                   -Value $p_connectiontype
```

To change the object passed to the function, we need to use the object's Value property, $p_connection.value. The Add-Member cmdlet adds properties and methods to the object. MemberType specifies what type of property or method we want to attach. In the previous code, we add a noteproperty, which is just a place to hold static data. The Name parameter assigns an externally visible name to the property. The Value parameter assigns an initial value to the property, and the Passthru parameter tells PowerShell to pass the property through the pipe. This same type of coding is used to create the following properties: DatabaseType, Server, DatabaseName, UseCredential, UserID, Password, DSNName, and Driver. Since the coding is identical except for Name and Value, I'm not going to list them all here.

AuthenticationType is handled a bit differently. To start, the property is created just like the other properties are. The code is as follows:

```
# AuthenticationType. Value must be in AuthenticationTypes.
    $p_connection.value | Add-Member    -MemberType noteproperty `
                                        -Name AuthenticationType `
                                        -Value 'NotAssigned' `
                                        -Passthru
```

However, AuthenticationType will not be set by directly assigning a value to it. Instead, a method named SetAuthenticationType will be called. This is so we can validate the AuthenticationType value before allowing it to be assigned. So, when we call SetAuthenticationType on the object as in "$myssint. SetAuthenticationType('Integrated')", an invalid value will be rejected. Let's look at the code that stores the valid list of values as an object property:

```
$p_authentiationtypes = ('Integrated','Logon','Credential', 'StoredCredential',
'DSN', 'DSNLess')

$p_connection.value | Add-Member    -MemberType noteproperty `
                                    -Name AuthenticationTypes `
                                    -Value $p_authentiationtypes
```

In this code, we are creating the array $p_authenticationtypes and loading it with values. Then, we use the Add-Member cmdlet to attach the array as a property named AuthenticationTypes to the object passed in to the function. Attaching the list to the object as a property enables the user to see what the valid values are.

Now, let's look at the code that sets the AuthenticationType:

```
$bauth = @'
    param([string]$p_authentication)

    if ($this.AuthenticationTypes -contains $p_authentication)
    {
        $this.AuthenticationType = $p_authentication
    }
    Else
    {
        Throw "Error - Invalid Authentication Type, valid values are " + $this.
        AuthenticationTypes
    }

    RETURN $this.AuthenticationType

'@
```

The here string is the script to be executed when the SetAuthenticationType is called. The only parameter is the authentication type to assign. To validate that the desired authentication type is valid, the code uses the object's AuthenticationTypes property. The special keyword $this refers to the current object— i.e., the object we are extending. The line "if ($this.AuthenticationTypes -contains $p_authentication)" is checking whether the value passed in is contained in the object's AuthenticationTypes hash table. If it is, the object $this.AuthenticationType is assigned the parameter passed in. If the value is not in the list, an error is thrown with a message telling the caller that the authentication type is not valid.

The code that follows attaches the script to the object as a script method named SetAuthenticationType:

```
$sauth = [scriptblock]::create($bauth)

$p_connection.value | Add-Member  -MemberType scriptmethod `
                                  -Name SetAuthenticationType `
                                  -Value $sauth `
                                  -Passthru
```

Then first statement, "$sauth = [scriptblock]::create($bauth)", converts the here string into a script block. Then the Add-Member cmdlet is used to attach the scriptblock to the object as a scriptmethod named SetAuthenticationType. The method takes one parameter—the value to set the AuthenticationType. You may be asking yourself, why is the code for the script method first defined as a here string and then converted to a script block? Why not just define it as a script block to start with? The reason is that a script block has limitations, including that it will not expand variables and it cannot define named parameters. By defining the code as a here string, which does support variable expansion, we can get the script block to support it too; i.e., when we convert it to the script block using the script block constructor create method. This technique gives our script methods the power of functions. I got this idea from a blog by Ed Wilson, the Scripting Guy:

http://blogs.technet.com/b/heyscriptingguy/archive/2013/05/22/variable-substitution-in-a-powershell-script-block.aspx

It is not always necessary to expand variables, so in some cases we could just directly define the script method as a script block. However, I prefer to code for maximum flexibility since requirements can change, so I make it a practice to always code script methods for my custom objects using this approach.

The next section of the New-UdfConnection function creates the script method BuildConnectionString, which creates the required connection string so as to connect to the database. Let's look at the code that follows:

```
$bbuildconnstring = @'
    param()

    If ($this.AuthenticationType -eq 'DSN' -and $this.DSNName -eq 'NotAssigned')
    { Throw "Error - DSN Authentication requires DSN Name to be set." }

    If ($this.AuthenticationType -eq 'DSNLess' -and $this.Driver -eq 'NotAssigned')
    { Throw "Error - DSNLess Authentication requires Driver to be set." }

    $Result = Get-UdfConnectionString $this.ConnectionType `
                $this.DatabaseType $this.Server $this.AuthenticationType `
                $this.Databasename $this.UserID $this.Password $this.DSNName $this.Driver

    If (!$Result.startswith("Err"))  { $this.ConnectionString = $Result } Else {
    $this.ConnectionString = 'NotAssigned' }

    RETURN $Result

'@
```

A here string is assigned the code to build the connection string. The script does not take any parameters. The first two lines do some validation to make sure that, if this is an ODBC DSN connection, the object's DSNName property has been set. Alternatively, if this is an ODBC DSNLess connection, it verifies that the Driver property is set. If something is wrong, an error is thrown. There could be any number of validations, but the idea here is to demonstrate how they can be implemented. Again, to access the object properties, we use the $this reference. If the script passes the validation tests, it calls function Get-UdfConnectionString, passing required parameters to build the connection string, which is returned to the variable $Result. If there was an error getting the connection string, a string starting with "Err" is returned. $Result is checked, and if it does not start with "Err", i.e., "If (!$Result.startswith("Err"))", the object's ConnectionString property is set to $Result. Remember, ! means NOT. Otherwise, the ConnectionString is set to 'NotAssigned'. The function Get-UdfConnectionString is not part of the object. It is just a function in the module, which means it is a static function—i.e., there is only one instance of it.

The example shows how we can mix instance-specific methods and properties with static ones. Get-UdfConnectionString can also be called outside of the object method, which might come in handy if someone just wants to build a connection string. We'll cover the code involved in Get-UdfConnectionString after we've finished covering New-UdfConnection. Now, let's take a look at the code that attaches the script to the script method:

```
$sbuildconnstring = [scriptblock]::create($bbuildconnstring)

$p_connection.value | Add-Member    -MemberType scriptmethod `
                                    -Name BuildConnectionString `
                                    -Value $sbuildconnstring `
                                    -Passthru
```

The first line converts the here string with the script into a scriptblock. Then the Add-Member cmdlet is used to attach the scriptblock to the scriptmethod BuildConnectionString. The Passthru parameter tells PowerShell to pass this scriptmethod through the pipe.

The next method, RunSQL, is the real powerhouse of the object, and yet it is coded in the same way. This method will execute any SQL statement passed to it, using the connection string generated by the BuildConnectionString method to connect to a database. Let's look at the script definition here:

```
# Do NOT put double quotes around the object $this properties as it messes up the values.
# **** RunSQL ***
$bsql = @'
    param([string]$p_insql,[boolean]$IsSelect)

  $this.BuildConnectionString()

  If ($this.ConnectionString -eq 'NotAssigned')  {Throw "Error - Cannot create connection
  string." }

  $Result = Invoke-UdfSQL $this.ConnectionType $this.DatabaseType $this.Server `
     $this.DatabaseName "$p_insql" `
     $this.AuthenticationType $this.UserID $this.Password `
     $this.ConnectionString $IsSelect `
     $this.DSNName $this.Driver

  RETURN $Result

'@
```

The script is assigned to a variable, $bsql, as a here string. The script takes two parameters, $p_insql, which is the SQL statement to be executed, and $IsSelect, a Boolean, which is $true if the SQL statement is a Select statement and $false if it is not a Select statement, such as an update statement. Statements that return results need to be handled differently than statements that do not. Just in case the user did not call the BuildConnectionString method yet, the script calls it to make sure we have a connection string. Then the script checks that the ConnectionString has been assigned a value, and, if not, it throws an error. Finally, Invoke-UdfSQL is called with the parameters for connection type, database type, server name, database name, SQL statement, authentication type, User ID, Password, Connection String, $true if the statement is a Select statement or $false if it is not, DSN Name, and Driver Name. If the SQL were a Select statement, $Result will hold the data returned. The code that follows attaches the script to the object:

```
$ssql = [scriptblock]::create($bsql)

$p_connection.value | Add-Member -MemberType scriptmethod `
                        -Name RunSQL `
                        -Value $ssql `
                        -Passthru
```

The here string holding the script is converted to a scriptblock variable $ssql. Then $ssql is attached to the object with the Add-Member cmdlet and becomes scriptmethod RunSQL. The Passthru parameter tells PowerShell to pass the scriptmethod through the pipe.

Supporting Functions

There are a few support functions used by the object that New-UdfConnection returns. The object user need not be aware of these functions, but they help the connection object perform tasks. If the user is familiar with these functions, they can call them directly rather than through the connection object. This adds flexibility to the module, as a developer can pick and choose what they want to use.

Get-UdfConnectionString

The connection object returned by New-UdfConnection calls Get-UdfConnectionString when the method BuildConnectionString is executed. This function creates a connection string based on the parameters passed to it.

Rather than write code that dynamically formats a connection string, why not read them from a text file? The format of a connection string is pretty static. Given the connection requirements—i.e., connection type, such as ADO.Net or ODBC, the database type, and the authentication method, such as Windows Integrated Security or logon credentials—the connection string format does not change. Only the variables like server name, database name, user ID, and password change. Ideally, we want to use connection strings in a file, like a template in which we can fill in the variable values. Fortunately, PowerShell makes this very easy to do. We'll use the CSV file named connectionstring.txt with the columns Type, Platform, AuthenticationType, and ConnectionString. Type, Platform, and AuthenticationType will be used to locate the connection string we need. Let's take a look at the contents of the file:

```
"Type","Platform","AuthenticationType","ConnectionString"
"ADO","SqlServer","Integrated","Data Source=$server;Integrated Security=SSPI;Initial
Catalog=$databasename"
"ADO","SqlServer","Logon","Data Source=$server;Persist Security Info=False;
IntegratedSecurity=false;Initial Catalog=$databasename;User ID=$userid;Password=$password"
"ADO","SqlServer","Credential","Data Source=$server;Persist Security Info=False;Initial
Catalog=$databasename"
```

```
"ADO","Azure","Logon","Data Source=$server;User ID=$userid;Password=$password;Initial
Catalog=$databasename;Trusted_Connection=False;TrustServerCertificate=False;Encrypt=True;"
"ODBC","PostgreSQL","DSNLess","Driver={$driver};Server=$server;Port=5432;Database=
$databasename;Uid=$userid;Pwd=$password;SSLmode=disable;ReadOnly=0;"
"ODBC","PostgreSQL","DSN","DSN=$dsn;SSLmode=disable;ReadOnly=0;"
```

Notice that we have what appear to be PowerShell variables in the data, prefixed with $, as values for things in the connection string that are not static.

Now, let's take a look at the code that uses the text file to build a connection string:

```
function Get-UdfConnectionString
{
[CmdletBinding()]
        param (
                [string] $type              ,   # Connection type, ADO, OleDB, ODBC, etc.
                [string] $dbtype            ,   # Database Type; SQL Server, Azure, MySQL.
                [string] $server            ,   # Server instance name
                [string] $authentication    ,   # Authentication method
                [string] $databasename      ,   # Database
                [string] $userid            ,   # User Name if using credential
                [string] $password          ,   # password if using credential
                [string] $dsnname           ,   # dsn name for ODBC connection
                [string] $driver                # driver for ODBC DSN Less connection
                )

  $connstrings = Import-CSV ($PSScriptRoot + "\connectionstrings.txt")

  foreach ($item in $connstrings)
  {

  if ($item.Type -eq $type -and $item.Platform -eq $dbtype -and $item.AuthenticationType
  -eq $authentication)
      {
          $connstring = $item.ConnectionString
          $connstring = $ExecutionContext.InvokeCommand.ExpandString($connstring)
          Return $connstring
      }
  }

  # If this line is reached, no matching connection string was found.
  Return "Error - Connection string not found!"

}
```

In this code, the function parameters are documented by comments; let's look at the first statement. The first line loads a list of connection strings from a CSV file into a variable named $connstrings. It looks for the file in the path pointed to by the automatic variable $PSScriptRoot, which is the folder the module umd_database is stored in. Make sure you copied the connectionstring.txt file to this folder. Using a foreach loop, we loop through each row in $connstrings until we find a row that matches the connection type, database type, and authentication type passed to the function. The matching row is loaded into $connstring. Now, a nice thing about PowerShell strings is that they automatically expand to replace variable names with their values. By having the function parameter names match the variable names used in the connection strings in the file, we can have PowerShell automatically fill in the values for us by expanding the string using the command $ExecutionContext.InvokeCommand.ExpandString. Then, the connection string is returned to the caller. If no match is found, the statement after the foreach loop will be executed, which returns a message "Error - Connection string not found!". Normally, creating connection strings is tedious, but this function can be extended to accommodate many different requirements just by adding new rows to the input file.

Invoke-UdfSQL

Invoke-UdfSQL is the function called by the connection object's RunSQL method. This function acts like a broker to determine which specific function to call to run the SQL statement. It currently supports ADO and ODBC, but you can easily add other types like OleDB. Let's take a look at the Invoke-UdfSQL function:

```
function Invoke-UdfSQL      ([string]$p_inconntype,
                            [string]$p_indbtype,
                            [string]$p_inserver,
                            [string]$p_indb,
                            [string]$p_insql,
                            [string]$p_inauthenticationtype,
                            [string]$p_inuser,
                                    $p_inpw, # No type defined; can be securestring or string
                            [string]$p_inconnectionstring,
                            [boolean]$p_inisselect,
                            [string]$p_indsnname,
                            [string]$p_indriver,
                            [boolean]$p_inisprocedure,
                                    $p_inparms)
{

  If ($p_inconntype -eq "ADO")
  {
    If ($p_inisprocedure)
    {
      RETURN Invoke-UdfADOStoredProcedure $p_inserver $p_indb $p_insql `
            $p_inauthenticationtype $p_inuser $p_inpw $p_inconnectionstring $p_inparms
    }
    Else
    {
      $datatab = Invoke-UdfADOSQL $p_inserver $p_indb $p_insql `
            $p_inauthenticationtype $p_inuser $p_inpw $p_inconnectionstring $p_inisselect
      Return $datatab
    }
  }
  ElseIf ($p_inconntype -eq "ODBC")
  {
    If ($p_inisprocedure)
    {

      RETURN Invoke-UdfODBCStoredProcedure $p_inserver $p_indb $p_insql `
            $p_inauthenticationtype $p_inuser $p_inpw $p_inconnectionstring $p_inparms
    }
```

```
    Else
    {
        $datatab = Invoke-UdfODBCSQL $p_inserver $p_indb $p_insql $p_inauthenticationtype `
                    $p_inuser $p_inpw $p_inconnectionstring $p_inisselect $p_indsnname $driver

        Return $datatab
    }
}
Else
{
    Throw "Connection Type Not Supported."
}

}
```

This function has an extensive parameter list. Some of them are not needed, but it's good to have the extra information in case we need it. Notice that parameter $p_inpw has no type defined. This is so the parameter can accept whatever is passed to it. As I will demonstrate later, the connection object can support either an encrypted or a clear-text password. An encrypted string is of type securestring, and clear text is of type string. Note: Depending on the connection requirements, some of the parameters may not have values. The function code consists of an If/Else block. If the parameter connection type $p_inconntype is 'ADO', then the Boolean is checked to see if this is a stored procedure call. If yes, the function Invoke-UdfADOStoredProcedure is called, otherwise Invoke-UdfADOSQL is called, with the results loaded into $datatab, which is then returned to the caller. If the parameter connection type $p_inconntype is 'ODBC', then the Boolean is checked to see if this is a stored procedure call. If yes, the function Invoke-UdfODBCStoredProcedure is called, otherwise Invoke-UdfODBCSQL is called, with the results loaded into $datatab, which is returned to the caller. If the connection type is neither of these, a terminating error is thrown.

Invoke-UdfADOSQL

Invoke-UdfADOSQL uses ADO.Net to execute the SQL statement and the connection string passed in. ADO.Net is a very flexible provider supported by many vendors, including Oracle, MySQL, and PostgreSQL. Let's look at the function Invoke-UdfADOSQL code:

```
function Invoke-UdfADOSQL
{
[CmdletBinding()]
    param (
            [string] $sqlserver              ,   # SQL Server
            [string] $sqldatabase            ,   # SQL Server Database.
            [string] $sqlquery               ,   # SQL Query
            [string] $sqlauthenticationtype  ,   # $true = Use Credentials
            [string] $sqluser                ,   # User Name if using credential
            $sqlpw                           ,   # password if using credential
            [string] $sqlconnstring          ,   # Connection string
            [boolean]$sqlisselect            # true = select, false = non select statement
        )
```

```
if ($sqlauthenticationtype -eq 'Credential')
{
    $pw =  $sqlpw
    $pw.MakeReadOnly()

    $SqlCredential = new-object System.Data.SqlClient.SqlCredential($sqluser,  $pw)
    $conn = new-object System.Data.SqlClient.SqlConnection($sqlconnstring, $SqlCredential)
}
else
{
    $conn = new-object System.Data.SqlClient.SqlConnection($sqlconnstring)
}

$conn.Open()

$command = new-object system.data.sqlclient.Sqlcommand($sqlquery,$conn)

if ($sqlisselect)
{
    $adapter = New-Object System.Data.sqlclient.SqlDataAdapter $command
    $dataset = New-Object System.Data.DataSet
    $adapter.Fill($dataset) | Out-Null
    $conn.Close()
    RETURN $dataset.tables[0]
}
Else
{
    $command.ExecuteNonQuery()
    $conn.Close()
}
```

This function takes a lot of parameters, but most of them are not needed; rather, they are included in case there is a need to extend the functionality. Let's take a closer look at the first section of code that handles credentials:

```
if ($sqlauthenticationtype -eq 'Credential')
{
    $pw =  $sqlpw
    $pw.MakeReadOnly()

    $SqlCredential = new-object System.Data.SqlClient.SqlCredential($sqluser,  $pw)
    $conn = new-object System.Data.SqlClient.SqlConnection($sqlconnstring, $SqlCredential)
}
else
{
    $conn = new-object System.Data.SqlClient.SqlConnection($sqlconnstring);
}
```

We can see that if the authentication type passed is equal to Credential, it indicates that the caller wants to use a credential object to log in. A credential object allows us to separate the connection string from the user ID and password so no one can see them. Note: This concept can also be used in making web-service requests. If the authentication type is Credential, the password parameter, $sqlpw, is assigned to $pw, and then this variable is set to read only. This is required by the credential object. Then, we create an instance of the SqlCredential object, passing the user ID and password as parameters, which returns a reference to the variable $SqlCredential. Finally, the connection object is created as an instance of SqlConnection with the connection string, $sqlconnectonstring, and the credential object, $SqlCredential, as parameters. The connection reference is returned to $conn. If the authentication type is not equal to Credential, the connection is created by passing only the connection string to the SqlConnection method. Note: The user ID and password would be found in the connection string if the authentication type were Logon or DSNLess.

Now the function is ready to open the connection as shown here:

```
$conn.Open()

$command = new-object system.data.sqlclient.Sqlcommand($sqlquery,$conn)
```

First, the connection must be opened. Then, a command object is created via the SqlCommand method, and the SQL statement and connection object are passed as parameters, returning the object to $command. The code to execute the SQL statement is as follows:

```
if ($sqlisselect)
{
    $adapter = New-Object System.Data.sqlclient.SqlDataAdapter $command
    $dataset = New-Object System.Data.DataSet
    $adapter.Fill($dataset) | Out-Null
    $conn.Close()
    RETURN $dataset.tables[0]
}
Else
{
    $command.ExecuteNonQuery()
    $conn.Close()
}
```

Above, the Boolean parameter $sqlisselect is tested for a value of true—i.e., "if ($sqlisselect)". Since it is a Boolean type, there is no need to compare the value to $true or $false. If true, this is a select statement and it needs to retrieve data and return it to the caller. We can see a SQL data adapter being created, with the SqlDataAdapter method call passing the command object as a parameter. Then a dataset object, DataSet, is created to hold the results. The data adapter—$adapter—Fill method is called to load the dataset with the results. The connection is closed, as we don't want to accumulate open connections. It is important to take this cleanup step. A dataset is a collection of tables. A command can submit multiple select statements, and each result will go into a separate table element in the dataset. This function only supports one select statement so as to keep things simple. Therefore, only the first result set is returned, as in the statement "RETURN $dataset.table[0]". If $issqlselect is false, the statement just needs to be executed. No results are returned. Therefore, the command method ExecuteNonQuery is called. Then, the connection is closed. There is nothing to return to the caller.

Using the Credential Object

The credential object provides good protection of the user ID and password. On-premises SQL Server supports using a credential object at logon, but Azure SQL does not. As we saw, the object returned by Get-UdfConnection supports using a credential. However, using it requires a slightly different set of statements. Let's look at the following example:

```
[psobject] $myconnection = New-Object psobject
New-UdfConnection ([ref]$myconnection)

$myconnection.ConnectionType = 'ADO'
$myconnection.DatabaseType = 'SqlServer'
$myconnection.Server = '(local)'
$myconnection.DatabaseName = 'AdventureWorks'
$myconnection.UseCredential = 'Y'
$myconnection.UserID = 'bryan'
$myconnection.Password = Get-Content 'C:\Users\BryanCafferky\Documents\password.txt' |
convertto-securestring

$myconnection.SetAuthenticationType('Credential')
$myconnection.BuildConnectionString()  # Should return the connection string.
```

These statements will set all the properties needed to run queries against our local instance of SQL Server. Most of this is the same as what we did before. The line I want to call your attention to is copied here:

```
$myconnection.Password = Get-Content 'C:\Users\BryanCafferky\Documents\password.txt' |
convertto-securestring
```

This line loads the password from a file that is piped into the ConvertTo-Securestring cmdlet to encrypt it. If you try to display the password property of $myconnection, you will just see 'System.Security.Securestring'. You cannot view the contents. So the password is never readable to anyone once it has been saved. Other than that difference, the connection object is used the same way as before. We can submit a query such as the one here:

```
$myconnection.RunSQL("SELECT top 20 * FROM [HumanResources].[EmployeeDepartmentHistory]",
$true) | Select-Object -Property BusinessEntityID, DepartmentID, ShiftID, StartDate |
Out-GridView
```

The query results will be returned and piped into the Select-Object cmdlet, which selects the columns desired, and then will be piped into the Out-GridView for display.

Encrypting and Saving the Password to a File

We have not seen how to save the password to a file. We can do that with this statement:

```
Save-UdfEncryptedCredential
```

This statement calls a module function that will prompt us for a password and, after we enter it, will prompt us for the filename to save it to with the Window's Save File common dialog. Let's take a look at the code for this function:

```
function Save-UdfEncryptedCredential {
[CmdletBinding()] param ()

    $pw = read-host -Prompt "Enter the password:" -assecurestring

    $pw | convertfrom-securestring |
    out-file (Invoke-UdfCommonDialogSaveFile  ("c:" + $env:HOMEPATH + "\Documents\" ) )

}
```

The first executable line prompts the user for a password, which is not displayed as typed because the `assecurestring` parameter to `Read-Host` suppresses display of the characters. The second line displays the Save File common dialog so the user can choose where to save the password. Because the call to `Invoke-UdfCommonDialogSaveFile` is in parentheses, it will execute first, and the password will be stored to the file specified by the user. The password entered is piped into `ConvertFrom-SecureString`, which obfuscates it by making it a readable series of numbers that is piped into the `Out-File` cmdlet, which saves the file.

For completeness, the function `Invoke-UdfCommonDialogSaveFile`, which displays the Save File common dialog form, is listed here:

```
function Invoke-UdfCommonDialogSaveFile($initialDirectory)
{
 [System.Reflection.Assembly]::LoadWithPartialName("System.windows.forms") |
 Out-Null

 $OpenFileDialog = New-Object System.Windows.Forms.SaveFileDialog
 $OpenFileDialog.initialDirectory = $initialDirectory
 $OpenFileDialog.filter = "All files (*.*)| *.*"
 $OpenFileDialog.ShowDialog() | Out-Null
 $OpenFileDialog.filename
}
```

This function uses the Window's form `SaveFileDialog` to present a user with the familiar Save As dialog. The only parameter is the initial directory the caller wants the dialog to default to. The last line returns the selected folder and filename entered.

Calling Stored Procedures

In simple cases, stored procedures can be called like any other SQL statement. If the procedure returns a query result, it can be executed as a `select` query. For example, consider the stored procedure in Listing 7-2 that returns a list of employees.

Listing 7-2. The stored procedure HumanResources.uspListEmployeePersonalInfoPS

```
Create PROCEDURE [HumanResources].[uspListEmployeePersonalInfoPS]
    @BusinessEntityID [int]
WITH EXECUTE AS CALLER
AS
BEGIN
    SET NOCOUNT ON;

    BEGIN TRY

            select *
            from [HumanResources].[Employee]
            where [BusinessEntityID] = @BusinessEntityID;

    END TRY
    BEGIN CATCH
        EXECUTE [dbo].[uspLogError];
    END CATCH;
END;

GO
```

The procedure in Listing 7-2 will return the list of employees that have the `BusinessEntityID` passed to the function—i.e., one employee, since this is the primary key. We can test it on SQL Server as follows:

```
exec [HumanResources].[uspListEmployeePersonalInfoPS] 1
```

One row is returned. Using the connection object returned by `New-UdfConnection`, we can code the call to this stored procedure, as shown in Listing 7-3. Note: Change properties as needed to suit your environment.

Listing 7-3. Calling a SQL Server stored procedure

```
Import-Module umd_database -Force

[psobject] $myconnection = New-Object psobject
New-UdfConnection ([ref]$myconnection)

$myconnection.ConnectionType = 'ADO'
$myconnection.DatabaseType = 'SqlServer'
$myconnection.Server = '(local)'
$myconnection.DatabaseName = 'AdventureWorks'
$myconnection.UseCredential = 'N'

$myconnection.SetAuthenticationType('Integrated')
$myconnection.BuildConnectionString()
$empid = 1

$myconnection.RunSQL("exec [HumanResources].[uspListEmployeePersonalInfoPS] $empid", $true)
```

Since the result set is passed back from a select query within the stored procedure, the call to the procedure is treated like a select statement. Notice that we can even include input parameters by using PowerShell variables.

Calling Stored Procedures Using Output Parameters

When we want to call a stored procedure that uses output parameters to return results, we need to add the parameters object to the database call. To demonstrate, let's consider the stored procedure that follows that takes the input parameters BusinessEntityID, NationalIDNumber, BirthDate, MaritalStatus, and Gender and returns the output parameters JobTitle, HireDate, and VacationHours. This is a modified version of an AdventureWorks stored procedure named [HumanResources].[uspUpdateEmployeePersonalInfo], with PS appended to the name, indicating it is for use by our PowerShell script. The input parameters are used to update the employee record. The output parameters are returned from the call. Let's review the stored procedure in Listing 7-4.

Listing 7-4. A stored procedure with output parametersq

```
USE [AdventureWorks]
GO

SET ANSI_NULLS ON
SET QUOTED_IDENTIFIER ON
GO

Create PROCEDURE [HumanResources].[uspUpdateEmployeePersonalInfoPS]
    @BusinessEntityID [int],
    @NationalIDNumber [nvarchar](15),
    @BirthDate [datetime],
    @MaritalStatus [nchar](1),
    @Gender [nchar](1),
    @JobTitle [nvarchar](50) output,
    @HireDate [date] output,
    @VacationHours [smallint] output
WITH EXECUTE AS CALLER
AS
BEGIN
    SET NOCOUNT ON;

    BEGIN TRY
        UPDATE [HumanResources].[Employee]
        SET [NationalIDNumber] = @NationalIDNumber
            ,[BirthDate] = @BirthDate
            ,[MaritalStatus] = @MaritalStatus
            ,[Gender] = @Gender
        WHERE [BusinessEntityID] = @BusinessEntityID;

        select @JobTitle = JobTitle, @HireDate = HireDate, @VacationHours = VacationHours
        from [HumanResources].[Employee]
        where [BusinessEntityID] = @BusinessEntityID;
```

```
    END TRY
    BEGIN CATCH
        EXECUTE [dbo].[uspLogError];
    END CATCH;
END;

GO
```

Listing 7-4 is a simple stored procedure, but it allows us to see how to pass input and output parameters of different data types. We can see that the Update statement will update the employee record with the input parameters. Then a select statement will load the values for JobTitle, HireDate, and VacationHours into the output parameters @JobTitle, @HireDate, and @VacationHours. Let's look more closely at how the parameters are defined:

```
@BusinessEntityID [int],
@NationalIDNumber [nvarchar](15),
@BirthDate [datetime],
@MaritalStatus [nchar](1),
@Gender [nchar](1),
@JobTitle [nvarchar](50) output,
@HireDate [date] output,
@VacationHours [smallint] output
```

Parameters can be of three possible types, which are Input, Output, or InputOutput. Input parameters can be read but not updated. Output parameters by definition should only be updatable but not read. InputOutput parameters can be read and updated. SQL Server does not support an Output parameter that can only be updated. Rather, it treats Output parameters as InputOutput parameters. By default, a parameter is Input, so it does not need to be specified. Notice that for the Output parameters, the word 'output' is specified after the data type.

Before we look at how to call this stored procedure with PowerShell, let's review how we would call it from SQL Server. Actually, it's a good idea to test calls to SQL from within a SQL Server tool like SQL Server Management Studio before trying to develop and test PowerShell code to do the same thing. The short SQL script in Listing 7-5 executes our stored procedure.

Listing 7-5. A SQL script to call a stored procedure

```
Use AdventureWorks
go

Declare  @JobTitle                    [nvarchar](50)
Declare @HireDate            [date]
Declare @VacationHours       [smallint]

exec  [HumanResources].[uspUpdateEmployeePersonalInfoPS] 1, 295847284, '1963-01-01', 'M',
'M',  @JobTitle Output, @HireDate Output, @VacationHours Output

print  @JobTitle
print  @HireDate
print  @VacationHours
```

When you run this script, you should see the following output:

```
Chief Executive Officer
2003-02-15
42
```

Don't worry if the actual values are different. It will be whatever is in the database at the time you execute this.

PowerShell Code to Call a Stored Procedure with Output Parameters

Now that we know we can execute the stored procedure with T-SQL, let's do the same thing using PowerShell. Let's look at the PowerShell script in Listing 7-6 that runs the stored procedure. Note: To get the ideas across, the script is pretty hard coded.

Listing 7-6. PowerShell code to call a stored procedure with output parameters

```
Import-Module umd_database

$SqlConnection = New-Object System.Data.SqlClient.SqlConnection
$SqlConnection.ConnectionString = "Data Source=(local);Integrated Security=SSPI;Initial
Catalog=AdventureWorks"
$SqlCmd = New-Object System.Data.SqlClient.SqlCommand
$SqlCmd.CommandText = "[HumanResources].[uspUpdateEmployeePersonalInfoPS]"
$SqlCmd.Connection = $SqlConnection
$SqlCmd.CommandType = [System.Data.CommandType]'StoredProcedure'
$SqlCmd.Parameters.AddWithValue("@BusinessEntityID", 1) >> $null
$SqlCmd.Parameters.AddWithValue("@NationalIDNumber", 295847284) >> $null
$SqlCmd.Parameters.AddWithValue("@BirthDate", '1964-02-02') >> $null
$SqlCmd.Parameters.AddWithValue("@MaritalStatus", 'S') >> $null
$SqlCmd.Parameters.AddWithValue("@Gender", 'M') >> $null

#  -- Output Parameters ---
# JobTitle
$outParameter1 = new-object System.Data.SqlClient.SqlParameter
$outParameter1.ParameterName = "@JobTitle"
$outParameter1.Direction = [System.Data.ParameterDirection]::Output
$outParameter1.DbType = [System.Data.DbType]'string'
$outParameter1.Size = 50
$SqlCmd.Parameters.Add($outParameter1) >> $null

# HireDate
$outParameter2 = new-object System.Data.SqlClient.SqlParameter
$outParameter2.ParameterName = "@HireDate"
$outParameter2.Direction = [System.Data.ParameterDirection]::Output
$outParameter2.DbType = [System.Data.DbType]'date'
$SqlCmd.Parameters.Add($outParameter2) >> $null

# VacationHours
$outParameter3 = new-object System.Data.SqlClient.SqlParameter
$outParameter3.ParameterName = "@VacationHours"
$outParameter3.Direction = [System.Data.ParameterDirection]::Output
```

```
$outParameter3.DbType = [System.Data.DbType]'int16'
$SqlCmd.Parameters.Add($outParameter3) >> $null

$SqlConnection.Open()
$result = $SqlCmd.ExecuteNonQuery()
$SqlConnection.Close()

$SqlCmd.Parameters["@jobtitle"].value
$SqlCmd.Parameters["@hiredate"].value
$SqlCmd.Parameters["@VacationHours"].value
```

There's a lot of code there, but we'll walk through it. As before, first we import the umd_database module. Then, we define the parameters. First, let's look at the code that creates the SQL connection and command objects:

```
$SqlConnection = New-Object System.Data.SqlClient.SqlConnection
$SqlConnection.ConnectionString = "Data Source=(local);Integrated Security=SSPI;Initial
Catalog=AdventureWorks"
$SqlCmd = New-Object System.Data.SqlClient.SqlCommand
$SqlCmd.CommandText = "[HumanResources].[uspUpdateEmployeePersonalInfoPS]"
$SqlCmd.Connection = $SqlConnection
$SqlCmd.CommandType = [System.Data.CommandType]'StoredProcedure';
```

We've seen the first few lines before—creating the connection, assigning the connection string, and creating a command object. Notice that for the command's CommandText property, we're just giving the name of the stored procedure, i.e., = [HumanResources].[uspUpdateEmployeePersonalInfoPS]. Then, we connect the command to the connection with the line "$SqlCmd.Connection = $SqlConnection". Finally, the last line assigns the CommandType property as 'StoredProcedure'. This is critical in order for the command to be processed correctly. The Input parameters are assigned by the code here:

```
$SqlCmd.Parameters.AddWithValue("@BusinessEntityID", 1) >> $null
$SqlCmd.Parameters.AddWithValue("@NationalIDNumber", 295847284) >> $null
$SqlCmd.Parameters.AddWithValue("@BirthDate", '1964-02-02') >> $null
$SqlCmd.Parameters.AddWithValue("@MaritalStatus", 'S') >> $null
$SqlCmd.Parameters.AddWithValue("@Gender", 'M') >> $null
```

Input parameters can use the abbreviated format for assignment. The parameters collection of the command object holds the parameter details. The AddWithValue method adds each parameter with value to the collection. To suppress any output returned from the AddWithValue method, we direct it to $null. Output parameters need to be coded in a manner that provides more details. Now, let's look at the code that creates the JobTitle output parameters:

```
# <---- Output Parameters ----->
# JobTitle
$outParameter1 = new-object System.Data.SqlClient.SqlParameter
$outParameter1.ParameterName = "@JobTitle"
$outParameter1.Direction = [System.Data.ParameterDirection]::Output
$outParameter1.DbType = [System.Data.DbType]'string'
$outParameter1.Size = 50
$SqlCmd.Parameters.Add($outParameter1) >> $null
```

In the first non-comment line above, we create a new SQL parameter object instance to hold the information about the parameter. Once created, we just assign details about the parameter, such as `ParameterName`, `Direction`, `DbType`, and `Size`, to the associated object properties. The `ParameterName` is the name defined in the stored procedure, which is why it has the @ sign prefix, as SQL Server variables and parameters have. The `Direction` property tells whether this is an `Input`, `Output`, or `InputOutput` parameter. Note: Although SQL Server does not support an `InputOutput` direction, ADO.Net does. We define the direction as `Output`. The `DbType` property is not of the SQL Server data type. Rather, it is an abstraction that will equate to a SQL Server data type in our case. For another type of database, the underlying database-type columns may be different. For a complete list of `DbType` to SQL Server data-type mappings, see the link: `https://msdn.microsoft.com/en-us/library/cc716729%28v=vs.110%29.aspx`

We use the `DbType` `'string'` for the `JobTitle`, which is defined as `nvarchar(50)`. For string types, we need to assign the `Size` property, which is the length of the column. Finally, we use the `Parameters` collection `Add` method to add the parameter to the collection. Table 7-1 shows some of the most common SQL Server data types and their ADO.Net corresponding `DbType`.

Table 7-1. *Common Data Types*

SQL Server Database Format	ADO.Net DbType
int	Int32
Smallint	Int16
bigint	Int64
varchar	String or Char[]
nvarchar	String or Char[]
char	String or Char[]
bit	Boolean
date	Date
decimal	Decimal
text	String or Char[]
ntext	String or Char[]

Now, let's look at the code that creates the remaining two output parameters:

```
# HireDate
$outParameter2 = new-object System.Data.SqlClient.SqlParameter
$outParameter2.ParameterName = "@HireDate"
$outParameter2.Direction = [System.Data.ParameterDirection]::Output
$outParameter2.DbType = [System.Data.DbType]'date'
$SqlCmd.Parameters.Add($outParameter2) >> $null

# VacationHours
$outParameter3 = new-object System.Data.SqlClient.SqlParameter
$outParameter3.ParameterName = "@VacationHours"
$outParameter3.Direction = [System.Data.ParameterDirection]::Output
$outParameter3.DbType = [System.Data.DbType]'int16'
$SqlCmd.Parameters.Add($outParameter3) >> $null
```

The code to assign the HireDate and VacationHours parameters is not very different from the code we saw to define the JobTitle parameter. Notice that the DbTypes of date and int16 do not require a value for the size property. Now, let's look at the code to execute the stored procedure:

```
$SqlConnection.Open();
$result = $SqlCmd.ExecuteNonQuery()
$SqlConnection.Close();
```

First, we open the connection. Then, we use the ExecuteNonQuery method of the command object to run the stored procedures, returning any result to $result. The returned value is usually -1 for success and 0 for failure. However, when there is a trigger on a table being inserted to or updated, the number of rows inserted and/or updated is returned.

We can see the Output parameters by getting their Value property from the Parameters collection, as shown here:

```
$SqlCmd.Parameters["@jobtitle"].value
$SqlCmd.Parameters["@hiredate"].value
$SqlCmd.Parameters["@VacationHours"].value
```

Notice that although the connection is closed, we can still retrieve the Output parameters.

Calling Stored Procedures the Reusable Way

We have seen how we can use PowerShell to call stored procedures. Now, let's take a look at how we can incorporate those ideas as reusable functions in the umd_database module. Overall, executing a stored procedure is like executing any SQL statement, except we need to provide the Input and Output parameters. The challenge here is that there can be any number of parameters, and each has a set of property values. How can we provide for passing a variable-length list of parameters to a function? Since PowerShell supports objects so nicely, why not create the parameter list as a custom object collection? The function that gets the object collection as a parameter can iterate over the list of parameters to create each SQL command parameter object. To help us build this collection, we'll use the helper function Add-UdfParameter, which creates a single parameter as a custom object:

```
function Add-UdfParameter {
[CmdletBinding()]
    param (
            [string] $name       ,   # Parameter name from stored procedure, i.e. @myparm
            [string] $direction  ,   # Input or Output or InputOutput
            [string] $value      ,   # parameter value
            [string] $datatype   ,   # db data type, i.e. string, int64, etc.
            [int]    $size           # length
    )

    $parm = New-Object System.Object
    $parm | Add-Member -MemberType NoteProperty -Name "Name" -Value "$name"
    $parm | Add-Member -MemberType NoteProperty -Name "Direction" -Value "$direction"
    $parm | Add-Member -MemberType NoteProperty -Name "Value" -Value "$value"
    $parm | Add-Member -MemberType NoteProperty -Name "Datatype" -Value "$datatype"
    $parm | Add-Member -MemberType NoteProperty -Name "Size" -Value "$size"

    RETURN $parm

}
```

This function takes the parameters for each of the properties of the SQL parameter object required to call a stored procedure. The first executable line in the function stores an instance of System.Object into $parm, which gives us a place to which to attach the properties. We then pipe $parm into the Add-Member cmdlet to add each property with a value from each of the parameters passed to the function. Finally, we return the $parm object back to the caller. Let's see how we would use the Add-UdfParameter in Listing 7-7.

Listing 7-7. Using Add-UdfParameter

```
Import-Module umd_database

$parmset = @()    # Create a collection object.

# Add the parameters we need to use...
$parmset += (Add-UdfParameter "@BusinessEntityID" "Input" "1" "int32" 0)
$parmset += (Add-UdfParameter "@NationalIDNumber" "Input" "295847284" "string" 15)
$parmset += (Add-UdfParameter "@BirthDate" "Input" "1964-02-02" "date" 0)
$parmset += (Add-UdfParameter "@MaritalStatus" "Input" "S" "string" 1)
$parmset += (Add-UdfParameter "@Gender" "Input" "M" "string" 1)
$parmset += (Add-UdfParameter "@JobTitle" "Output" "" "string" 50)
$parmset += (Add-UdfParameter "@HireDate" "Output" "" "date" 0)
$parmset += (Add-UdfParameter "@VacationHours" "Output" "" "int16" 0)

$parmset | Out-GridView  # Verify the parameters are correctly defined.
```

Listing 7-7 starts by importing the umd_database module. Then, we create an empty collection object named $parmset by setting it equal to @(). We load this collection with each parameter by calling the function Add-UdfParameter. There are a few things to notice here. We enclose the function call in parentheses to make sure that the function is executed first. We use the += assignment operator to append the object returned to the $parmset collection. Normally, the += operator is used to increment the variable on the left side of the operator with the value on the right side, i.e., x += 1 is the same as saying x = x + 1. However, in the case of objects, it appends the object instance to the collection. The last statement pipes the parameter collection $parmset to Out-Gridview so we can see the list. We should see a display like the one in Figure 7-1.

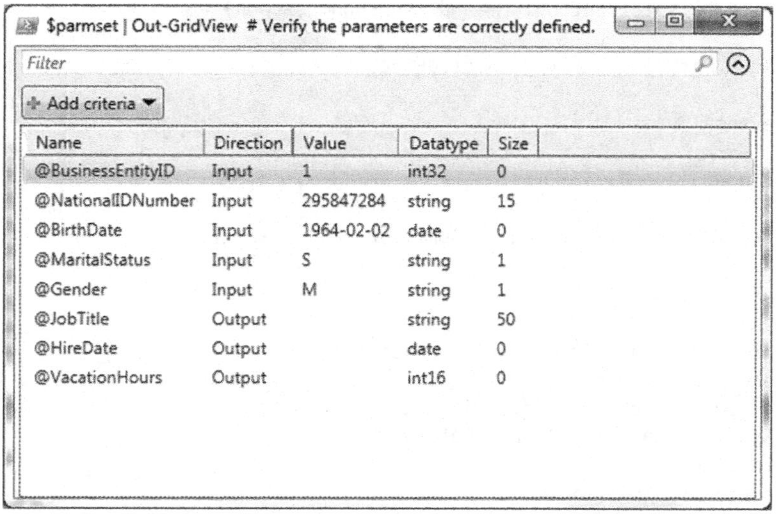

Figure 7-1. Out-GridView showing the parameter collection

Now that we have the parameter collection, we want to pass this to a function that will execute the stored procedure. Let's look at the code to do this:

```
function Invoke-UdfADOStoredProcedure
{
[CmdletBinding()]
    param (
            [string] $sqlserver            ,    # SQL Server
            [string] $sqldatabase          ,    # SQL Server Database.
            [string] $sqlspname            ,    # SQL Query
            [string] $sqlauthenticationtype ,   # $true = Use Credentials
            [string] $sqluser              ,    # User Name if using credential
            $sqlpw                         ,    # password if using credential
            [string] $sqlconnstring        ,    # Connection string
            $parameterset                       # Parameter properties
        )

  if ($sqlauthenticationtype -eq 'Credential')
  {
     $pw =  $sqlpw
     $pw.MakeReadOnly()

     $SqlCredential = new-object System.Data.SqlClient.SqlCredential($sqluser,  $pw)
     $conn = new-object System.Data.SqlClient.SqlConnection($sqlconnstring, $SqlCredential)
  }
  else
  {
     $conn = new-object System.Data.SqlClient.SqlConnection($sqlconnstring);
  }

  $conn.Open()

  $command = new-object system.data.sqlclient.Sqlcommand($sqlspname,$conn)

  $command.CommandType = [System.Data.CommandType]'StoredProcedure';

  foreach ($parm in $parameterset)
  {
    if ($parm.Direction -eq 'Input')
    {
        $command.Parameters.AddWithValue($parm.Name, $parm.Value) >> $null;
    }
    elseif ($parm.Direction -eq "Output" )
    {
        $outparm1 = new-object System.Data.SqlClient.SqlParameter;
        $outparm1.ParameterName = $parm.Name
        $outparm1.Direction = [System.Data.ParameterDirection]::Output;
        $outparm1.DbType = [System.Data.DbType]$parm.Datatype;
        $outparm1.Size = $parm.Size
        $command.Parameters.Add($outparm1) >> $null
    }
  }
```

```
$command.ExecuteNonQuery()
$conn.Close()

$outparms = @{}

foreach ($parm in $parameterset)
{
  if ($parm.Direction -eq 'Output')
  {
      $outparms.Add($parm.Name, $command.Parameters[$parm.Name].value)
  }
}

RETURN $outparms

}
```

Let's review this code in detail. The first executable block of lines should look familiar, as it is the same code used in the function earlier to run a SQL statement, i.e., Invoke-UdfADOSQL:

```
if ($sqlauthenticationtype -eq 'Credential')
{
   $pw =  $sqlpw
   $pw.MakeReadOnly()

   $SqlCredential = new-object System.Data.SqlClient.SqlCredential($sqluser,  $pw)
   $conn = new-object System.Data.SqlClient.SqlConnection($sqlconnstring, $SqlCredential)
}
else
{
   $conn = new-object System.Data.SqlClient.SqlConnection($sqlconnstring);
}

$conn.Open()

$command = new-object system.data.sqlclient.Sqlcommand($sqlspname,$conn)
```

First, we check if we need to use a credential object. If yes, then we make the password read only and create the credential object, passing in the user ID and password. Then, we create the connection object using the connection string and credential object. If no credential object is needed, we just create the connection object using the connection string. Then, we open the connection using the Open method. By now the code should be looking familiar.

The next statement sets the CommandType property to 'StoredProcedure':

```
$command.CommandType = [System.Data.CommandType]'StoredProcedure';
```

From here we are ready to create the stored procedure parameters, which we do with the code that follows:

```
foreach ($parm in $parameterset)
  {
    if ($parm.Direction -eq 'Input')
    {
        $command.Parameters.AddWithValue($parm.Name, $parm.Value) >> $null;
    }
    elseif ($parm.Direction -eq "Output" )
    {
        $outparm1 = new-object System.Data.SqlClient.SqlParameter;
        $outparm1.ParameterName = $parm.Name
        $outparm1.Direction = [System.Data.ParameterDirection]::Output;
        $outparm1.DbType = [System.Data.DbType]$parm.Datatype;
        $outparm1.Size = $parm.Size
        $command.Parameters.Add($outparm1) >> $null
    }
  }
```

The foreach loop will iterate over each object in the collection $parameterset that was passed to this function. On each iteration, $parm will hold the current object. Remember, we created this parameter by using the helper function Add-UdfParameter. On each iteration, if the parameter's direction property is Input, we use the AddWithValue method to add the parameter to the command's parameters collection. Otherwise, if the direction is Output, we create a new SqlParameter object instance and assign the required property values from those provided in $parm.

Then, we execute the stored procedure with the statements here:

```
$command.ExecuteNonQuery()
$conn.Close()
```

Now, we need to return the Output parameters back to the caller. There are a number of ways this could be done. One method I considered was updating the parameter object collection passed into the function. However, that would make the caller do a lot of work to get the values. Instead, the function creates a hash table and loads each parameter name as the key and the return value as the value. Remember, hash tables are just handy lookup tables. Let's look at the code for this:

```
$outparms = @{}

  foreach ($parm in $parameterset)
  {
    if ($parm.Direction -eq 'Output')
    {
        $outparms.Add($parm.Name, $command.Parameters[$parm.Name].value)
    }
  }

  RETURN $outparms
}
```

Here, $outparms is created as an empty hash table by the statement "$outparms = @{}". Then, we iterate over the parameter set originally passed to the function. For each parameter with a direction of Output, we add a new entry into the $outparms hash table with the key of the parameter name and the value taken from the SQL command parameters collection. Be careful here not to miss what is happening. We are not using the value from the parameter collection passed to the function. We are going into the SQL command object and pulling the return value from there.

Now we have nice, reusable functions to help us call stored procedures. Wouldn't it be nice to integrate this with the umd_database module's connection object we covered earlier? That object was returned by New-UdfConnection. Let's integrate the functions to call a stored procedure with New-UdfConnection so that we have one nice interface for issuing SQL commands. To do that, we'll need to add a method to the connection object returned by New-UdfConnection. The code that follows creates that function and attaches it to the object:

```
# For call, $false set for $IsSelect as this is a store procedure.
# $true set for IsProcedure
 $bspsql = @'
    param([string]$p_insql, $p_parms)

    $this.BuildConnectionString()

    If ($this.ConnectionString -eq 'NotAssigned')
       {Throw "Error - Cannot create connection string." }

    $Result = Invoke-UdfSQL $this.ConnectionType $this.DatabaseType `
                    $this.Server $this.DatabaseName "$p_insql" `
                    $this.AuthenticationType $this.UserID $this.Password `
                    $this.ConnectionString  $false `
                    $this.DSNName $this.Driver $true $p_parms

    RETURN $Result

'@
    $sspsql = [scriptblock]::create($bspsql)

    $p_connection.value | Add-Member -MemberType scriptmethod `
                    -Name RunStoredProcedure `
                    -Value $sspsql `
                    -Passthru
```

As with other object methods, we first assign the code block to a here string variable, which is called $bsqlsql in this case. The code block shows that two parameters are accepted by the function: $p_insql, which is the name of the stored procedure, and $p_parms, which is the parameter collection we created using Add-UdfParameter. The first executable line of the function uses the object's BuildConnectionString to create the connection string so as to connect to the database. If there is a problem creating the connection string, as indicated by a value of 'NotAssigned', an error is thrown. Finally, the function Invoke-UdfSQL is called, passing the object properties and the parameters. Notice two Boolean values are being passed. The first, which is $false, is the $IsSelect parameter, so we are saying this is not a select query. The second, which is $true, is for a parameter that tells the function this is a stored procedure call.

We're almost there, but there is one piece missing. We need to discuss the function being called, Invoke-UdfSQL. This function acts as a broker to determine which specific function to call, i.e., for ADO or ODBC. To see how the function determines which call to make, let's look at the code for Invoke-UdfSQL:

```
function Invoke-UdfSQL        (
                [string]$p_inconntype,
                [string]$p_indbtype,
                [string]$p_inserver,
                [string]$p_indb,
                [string]$p_insql,
                [string]$p_inauthenticationtype,
                [string]$p_inuser,
                    $p_inpw,    # No type defined; can be securestring or string
                [string]$p_inconnectionstring,
                [boolean]$p_inisselect,
                [string]$p_indsnname,
                [string]$p_indriver,
                [boolean]$p_inisprocedure,
                    $p_inparms)
{

   If ($p_inconntype -eq "ADO")
   {
     If ($p_inisprocedure)
     {
       RETURN Invoke-UdfADOStoredProcedure $p_inserver $p_indb $p_insql `
            $p_inauthenticationtype $p_inuser $p_inpw $p_inconnectionstring $p_inparms
     }
     Else
     {
       $datatab = Invoke-UdfADOSQL $p_inserver $p_indb $p_insql $p_inauthenticationtype `
            $p_inuser $p_inpw $p_inconnectionstring $p_inisselect

       Return $datatab
     }
   }
   ElseIf ($p_inconntype -eq "ODBC")
   {
      If ($p_inisprocedure)
      {
        write-host 'sp'
        RETURN Invoke-UdfODBCStoredProcedure $p_inserver $p_indb $p_insql `
            $p_inauthenticationtype $p_inuser $p_inpw $p_inconnectionstring $p_inparms
      }
      Else
      {
        $datatab = Invoke-UdfODBCSQL $p_inserver $p_indb $p_insql $p_inauthenticationtype `
                 $p_inuser $p_inpw $p_inconnectionstring $p_inisselect $p_indsnname $driver

       Return $datatab
     }
   }
```

```
   Else
   {
      Throw "Connection Type Not Supported."
      Return "Failed - Connection type not supported"
   }
}
```

Don't be intimidated by this code. It's really just a set of if conditions. There are a lot of parameters, but some of them are just to support later expansion of the function. This function supports two types of SQL calls: ADO.Net and ODBC. Once it determines that this call is ADO.Net, it checks the Boolean passed in, $p_inisprocedure, to determine if this is a stored procedure call. If this is true, then the function Invoke-UdfADOStoredProcedure is called. Since Invoke-UdfADOStoredProcedure returns a value, i.e., a hash table of the output parameter values, the RETURN statement makes the function call. We've seen the other statements before, which have to do with non–stored procedure calls.

Now that we've covered how all this works, let's look at the code in Listing 7-8 that uses the connection object to call the stored procedure.

Listing 7-8. Using the umd_database module's connection object to call a stored procedure

```
Import-Module umd_database

[psobject] $myconnection = New-Object psobject
New-UdfConnection([ref]$myconnection)

$myconnection.ConnectionType = 'ADO'
$myconnection.DatabaseType = 'SqlServer'
$myconnection.Server = '(local)'
$myconnection.DatabaseName = 'AdventureWorks'
$myconnection.UseCredential = 'N'
$myconnection.UserID = 'bryan'
$myconnection.Password = 'password'

$myconnection.SetAuthenticationType('Integrated')

$myconnection.BuildConnectionString()

$parmset = @()   # Create a collection object.
# Add the parameters we need to use...
$parmset += (Add-UdfParameter "@BusinessEntityID" "Input" "1" "int32" 0)
$parmset += (Add-UdfParameter "@NationalIDNumber" "Input" "295847284" "string" 15)
$parmset += (Add-UdfParameter "@BirthDate" "Input" "1964-02-02" "date" 0)
$parmset += (Add-UdfParameter "@MaritalStatus" "Input" "S" "string" 1)
$parmset += (Add-UdfParameter "@Gender" "Input" "M" "string" 1)
$parmset += (Add-UdfParameter "@JobTitle" "Output" "" "string" 50)
$parmset += (Add-UdfParameter "@HireDate" "Output" "" "date" 0)
$parmset += (Add-UdfParameter "@VacationHours" "Output" "" "int16" 0)

$myconnection.RunStoredProcedure('[HumanResources].[uspUpdateEmployeePersonalInfoPS]',
$parmset)
$parmset  # Lists the output parameters
```

Listing 7-8 shows how we use our custom functions to call a stored procedure that returns Output parameters. First, we create a new PSObject variable, i.e., $myconnection. A reference to this object is passed to the function New-UdfConnection, which attaches our custom connection methods and properties. Then, a series of statements sets the properties of our connection object. We call the BuildConnectionString method to generate the connection string needed to access the database. Then, the statement $parmset = @() creates an empty object collection named $parmset. Subsequent statements append custom parameter objects to the collection using Add-UdfParameter. Finally, the stored procedure is executed, passing the stored procedure name and the parameter collection. The results should be written to the console. The last line just displays the parameter set, i.e., $parmset.

Summary

In this chapter we explored executing queries using ADO.Net, which will handle most database platforms, including SQL Server, MS Access, Oracle, MySQL, and PostgreSQL. This chapter bypassed using the SQLPS module in favor of writing our own custom module that provides a generic and easy-to-use set of functions to run queries. To provide one point of interaction with these functions, the module provides a database connection object that can use ADO.Net or ODBC to execute any SQL statement. The first part of this chapter focused on running select statements and queries that yield no results, such as an update statement. We covered different authentication modes to provide the most secure connection possible. Then, we discussed calling stored procedures and how to support Output parameters using the SQL Command Parameters collection. We stepped through how the umd_database module integrates these features into one consistent interface. Beyond showing how to connect to databases and execute queries, the goal of this chapter was to demonstrate how to create reusable code to extend PowerShell and simplify your development work.

CHAPTER 8

■ ■ ■

Customizing the PowerShell Environment

PowerShell provides an amazing level of customization and transparency. In this chapter, we will discuss how PowerShell supports configuration using three types of variables: automatic, preference, and environment. Automatic variables are created and used by PowerShell to support its operations and can be read by scripts to get context-specific information. Preference variables control PowerShell's behavior and can be modified to suit our needs. Environment variables are not specific to PowerShell. They are variables used by Windows applications including PowerShell and can be created, read, and set by PowerShell scripts. We'll review how to use aliases to create our own names for PowerShell cmdlets. We will use PowerShell drives to dynamically create short names for provider locations. Finally, we'll discuss how to use all these features to customize PowerShell sessions on startup using a special script called a profile.

PowerShell Variables

Thus far, we've done a lot with user-defined variables. Three other types of variables PowerShell supports are automatic variables, preference variables, and environment variables. Automatic variables are created by PowerShell and store the state of the PowerShell session. Preference variables are created and assigned default values when a PowerShell session starts. The values of these variables can be changed to suit the user's needs. Environment variables are not PowerShell specific. They are variables used to configure the Windows environment and applications, which include the command shell (CMD.EXE) and PowerShell. Although PowerShell can create and maintain environment variables, they can also be created and changed outside of PowerShell. An interesting feature is that PowerShell has a provider for variables, which means we can navigate variables like we do a system folder. For example, enter the following command at the console prompt:

```
Get-ChildItem Variable:
```

A partial listing of the output follows:

```
Name                    Value
----                    -----
$                       cls
?                       True
^                       cls
args                    {}
ConfirmPreference       High
```

```
ConsoleFileName
DebugPreference                   SilentlyContinue
Error                             {The term 'now' is not recognized as the name of a cmdlet...
ErrorActionPreference             Continue
ErrorView                         NormalView
ExecutionContext                  System.Management.Automation.EngineIntrinsics
false                             False
FormatEnumerationLimit            4
HOME                              C:\Users\BryanCafferky
Host                              System.Management.Automation.Internal.Host.InternalHost
input                             System.Collections.ArrayList+ArrayListEnumeratorSimple
MaximumAliasCount                 4096
MaximumDriveCount                 4096
MaximumErrorCount                 256
MaximumFunctionCount              4096
MaximumHistoryCount               4096
MaximumVariableCount              4096
```

As we can see from this list, there are a lot of PowerShell variables, and the Variable provider gives us an easy way to access them.

Automatic Variables

Automatic variables are created, assigned values, and used by PowerShell. We've used some of them already. For example, the $_ variable references the current object in the pipeline. $Args contains an array of undeclared parameters for a script or function. When we discussed error handling, we used $Error, which is an automatic variable that contains information about errors that occurred. Let's review some of the other interesting automatic variables.

$?

$? contains true if the last statement executed was successful and false if it failed. It can be used as a way to check for a failed statement. Consider the code here:

```
Get-Date

If ($?) { 'Succeeded' } Else { 'Failed' }

Gibberish   # Gibberish to force an error.

If ($?) { 'Succeeded' } Else { 'Failed' }
```

The first line executes the Get-Date cmdlet. The next line evaluates $?, which returns true if the last statement executed successfully. Since it did, 'Succeeded' displays on the console. The third line, Gibberish, is not a valid command, so it fails. The line after that will write 'Failed' to the console after a series of error messages. The output should look similar to the output here:

```
Friday, August 14, 2015 3:07:04 PM
Succeeded
Gibberish: The term ' Gibberish' is not recognized as the name of a cmdlet, function, script
file, or operable program.
```

```
Check the spelling of the name, or if a path was included, verify that the path is correct
and try again.
At line:5 char:1
+ Gibberish   #  Gibberish to force an error.
+ ~~~~
    + CategoryInfo          : ObjectNotFound: (Gibberish:String) [], CommandNotFoundException
    + FullyQualifiedErrorId: CommandNotFoundException
Failed
```

$Host

The variable $Host points to the host application for PowerShell and has a number of methods and properties. Some of the properties can be used to change the behavior of PowerShell or to find out information about the PowerShell environment. Some examples of how we can use this variable follow:

```
$Host.Name            # ISE displays 'Windows PowerShell ISE Host', CLI displays 'ConsoleHost'
$Host.Version         # The version of PowerShell host
$Host.CurrentUICulture # The localization, i.e. language setting.
```

To make accessing $Host easier, we can use the cmdlet Get-Host as shown here:

```
Get-Host
```

And you should see output similar to the display here:

```
Name              : Windows PowerShell ISE Host
Version           : 4.0
InstanceId        : 626a51e9-e433-4282-ac58-bdb2dc38b820
UI                : System.Management.Automation.Internal.Host.InternalHostUserInterface
CurrentCulture    : en-US
CurrentUICulture  : en-US
PrivateData       : Microsoft.PowerShell.Host.ISE.ISEOptions
IsRunspacePushed  : False
Runspace          : System.Management.Automation.Runspaces.LocalRunspace
```

Get-Host will return a reference to $Host, which can be stored in a variable. The variable can then be used to set the properties of $Host as shown here:

```
$myhost = Get-Host
$myhost.currentculture.DateTimeFormat # List the localized date and time formats
$myhost.UI.RawUI.WindowTitle = "Bryan's Window"   # Sets the window title of the host
```

In the first line in this code, we set $myhost to point to $host by using the Get-Host cmdlet. The next line displays a list of date and time formats for the machine's localization. Finally, we set the host window's title to "Bryan's Window". In the CLI, that will show up as in Figure 8-1, but this works in the ISE as well.

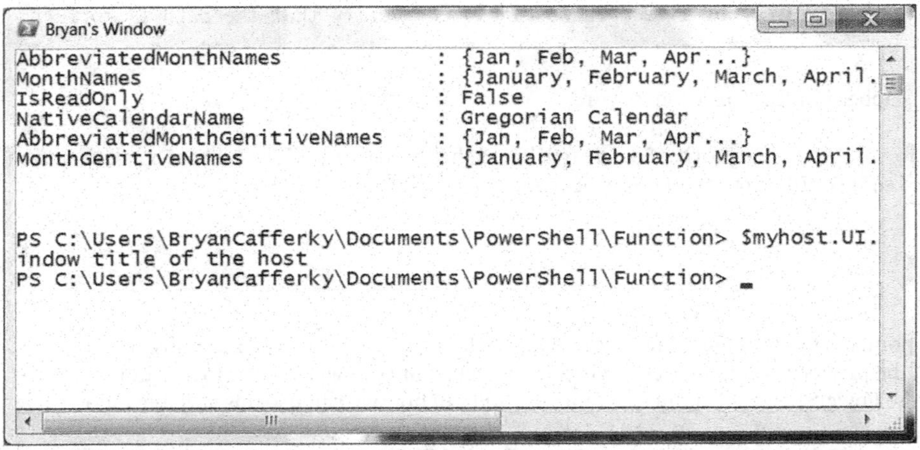

Figure 8-1. *The PowerShell CLI with custom window title*

As we can see in Figure 8-1, we changed the title of the CLI window by changing a property of $host.

$Input

$Input is available only within a function or script block. It enumerates the collection in the pipeline. If there is a Process block, $Input is enumerated through that block, and the End block receives an empty collection. If there is no process block, $Input is passed to the End block once, i.e., as the pipeline collection. $Input gives us greater control processing the pipeline than using $_ does. Let's look at some examples in Listing 8-1 to illustrate.

Listing 8-1. Using $Input

```
function Invoke-UdfProcessPipeline() {
  Begin {
    # Executes once, before the pipeline is loaded, i.e., $input is empty.
    "Begin block pipeline..."
    $Input
  }

  Process {
    # Executes after pipeline is loaded, i.e., enumerates through each item in the collection.
    "Process block pipeline..."
    $Input
  }

  End {
    # Executes once after the Process block has finished. Since there is a Process block,
      $input is emptied.
    "End block pipeline..."
    $Input
  }
}

#  Pipe data into the function Invoke-UdfProcessPipeline
("A", "B", "C") | Invoke-UdfProcessPipeline
```

When we pipe data into this function, the following messages display on the console:

```
Begin block pipeline...
Process block pipeline...
A
Process block pipeline...
B
Process block pipeline...
C
End block pipeline...
```

We see in this example that the Begin block has no data in $Input. The Begin block is used to do work before the pipeline is passed into the function, and it only executes once. The Process block is called once for each item in the pipeline, so $Input contains one item each time the Process block is called. Therefore, we see the "Process block pipeline" message displayed multiple times. The End block is executed once after the Process block has executed. Because there is a Process block, $Input is exhausted, i.e., has no data, which is why we do not see the End process message. What if we don't include a process block? Let's look at that scenario in Listing 8-2.

Listing 8-2. Processing pipeline end block

```
function Invoke-UdfProcessPipelineEndBlock() {
  Begin {
    # Executes before the pipeline is loaded, i.e., $input is empty.
    "Begin block pipeline..."
    $Input
  }

  #  No process block.

  End {
    # Since the Process block
    "End block pipeline..."
    $Input
  }
}
```

```
#  Pipe data into the function Invoke-UdfProcessPipeline
("A", "B", "C") | Invoke-UdfProcessPipelineEndBlock
```

When we pipe data into this function, the messages that follow display on the console:

```
Begin block pipeline...
End block pipeline...
A
B
C
```

In Listing 8-2, there is no Process block. Therefore, the pipeline is still full when the End block is executed, and $Input contains the entire pipeline. However, the End block is only executed once, so the entire collection in $Input sent to the End block—i.e., it is not enumerated. This is why we only see "End block pipeline" once in the output. What if we want to process the pipeline both in the Process block and the End block? We can do this by resetting the $Input enumerators, as shown in Listing 8-3.

Listing 8-3. Resetting $Input

```
function Invoke-UdfProcessPipelineEndBlockReset() {
  Begin {
    # Executes before the pipeline is loaded, i.e., $input is empty.
    "Begin block pipeline..."
    $Input
  }

  End {
    # Since the Process block
    "End block pipeline..."
    "Iterate through first time to process..."
    $Input | ForEach-Object {$_}
    $Input.Reset()  # Reset to top of the pipeline
    "Show the pipeline has been reset by listing it again..."
    $Input
  }
}

#  Pipe data into the function Invoke-UdfProcessPipeline
"A", "B", "C") | Invoke-UdfProcessPipelineEndBlockReset
```

When we pipe data into this function, the messages that follow display on the console:

```
Begin block pipeline...
End block pipeline...
Iterate through first time to process...
A
B
C
Show the pipeline has been reset by listing it again...
A
B
C
```

Here, we see there is no Process block. Instead, we need to completely control the pipeline through the End block. Recall that the End block is only called once. Therefore, to process each item in the pipeline we need to iterate through $input, which is what the statement $input | Foreach-Object {$_} does. However, that means the pipeline will be exhausted, so in the next line we reset it with the Reset method of $Input. To prove we really did reset the pipeline, we display it again. The point of this discussion is to be aware that you can take direct control of the pipeline when needed. For more information on pipeline processing, see the following link:

https://www.simple-talk.com/dotnet/.net-tools/down-the-rabbit-hole--a-study-in-powershell-pipelines,-functions,-and-parameters/

$MyInvocation

$MyInvocation provides a wealth of information about the content of the currently executing code. To get an idea of the information available, let's try the code in Listing 8-4.

Listing 8-4. Showing $MyInvocation

```
function Invoke-UdfMyFunction ([string]$parm1, [int]$parm2, $parm3 )
{

    $MyInvocation

#  Do some work...
}
```

We call this function with the statement here:

```
Invoke-UdfMyFunction "test" 1 "something"
```

A version of the function Invoke-UdfMyFunction is defined that simply displays the contents of $MyInvocation. We should get output similar to what is shown here:

```
MyCommand            : Invoke-UdfMyFunction
BoundParameters      : {[parm1, test], [parm2, 1], [parm3, something]}
UnboundArguments     : {}
ScriptLineNumber     : 10
OffsetInLine         : 1
HistoryId            : 100
ScriptName           : C:\Users\BryanCafferky\Documents\Book\Code\Chapter08\scr_
                       myinvokation.ps1
Line                 : Invoke-UdfMyFunction "test" 1 "something"
PositionMessage      : At C:\Users\BryanCafferky\Documents\Book\Code\Chapter08\scr_
                       myinvokation.ps1:10 char:1
                       + Invoke-UdfMyFunction "test" 1 "something"
                       + ~~~~~~~~~~~~~~~~~~~~~~~~~~~~~~~~~~~~~~~~~~~
PSScriptRoot         : C:\Users\BryanCafferky\Documents\Book\Code\Chapter08
PSCommandPath        : C:\Users\BryanCafferky\Documents\Book\Code\Chapter08\scr_
                       myinvokation.ps1
InvocationName       : Invoke-UdfMyFunction
PipelineLength       : 1
PipelinePosition     : 1
ExpectingInput       : False
CommandOrigin        : Internal
DisplayScriptPosition :
```

Here, we can see that $MyInvocation has a lot of information. We can see the function name is in the MyCommand property, the parameters are in BoundParameters, the path to the script is in ScriptName, and the full path to the script is in PSCommandPath, and we can see a number of other properties containing other attributes. This information can be used generally when you need to locate files related to the executing script. For example, it could be used to execute or load other scripts in the same folder as the called function. Suppose we wanted to log details about each call to a function and we don't want to hard code the path to the log file. Instead, regardless of where the script with the called function is stored, we will write to a log in the same folder as the called function. Let's look at Listing 8-5 to see this in action.

Listing 8-5. Logging using $MyInvocation.PSScriptRoot

```
function Invoke-UdfMyFunctionWithlogging ([string]$parm1, [int]$parm2, $parm3 )
{

  $logfilepath = $MyInvocation.PSScriptRoot + '\logfile.txt'

  $logline = "function called: " + $MyInvocation.InvocationName + " at " `
             + (Get-Date -Format g) + " with parms: " + $MyInvocation.BoundParameters.Keys

  $logline  >> $logfilepath
  $logline

}

Invoke-UdfMyFunctionWithlogging "test" 1 "something"
```

In Listing 8-5, three parameters are accepted: a string named $parm1, an integer named $parm2, and an object named $parm3. The first executable line stores the full path to the log file as the current script's folder, i.e., $MyInvocation.PSScriptRoot concatenated with a backslash and the file name 'logfile.txt'. Then, we format a string to be written to the log file, which uses $MyInvocation.InvocationName to get the function called, Get-Date, to get the current date and time, and $MyInvocation.BoundParameters.Keys to get the names of the function parameters. Notice that the Get-Date Format parameter is used. This is required because without it a carriage return and line feed precede the value—the log row is broken into two rows. Then the log string is appended to the log file pointed to by $logfilepath. The last line just displays the variable $logline.

The content of the log file should look like the contents here:

```
function called: Invoke-UdfMyFunction_withlogging at 2/8/2015 4:13 PM with parms:
parm1 parm2 parm3
function called: Invoke-UdfMyFunction_withlogging at 2/8/2015 4:13 PM with parms:
parm1 parm2 parm3
```

Note: By default, Get-Date prepends the value with a carriage return and line feed. Use the Format parameter to eliminate this.

$null

Database developers in particular should beware the $null automatic variable. In T-SQL, a null is an unknown value and will never equal another value, even another null—null <> null. In PowerShell, null is not like the SQL Server null. Instead it represents a default minimum value for a given data type. Let's look at Listing 8-6 to see how $null works.

Listing 8-6. Experimenting with $null

```
function Invoke-UdfMyFunctionWithlogging ([string]$parm1, [int]$parm2 = 3, $parm3 )
{

  "The value of `$parm2 is $parm2"

  if ($parm1) {"Has a value"} else {"No value"}
```

```
    if ($parm1 -eq $null) {"No parm passed equals `$null"} else {"No value does not equal
`$null"}

    "Let's get the string version of null and try again."
    if ($parm1 -eq [string]$null) {"`$null test worked"} else {"A real value was passed"}

    "Default for `$parm1 is '$parm1'"
    "Default for `$parm2 is $parm2"
    "Default for `$parm3 is $parm3"

    "Notice that `$null equals `$null"
    ($null -eq $null)

    "If we concatenate a $null with other strings, we do not get `$null back"
    $myvar = "Bryan " + $null + "Cafferky"
    $myvar

    [string]$mystr = $null
    "`$null assigned to a string = '$mystr'."
    [int]$myint = $null
    "`$null assigned to a number = $myint."

}

#  Call the function...
Invoke-UdfMyFunctionWithlogging
```

When we run this code, we should get the following output:

```
The value of $parm2 is 3
No value
No value does not equal $null
Let's get the string version of null and try again.
$null test worked
Default for $parm1 is ''
Default for $parm2 is 3
Default for $parm3 is
Notice that $null equals $null
True
If we concatenate a  with other strings, we do not get $null back
Bryan Cafferky
$null assigned to a string = ''.
$null assigned to a number = 0.
```

The purpose of the function in Listing 8-6 is to show how $null and unassigned parameters get values. The function call omits all parameters. The first line of the function displays the value of $parm2. Since $parm2 has a default value assigned, it displays that value, which is 3. The next line just tests for the $parm1 parameter, and since none was passed, displays the message "No value". The next line is interesting, so let's look at it closely:

```
if ($parm1 -eq $null) {"No parm passed equals `$null"} else {"No value does not equal `$null"}
```

We might think that no parameter value is the same as $null, but, as the output confirms, it is not. $null is a type-specific default value. For a string it is a zero-length string, and for a number it is zero. So, if we want to test for a $null, we need to convert it to the data type first by putting the data type just before the variable, as shown in the line here:

```
if ($parm1 -eq [string]$null) {"`$null test worked"} else {"A real value was passed"}
```

We are comparing $parm's default value to $null, cast to a string data type. The default for a string parameter is a zero-length string, and a $null type cast to a string is also a zero-length string. They are equal, so we get the message "$null test worked".

Then we have three lines just meant to show us the parameter default values.

Just to show that $null is not like the database null, we see the lines here:

```
"Notice that `$null equals `$null"
($null -eq $null)
```

The test "$null -eq $null" returns True.

In T-SQL, if you concatenate a null value with other strings, a null is returned. The lines that follow test this in PowerShell:

```
"If we concatenate a $null with other strings, we do not get `$null back"
$myvar = "Bryan " + $null + "Cafferky"
$myvar
```

The $null is just a zero-length string and has no effect. We still get the concatenated value of the other strings.

Finally, just to show the $null has different values depending on the data type, we see the lines shown here:

```
[string]$mystr = $null
"`$null assigned to a string = '$mystr'."
[int]$myint = $null
"`$null assigned to a number = $myint."
```

$mystr is assigned a zero-length string, and $myint is assigned a value of zero.

Let's call the function again, passing $null as the value for all three parameters:

```
Invoke-UdfMyFunctionWithlogging $null $null $null
```

We should see the output shown here:

```
The value of $parm2 is 0
No value
No value does not equal $null
Let's get the string version of null and try again.
$null test worked
Default for $parm1 is ''
Default for $parm2 is 0
Default for $parm3 is
Notice that $null equals $null
True
```

```
If we concatenate a with other strings, we do not get $null back
Bryan Cafferky
$null assigned to a string = ''.
$null assigned to a number = 0.
```

Notice that the first line of output shows $parm2, which is assigned a default value of 3 in the function, has a value of zero. This is because the $null overrode the parameter's default value. The point is that $null is a value and is not the same as not passing a value.

I hope the point here is clear—$null can be useful, but its behavior may not be what you expect.

Caution: $null can be misleading as it represents a value, not an unknown as in SQL Server. Be very careful when using $null as it may not behave as you would expect.

$OFS

$OFS is the string used by PowerShell to separate values when an array in converted to a string. Depending on your requirements, this could come in handy. For example, if you need to convert arrays to strings to be consumed by an application, you could use $OFS to help. Let's review in the example that follows.

First, let's set $OFS to its default value of a space, load an array, convert the array to a string, and write the string to the console:

```
$OFS = ' '  # Setting to the original default value.
$myarray ="Bob","Mary","Harry","Sue"
[string] $mystring1 = $myarray
$mystring1
```

The output for this code is shown next. Each element is separated by a space:

```
Bob Mary Harry Sue
```

Now let's set $OFS to a comma, load an array, convert the array to a string, and write the string to the console. This makes outputting a CSV file easy:

```
$OFS = ','
$myarray ="Bob","Mary","Harry","Sue"
[string] $mystring2 = $myarray
$mystring2
```

The output for this code is shown next. Each element is separated by a comma:

```
Bob,Mary,Harry,Sue
```

Next, we set $OFS to a tab control character, load an array, convert the array to a string, and write the string to the console:

```
$OFS = "`t"
$myarray ="Bob","Mary","Harry","Sue"
[string] $mystring3 = $myarray
$mystring3
```

The output for this code is shown next. Each element is separated by a tab:

```
Bob     Mary    Harry    Sue
```

Next, we set $OFS to a string 'XXXX', load an array, convert the array to a string, and write the string to the console. This example shows how you can use $OFS to do some very custom output:

```
$OFS = 'XXXX'
$myarray ="Bob","Mary","Harry","Sue"
[string] $mystring4 = $myarray
$mystring4
```

The output for this code is shown next. Each element is separated by the string 'XXXX':

```
BobXXXXMaryXXXXHarryXXXXSue
```

What's significant about the $OFS variable beyond how handy it is to be able to define the value separator is that we are not limited to one character. We can use escape characters, strings, and even embed variables and functions into the value. Consider the odd example here:

```
$OFS = "- field separators like " + (get-date) + " are odd - "
$myarray ="Bob","Mary","Harry","Sue"
[string] $mystring5 = $myarray
$mystring5
```

Which produces the following output:

```
Bob- field separators like 02/07/2015 17:45:49 are odd - Mary- field separators like
02/07/2015 17:45:49 are odd - Harry- field separators like 02/07/2015 17:45:49 are odd - Sue
```

In this example, we are embedding the current date and time by concatenating the Get-Date cmdlet into the $OFS string we assign.

$PSBoundParameters

The $PSBoundParameters variable is a handy one for testing and debugging. $PSBoundParameters gets loaded with a dictionary object of each parameter name and value when a function is called. From within the function, we can use it to see what was passed in. Consider the code in Listing 8-7.

Listing 8-7. Inspecting $PSBoundParameters

```
function Invoke-UdfMyFunction ([string]$parm1, [int]$parm2, $parm3 )
{

    $PSBoundParameters

#  Do some work...
}

Invoke-UdfMyFunction "test" 1 "something"
```

In Listing 8-7 we can see the definition for the function Invoke-UdfMyFunction. The only executable statement displays the value of $PSBoundParameters. Then, we call the function seen in the last line; we should see the following output:

```
Key                                                         Value
---                                                         -----
parm1                                                       test
parm2                                                       1
parm3                                                       something
```

We can see each parameter name in the Key column and its value in the Value column. This can be very useful when debugging code.

$PSCmdlet

The $PSCmdlet object is rich with function execution-context information. The function in Listing 8-8 will help us explore this variable.

Listing 8-8. Exploring $PSCmdlet

```
function Invoke-UdfPSCmdlet {
 [CmdletBinding()]
        param (
          )

    Write-Host "Here is a dump of `$PSCmdLet..."
    $PSCmdlet

    Write-Host "Here is a list of the MyInvocaton attributes..."
    $PSCmdlet.MyInvocation

    if($PSCmdlet.ShouldContinue('Click Yes to see GridView of methods and properties...',
    'Show GridView'))
    {
        $PSCmdlet | Get-Member | Out-GridView
    }

}

Invoke-UdfPSCmdlet
```

$PSCmdlet is initialized with data when code that includes the CmdletBinding attribute is executed, and it is only available within the called code. The function in Listing 8-8 will do three things to help us see what is available in $PSCmdlet. First, it writes the object to the console. Then, it writes just the MyInvocation property, which is a set of very useful information about the calling context. Finally, the ShouldContinue method of $PSCmdlet is called to prompt us as to whether we want to continue, end, or suspend the script. This is the same behavior as when we use the Confirm common parameter. The output is shown here:

```
Here is a dump of $PSCmdLet...
ParameterSetName        : __AllParameterSets
MyInvocation            : System.Management.Automation.InvocationInfo
PagingParameters        :
```

```
InvokeCommand        : System.Management.Automation.CommandInvocationIntrinsics
Host                 : System.Management.Automation.Internal.Host.InternalHost
SessionState         : System.Management.Automation.SessionState
Events               : System.Management.Automation.PSLocalEventManager
JobRepository        : System.Management.Automation.JobRepository
JobManager           : System.Management.Automation.JobManager
InvokeProvider       : System.Management.Automation.ProviderIntrinsics
Stopping             : False
CommandRuntime       : Invoke-UdfPSCmdlet
CurrentPSTransaction :
CommandOrigin        : Internal

Here is a list of the MyInvocaton attributes...
MyCommand            : Invoke-UdfPSCmdlet
BoundParameters      : {}
UnboundArguments     : {}
ScriptLineNumber     : 20
OffsetInLine         : 1
HistoryId            : 210
ScriptName           : C:\Users\BryanCafferky\Documents\Book\Code\Invoke-UdfPSCmdlet.ps1
Line                 : Invoke-UdfPSCmdlet
PositionMessage      : At C:\Users\BryanCafferky\Documents\Book\Code\Chapter08\Invoke-
                       UdfPSCmdlet.ps1:20 char:1
                       + Invoke-UdfPSCmdlet
                       + ~~~~~~~~~~~~~~~~~~
PSScriptRoot         : C:\Users\BryanCafferky\Documents\Code\Chapter08
PSCommandPath        : C:\Users\BryanCafferky\Documents\Code\Chapter08\Invoke-UdfPSCmdlet.ps1
InvocationName       : Invoke-UdfPSCmdlet
PipelineLength       : 1
PipelinePosition     : 1
ExpectingInput       : False
CommandOrigin        : Internal
DisplayScriptPosition :

True
```

Then you are prompted as shown in Figure 8-2.

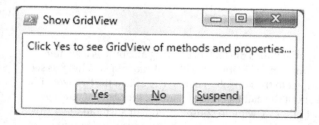

Figure 8-2. *The Confirmation method causes the execution to stop so the user can decide on an action*

If you click Yes, True is returned to the `if` expression and the code in the braces executes—i.e., `$PSCmdlet` is piped into `Get-Member`, which is piped into `Out-Gridview`. If you click No, the program stops. If you click Suspend, the program suspends running and you are able to enter commands into the console until you type `'exit'` to resume program execution.

$PsCulture

`$PsCulture` contains the culture name, language code, and country code currently in use, such as `'en-US'` for United States English.

```
$PsCulture
```

The value of `$PsCulture` will display as shown here:

```
En-US
```

The value is obtained from `System.Globalization.CultureInfo.CurrentCulture.Name`. We can use the cmdlet `Get-Culture` to get a reference to this object, as shown:

```
$myculture = Get-Culture
```

Try the statements that follow to explore the information returned by `Get-Culture`:

```
$myculture | Get-Member
```

The output of this command shows that there is a lot of information in this object:

```
Name                         MemberType Definition
----                         ---------- ----------
ClearCachedData              Method     void ClearCachedData()
Clone                        Method     System.Object Clone(), System.Object ICloneable...
Equals                       Method     bool Equals(System.Object value)
GetConsoleFallbackUICulture  Method     cultureinfo GetConsoleFallbackUICulture()
GetFormat                    Method     System.Object GetFormat(type formatType),
GetHashCode                  Method     int GetHashCode()
GetType                      Method     type GetType()
ToString                     Method     string ToString()
Calendar                     Property   System.Globalization.Calendar Calendar {get;}
CompareInfo                  Property   System.Globalization.CompareInfo CompareInfo
CultureTypes                 Property   System.Globalization.CultureTypes CultureTypes
DateTimeFormat               Property   System.Globalization.DateTimeFormatInfo
DisplayName                  Property   string DisplayName {get;}
EnglishName                  Property   string EnglishName {get;}
IetfLanguageTag              Property   string IetfLanguageTag {get;}
IsNeutralCulture             Property   bool IsNeutralCulture {get;}
IsReadOnly                   Property   bool IsReadOnly {get;}
KeyboardLayoutId             Property   int KeyboardLayoutId {get;}
LCID                         Property   int LCID {get;}
Name                         Property   string Name {get;}
NativeName                   Property   string NativeName {get;}
NumberFormat                 Property   System.Globalization.NumberFormatInfo NumberFormat
```

```
OptionalCalendars                   Property    System.Globalization.Calendar[] OptionalCalendars
Parent                              Property    cultureinfo Parent {get;}
TextInfo                            Property    System.Globalization.TextInfo TextInfo {get;}
ThreeLetterISOLanguageName          Property    string ThreeLetterISOLanguageName {get;}
ThreeLetterWindowsLanguageName      Property    string ThreeLetterWindowsLanguageName {get;}
TwoLetterISOLanguageName            Property    string TwoLetterISOLanguageName {get;}
UseUserOverride                     Property    bool UseUserOverride {get;}
```

We can get information about the calendar by displaying the Calendar property:

$myculture.Calendar

The contents are written to the console as shown here:

```
MinSupportedDateTime : 1/1/0001 12:00:00 AM
MaxSupportedDateTime : 12/31/9999 11:59:59 PM
AlgorithmType        : SolarCalendar
CalendarType         : Localized
Eras                 : {1}
TwoDigitYearMax      : 2029
IsReadOnly           : False
```

To display information about the culture-specific date and time, use the DateTimeFormat property, as shown here:

$myculture.DateTimeFormat

The following detailed date and time format information is then displayed:

```
AMDesignator                      : AM
Calendar                          : System.Globalization.GregorianCalendar
DateSeparator                     : /
FirstDayOfWeek                    : Sunday
CalendarWeekRule                  : FirstDay
FullDateTimePattern               : dddd, MMMM dd, yyyy h:mm:ss tt
LongDatePattern                   : dddd, MMMM dd, yyyy
LongTimePattern                   : h:mm:ss tt
MonthDayPattern                   : MMMM dd
PMDesignator                      : PM
RFC1123Pattern                    : ddd, dd MMM yyyy HH':'mm':'ss 'GMT'
ShortDatePattern                  : M/d/yyyy
ShortTimePattern                  : h:mm tt
SortableDateTimePattern           : yyyy'-'MM'-'dd'T'HH':'mm':'ss
TimeSeparator                     : :
UniversalSortableDateTimePattern  : yyyy'-'MM'-'dd HH':'mm':'ss'Z'
YearMonthPattern                  : MMMM, yyyy
AbbreviatedDayNames               : {Sun, Mon, Tue, Wed...}
ShortestDayNames                  : {Su, Mo, Tu, We...}
DayNames                          : {Sunday, Monday, Tuesday, Wednesday...}
AbbreviatedMonthNames             : {Jan, Feb, Mar, Apr...}
MonthNames                        : {January, February, March, April...}
```

```
IsReadOnly                      : False
NativeCalendarName              : Gregorian Calendar
AbbreviatedMonthGenitiveNames   : {Jan, Feb, Mar, Apr...}
MonthGenitiveNames              : {January, February, March, April...}
```

We can use the `ThreeLetterISOLanguageName` property to get the ISO standard three-character code for the language:

```
$myculture.ThreeLetterISOLanguageName
```

For my machine, I see the value here:

```
eng
```

This code stands for English.

To get a longer, more descriptive name, we can use the `DisplayName` property as shown here:

```
$myculture.DisplayName
```

This will show the following value on my machine:

```
English (United States)
```

Piping the `$myculture` object to `Get-Member` shows us that it contains a lot of information. The statements after that show information about the calendar, data/time formats, the ISO three-character code, and the descriptive display name.

Other Automatic Variables

Table 8-1 describes some other potentially useful automatic variables.

Table 8-1. *Useful Automatic Variables*

Variable	Description
$HOME	Path to user's home directory.
$LastExitCode	Contains the Exit code of the last Windows program that ran.
$PSCommandPath	The path of where the currently executing script is located.
$PSDebugContext	When debugging, this object provides information about the debugging session.
$PsHome	The full path to the PowerShell installation directory.

For more information on automatic variables, see the following link:

```
https://technet.microsoft.com/en-us/library/hh847768.aspx
```

Preference Variables

Some of PowerShell's behavior that can be changed is controlled by preference variables, which are created and assigned values when a PowerShell session starts. There are many preference variables, but let's focus on those that have significant value for development. For a complete list of all the preference variables, see the following link: `https://technet.microsoft.com/en-us/library/hh847796.aspx`. Let's take a look at `$ConfirmPreference`.

$ConfirmPreference

The `$ConfirmPreference` variable has a default value of `High`. This means that when a cmdlet is used that PowerShell considers to pose a high risk if performed incorrectly, the user will be asked to confirm they want to continue with the operation before it is actually performed. Consider the code here:

```
"junk" > myjunk.txt

Remove-Item myjunk.txt  # The file is deleted with no prompt.
```

If you run these two lines, a file is created in the first line and deleted in the second line. Let's try this again, first changing the `$ConfirmPreference` variable as shown here:

```
$ConfirmPreference = "Low"

"junk" > myjunk.txt

Remove-Item myjunk.txt  # you are asked to confirm this action before it is executed.
```

In the first line, we set the `$ConfirmPreference` variable to `"Low"`, thus telling PowerShell to prompt us to confirm the execution of any cmdlet with a `"Low"` or higher risk. When the lines that try to either write to the file or delete it execute, a popup dialog appears asking us to confirm the operation.

What if we wanted to override the `$ConfirmPreference` value? We can do that by passing the `Confirm` parameter on the cmdlet call, as shown here:

```
Remove-Item myjunk.txt -Confirm:$false # Confirm default is overridden.
```

The notation `Confirm:$false` passed a false value to the `Confirm` parameter. Normally a switch parameter like `Confirm` is not passed when a false value is desired, but when we need to override a default value for it, we can pass `false` using this notation. For example, in a custom function, we could pass a false value to a switch parameter as shown here:

```
function Invoke-MyTest ([switch]$test)
{
  if ($test) { "Swell" } else { "Doh!" }
}

Invoke-MyTest -test:$false
```

We should see the following output:

```
Doh!
```

The output shows that we successfully passed a value of `false` to the `$test` parameter.

$DebugPreference

By default, if you want `Write-Debug` output statements to display on the console, you need to pass the Debug common cmdlet parameter. The $DebugPreference variable affects not only the display of messages but also whether processing should continue. The default value is `SilentlyContinue`, which suppresses messages and continues processing as if they were not there.

■ **Note** You must include the `CmdletBinding` attribute in code for it to support the `Write-Debug` and `Write-Verbose` statements.

Setting the $DebugPreference variable is a convenient way to configure an environment to display or suppress debug messages without changing any code. For example, in the development environment, it might be useful to set this variable to `Continue` so we can see the messages. In production, we could let this variable default to `SilentlyContinue`, which ignores the `Write-Debug` statements. The $DebugPreference valid values and related effects are listed in Table 8-2.

Table 8-2. *DebugPreference Valid Values*

Value	Effect
Stop	Displays the message, stops execution, and outputs an error message to the console
Inquire	Displays the message and asks the user if they want to continue. If the cmdlet call overrides the preference variable with the Debug common parameter, PowerShell changes the $DebugPreference variable to Inquire and will ask the user if they want to continue processing.
Continue	Displays the message and continues execution
SilentlyContinue	This is the default value. Suppresses messages and continues processing, i.e., ignores the `Write-Debug` or `Write-Verbose` statements, respectively.

Be aware that if the $DebugPreference setting is overridden by a cmdlet call that uses the Debug common parameter, the $DebugPreference variable is changed to Inquire for the duration of the call. This means that the current and all subsequent `Write-Debug` statements will cause processing to halt while the user is prompted to continue, suspend, or stop processing. Let's look at Listing 8-9 to see how this works.

Listing 8-9. Experimenting with $DebugPreference

```
$DebugPreference = "SilentlyContinue"

function Show-UdfMyDebugMessage {
[CmdletBinding()]
      param ()

  Write-Debug "Debug message"

  $DebugPreference

  Write-Debug "2nd Debug message"

}
```

Let's call the function in Listing 8-9 with no parameters:

```
Show-UdfMyDebugMessage
```

The `Write-Debug` statements in the function were ignored and all we get is the value of `$DebugPreference`, which is `SilentlyContinue`.

Now, let's make the call passing the Debug common parameter:

```
Show-UdfMyDebugMessage –Debug
```

We should see the following lines written to the console. Not only are the `Write-Debug` messages being written to the console, but we also get prompted on each `Write-Debug` message about whether we want execution to continue, halt, or be suspended. Notice that the value of $DebugPreference is `Inquire`. It was set to this because we passed the Debug common parameter. See the following:

```
DEBUG: Debug message
Inquire
DEBUG: 2nd Debug message
```

So, did the value of $DebugPreference stay Inquire? Let's test that by calling the function again without the Debug parameter:

```
Show-UdfMyDebugMessage
```

We see the following output on the console, which proves the value has returned to its original value:

```
SilentlyContinue
```

Finally, just to prove `$DebugPreference` is really back to its original value, let's display it as shown here:

```
$DebugPreference
```

The behavior of PowerShell temporarily changing the value of `$DebugPreference` is called out, as it may cause unanticipated behavior.

$VerbosePreference

By default, if you want `Write-Verbose` output statements to write to the console, you need to pass the Verbose common cmdlet parameter. This preference variable affects not only the display of messages, but also whether processing should continue. The default value is `SilentlyContinue`, which suppresses the messages and continues processing as if they were not there. Remember, you must include the `CmdletBinding` attribute in any code that you want to support the `Write-Debug` and `Write-Verbose` statements. Table 8-3 lists the possible `$VerbosePreference` values and the effect of each value.

Table 8-3. *$VerbosePreference Valid Values*

Value	Effect
Stop	Displays the message, stops execution, and outputs an error message to the console
Inquire	Displays the message and asks the user if they want to continue
Continue	Displays the verbose message and continues processing
SilentlyContinue	This is the default value. Suppresses messages and continues processing, i.e., ignores the Write-Verbose statement

Log Event Variables

Some PowerShell events are written to the Windows event log. To see what is logged, enter the command seen here:

```
Get-EventLog "Windows PowerShell"
```

You should see a list of PowerShell events that were logged. There are two Windows event logs, which are the classic and the new event logs. The log PowerShell writes to is the classic event log. Starting with Windows Vista, Windows added a new event log that was redesigned to use XML, and a new viewer was added to support viewing the new format.

The PowerShell events that are logged by default are listed here:

$LogEngineHealthEvent	Logs PowerShell session errors and failures
$LogEngineLifecycleEvent	Logs when PowerShell is started and stopped
$LogProviderLifecycleEvent	Logs the starting and stopping of Providers
$LogProviderHealthEvent	Logs any Provider errors

To stop logging any of these events, just set the associated variable to $false. The events that follow are not logged by default:

$LogCommandHealthEvent	Logs any command errors
$LogCommandLifecycleEvent	Logs when commands start and end

The log event preference variables have either a true or false value. To turn on logging for an event, set its corresponding preference variable to true, i.e., $LogCommandHealthEvent = $true will start the logging of command errors. To turn off logging for an event, set its corresponding preference variable to true, i.e., $LogEngineHealthEvent = $false will stop the logging of session errors and failures

The following cmdlets can be used to manage the PowerShell event log. You must be running PowerShell with administrator rights to use these cmdlets.

Clear-EventLog	Deletes all the entries in the log(s) specified on the machine specified.
Limit-EventLog	Sets limits on how big the log can grow and how long to retain entries.
New-EventLog	Creates a custom event log.
Remove-EventLog	Removes an event log. This does not just clear entries, it actually deletes the log.
Show-EventLog	Opens up the Classic Event Viewer.
Write-EventLog	Writes an entry to the specified event log.

Using these cmdlets, we can create custom logs and write to them in our applications. Let's look at the example in Listing 8-10. Note: To run this script you need to start PowerShell as administrator.

Listing 8-10. Creating a custom log

```
New-EventLog -LogName DataWarehouse -Source ETL

Limit-EventLog -LogName DataWarehouse -MaximumSize 10MB -RetentionDays 10

For ($i=1; $i -le 5; $i++)
{
   Write-EventLog -LogName DataWarehouse -Source ETL -EventId 9999 -Message ("DW Event
   written " + (Get-Date))
}

Get-EventLog -LogName DataWarehouse
```

The first line in Listing 8-10 creates a new event log named DataWarehouse with a source of ETL. The next line limits the log to 10 megabytes and a 10-day retention of entries. Then the For loop writes some entries to the log. Finally, we view the log entries with the Get-EventLog cmdlet. The display should look similar to the output here:

```
Index   Time          EntryType    Source   InstanceID    Message
-----   ----          ---------    ------   ----------    -------
13      Feb 23 17:03  Information ETL       9999          DW Event written 02/23/2015 17:03:27
12      Feb 23 17:03  Information ETL       9999          DW Event written 02/23/2015 17:03:27
11      Feb 23 17:03  Information ETL       9999          DW Event written 02/23/2015 17:03:27
10      Feb 23 17:03  Information ETL       9999          DW Event written 02/23/2015 17:03:27
9       Feb 23 17:03  Information ETL       9999          DW Event written 02/23/2015 17:03:27
```

Let's clear and remove the log with the statements here:

```
Clear-EventLog -LogName DataWarehouse

Remove-EventLog -LogName DataWarehouse
```

The first line deletes all entries from the log, but the log is still available to be written to. The Remove-EventLog cmdlet deletes the log itself so it can no longer be written to.

The EventLog cmdlets make creating and using custom event logs easy. In production environments this can be a good way to audit applications and log information to help debug problems.

$PSDefaultParameterValues

$PSDefaultParameterValues provides a way to define values to be used for cmdlet parameters when they are omitted from the call. To get an idea of how this works, let's look at the following example:

```
$PSDefaultParameterValues=@{
"Get-EventLog:logname"="Windows PowerShell";
"Get-EventLog:EntryType"="Warning";
}

Get-EventLog
```

$PSDefaultParameterValues is a hash table, so it is loaded with the standard hash table assignment we've seen before. It is loaded using a series of name/value pairs. The name is the cmdlet name you want to assign the default value to, followed by a colon and the parameter name, i.e., Get-ChildItem:Path. This is assigned the value on the opposite side of the equal sign. In our example, we are assigning a default value for the LogName parameter and the EntryType parameter of Get-EventLog. When we run the statement Get-EventLog, we will only see the PowerShell log's Warning messages.

We can use wildcards on the cmdlet name, and we are not limited to built-in cmdlets. We can create default parameter values for our own functions, as shown in Listing 8-11.

Listing 8-11. Using $PSDefaultParameterValues

```
function Invoke-UdfSomething
{
[CmdletBinding()]
        param (
                [string] $someparm1,
                [string] $someparm2
                 )

   Write-Host "`$someparm1 is $someparm1"
   Write-Host "`$someparm2 is $someparm2"
}

$PSDefaultParameterValues=@{
"Invoke-Udf*:someparm1"="my paramater value";
}

Invoke-UdfSomething
```

Invoke-UdfSomething is defined with the parameters $someparm1 and $someparm2. The function just displays the parameter values. Then we assign a default value for $someparm1 for any cmdlets that begin with "Invoke-Udf", which limits this to our custom code. Finally, we call Invoke-UdfSomething, and we should see the output that follows:

```
$someparm1 is my parmater value
$someparm2 is
```

We can see $someparm1 has the default value, but $someparm2 does not. Bear in mind, any other functions with a name that starts with "Invoke-Udf" and has a parameter named $someparm1 will also get the default value when no value is passed. However, we cannot use wildcards for parameter names. PowerShell will let you load the default, but it will generate an error when it sees more than one parameter matching the name. Consider the code here:

```
$PSDefaultParameterValues=@{
"Invoke-Udf*:someparm*"="my parmater value";
}

Invoke-UdfSomething
```

When we run this code, we see the output that follows. PowerShell saw the conflict and did not supply the default to either parameter:

```
WARNING: The following name or alias defined in $PSDefaultParameterValues for this cmdlet
resolves to multiple parameters: somepar
m*. The default has been ignored.
$someparm1 is
$someparm2 is
```

$PSDefaultParameterValues offers some interesting possibilities. However, it a good idea to restrict the parameters being defaulted as narrowly as possible to avoid unintended side effects.

Environment Variables

Windows environment variables are exposed in PowerShell as a file-system drive through the environment provider. We can access them using the Env: drive, as shown here:

```
Get-ChildItem Env:
```

This command will list all the environment variables. On my machine, the list of environment variables is as follows:

```
Name                          Value
----                          -----
ALLUSERSPROFILE               C:\ProgramData
AMDAPPSDKROOT                 c:\Program Files (x86)\AMD APP\
APPDATA                       C:\Users\BryanCafferky\AppData\Roaming
COMPUTERNAME                  BRYANCAFFERKYPC
HOMEDRIVE                     C:
HOMEPATH                      \Users\BryanCafferky
LOGONSERVER                   \\BRYANCAFFERKYPC
Path                          C:\Program Files\Common Files\Microsoft Shared\Windows Live;
PATHEXT                       .COM;.EXE;.BAT;.CMD;.VBS;.VBE;.JS;.JSE;.WSF;.WSH;.MSC;.CPL
PSModulePath                  C:\Users\BryanCafferky\Documents\WindowsPowerShell\Modules;
USERDOMAIN                    BRYANCAFFERKYPC
USERNAME                      BryanCafferky
windir                        C:\Windows
```

We can use the environment variables in our scripts to make them more robust and flexible. The code that follows is an example of this:

```
$filepath = "$Env:HOMEDRIVE$env:HOMEPATH\Documents\mylogfile.txt"

"Writing row for $Env:UserName." | Out-File -FilePath $filepath -Append
```

The first line assigns $filepath as the current user's documents folder and sets the file name as mylogfile.txt. The next line writes a line to the file that includes the current user's name, which is in $Env:UserName. Using this technique, the code can run on any machine and store the file in the appropriate folder for that user.

Using PS Drives

PowerShell drives are similar to network drive mappings except they are specific to PowerShell in creation and usage. They are handy for creating easy-to-remember short names for locations we frequently refer to, like FTP folders, network drives, and UNC paths. By default, PowerShell drives automatically go away when the PowerShell session ends. What is interesting about PowerShell drives is that unlike Windows drive mappings, PowerShell drives can be used for any provider, which includes things like the Windows registry and the certificates store.

Here is an example of creating and using a PS drive:

```
New-PSDrive -name myps -psprovider FileSystem -root C:\Users\

Get-ChildItem myps:    # Get a list of files where the psdrive points.
```

The first line creates a new PS drive called myps. The psprovider parameter tells PowerShell what provider is being used, which in this case is FileSystem. The Root parameter is the path to be used as the root of the drive. The second line lists all the files in the folder the PS drive myps points to. Notice the colon suffix to the drive name. This is required, because a provider simulates a file system, which requires the drive notation.

Since the SQLPS modules create a provider named SqlServer, once we have loaded the module, we can create a drive that maps to a level in the SQL Server hierarchy. Let's look at an example of this:

```
Import-Module SQLPS -DisableNameChecking

New-PsDrive -name at -psprovider SqlServer -root ` SQLSERVER:\SQL\Machine\DEFAULT\Databases\
Adventureworks\Tables

Get-ChildItem aworks:
```

After the SQLPS module has been imported, a PS drive named aworks is created that points to the tables in the AdventureWorks database on the default instance of SQL Server. Note: You will need to change the path to the instance of where your copy of AdventureWorks is located. The second line will list all the AdventureWorks tables. PowerShell provides a number of built-in PS drives to make accessing resources easier. Let's enter the command you see here:

```
Get-PSDrive
```

When we enter this command, we should see something like the output here:

Name	Used (GB)	Free (GB)	Provider	Root
Alias			Alias	
at			SqlServer	SQLSERVER:\SQL\User\D...
C	267.97	648.33	FileSystem	C:\
Cert			Certificate	\
D			FileSystem	D:\
Env			Environment	
F			FileSystem	F:\
Function			Function	
HKCU			Registry	HKEY_CURRENT_USER
HKLM			Registry	HKEY_LOCAL_MACHINE

```
myps                    648.33    FileSystem    C:\Users\BryanCafferky\Documents...
SQLSERVER                         SqlServer     SQLSERVER:\
Variable                          Variable
WSMan                             WSMan
```

These predefined drives provide an easy way to query about the environment. Notice there is a PS drive automatically created for the physical drives on your machine. To get a list of all defined aliases, we can enter the command Get-ChildItem Alias:, or to see all the environment variables, we just enter Get-ChildItem Env:. We can also see the provider names for the predefined drives, which we can use to create more drives of the same type. Another way to get the provider names is with the Get-PSProvider cmdlet, as shown here:

```
Get-PSProvider
```

You should see the provider list as follows. Notice that because we loaded the SQLPS module, SqlServer shows as a provider:

```
Name            Capabilities                          Drives
----            ------------                          ------
Alias           ShouldProcess                         {Alias}
Environment     ShouldProcess                         {Env}
FileSystem      Filter, ShouldProcess, Credentials    {C, myps, D, F}
Function        ShouldProcess                         {Function}
Registry        ShouldProcess, Transactions           {HKLM, HKCU}
Variable        ShouldProcess                         {Variable}
SqlServer       Credentials                           {SQLSERVER, at}
Certificate     ShouldProcess                         {Cert}
WSMan           Credentials                           {WSMan}
```

If we want to delete a PS drive, we can use the Remove-PSDrive cmdlet. Let's assume we want to remove the myps drive we created earlier and add it back, but this time mapped to a network drive and persisted like a standard drive mapping, and we also want to make it global, which means all our PowerShell sessions can access it. We can do that with the statements here:

```
Remove-PSDrive myps
New-PSDrive -name myps -psprovider FileSystem -root \\Server\Share -Persist -Scope global
```

The first line removes the PS drive myps. The line after that creates it again, but this time pointing to a network share named \\Server\Share. The Persist parameter tells PowerShell not to remove the drive when we exit PowerShell, and the global scope makes the drive available to all our PowerShell sessions. PowerShell will not let you persist a local drive mapping—it must be a remote connection. Be sure to replace \\Server\Share with a shared location in your environment.

PS drives are a powerful feature not only for being more productive in PowerShell but also as a means to configure the environment for applications. For example, if a number of scripts need to use an FTP folder, a PS drive could be created that all the scripts use. In the development environment, perhaps it points to a test folder, but in production it would point to the production folder. If an FTP server needed to be renamed, only the path pointed to by the PS drive would need to be changed. This is an important consideration for application deployments.

Aliases

PowerShell allows us to map commands to other names. For example, we could map the word showfiles to the cmdlet Get-ChildItem. Then, whenever we want a directory listing, we just enter showfiles. This alternate name for a cmdlet is called an *alias*. This is a powerful feature that can greatly help productivity when using PowerShell interactively. In fact, PowerShell has many built-in aliases that map cmdlets to Linux and DOS aliases to make the transition easier. To see a list of all the aliases that are defined in your PowerShell environment, enter the following command:

```
Get-Alias
```

A list of all the defined aliases is displayed. Let's take a look at the alias dir by entering the command here:

```
Get-Alias dir
```

We should see the following output:

```
CommandType    Name                          ModuleName
-----------    ----                          ----------
Alias          dir -> Get-ChildItem
```

The Name column shows that dir is mapped to Get-ChildItem. This means that dir and Get-ChildItem will both do the same thing. In addition to allowing us to map PowerShell commands to commands more familiar to us, aliases are used to create abbreviations for commands. For example, gci is a built-in alias for Get-ChildItem. Table 8-4 shows some of the more commonly used aliases that you should be aware of. Notice that many DOS and Linux commands have aliases provided. Other aliases are abbreviations, and you need to know them as you may run across them in other people's code.

Table 8-4. *Built-in aliases and the related cmdlets*

Alias	PowerShell Cmdlet
%	ForEach-Object
?	Where-Object
cat	Get-Content
cd	Set-Location
cls	Clear-Host
copy	Copy-Item
cp	Copy-Item
del	Remove-Item
dir	Get-ChildItem
echo	Write-Output
erase	Remove-Item
foreach	ForEach-Object
gc	Get-Content

(*continued*)

Table 8-4. *(continued)*

Alias	PowerShell Cmdlet
gci	Get-ChildItem
ls	Get-ChildItem
pwd	Get-Location
rd	Remove-Item
ren	Rename-Item
rm	Remove-Item
rmdir	Remove-Item
select	Select-Object
where	Where-Object

See the following link by Microsoft for guidelines on creating aliases:

```
https://msdn.microsoft.com/en-us/library/dd878329%28v=vs.85%29.aspx
```

While aliases are great for increasing productivity when working interactively in PowerShell, I would not recommend using them in your PowerShell programs. A key objective of good programming is to make your code as easy to understand as possible. Aliases that are abbreviations make code cryptic, while aliases that remap cmdlets to different words make it hard for someone reading your code to know which cmdlets are being called.

Customizing the Console

You've seen how to change the settings in the ISE. However, we can change settings in the console just as easily. Start the PowerShell CLI, click on the PowerShell icon in the upper left corner of the window, and select Properties, as shown in Figure 8-3.

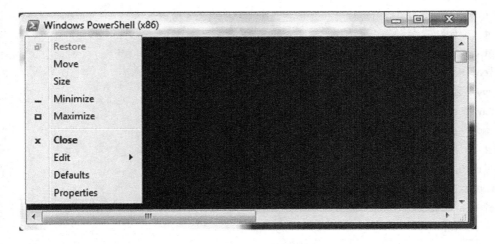

Figure 8-3. *Click on the Properties item in the PowerShell Console drop-down menu to change settings*

The Properties window is displayed; this is where we can customize much of the behavior of the console to fit our needs. On the Options tab, shown in Figure 8-4, we can set the cursor size to small, medium, or large. We can also set the amount of command history to be maintained and whether we want duplicate commands in the history deleted. QuickEdit mode lets you use the mouse to select and copy text in the console. Insert mode adds new text into a line rather than replacing the text.

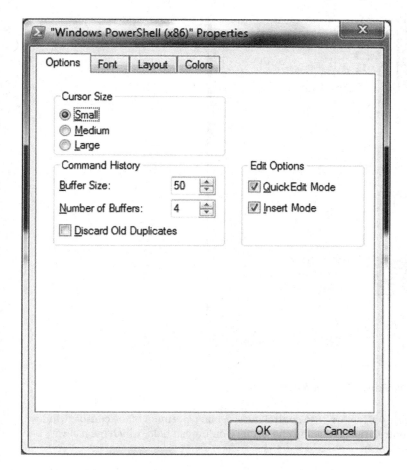

Figure 8-4. *The PowerShell Console Properties window Options tab*

If we click on the Font tab, shown in Figure 8-5, we can select the font and point size of text displayed in the console.

Figure 8-5. *The PowerShell Console Properties window Font tab*

The Layout tab, shown in Figure 8-6, allows us to control the size and placement of the console window. Screen Buffer Size, for example, controls how much text the virtual window can hold, which must always be at least one physical Window Size's worth.

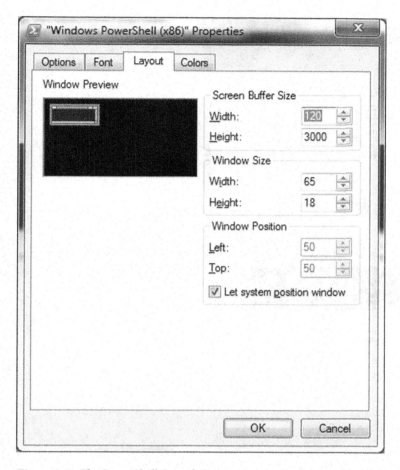

Figure 8-6. *The PowerShell Console Properties window Layout tab*

The Colors tab, shown in Figure 8-7, allows us to set the text and background colors used by the ISE.

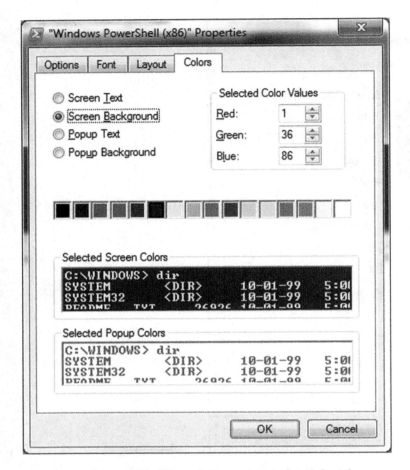

Figure 8-7. *The PowerShell Console Properties window Color tab*

Profiles

The PowerShell environments support the inclusion of a special startup script called a *profile*. The purpose of this script is to customize the environment for your needs. For example, a database developer may want to load the SQLPS module automatically when PowerShell starts. A developer may want to set some default environment values, such as the name of the development database server, so they can be used in scripts and on the command line. In the old DOS days, the equivalent script file was named Autoexec.bat. A profile can be defined for the current user or for all users of the computer. A profile can also be created to apply to a specific host like the ISE or the CLI or to be used for all hosts. The variable $Profile is an object with a property that stores the path to each type of possible profile script, whether or not the script actually exists. To see the values of these properties enter the following command:

```
$profile | Get-Member -MemberType NoteProperty
```

In the ISE, I get the output here:

```
Name                   MemberType   Definition
----                   ----------   ----------
AllUsersAllHosts       NoteProperty System.String
                                    AllUsersAllHosts=C:\Windows\System32\WindowsPowerShell\
                                    v1.0\profile.ps1
AllUsersCurrentHost    NoteProperty System.String
                                    AllUsersCurrentHost=C:\Windows\System32\
                                    WindowsPowerShell\v1.0\Microsoft.Pow...
CurrentUserAllHosts    NoteProperty System.String
                                    CurrentUserAllHosts=C:\Users\BryanCafferky\Documents\
                                    WindowsPowerShell\profi...
CurrentUserCurrentHost NoteProperty System.String
                                    CurrentUserCurrentHost=C:\Users\BryanCafferky\Documents\
                                    WindowsPowerShell\Mi...
```

If you reference just `$profile`, it references the `CurrentUserCurrentHost` value. Let's try a quick demonstration to see how this works. If the ISE is not already started, start it now. In the ISE console, enter the command seen here:

```
Notepad $profile
```

Assuming you have not created a profile previously, you will get prompted to create one with a dialog box similar to the one in Figure 8-8.

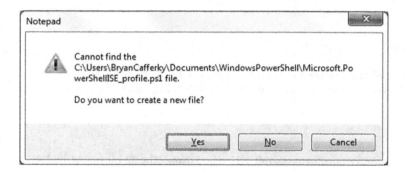

Figure 8-8. *Dialog to create the profile script*

Click Yes and you will be presented with an empty document in Notepad. Enter the commands seen here:

```
write-host 'The CurrentUserCurrentHost profile has started...'
write-host "Welcome $env:username." -Foreground Yellow
```

Save the file and exit Notepad. Then exit the ISE and restart it. After the ISE starts, you should see messages displayed to the console similar to the ones here:

```
The CurrentUserCurrentHost profile has started...
Welcome BryanCafferky.
```

The profile script we created will run every time we start the ISE but it will not execute when we enter the PowerShell CLI. If we had created the profile while we were in the CLI, the profile would execute when the CLI was started. This profile is specific to the user who created it. To create a profile that would be executed for all users, we need to start the ISE as an Administrator. Otherwise, Windows will not let us create the file. After starting the ISE as an administrator, we can create a profile that applies to all ISE users by entering:

```
Notepad $profile.AllUsersCurrentHost
```

Then we could enter the script and save it.

An important concept here is that there can be a layering of profiles. If there is a profile of each type, we could have up to four profile scripts execute when we start a host. To demonstrate, I created a short script of each type that just wrote to the console, showing the profile type it was running from. The output is shown here:

```
The AllUsersAllHosts profile has started...
The AllUsersCurrentHost profile has started...
The CurrentUserAllHosts profile has started...
The CurrentUserCurrentHost profile has started...
Welcome BryanCafferky.
```

The point of this is to show that multiple profiles can execute and that they do so in order of broadest scope to most specific scope. If we were to run the CLI, we should see the first three lines display but not the last two, because those are specific to the ISE.

Profiles are generally used to make working interactively with PowerShell easier. For example, we can have modules we use often load automatically or we can customize the console prompt. However, we can also use them to configure the PowerShell environment to execute scripts in a consistent manner. If we have a dedicated Windows account to run the PowerShell scripts, we can customize the current user current host profile to optimize the way scripts are deployed and executed.

Current User Current Host

As we saw earlier, the narrowest scoped profile is for the current user current host. When we reference $profile, the location of this profile is the value returned. Start the PowerShell ISE, and in the console enter the command here:

```
Notepad.exe $profile
```

This command opens the profile for the current user's ISE in Notepad. Note: The 32-bit and 64-bit ISE share the same profile. And the 32-bit and 64-bit CLI share the same profile.

Now, let's enter the following lines into the profile and save it:

```
write-host 'The CurrentUserCurrentHost profile has started...'
Write-host "Welcome $env:username." -Foreground Yellow

$Host.UI.RawUI.WindowTitle = "$env:UserName"
```

■ **Note**   Remember both the CLI and the ISE provide windows to configure the fonts, window sizes and placement, and other environment features, so a profile may not be needed in some cases.

Current User All Hosts

When we are running PowerShell from our own user account, the current user current host profile, $Profile.CurrentUserAllHosts, is our own personal profile, and we are free to do whatever we want in it without affecting others. It is the place to customize PowerShell to suit our tastes and make ourselves more productive. Let's look at the simple profile that follows to customize PowerShell to our needs:

```
write-host 'The CurrentUserAllHosts profile has started...'
# Simple script to establish commonly used PowerShell custom functions...
Import-Module umd_database

New-Alias GetFileName Invoke-UdfCommonDialogSaveFile

$PSDefaultParameterValues=@{
"*:dbservername"="(local)";
}

$global:pscodepath = $env:HomeDrive + $env:HomePath + "\Documents\PowerShell\Scripts"

Set-Location $global:pscodepath
```

In this code, the first line writes a message to the console stating that the CurrentUserAllHosts profile has been executed. The module umd_database is imported. A new alias GetFileName is created for the function Invoke-UdfCommonDialogSaveFile. A default parameter value for dbservername for all cmdlets is added to $PSDefaultParameterValues. Then, a globally scoped variable, $global:pscodepath, is created and assigned the concatenation of $env:HomeDrive, $env:HomePath, and the string "\Documents\ PowerShell\Scripts". The current location is then set to $global:pscodepath. Note: To use this alias, the module containing the related function, umd_database, must be imported.

All Users Current Host

To create or change the $Profile.AllUsersCurrentHost, we need to start PowerShell as the Administrator. Then execute the following command:

```
Notepad.exe $Profile.AllUsersCurentHost
```

This profile will execute for all users, but only for the host from which we invoked the editor. Following is an example of a customization we might want to make in this profile:

```
Write-Host "The AllUsersCurrentHost profile has started..."
$Host.UI.RawUI.BufferSize.Width = 100
$Host.UI.RawUI.BufferSize.Height = 1000
```

After we display the message that the profile has started, we set the buffer width and size properties to give all users a little extra space. BufferHeight refers to how many lines of screen output is retained for scrolling backward.

All Users All Hosts

There may be some configuration settings that are common to all users and not specific to the host—things such as the mail server and the company name. It may be a security requirement to log the start of all PowerShell sessions with information such as the user ID, date, and time. These are things we can handle in the all users all hosts profile. See here:

```
# Import Modules...
Import-Module umd_database

$global:dbserver = '(local)'
$global:dbname   = 'Adventureworks'

# Some useful aliases
Set-Alias edit   notepad.exe
Set-Alias open   Invoke-Item
Set-Alias now    Get-Date
Set-Alias rsql   Invoke-UdfSQLQuery

$PSDefaultParameterValues = @{"*:Verbose"=$true;
                "Invoke-UdfSQLQuery:sqlserver"=$global:dbserver;
                "Invoke-UdfSQLQuery:sqldatabase"=$global:dbname}

"Current User Current Machine Default Parameter Values set are..."
$PSDefaultParameterValues
```

The first non-comment line loads the umd_database module so its functions are available to us when we start PowerShell. Then we see two statements assigning values to global variables dbserver and dbname. Having these available to us means we can pass them into any functions we call. On each machine, such as development, QA, and production, we would set the values as required. Then we see some handy aliases being declared. For example, rather than type "notepad.exe", we can just type "edit". The Invoke-Item cmdlet is handy to open files of different types because it launches the program registered for the file type. However, it is not intuitively named, so the alias "open" is created for it. We often need the current date, so we have a convenient alias of "now" for Get-Date. The function Invoke-UdfSQLQuery will submit a query to a SQL Server database and return the results. For convenience in the CLI, we create the "rsql" alias. It would be nice if we could include parameter values for an alias, but that is not supported. Aliases are just a different name for a cmdlet. The use of $PSDefaultParameterValues demonstrates how we can set default values based on variables in the profile. We could copy this profile to another machine and change the variables appropriately. Note: The modules you want to load depend on what you use most often, but I have found some modules such as SQLPS take a long time to load, and so I do not load it in my profile.

Summary

In this chapter we saw the many ways PowerShell provides customization and transparency. We discussed how PowerShell supports configuration through automatic, preference, and environment variables. We learned how to use automatic variables to get session and execution context–specific information. Preference variables control PowerShell's behavior and can be modified to suit our needs. Environment variables are used by various applications including PowerShell and can be created, read, and set by PowerShell scripts. We learned how to use aliases to create our own names for PowerShell cmdlets. We saw how PowerShell drives allow us to dynamically create short names for any provider location. Finally, we discussed how to use all these features in a special script called a profile that executes when a session starts.

CHAPTER 9

■ ■ ■

Augmenting ETL Processes

This chapter will cover how to use PowerShell to augment ETL development. We often need to load external files into a SQL Server database. However, these files usually need to go through some preparation before they can be loaded. Perhaps they arrive via FTP from an external source. Such files may be compressed. Perhaps they need to be scrubbed of bad values or modified to make them easier to load. After being loaded, the business may want the files archived and retained for a period of time. Before PowerShell, legacy-style batch files were often employed to do these tasks. However, batch files are cryptic, difficult to maintain, and lack support for reusability. In this chapter, we will see how PowerShell scripts can be used to accomplish these tasks. Rather than define a specific business scenario for these tasks, we consider this a common ETL pattern in which we can choose to employ the given tasks that apply. In this pattern, files arrive in a folder and copied to a local server, then are decompressed, loaded, and archived. Typically, when the job starts and ends, email notifications are sent out. Sometimes there are additional requirements. We will discuss functions that help with these tasks. Let's consider the potential ETL steps already mentioned as a template from which we can pick what we need. Figure 9-1 shows a common ETL pattern.

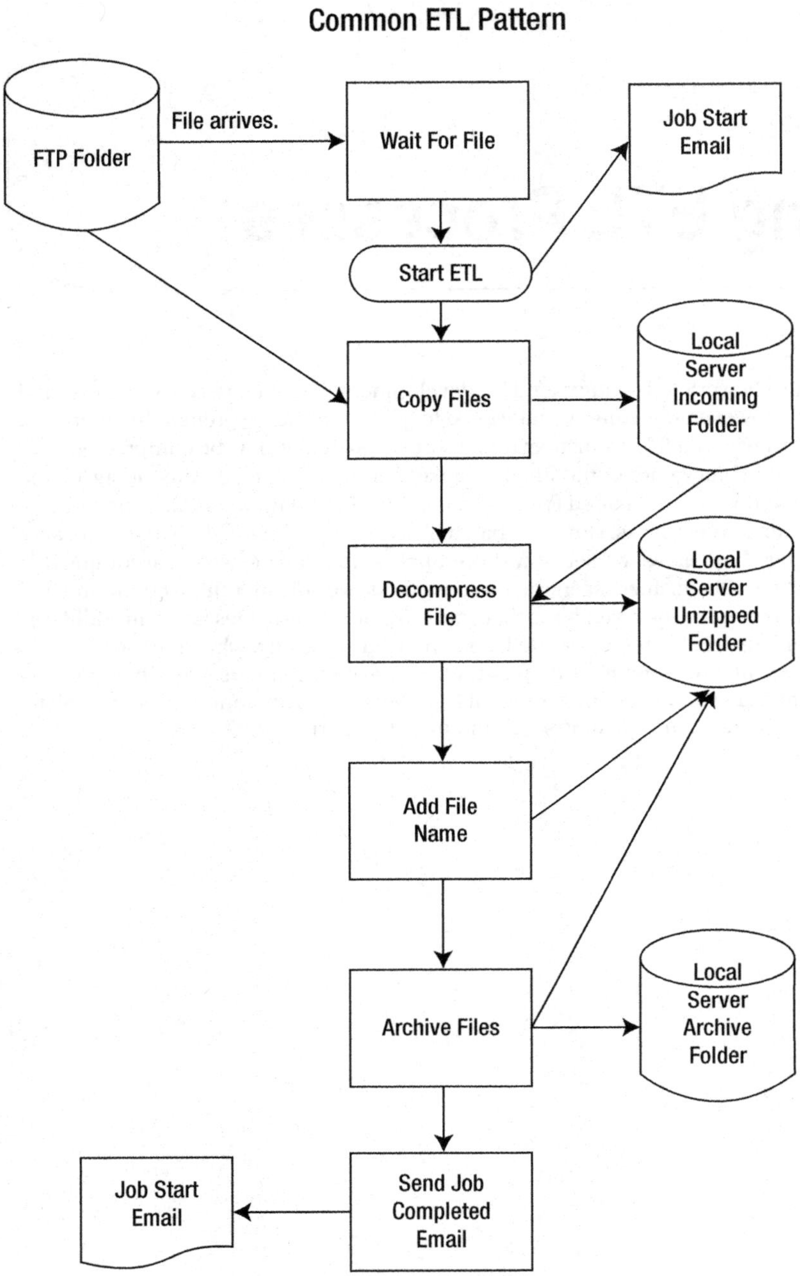

Common ETL Pattern

Figure 9-1. *A common ETL pattern*

We will start by reviewing functions that perform the steps in the ETL pattern: wait for a file, copy the file, decompress the file, add the file name as a column so it can be tracked, load the file into SQL Server, and send email notifications. These are presented without a context to show how they can be accomplished. Then we will review a script that orchestrates these functions into a complete ETL load process. In practice, an SSIS package would probably load the data, but we'll use a PowerShell script to show how that can be done by PowerShell. This will be followed by additional ETL-related functions that validate data, combine files, add column headings to files, and encrypt passwords to send email securely. By the end of this chapter we will know how to use PowerShell to augment our ETL development and have a set of functions we can apply immediately.

The Functions

In this section, we will review reusable functions that prepare the files for load and then archive the files afterward. The first task in an ETL job is often to wait for the file to arrive, which we will do using the Wait-UdfFileCreation function. This function will suspend the ETL process until it sees that a file matching the specified name pattern has arrived. Then we need to copy the file to a local folder to be processed, which we do using Copy-UdfFile. We unzip the file using Expand-UdfFile. To make it easier to track down data problems, we use Add-UdfColumnNameToFile to append a new column to the file that has the name of the flat file. We load the file to a SQL Server table. Finally, we archive the file using Move-UdfFile. We will use Send-UdfMail to send start and end job notifications. We'll start by reviewing each function in detail. Then we'll assemble them into an ETL process. All the functions in this chapter are in the module umd_etl_functions except Save-UdfEncryptedCredential, which is in umd_database.

Wait for a File

Our ETL load process begins when a file arrives. If this occurs on a reliable schedule, then a tool like SQL Agent can be used to run the ETL process based on that schedule. However, often files are not received on a fixed schedule, and the ETL process needs to run as the files come in. In Chapter 3 we saw how to use the FileSystemObject to register code to execute when a new file arrives. Here, we will discuss an alternative method of monitoring for a new file. The function that follows periodically checks for a file matching a given file name pattern in the specified folder. If a match is found, the function ends; otherwise, it waits for two seconds and then tries again. This technique works well with SQL Agent. By making the wait for file function the first job step, the job will just stay in that step until a file arrives. The job schedule can be set to run periodically–say, hourly–so once the job has executed, it will automatically schedule itself again within an hour. Since SQL Agent will not queue up a job that is already running, there's no issue of getting duplicate jobs in the queue. Let's review the function:

```
function Wait-UdfFileCreation
{
 [CmdletBinding()]
      param (
              [string] $path,   # Folder to be monitored
              [string] $file    # File name pattern to wait for.
          )

  $theFile = $path + $file

  #  $theFile variable will contain the path with file name of the file we are waiting for.
  While ($true) {
      Write-Verbose $theFile
      If (Test-Path $theFile) {
          #file exists. break loop
          break
      }
```

```
        #sleep for 2 seconds, then check again - change this to fit your needs...
        Start-Sleep -s 2
    }
    Write-Verbose 'File found.'
}
```

```
# Example call below...
Wait-UdfFileCreation ($env:HOMEDRIVE + $env:HOMEPATH + '\Documents\') 'filecheck.txt'
-Verbose
```

Let's review this function in detail. First, let's look at the function declaration:

```
function Wait-UdfFileCreation
{
  [CmdletBinding()]
        param (
                [string] $path,    # Folder to be monitored
                [string] $file     # File name pattern to wait for.
            )
```

Notice the CmdletBinding attribute, which adds a number of features including support for common parameters and parameter validation. It is good practice to use CmdletBinding in our functions. The function declaration declares the function Wait-UdfFileCreation and tells us :that it supports the string parameters $path and $file.

The line '$theFile = $path + $file' just concatenates the variables $path and $file and stores the result in $theFile.

The following code does the real work:

```
#  $theFile variable will contain the path with file name of the file we are waiting for.
While ($true)
{
        Write-Verbose $theFile
        IF (Test-Path $theFile)
        {
            #file exists. break loop
            break
        }
        #sleep for 2 seconds, then check again - change this to fit your needs...
        Start-Sleep -s 2
}
    Write-Verbose 'File found.'
}
```

The While loop will never end, because the comparison is the constant $true. We do this because we only want to exit when a file is found. The statement 'Write-Verbose $theFile' will write the variable $theFile to the console if the Verbose parameter was passed on the function call. This is great for testing, but when we move the code to production, we need to remove the Verbose parameter. SQL Agent will fail a PowerShell script that tries to write to the console. The line 'IF (Test-Path $theFile)' uses the cmdlet Test-Path to check whether a file matching the file name pattern exists in the folder. Test-Path returns $true if the file does exist and $false if it does not. Notice that since only true or false can be returned, we don't need to compare the return value to true or false—i.e., Test-Path –eq $true. This is because the IF test expression evaluates to a true or false value, so there's no need for extra verbiage. In other words, "if ($return -eq $true)" is the same as writing "if ($return)". If the Test-Path returns true, the break statement is executed, which exits the While loop, resulting in the 'Write-Verbose 'File found.' message being displayed. Otherwise, the 'Start-Sleep 2' statement executes, which just waits for two seconds and then returns to the start of the loop again.

The wait for file function is useful in many situations and is easy to implement. As a first step in a SQL Agent job, it's the ideal way to dynamically load files as they arrive. The job is suspended until a file arrives, and then it executes the steps to load the file. The SQL Agent scheduler will automatically restart the job based on whatever time frame you need. It may seem that having a job suspended while polling for a file will take up significant resources. However, in practice, I have found the overhead not to be an issue. The duration between each file existence check should be set to something reasonable, like ten minutes. I've used this approach successfully for a number of jobs. If you have many jobs that need to start when a file arrives, you might consider a different approach, such as using the FileSystemWatcher to trap the file-creation event. This approach is discussed in Chapter 13 as part of the discussion on :work flows.

Copy File

Once a file has arrived in the FTP folder, it's a good idea to copy it to a local server folder to be processed. We could just use the Copy-Item cmdlet, but having a function allows for extensibility and for trapping errors. Let's look at the code to copy files::

```
function Copy-UdfFile {
 [CmdletBinding(SupportsShouldProcess=$true)]
        param (
             [string]$sourcepathandfile,
             [string]$targetpathandfile,
             [switch]$overwrite
           )

  $ErrorActionPreference = "Stop"
  $VerbosePreference = "Continue"

  Write-Verbose "Source: $sourcepathandfile"
  Write-Verbose "Target: $targetpathandfile"

  try
  {
   If ($overwrite)    {
    Copy-Item -Path $sourcepathandfile -Destination $targetpathandfile -Force }
   else {
    Copy-Item - Path $$sourcepathandfile -Destination $targetpathandfile }
   }
  catch
  {
     "Error moving file."
  }
}
```

As we've already seen, we use CmdletBinding to define the function parameters. Then we set $ErrorActionPreference = "Stop", telling PowerShell to treat non-terminating errors as if they were terminating. This is so we can trap these errors. The line '$VerbosePreference = "Continue"' tells

PowerShell to display any Verbose messages output by the script providers or cmdlets and continue executing the script. The Write-Verbose message just displays the source and target file path. The real work happens in the Try/Catch block:

```
try
{
 If ($overwrite)   {
  Copy-Item -Path $$sourcepathandfile -Destination $targetpathandfile -Force }
 else {
  Copy-Item -Path $$sourcepathandfile -Destination $targetpathandfile }
 }
catch
{
   "Error moving file."
 }
}
```

The code ::between the try statement and the catch statement will be executed. We use the switch parameter $overwrite to determine if any existing file should be overwritten by the copy–i.e., if $overwrite is true, the file will be overwritten because the Force parameter is passed to the Copy-Item cmdlet. Otherwise, the file is copied without the Force parameter, which will trigger an error if a file already exists with the destination file name. When an error is raised, the code in the catch block will execute.

The copy file function is simple yet useful and extensible. Depending on our needs, we can extend this function to include logging, notifications, or to meet any other requirements that come up. Best of all, as a common function, we only need to maintain it in one place.

Unzip the File

Usually external files sent via FTP are compressed to save space and reduce network traffic. There are a number of compression formats available, but for demonstration purposes we will use the Zip format. The interesting thing about this function is that it uses the Windows Explorer API to do the work. The function uses a file-name mask to get the list of files to unzip rather than just supporting a single file.

The function that follows decompresses a file that is compressed into zip format:

```
function Expand-UdfFile
{
[CmdletBinding(SupportsShouldProcess=$true)]
        param (
            [string]$sourcefile,
            [string]$destinationpath,
            [switch]$force
        )

    $shell=new-object -com shell.application
    $zipfile = $shell.NameSpace($sourcefile)

    if ($force) {$zipparm = 0x14 }  else { $zipparm = $null }
```

```
foreach ($item in $zipfile.items())
{
    Try
    {
        $shell.NameSpace($destinationpath).CopyHere($item, $zipparm)
    }
    Catch {
            Write-Verbose "File exists already and was overwritten."
            }
    }
}
```

In this code, the CmdletBinding defines the function parameters, which are the $sourcefile (the path to the files to be unzipped), $destinationpath (the path and file name of the unzipped file), and the switch $force, which, if passed, tells the function to replace the file if it already exists. The next line is interesting:

```
$shell=new-object -com shell.application
```

Using the New-Object cmdlet, we are creating an interface to Windows Explorer using the Shell. Application object. This exposes the functionality of Windows Explorer to our script. It seems a bit odd that PowerShell is itself an interface to Windows, yet here we create a different interface to Windows. However, Windows Explorer exposes methods and properties not readily available in PowerShell.

The line that follows sets the source path and file name for the zipped file:

```
$zipfile = $shell.NameSpace($sourcefile)
```

The next line sets whether we want to overwrite the destination files if it already exists:

```
if ($force) {$zipparm = 0x14 }  else { $zipparm = $null }
```

In this line, we are testing the $force switch parameter and setting the value of $zipparm to hexadecimal value '0x14' if it is true and null if it is false, i.e., switch was not passed. This value is to be passed with the unzip operation to control how the command behaves. Note: This type of parameter defines a set of flags that are based on a bit value in a given position within a byte. See the link that follows for more information on all the possible values for this parameter:

```
http://msdn.microsoft.com/en-us/library/windows/desktop/bb787866(v=vs.85).aspx
```

The next block of code loops through each file in the compressed folder, unzipping each:

```
foreach ($item in $zipfile.items())
{
    Try
    {
        $shell.NameSpace($destinationpath).CopyHere($item, $zipparm)
    }
    Catch
    {
        Write-Verbose "File exists already and was overwritten."
    }
}
```

The object $zipfile.items() is a collection, and we iterate through each compressed file it contains using the foreach statement. Each file will be placed in the $item variable. The Try statement will use the $shell object to unzip the file by calling the CopyHere method and passing the file object to unzip and the optional parameter in $zipparm. The Catch statement will display "File exists already and was overwritten." if the destination file already exists.

The unzip function showed how we can easily decompress files using the Windows Explorer API. The function supports a file-name mask, so it does not matter how many files need to be unzipped.

If your installation uses Window Server Core, which is a subset of the full Windows installation, the function will not work. Instead, you can use a .NET class available as of .NET 4.5 that will extract files. The blog link here provides an explanation on how to do this:

https://vcsjones.com/2012/11/11/unzipping-files-with-powershell-in-server-core-the-new-way/

For information on what Windows Server Core is, see the link here:

https://msdn.microsoft.com/en-us/library/hh846323%28v=vs.85%29.aspx

Add the File Name to a Flat File

Typically, files are sent on a periodic basis and from different sources. If there is a problem with the data in one of the files, it can be difficult to track down which file contains the bad data. The function that follows adds the file name as a column to the CSV file so it can be loaded along with the other data into the target SQL Server table. This is particularly useful if the file names have identifying values, such as ABCCompany_Claims_20140101.csv. Knowing where bad data is coming from allows you to take action, such as requesting the source entity resend the file or correct bugs in their extract process.

The code here adds the file name as a column to the CSV file:

```
function Add-UdfColumnNameToFile
{
[CmdletBinding(SupportsShouldProcess=$true)]
        param (
             [string]$sourcepath,
             [string]$targetpath,
             [string]$filter
           )

    $filelist = Get-ChildItem -Path $sourcepath -include $filter

    foreach ($file in $filelist)
    {
      $csv = get-content $file

      $start = 0

      $file_wo_comma = $file.name.Replace(',','_')
      $file_wo_comma = $file_wo_comma.Replace(' ','')

      $targetpathandfile = $targetpath +  $file_wo_comma
```

```
    foreach ($line in $csv)
       {
       if ($start -eq 0)
          {
             $line += ",filename"
             $line > $targetpathandfile
          }
       else
          {
             $line +=",$file_wo_comma"
             $line >> $targetpathandfile
          }

       $start = 1

       }
    }
}
```

Let's look at the function header:

```
function Add-UdfColumnNameToFile
{
[CmdletBinding(SupportsShouldProcess=$true)]
     param (
          [string]$sourcepath,
          [string]$targetpath,
          [string]$filter
        )
```

The CmdletBinding shows three string parameters: $sourcepath is the folder path where the source file is located, $targetpath is the destination path where the new file (with file name column) will be written, and $filter is the file name filter to match on; i.e., any files matching the pattern will be processed.

We will need to get a list of files to process, which we do with the statement here:

```
$filelist = Get-ChildItem -Path $sourcepath -Include $filter
```

We will need to iterate over the files in the list returned, which we do by using a foreach loop, as shown here:

```
foreach ($file in $filelist)
{
  $csv = Get-Content $file
```

This statement will execute for each file in $filelist and place the current file reference into $file. Then, we load the current iteration's file into $csv using the Get-Content cmdlet.

Since this is a CSV file, the first row will be column headings. Therefore, we need to handle the first row differently than we do the other rows. For the first row, we want to add a column heading for the file name. To identify which iteration is the first, we set the variable $start = 0 before we enter the loop that processes the rows, as shown here:

```
$start = 0
```

Note: After the first row of the file has been processed, we will set $start = 1 to signal we are done processing the first row.

File names with commas or spaces in the name can cause problems, so we'll replace the comma with an underscore and remove spaces in the target file name with the statements seen here:

```
$file_wo_comma = $file.name.Replace(',','_')
$file_wo_comma = $file_wo_comma.Replace(' ','')
```

Now we can concatenate the target file path with the scrubbed file name, as shown:

```
$targetpathandfile = $targetpath + $file_wo_comma
```

Since we want to add a new column to each row in each file, we need to iterate over the rows, which we can do with the foreach statement:

```
foreach ($line in $csv)
    {
```

This statement will cause each row in the file to be placed into $line.

The block of code that follows does the actual work of adding the new column:

```
if ($start -eq 0)
    {
        $line += ",filename"
        $line > $targetpathandfile
    }
else
    {
        $line +=",$file_wo_comma"
        $line >> $targetpathandfile
    }
```

```
$start = 1
```

If $start = 0, we know this is the first iteration and therefore the first row in the file. Therefore, we want to add the column name filename, prefixed with a comma, to the output file. The variable $line is written to the output file using the > operator, which will cause any existing file with the same name to be overwritten. If the else code block executes, we know this is not the first line and that we want to append the file name value to the row. (Note: += means append what is to the right of the += to the variable on the left.) Then, the revised row in variable $line is appended to the target output file using the >> operator. Immediately after the If code block, $row is set to 1. Since this comes after the code block, the first iteration will have a value of 0, indicating the first line.

Adding the file name to the file and loading it into the target SQL Server table is very useful in tracking down data issues. It's primarily beneficial when files come frequently or from different sources. If the files do not have distinct file names, you may want to rename them before using this function. For example, you could append the current date and, if you can identify the source, perhaps prefix an identifier like ABCCompany. The renamed files should be archived to a folder where you can access them later if needed.

There are other ways to accomplish the same thing. In the actual situation where I used this function, I needed to add the file name to each flat file before merging them all into one file. The ETL tool being used did not support iteration over multiple files. A single, fixed file name had to be mapped in the ETL as the input source. Having the originating file name available in the SQL Server table was helpful for troubleshooting data issues.

Move the Files

Moving a file differs from copying one in that we do not leave the original file behind. This would typically be done as a means of archiving the file in case we need it later. It may not seem necessary to write a function to move a file when the cmdlet Move-Item can be called directly to do this. However, wrapping the Move-Item statement into a function allows the function to be extended to include additional functionality, such as logging and displaying informational messages. Also, I find it is easier to remember how to use my own function since it is customized to my task. Let's look at the following function:

```
function Move-UdfFile
{
[CmdletBinding(SupportsShouldProcess=$true)]
        param (
            [string]$sourcepathandfile,
            [string]$targetpathandfile,
            [switch]$overwrite
          )

        Write-Verbose 'Move file function...'

        try
        {
          If ($overwrite)
          {
           Move-Item -PATH $sourcepathandfile -DESTINATION $targetpathandfile -Force
          }
          else
          {
           Move-Item -PATH $sourcepathandfile -DESTINATION $targetpathandfile
          }
        }
        catch
        {
           "Error moving file."
           break
        }
}
```

We use CmdletBinding to define the function parameters: $sourcepathandfile to name the object we want to move, $targetpathandfile to define where we want the object moved to, and $overwrite, which is a switch that, if passed, will cause the function to overwrite the destination object if it already exists. The try statement executes the code between the braces that follow. If ($overwrite) will execute the code in the braces that follow only if the overwrite switch was passed. Otherwise, the code in the braces after the else statement is executed. If an error is raised, the code in the catch block is executed, i.e., the message "Error moving file". is displayed and the function is exited using the break statement.

The move file function copies the file to the destination and deletes it from the source, which is why it is ideal for archiving files.

Send Email

Many times an ETL process needs to notify users of events such as the loading of a file or failure of a process. PowerShell has the built-in cmdlet Send-MailMessage to support this. If you are sending email through a local email server behind a firewall, the call does not require authentication, but as a consultant I prefer the ability to develop and test without being logged in to a client's network. Therefore, I developed the function that follows to send email using a service provider like Google or Outlook. To do this, credentials—i.e., user ID and password—must be provided. Note: The mail will be sent using the same type of configuration information a smartphone would use. Let's look at the code:

```
function Send-UdfMail
{
[CmdletBinding(SupportsShouldProcess=$false)]
        param (
               [Parameter(Mandatory = $true, Position = 0)]
               [string]$smtpServer,
               [Parameter(Mandatory = $true, Position = 1)]
               [string]$from,
               [Parameter(Mandatory = $true, Position = 2)]
               [string]$to,
               [Parameter(Mandatory = $true, Position = 3)]
               [string]$subject,
               [Parameter(Mandatory = $true, Position = 4)]
               [string]$body,
               [Parameter(Mandatory = $true, Position = 5)]
               [string]$port,
               [Parameter(Mandatory = $false, Position = 6, ParameterSetName = "usecred")]
               [switch]$usecredential,
               [Parameter(Mandatory = $false, Position = 7, ParameterSetName = "usecred")]
               [string]$emailaccount,
               [Parameter(Mandatory = $false, Position = 8, ParameterSetName = "usecred")]
               [string]$password
               )

   if ($usecredential)
   {
     Write-Verbose "With Credential"
     $secpasswd = ConvertTo-SecureString "$password" -AsPlainText -Force
     $credential = New-Object System.Management.Automation.PSCredential
         ("$emailaccount", $secpasswd)

     Send-MailMessage -smtpServer $smtpServer -Credential $credential -from $from -to $to
     -subject $subject -Body $body -Usessl -Port $port
   }
   Else
   {
     Write-Verbose "Without Credential"
     Send-MailMessage -smtpServer $smtpServer -from $from -to $to -subject $subject -Body
     $body -Usessl -Port $port
   }
}
```

The CmdletBinding has some added parameters we have not seen yet. Let's review:

```
[CmdletBinding(SupportsShouldProcess=$false)]
      param (
          [Parameter(Mandatory = $true, Position = 0)]
          [string]$smtpServer,
          [Parameter(Mandatory = $true, Position = 1)]
          [string]$from,
          [Parameter(Mandatory = $true, Position = 2)]
          [string]$to,
          [Parameter(Mandatory = $true, Position = 3)]
          [string]$subject,
          [Parameter(Mandatory = $true, Position = 4)]
          [string]$body,
          [Parameter(Mandatory = $true, Position = 5)]
          [string]$port,
          [Parameter(Mandatory = $false, Position = 6,
           ParameterSetName = "usecred")]
          [switch]$usecredential,
          [Parameter(Mandatory = $false, Position = 7,
           ParameterSetName = "usecred")]
          [string]$emailaccount,
          [Parameter(Mandatory = $false, Position = 8,
           ParameterSetName = "usecred")]
          [string]$password
          )
```

The Mandatory parameter attribute defines whether the parameter must be provided or not. The Position parameter attribute identifies the sequence of the parameter if it is not passed by name. Normally, we can just let this default, but in this case we are using ParameterSetName, which lets us group parameters. The idea here is that if the switch usecredential is passed, the other parameters in the set usecred should also be provided. So, if we just want to send mail behind the firewall where credentials are not needed, we can just pass parameters 0 through 5. If we want to send email and use credentials, we would add the usecredential switch parameter to the call, along with the user ID and password. Parameter sets are often used to simulate polymorphism, also known as function overloading. The idea is that the function can be passed different types of parameters to cause different behavior. This was covered in detail in Chapter 5.

As shown next, we can see in the line if ($usecredential) { that if the switch –usecredential is passed, the code in the braces will be executed:

```
if ($usecredential)
{
  Write-Verbose "With Credential"
  $secpasswd = ConvertTo-SecureString "$password" -AsPlainText -Force
  $credential = New-Object System.Management.Automation.PSCredential
    ("$emailaccount", $secpasswd)

  Send-MailMessage -smtpServer $smtpServer -Credential $credential -from $from -to $to
  -subject $subject -Body $body -Usessl -Port $port
}
```

Write-Verbose just displays the message if the Verbose parameter is passed. It may be acceptable to have the password passed to the function, since that is behind the firewall, but when the function passes it to the outside it could be read; thus, we need to encrypt it with the ConvertTo-SecureString cmdlet. The line $secpasswd = ConvertTo-SecureString "$password" -AsPlainText –Force is encrypting the clear-text string $password and storing the result in $secpasswd. Then, we create a Credential object using New-Object. We pass the email account and encrypted password and store the object reference in $credential.

The format of a call to the Send-MailMessage cmdlet is shown here:

```
Send-MailMessage -smtpServer $smtpServer -Credential $credential -from $from -to
$to -subject $subject -Body $body -Usessl -Port $port
```

To use the function, we need to know the SMTP server name and port. I had to search around to find what the correct settings are for Outlook and Google. You can get the settings for Outlook at:

```
http://email.about.com/od/Outlook.com/f/What-Are-The-Outlook-com-Smtp-Server-Settings.htm
```

For Google, the settings can be found at:

```
http://email.about.com/od/accessinggmail/f/Gmail_SMTP_Settings.htm
```

We can call our send mail function using Outlook as shown here:

```
Send-UdfMail  -verbose "smtp.live.com" "myaccount@msn.com" "useremail@gmail.com" "Hellow"
"Email sent from PowerShell." "587" -usecredential " myaccount@msn.com " "mypassword"
```

And we can call our send mail function using Google as shown here:

```
Send-UdfMail  -verbose "smtp.gmail.com" "myaccount@gmail.com" "useremail@gmail.com" "Hello"
"Email sent from PowerShell." "587" -usecredential " myaccount@gmail.com " "mypassword"
```

The email user name for the credential is just your email address for that service, and the password is the password you would use to log into your mail. We can send the email anywhere we want. The example sends the mail to a Google account. Note: I found that for both Outlook and Google you must specify the port, which is 587 for both services.

If the switch parameter usecredential is not passed to the function, the code shown here will execute:

```
Else
{
  Write-Verbose "Without Credential"
  Send-MailMessage -smtpServer $smtpServer -from $from -to $to -subject $subject -Body
  $body -Usessl -Port $port
```

Note: The only difference between when usecredential is passed versus not passed is that when it is not passed, no credential is passed to the Send-MailMessage cmdlet. If you specify the usecredential parameter, you must also pass the email account and password. If you do not pass usecredential, do not pass email account and password. Also, when credentials are not used, I found it was necessary to specify the Usessl parameter.

Many situations require sending email notifications. The send mail function wraps the Send-MailMessage cmdlet up to make it is easier to use and supports two variations. It can be called without supplying credentials, which is often done behind an internal network, or with credentials, which allows us to use public services like Outlook or Google.

Load the Files

The scenario is this example assumes CSV files containing sales data will be arriving in an FTP folder, and that we need to load these files into a SQL Server table. The file-naming format of the external files is sales_COMPANYNAME_YYYYMMDD.csv, where COMPANYNAME is the company sending the data and YYYYMMDD is the date as year, month, and day.

The SQL Server table we will load is on a database named Development. Change this to whatever database you want to run this example on. You can create the table with the statement here:

```
CREATE TABLE [dbo].[sales](
        [SalesPersonID] [int] NOT NULL,
        [FirstName] [varchar](50) NOT NULL,
        [LastName] [varchar](50) NOT NULL,
        [TotalSales] [decimal](32, 2) NULL,
        [AsOfDate] [date] NOT NULL,
        [SentDate] [date] NULL
) ON [PRIMARY]
SET ANSI_PADDING ON
ALTER TABLE [dbo].[sales] ADD [FileName] [varchar](150) NULL
PRIMARY KEY CLUSTERED
(
        [SalesPersonID] ASC
)
```

We could use SSIS to load the files, but I think it is better to keep this all in PowerShell since our goal is to learn about PowerShell. In Chapter 11, we will discuss using PowerShell for ETL, so this will provide an introduction to that topic. The following function loads the files into a SQL Server table:

```
function Invoke-UdfSalesTableLoad
{
 [CmdletBinding()]
        param (
                [string] $path,    # Folder to be monitored
                [string] $filepattern    # File name pattern to wait for.
            )

$conn = new-object System.Data.SqlClient.SqlConnection("Data Source=(local);Integrated
Security=SSPI;Initial Catalog=Development");
$conn.Open()

$command = $conn.CreateCommand()

# Clear out the table first...
$command.CommandText = "truncate table dbo.sales;"
$command.ExecuteNonQuery()
write-verbose $path
write-verbose $filepattern

$loadfilelist = Get-ChildItem $path $filepattern

write-verbose $loadfilelist
```

255

```
foreach ($loadfile in $loadfilelist)
{

    $indata = Import-Csv $loadfile.FullName
    $indata

    foreach ($row in $indata)
    {

    $rowdata = $row.SalesPersonID + ", '" + $row.FirstName + "', '" + $row.LastName + "',
    " + $row.TotalSales + ", '" + $row.AsOfDate + "', '" + $row.SentDate + "', '" + $row.
    filename + "'"

    Write-Verbose $rowdata

    $command.CommandText = "INSERT into dbo.sales VALUES ( " + $rowdata + ");"
    $command.ExecuteNonQuery()
    }

}

$conn.Close()

}
```

The CmdletBinding shows two supported parameters: $path, which is the path to the source files to be loaded, and $filepattern, which is the file-name mask of what files to load—i.e., sales*.csv, or all files that start with sales and end with .csv. Let's take a look:

```
function Invoke-UdfSalesTableLoad
{
 [CmdletBinding()]
       param (
              [string] $path,    # Folder to be monitored
              [string] $filepattern    # File name pattern to wait for.
           )
```

We're going to use the SQL Server .NET objects to load the data, as shown here:

```
$conn = new-object System.Data.SqlClient.SqlConnection("Data Source=(local);Integrated
Security=SSPI;Initial Catalog=Development");
$conn.Open()
```

In this code, we create a SQL connection object using System.Data.SqlClient.SqlConnection and storing the reference in $conn. Then, we open the connection using the $conn Open method, i.e., $conn.Open().

Using the connection object, we can execute SQL commands. To make this rerunnable, we need to truncate the target table. This would be a common practice if we were loading to a staging table. Let's look at the code to do this:

```
$command = $conn.CreateCommand()

#  Clear out the table first...
$command.CommandText = "truncate table dbo.sales;"
$command.ExecuteNonQuery()
```

First, we use the connection object's :CreateCommand method to create a Command subobject. Then, we can assign a SQL statement to execute, i.e., $command.CommandText = "truncate table dbo. sales;". Finally, we use the ExecuteNonQuery method to execute the truncated table statement. Note: ExecuteNonQuery is used because the query does not return data.

We need to get a list of the files to load, which we do with the following statement:

```
$loadfilelist = Get-ChildItem $path $filepattern
```

The heart of the load cannot easily be broken into pieces, so let's look at the whole thing:

```
foreach ($loadfile in $loadfilelist)
{

    $indata = Import-Csv $loadfile.FullName
    Write-Verbose $indata

    foreach ($row in $indata)
    {

    $rowdata =  $row.SalesPersonID + ", '" + $row.FirstName + "', '" + $row.LastName + "',
    " + $row.TotalSales + ", '" + $row.AsOfDate + "', '" + $row.SentDate + "', '" + $row.
    filename + "'"

    Write-Verbose $rowdata

    $command.CommandText = "INSERT into dbo.sales VALUES ( " + $rowdata + ");"
    $command.ExecuteNonQuery()
    }

}
```

The first statement, foreach, creates an outer loop that will cycle through all the files in $loadfilelist. The variable $loadfile will contain each individual file. We use Import-CSV to load $loadfile.FullName into $indata. Note: The property FullName is the fully qualified path and file name.

Now that we have each file, we loop through every row in the file with the inner foreach loop, i.e., foreach ($row in $indata). To load the data, we need to format it into an Insert statement. To prepare for this we need to string all the column values together and include quotes and commas as needed. We do this with the following statement:

```
$rowdata =  $row.SalesPersonID + ", '" + $row.FirstName + "', '" + $row.LastName + "', " +
$row.TotalSales + ", '" + $row.AsOfDate + "', '" + $row.SentDate + "', '" + $row.filename +
"'".
```

Note We need to add single quotes around string and date columns.

Then, we assign the CommandText as a prefix of INSERT into dbo.sales VALUES followed by the variable $rowdata we created earlier. Then, we just execute the command object's ExecuteNonQuery method, and the row is inserted.

Finally, we close the connection, as show here:

```
$conn.Close()
```

The load file function demonstrates that PowerShell can be used as an ETL tool, but we could also call an SSIS package to load the data. We could have used the SQLPS module to help load the data, but using the SQLClient library directly demonstrates how easy it is to access SQL Server directly. Now, let's discuss how to use the functions we just discussed in an ETL process.

Let's Process Some Files

Now that we've reviewed the individual functions we plan to use in our ETL process, let's see how it all comes together. We want to perform all the steps, from receiving new files from an external source to loading the files into SQL Server tables. The steps to process these files are as follows:

- File is transferred from external source to your company.
- A polling process identifies that a new file has arrived and starts the load process.
- Send an email notification that the load job has started.
- Copy the files to a local drive on the server.
- Unzip the files to an unzipped folder.
- Add the file name as a new column to the file.
- Load the file into SQL Server.
- Archive the original file to an archive folder.
- Send an email notification that the load job has ended.

To make using the script easier to follow, I packaged up the functions we will need into a module named umd_etl_functions. Copy this to a folder where Windows looks for modules, such as \Windows\ PowerShell in your Documents folder. Create a folder named umd_etl_functions and copy the module from the code disk to this folder. Normally, I would probably not include the actual load script in a module since it is not generic, but doing so here makes it easier to run the example.

Now, let's take a look at the ETL load script in Listing 9-1.

Listing 9-1. ETL load script

```
Import-Module umd_etl_functions -Force
Clear-Host  # So we can see the messages easily.

$rootfolder = $env:HOMEDRIVE + $env:HOMEPATH + "\Documents"
$ftppath = $rootfolder + "\FTP\sales_*.zip"
$inbound =  $rootfolder + "\Inbound\"
$zippath = $inbound + "\sales_*.zip"
```

```
$unzippedpath = $rootfolder + "\unzipped\"
$processpath = $rootfolder + "\Process\"
$archivepath = $rootfolder + "\Archive\"

# Wait for the files...
Wait-UdfFileCreation $ftppath  -Verbose

# Notify users the job has started using Outlook...
Send-UdfMail  "smtp.live.com" "emailaddress@msn.com" "emailaddress@msn.com" "ETL Job: Sales
Load has Started" "The ETL Job: Sales Load has started." "587" -usecredential "emailaddress@
msn.com" "password"

# Copy the files...
Copy-UdfFile $ftppath $inbound -overwrite

$filelist = Get-ChildItem $zippath

#  Unzip the files...
Foreach ($file in $filelist)
{
    Expand-UdfFile $file.FullName $unzippedpath -force
}

# Add file name to file...
Add-UdfColumnNameToFile $unzippedpath  $processpath "sales*.csv" -Verbose

# Load the files...
Invoke-UdfSalesTableLoad $processpath "sales*.csv" -Verbose

# Archive files...
Move-UdfFile $ftppath $archivepath  -overwrite

# Notify users the job has finished...
Send-UdfMail  "smtp.live.com" "emailaddress@msn.com" "emailaddress@msn.com" "ETL Job:
Sales Load has ended" "The ETL Job: Sales Load has ended." "587" -usecredential
"emailaddress@msn.com" "password"
```

The nice thing about using functions is that we can create a high-level script like the one here that is easy to understand. If there is a problem, we can focus on the specific function where the error is occurring. Let's take a closer look at the script:

```
Import-Module umd_etl_functions
```

This line just imports our module, making all its functions available to us.

Then, we create some variables to help us with the function parameters we'll need, as shown here:

```
$rootfolder = $env:HOMEDRIVE + $env:HOMEPATH + "\Documents"
$ftppath = $rootfolder + "\FTP\sales_*.zip"
$inbound =  $rootfolder + "\Inbound\"
$zippath = $inbound + "\sales_*.zip"
$unzippedpath = $rootfolder + "\unzipped\"
$processpath = $rootfolder + "\Process\"
$archivepath = $rootfolder + "\Archive\"
```

To make this easier to set up, we use subfolders of your Documents folder. I like to keep folders separate when I process external files. The subfolders we will use are:

FTP = The initial folder from which the files arrive.

Inbound = The local server folder to which files from the FTP folder are copied for processing.

Unzipped = The folder to which the compressed files are expanded.

Process = The folder to which modified versions of the files are written; i.e., when we add the file name as a new column, we write the file out as a new version to \Process.

Archive = Folder to which the original files are moved and then retained.

Now, let's look at the code that polls for new files:

```
# Wait for the files...
Wait-UdfFileCreation $ftppath  -Verbose
```

We're calling the Wait-UdfFileCreation function, passing the full folder path and file-name pattern to watch for. The Verbose parameter causes the function to display any Write-Verbose statements in the function. The messages just display the file name being checked for on each iteration of the loop. Once a file matching the requested pattern is found, the function simply exits, allowing the rest of the load process to take place. To test this, run the script. It will wait for the file. Copy the zipped file sales_abccompany_20141101 to the FTP subfolder. That will trigger the script to run.

When a job starts, it's good practice to send a notification to interested parties, which the statement here does:

```
# Notify users the job has started using Outlook...
Send-UdfMail  "smtp.live.com" "emailaddress@msn.com" "emailaddress@msn.com" "ETL Job:
Sales Load has Started" "The ETL Job: Sales Load has started." "587" -usecredential
"emailaddress@msn.com" "password"
```

You will need to replace the credentials with the desired email address and password for your use. If you do not require authentication, just remove the switch –usecredential and the parameters after it.

The next statement just copies the file from the FTP folder to the local folder:

```
# Copy the files...
Copy-UdfFile $ftppath $inbound -overwrite
```

For demonstration purposes, all the folders are local. In practice, you'll want to change this to the FTP folder in your organization. The file is compressed, so we need to unzip it, which we do with these statements:

```
$filelist = Get-ChildItem $zippath

#  Unzip the files...
Foreach ($file in $filelist)
{
    Expand-UdfFile $file.FullName $unzippedpath -force
}
```

The first line just stores the list of zip files we need to unzip in the variable $filelist. Then, we loop through these files using the Foreach statement. Each file item is stored in $file. We pass the FullName property to the Expand-UdfFile, followed by the path at which to store the unzipped files. We also pass the Force switch, which causes any existing files of the same name to be overwritten. As mentioned previously, having the name of the file from which each row came is useful for tracking down problems.

We call the function that follows to add the file name as a column to each file:

```
# Add file name to file...
Add-UdfColumnNameToFile $unzippedpath  $processpath "sales*.csv" -Verbose
```

The input files are in the folder specified by $unzippedpath. A new file, with the file-name column included, is written out to the folder specified by $processpath.

Then, we load the files with the statement here:

```
# Load the files...
Invoke-UdfSalesTableLoad $processpath "sales*.csv" –Verbose
```

The variable $processpath is the folder holding the files to be loaded. sales*.csv is the file-name pattern to load—i.e., any file that starts with sales and ends with .csv. Finally, we can archive the files with the following statement:

```
# Archive files...
Move-UdfFile $ftppath $archivepath  -overwrite
```

We are moving the files in folder $ftppath to the folder specified in $archivepath, and overwriting any files that are already there.

Now we can send an email notifying users the job has finished, as shown here:

```
# Notify users the job has finished...
Send-UdfMail  "smtp.live.com" "emailaddress@msn.com" "emailaddress@msn.com" "ETL Job:
Sales Load has ended" "The ETL Job: Sales Load has ended." "587" -usecredential
"emailaddress@msn.com" "password"
```

Using functions has enabled us to create a job flow that is easy to read and maintain. If you need to do more work, we can just add in more functions. If files will be coming from multiple sources but follow the same pattern, we can make the job script a function so it can be reused for different sources. The purpose of this script is to demonstrate how effectively PowerShell scripts can orchestrate your ETL processes.

More Useful ETL Functions

Sometimes you will need additional functions to get the job done. For example, we often need to validate the data coming in before loading it. Maybe we need to merge multiple files together. Perhaps the files coming in have no column headings, so we need to add them. We may want to make the send email function more secure by encrypting the password to a file where it can be read by the function. In this section, we will review how to accomplish these tasks.

Data Validation

PowerShell provides many ways to validate our data. Since data validation is a common ETL requirement, let's look at the following function, that provides a set of standard column validations:

```
function Invoke-UdfColumnValidation
{
 [CmdletBinding()]
      param (
              [string] $column,       # value to be checked.
              [ValidateSet("minlength","maxlength","zipcode", "phonenumber", "emailaddress",
                        "ssn", "minintvalue", "maxintvalue")]
```

```
                [string] $validation,
                [parameter(Mandatory=$false)]
                [string] $validationvalue
        )

    [boolean] $result = $false;

    Switch ($validation)
    {

        "minlength"     { $result = ($column.Length -ge [int] $validationvalue); break  }
        "maxlength"     { $result = ($column.Length -le [int] $validationvalue); break  }
        "zipcode"       { $result = $column -match ("^\d{5}(-\d{4})?$")           ; break }
        "phonenumber"   { $result = $column -match ("\d{3}-\d{3}-\d{4}")          ; break }
        "emailaddress" { $result = $column -match
            ("^[_a-z0-9-]+(\.[_a-z0-9-]+)*@[a-z0-9-]+(\.[a-z0-9-]+)*(\.[a-z]{2,4})$"); break }
        "ssn"           { $result = $column -match ("^\d{3}-?\d{2}-?\d{4}$")      ; break }
        "minintvalue"   { $result = ([int]$column -ge [int] $validationvalue); break }
        "maxintvalue"   { $result = ([int]$column -le [int] $validationvalue); break }

    }

    Write-verbose "$column $validation $validationvalue"

    Return $result

}
```

Let's look closely at the function's CmdletBinding:

```
function Invoke-UdfColumnValidation  :
{
 [CmdletBinding()]
        param (
                [string] $column,        # value to be checked.
                [ValidateSet("minlength","maxlength","zipcode", "phonenumber", "emailaddress",
                 "ssn", "minintvalue", "maxintvalue")]
                [string] $validation,    # File name pattern to wait for.
                [parameter(Mandatory=$false)]
                [string] $validationvalue
        )
```

We can see that this function supports parameters $column, $validation, and $validationvalue. Parameter $column is the value you want to validate. This is always passed as a string, so if the value is not a string, cast it to a string before passing it into the function. Note: You can cast a value by placing the desired data type before it; i.e., [string] myintegervariable. Parameter $validation is the type of :validation we want performed. Notice we use the ValidateSet binding attribute, which will restrict the values allowed into the function to the list of values in the parentheses. This list of values will be displayed by Intellisense when you specify the Validation parameter, as shown in Figure 9-2.

```
Invoke-UdfColumnValidation "test" -validation
```

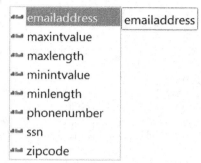

Figure 9-2. Intellisense showing the list of valid values for a function parameter

The parameter $validationvalue: is optional (the Mandatory attribute is $false) and should only be passed by a validation that requires a comparison value, such as minlength. Format validations like phonenumber do not require a comparison value.

The function tells us whether the value passes the test (true) or fails (false)—it will return true or false when called. The line that follows creates the variable to hold the result and initializes it to false:

```
[boolean] $result = $false;
```

The function evaluates what validation is requested by checking the $validation parameter. The Switch statement provides an elegant way to do this, as shown here:

```
Switch ($validation)
{

    "minlength"     { $result = ($column.Length -ge [int] $validationvalue); break   }
    "maxlength"     { $result = ($column.Length -le [int] $validationvalue); break   }
    "zipcode"       { $result = $column -match ("^\d{5}(-\d{4})?$")         ; break }
    "phonenumber"   { $result = $column -match ("\d{3}-\d{3}-\d{4}")        ; break }
    "emailaddress"  { $result = $column -match
    ("^[_a-z0-9-]+(\.[_a-z0-9-]+)*@[a-z0-9-]+(\.[a-z0-9-]+)*(\.[a-z]{2,4})$");
                              break }
    "ssn"           { $result = $column -match ("^\d{3}-?\d{2}-?\d{4}$")      ; break }
    "minintvalue"   { $result = ([int]$column -ge [int] $validationvalue); break }
    "maxintvalue"   { $result = ([int]$column -le [int] $validationvalue); break }

}
```

The Switch statement is followed by an expression to be evaluated. Each possible value is listed, with related code in braces after the value. The comparison expression will return true or false, which gets stored in $result. Notice the break statement after each code block. We need this because without it the Switch statement will continue to be evaluated. Notice how we can use the properties of the $column parameter to do some tests, like checking the length. For the pattern matching, we are using regular expressions. Building regular expressions can be difficult, but there is a lot of help on the Internet. I found this site to be particularly rich with examples:

```
http://www.regexlib.com/
```

Finally, we return the result to the client, as shown here:

```
Return $result
```

Some example calls for these validations are provided here:

```
# Min/Max tests...
Invoke-UdfColumnValidation "test" -validation "minlength" -validationvalue "2"
Invoke-UdfColumnValidation "test" -validation "maxlength" -validationvalue "2"
Invoke-UdfColumnValidation "1" -validation "minintvalue" -validationvalue "2"
Invoke-UdfColumnValidation "1" -validation "maxintvalue" -validationvalue "2"

# Phone Number format...
Invoke-UdfColumnValidation "123" -validation "phonenumber"
Invoke-UdfColumnValidation "999-999-9999" -validation "phonenumber" -Verbose

# Zip Code format...
Invoke-UdfColumnValidation "02886" -validation "zipcode" -Verbose
Invoke-UdfColumnValidation "02886-1234" -validation "zipcode" -Verbose

# Social Security Number format...
Invoke-UdfColumnValidation "999-99-9999" -validation "ssn" -Verbose
Invoke-UdfColumnValidation "12345" -validation "ssn" -Verbose

# Email Address format—does not validate domain...
Invoke-UdfColumnValidation "022886-1234" -validation "emailaddress" -Verbose
Invoke-UdfColumnValidation "test@msn.com" -validation "emailaddress" -Verbose
Invoke-UdfColumnValidation "test@yahoo.org" -validation "emailaddress" -Verbose
```

Code that uses the validation function might look like this:

```
If (Invoke-UdfColumnValidation "test@yahoo.org" -validation "emailaddress" -Verbose)
{
  "Load the value."
}
Else
{
  "Reject the value."
}
```

This displays the following:

```
VERBOSE: test@yahoo.org emailaddress
Load the value
```

This function provides a starting point and can be extended to include whatever validations we need. We can be creative and add look-ups to find SQL Server tables, calculations, date dimensions, and so on. We can see that PowerShell has a lot of built-in support for validating data, thus allowing us to accomplish a lot with very little code. What we do when data fails validation depends on the requirements. We could filter the row out and write it to an error log, or we could try to fix the value automatically. The real value comes in when we combine this with other functions.

Combine Files

Sometimes it is useful to combine multiple files of the same format into one file. This could be to simplify the load or to consolidate a set of output files. The situation in which I developed this function was that the ETL tool did not support iterating over multiple files in a load. In fact, it required a fixed file name. The function that follows consolidates files into a folder that matches a given file-name pattern:

```
function Add-UdfFile {
[CmdletBinding()]
        param (
                [string] $source,
                [string] $destination,
                [string] $filter
            )

$filelist = Get-ChildItem -Path $source  $filter

write-verbose $source

write-verbose "$filelist"

try
{
 Remove-Item $destination -ErrorAction SilentlyContinue
 write-host "Deleted $destination ."
 }
catch
 {
    "Error:  Problem deleting old file."
 }

# Add-Content $destination "Column1`r`n"

  foreach ($file in $filelist)
  {
   write-verbose $file.FullName

  $fc = Get-Content $file.FullName

  Add-Content $destination $fc
  }
}
```

Let's take a closer look at the function parameters:

```
function Add-UdfFile {
[CmdletBinding()]
        param (
                [string] $source,
                [string] $destination,
                [string] $filter
            )
```

The parameters are $source, which is the source folder path; $destination, which is the path with the file name of the combined file to be written out; and $filter, which is the file-name pattern, such as *.txt.

An example of calling this function is seen here:

```
Add-UdfFile 'C:\Users\Documents\' 'C:\Users\ Documents\combined.txt' 'o*.txt' -Verbose
```

The first thing the function needs to do is get a list of the files that need to be combined, which it does as follows:

```
$filelist = Get-ChildItem -Path $source  $filter
```

Then, we need to delete the destination file if it already exists, which we do with the following Try/Catch block:

```
try
{
 Remove-Item $destination -ErrorAction SilentlyContinue
 write-host "Deleted $destination ."
 }
catch
 {
   "Error:  Problem deleting old file."
 }
```

Notice that the Remove-Item statement includes the ErrorAction SilientlyContinue parameter. This is so the code will not fail if the file does not exist. If there is a problem deleting the file, the catch block will display an error message.

Now, we need to loop through the file list to merge the files, as shown here:

```
foreach ($file in $filelist)
{
  Write-Verbose $file.FullName

  $fc = Get-Content $file.FullName

  Add-Content $destination $fc
}
```

The foreach statement will loop through each file in $filelist and store the item in $file. Get-Content is used to load the file contents using the $file.FullName (the path and file name). The Add-Content cmdlet is used to append the file contents in $fc to the destination file.

Combining files is not a common requirement when your ETL tool is SSIS. When I developed this function, I was using a different ETL tool that required it. This function could also be used to combine multiple output files to be used by an external user.

Add Column Headings

There may be times when the files you are sent do not have column headings, but you know what should be in each column. The function that follows adds column headings to a CSV file. The column headings are a single line at the top of the file, with column names separated by commas. See the code here:

```
function Add-UdfFileColumnHeading {
[CmdletBinding()]
        param (
                [string] $sourcefile,
                [string] $destinationfile,
                [string] $headingline
            )

if (Test-Path  $destinationfile)
{
    Remove-Item $destinationfile -Force
    write-verbose "Deleted $destinationfile ."
}

Add-Content $destinationfile "$headingline"

$fc = Get-Content  $sourcefile

Add-Content $destinationfile $fc
}
```

We can see that the CmdletBinding supports the parameters of $sourcefile, which is the path and file name of the input file; $destination, which is the path and file to the output file; and $headingline, which is the exact line you want inserted at the top of the file to serve as column headings—you need to include comma separators. If the output file already exists, we need to delete it, which we do with the code here:

```
if (Test-Path  $destinationfile)
{
    Remove-Item $destinationfile –Force
    Write-Verbose "Deleted $destinationfile ."
}
```

The Test-Path cmdlet, as we have seen, returns true if the path exists and false if it does not. So, the previous code will delete the destination file name if it already exists.

Next, we write the heading line to the output file name with this line:

```
Add-Content $destinationfile "$headingline"
```

Add-Content adds the second parameter, i.e., $headingline, to the first parameter, which is the destination file name. Now, we need to append the source file to the destination file, as follows:

```
$fc = Get-Content  $sourcefile

Add-Content $destinationfile $fc
```

In this code, first we load the source file into $fc using the Get-Content cmdlet. Then, we use Add-Content to append $fc to the destination file.

The function can be called as follows:

```
Add-UdfFileColumnHeading 'C:\Documents\outfile1.txt' 'C:\Documents\filewithheadings.txt' `
"firstname,lastname,street,city,state,zip" -Verbose
```

Sometimes files need to be loaded that do not have column headings. You can load them this way, but it is a lot easier to work with files that have column headings, especially when you want to use PowerShell's Import-CSV cmdlet. The function in this example is simple yet effectively adds column headings to a file and, best of all, can be used for any CSV file.

Securing Credentials

Some operations require secure information, like passwords. For example, in the send email function we used in the ETL job, the password was clear text which means anyone can see it. If you send clear text over the Internet, anyone can read it. It's not a good idea to have things like passwords available for anyone to read. A better idea is to encrypt the password and store it in a file so it can be safely used.

Before we look at the encryption function, we need to review a helper function that we will use to prompt the user for the destination file location and name. We're going to leverage the built-in Windows Save File Common Dialog for this purpose.

Let's review the code:

```
function Invoke-UdfCommonDialogSaveFile($initialDirectory)
{
 [System.Reflection.Assembly]::LoadWithPartialName("System.windows.forms") |
 Out-Null

 $OpenFileDialog = New-Object System.Windows.Forms.SaveFileDialog
 $OpenFileDialog.initialDirectory = $initialDirectory
 $OpenFileDialog.filter = "All files (*.*)| *.*"
 $OpenFileDialog.ShowDialog() | Out-Null
 $OpenFileDialog.filename
}
```

This function is just a helper function. It will invoke the Windows Save File common dialog so the user can use a GUI to specify the path and file name of the encrypted password file. The first line defines a reference to the Windows forms object library. Once that is done, we can use the statement copied next to create a new Windows Save File dialog object instance:

```
$OpenFileDialog = New-Object System.Windows.Forms.SaveFileDialog
```

Now that we have the Save File dialog reference, we can set the configuration properties for it, such as the initial directory and default file-name pattern, with the lines seen here:

```
$OpenFileDialog.initialDirectory = $initialDirectory
$OpenFileDialog.filter = "All files (*.*)| *.*"
```

Then, all we have to do to open the dialog box is execute the ShowDialog method, as follows:

```
$OpenFileDialog.ShowDialog() | Out-Null
```

In this code, we are piping the output of the ShowDialog method to Out-Null so as to suppress getting back any output from the command. The SaveFileDialog sets the object's filename property to the name of the file selected or entered by the user, so we want to return that to the caller with the line seen here:

```
$OpenFileDialog.filename
```

Now that we have the helper function defined, we can code a function to get and encrypt the password. Review the code that follows, which does this. Note: This function is in the module umd_database. See here:

```
function Save-UdfEncryptedCredential
{
[CmdletBinding()] param ()

  $pw = read-host -Prompt "Enter the password:" -assecurestring

  $pw | convertfrom-securestring |
  out-file (Invoke-UdfCommonDialogSaveFile  ($env:HOMEDRIVE + $env:HOMEPATH + "\Documents\"
) )
}
```

The function Save-UdfEncryptedCredential is very short yet does a lot of work. Notice this function does not take any parameters. When we call it, we are prompted to enter a password by the Read-Host cmdlet, which is masked and encrypted by the AsSecurestring parameter and returned to the variable $pw. The variable $pw is piped into ConvertFrom-SecureString, which converts the data into a string and pipes it into the Out-File cmdlet, which writes it to a file. Let's look more closely at the Out-File statement:

```
out-file (Invoke-UdfCommonDialogSaveFile  (($env:HOMEDRIVE + $env:HOMEPATH + "\Documents\" ) )
```

As in math, the parentheses control the order of execution. The code in the innermost parentheses, which defines the file default path, is executed before the code in the outer parentheses, which prompts us for a file path and name using the Windows Save File common dialog. The result of the Save File dialog is passed to the Out-File cmdlet, i.e., that is where the encrypted file is written.

There are times when we need to use a password to get a task done. It might be the password to connect to SQL Server or to log on to an account. It not a good practice to have passwords in clear text in a script for people to see. Instead, we can use the Save-UdfEncryptedCredential to encrypt the password and store it in a file. From there, it can be read securely and used by any code that needs it.

Send Secure Email

So, we have the password encrypted in a file. How do we use it? The Send Email function we saw earlier had a significant issue. The calling script had to pass the parameter password in clear text. Let's revisit the Send Mail function, which is enhanced to use an encrypted password file:

```
function Send-UdfSecureMail
{
[CmdletBinding(SupportsShouldProcess=$false)]
        param (
             [Parameter(Mandatory = $true)]
             [string]$smtpServer,
             [Parameter(Mandatory = $true)]
             [string]$from,
```

```
        [Parameter(Mandatory = $true)]
        [string]$to,
        [Parameter(Mandatory = $true)]
        [string]$subject,
        [Parameter(Mandatory = $true)]
        [string]$body,
        [Parameter(Mandatory = $true)]
        [string]$port,
        [Parameter(Mandatory = $true)]
        [string]$emailaccount,
        [Parameter(Mandatory = $true)]
        [string]$credentialfilepath
        )

    $credin = Get-Content $credentialfilepath | convertto-securestring

    write-verbose $credentialfilepath

    $credential = New-Object System.Management.Automation.PSCredential ("$emailaccount",  $credin)

    Send-MailMessage -smtpServer $smtpServer -Credential $credential -from $from -to $to
    -subject $subject -Body $body -Usessl -Port $port
}
```

Our new function, Send-UdfSecureMail, has a few differences from Send-UdfMail. From a parameters standpoint, the big change is that now instead of taking a password parameter, the function accepts a credential path ($credentialfilepath) parameter, which is the path and file of the credential file we created earlier. The line here loads the credential file:

```
$credin = Get-Content $credentialfilepath | convertto-securestring
```

Get-Content loads the file, which is piped into the ConvertTo-SecureString cmdlet to be encrypted. Note: Technically the file was not encrypted. Rather, the encrypted password was converted to an unintelligible string that could be written to a file. ConvertTo-SecureString encrypts it again so we can use it securely. The encrypted password is stored in $credin.

The line that follows is an example of how to call the secure email function:

```
Send-UdfSecureMail  -verbose "smtp.live.com" "fromemail" "toemail" "Yo!" "Email sent from
PowerShell." "587" "emailaccount" "c:\somedir\mycredential.txt"
```

The secure send email function is a big improvement over the version with a clear-text password parameter. The secure version reads the password from an encrypted file, thus allowing it to send email without exposing the password to anyone who reads the code. The method used here is very basic. You can pass the SecureKey parameter to the ConvertTo-SecureString cmdlet when you call it in order to provide a key to decode the string. If you require tighter security, you might want to look at third-party encryption tools.

Summary

This chapter focused on how to use PowerShell to augment your ETL development. We began by considering steps common to many ETL processes. We discussed functions to perform these tasks that you can incorporate into your ETL work. These functions include things such as polling a folder for the arrival of new files matching a file-name pattern, copying files, decompressing files, adding the file name as a column to the files, loading the file into SQL Server, and sending email notifications. This culminated in a complete ETL script that used these functions to process a flat file load from start to finish. Then, we discussed additional functions that are useful in ETL development—data validation, file merging, the addition of column headings, the encryption of credentials, and a secure-send email function. All these functions are provided in a module that can be used in your ETL development.

Summary

CHAPTER 10

■ ■ ■

Configurations, Best Practices, and Application Deployment

In this chapter, we are going to discuss several related topics: configuring PowerShell applications, development best practices, and application deployment. First, we will discuss how to configure PowerShell applications to so as maximize flexibility and ease of maintenance. A nice feature of SQL Server Integration Services (SSIS) is that it has a number of configuration methods. In this chapter, we will discuss how to achieve comparable functionality in PowerShell using several approaches. Then, we will discuss the goals of best practices and how to apply them to PowerShell. Finally, we will consider deploying PowerShell applications and ways to simplify this process.

Configuring PowerShell Applications

How we design a configuration depends on the technical environment we are working in. For example, at one company where I worked there were many development, integration, and QA environments for the same application. Each pointed to different database servers, but ultimately each was to deploy to the same production environment. The development and integration environments were split out by geographic region, while the QA environments were for different releases. New environments were created routinely, and others were removed. In this situation, a sophisticated configuration design was required. At a much smaller company, the data warehouse environments consisted of a development server and a production server. The configuration approach used was a simple one that employed environment variables. Let's consider several approaches to configuring PowerShell applications, each designed to support a different level of complexity. Note: You will need to start PowerShell as Administrator to run many of the scripts in this chapter.

Using Environment Variables

Windows environment variables are used by Windows itself and by many applications to store configuration settings. There are three environment variable levels, which are *machine*, *user*, and *process*. A level refers to who or what processes can access the variable and how long the variable persists on the machine. Machine- and user-level variables persist after the PowerShell session ends. In fact, they are stored in the Windows Registry and will be reloaded after a system reboot. Machine-level variables are visible to all users and all processes on the machine. User-level variables are visible only to the user that created the variable. Process-level variables only exist for the duration of the PowerShell session and are only visible to that session.

As we discuss how to create and maintain environment variables, we will also discuss what happens if there is an environment variable with the same name defined at the machine, user, and process levels. The issue is knowing which value we will see in our scripts. Let's test it out and see. Start PowerShell as Administrator and enter the following statement, which creates a machine-level environment variable named testvar:

```
[Environment]::SetEnvironmentVariable('testvar', 'machine', 'Machine')
Get-Process explorer | Stop-Process #  Line to address Windows bug
```

The first line creates a new machine-level environment variable. The line after it addresses a Windows bug. After creating a new machine- or user-level environment variable, Windows Explorer does not function correctly. In fact, in my testing, I found that none of the taskbar programs would work, and Windows said it could not find the program. I found the issue in a blog related to adding environment variables via the control panel, and the solution is to stop and restart Explorer. Hence, we have the second line. Interestingly, in the PowerShell environment, when you stop the Explorer process, it automatically restarts itself. Note: If Explorer does not restart, you can run the statement 'Start-Process Explorer' to start Windows Explorer. For other issues, rebooting your machine should correct the problem.

Now, exit PowerShell and restart it using the following command so you can see the new environment variable:

```
Get-Item env:testvar
```

You should see the following output:

```
Name                        Value
----                        -----
testvar                     machine
```

Now enter the statements seen here:

```
[Environment]::SetEnvironmentVariable("testvar", "user", "User")
Get-Process explorer | Stop-Process #  Line to address Windows bug
```

Exit PowerShell and restart it so you can see the new environment variable, as shown:

```
Get-Item env:testvar
```

You should see the following output confirming the user environment variable was created:

```
Name                        Value
----                        -----
testvar                     user
```

Now, add a process-level environment variable as follows:

```
[Environment]::SetEnvironmentVariable("testvar", "process", "Process")
```

Do not exit PowerShell, since this is only a process-level environment variable. Display the variable value as shown here:

```
Get-Item env:testvar
```

You should see the following output:

```
Name                       Value
----                       -----
testvar                    process
```

We can see from this exercise that each variable level overrides the next. This can be useful in testing, as we can set user-level variables to override the machine-level values and then remove them when we are done. We could also have different accounts run various scripts and set configuration variables at the user level so that they each get different values. To just override variables for a session, we can create process-level variables. However, be careful with this, because it may not be obvious to other developers or users of your code that there are both user-level and process-level variables, and they may become confused as to where the values are coming from.

If we need to remove a process-level environment variable, we can use the Remove-Item cmdlet, as shown next. This cmdlet will not work for user- or machine-level environment variables. See here:

```
# To remove a process-level environment variable.
Remove-Item Env:testvar
```

For user- and machine-level environment variables, the first executable statement that follows is the only way to remove the variable, and it will be visible until you restart PowerShell:

```
[Environment]::SetEnvironmentVariable("testvar",$null,"Machine")
Get-Process explorer | Stop-Process #  Line to address Windows bug
```

Although we can define and use environment variables to directly store all the configuration settings for PowerShell applications, a more flexible approach is to use them in combination with other tools. The previous discussion was simply to get acquainted with defining and using environment variables in PowerShell.

PowerShell Variables Scope

When a PowerShell session is started, it creates a global memory space we can think of as a container. The global container stores the built-in aliases, environment variables, preference variables, and PowerShell drives. When we execute a script, a sub-container is created within the global container to hold the objects created by the script. If a script or function is called from this script, a container within the script's memory is created. As scripts and functions are called, these containers continue to be nested. PowerShell does this so it can keep each memory area separate and protect us from inadvertently changing an object owned by another script or function. Figure 10-1 shows a visual representation of how PowerShell segregates these containers.

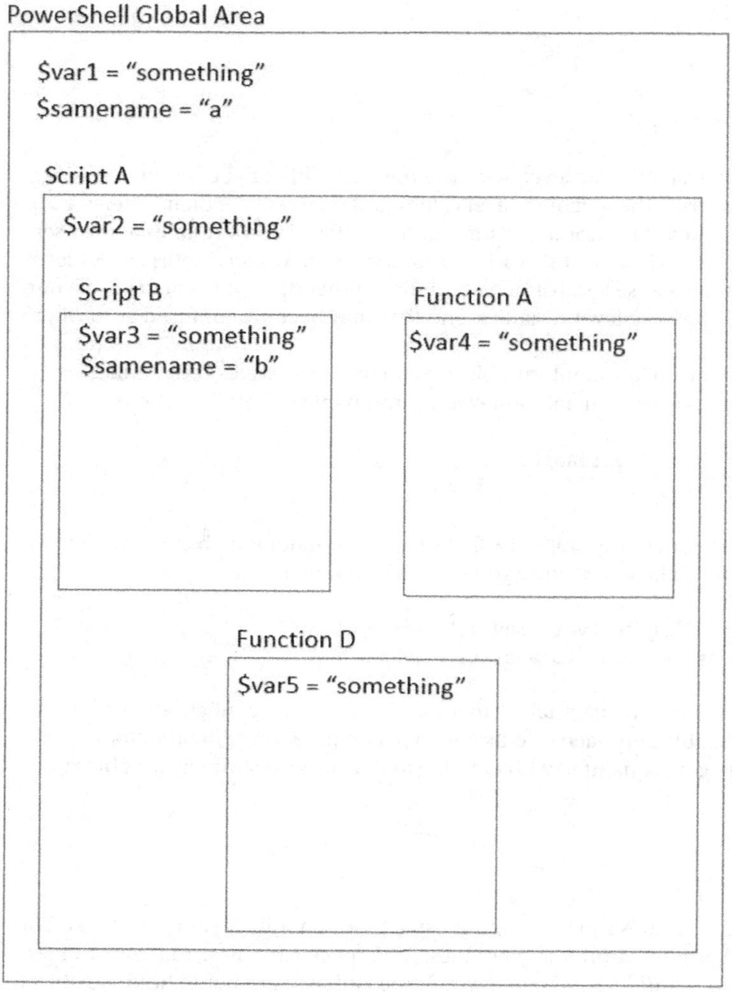

PowerShell Global Area

```
$var1 = "something"
$samename = "a"

  Script A

    $var2 = "something"

      Script B                        Function A

        $var3 = "something"             $var4 = "something"
        $samename = "b"


             Function D

               $var5 = "something"
```

Figure 10-1. *PowerShell memory to support scopes*

In Figure 10-1, we can see that each block of code has its own container, thus creating a hierarchy. Each level of the hierarchy is called a *scope*. The outermost scope is the global scope. Because the Script A container is within another container, i.e., the global container, the global scope is called the parent scope and Script A's scope is called the child scope. The containers are nested to form a hierarchy. Whether code in one container can see objects in another container is determined by whether the other container is in a parent or child scope. By default, code in the child scope can see objects in the parent scope, but code in the parent scope cannot see objects in a child scope. Containers at the same level are called *siblings*. Siblings cannot see each other's objects. In Figure 10-1, we can see that the containers Script B, Function A, and Function D are all children to Script A and are siblings to each other. Therefore, they can see the global variable $var1 and Script A's variable $var2. They cannot see each other's objects because they are siblings. The global scope can only see $var1. Script A can only see $var1 and $var2.

To access an object created by the currently executing script, we refer to it with the script scope. *Local scope* is a relative term that refers to the scope of the currently executing code. *Private scope* is explicitly defined by the code when access to the object is restricted. Private scope means that the object can only be seen within the scope in which it was created. There are two ways we can specify a variable's scope. One is to prefix the variable name with a scope, as shown:

```
$global:var1 = 'w'  # This is a global variable.
$script:var2 = 'x' # This is a script-scoped variable.
$private:var3 = 'y' # This is a privately scoped variable.
```

These statements reference variables at each scope. When no scope prefix is used, the default scope used depends on whether the variable is being read or assigned a value. If it is being read, PowerShell will search for a variable, starting in the current scope and going up the hierarchy until it is found. The statement here is an example:

```
If ($myvar -eq 'a') { "Yes" }
```

As a result of this statement, PowerShell will search for the variable $myvar in the current scope and move up the scope hierarchy.

When a variable is assigned a value without a scope prefix, the variable will be created in the current scope, if it was not already created there, and will be assigned a value. The statement here is an example of this:

```
$var4 = "z"
```

A new variable is created in the current scope because no scope prefix was defined.

The other way to reference a variable's scope is by using the Scope parameter of the variable cmdlets. Let's look at some examples of using the Scope parameter with Set-Variable:

```
Set-Variable -Name myvar -Value 'something' -Scope global
Set-Variable -Name myvar -Value 'something' -Scope script
Set-Variable -Name myvar -Value 'something'
```

The Set-Variable cmdlet assigns a value to a variable. If the variable does not exist, it creates it. The first line assigns a value to a globally scoped variable. The line after that assigns a value to a script-scoped variable. The third line assigns a value to a locally scoped variable. We can also use the New-Variable cmdlet to create a variable. Examples of using this cmdlet are seen here:

```
#  Note: we use the visibility parameter to set the scope to private.
New-Variable -name myvar2 -Visibility private -Value 'x'

New-Variable -name myvar3 -Scope global   -Value 'y'
```

The first non-comment statement uses New-Variable to create a privately scoped variable named $myva2 and assigns a value of 'x' to it. Notice: The statement does not use the Scope parameter. Instead, it uses the Visibility parameter to specify that the variable is private. The line after that creates a globally scoped variable named $myvar3 and assigns a value of 'y' to it.

The cmdlet Get-Variable can be used to retrieve the value of a variable. The statement that follows gets the value of $myvar3 in the global scope:

```
Get-Variable myvar3 -Scope global
```

Get-Variable can be used with a wildcard filter to get information on multiple variables. The example here demonstrates this:

```
Get-Variable -Name m*
```

This statement will show the name and value of all variables whose name begins with the letter *m*. If we want to see variables of a given scope, we can use the scope parameter as shown next. Note: In addition to variables we created, we will see variables called *automatic* and *preference* variables that are used by PowerShell to control preferences and configuration settings. See the scope parameter here:

```
Get-Variable -Scope global
```

This statement will get the names and values of all globally scoped variables.

The Clear-Variable cmdlet can be used to empty the variable of any value. The Remove-Variable cmdlet will delete the variable. Do not try to clear or remove PowerShell's automatic or preference variables.

Now that we've covered the basics of variable scopes, let's look at what happens when a variable of the same name is declared in multiple scopes. The script in Listing 10-1 creates and assigns values to the variable $myvar at different scopes. The goal is to demonstrate which scope we see by default when no scope prefix is used and to see if we can access the parent scopes. Listing 10-1 must be executed from the CLI. Running it from within the ISE will not produce the correct results.

Listing 10-1. Examining variable scope

```
# Some script
$global:myvar = 'global'   # All code in the session can access this.
"`$myvar is at the global scope - value is '$myvar'"

'Creating a new variable $myvar'
$myvar = 'script'   # Creates a new variable, which hides the global variable.
"By default `$myvar is at the script scope - value is '$script:myvar'"

"We can still access the global variable using the scope prefix `$global:myvar - value is
'$global:myvar'"

function Invoke-UdfSomething
{
  "Now in the function..."
  "`$myvar in the function sees the script scope - value is '$myvar'"

  # If we assign a value to $myvar we create a new variable in the function scope.
  'We assign a value to $myvar creating a function-scoped variable'
  $myvar = 'function'

  "The default scope for `$myvar is now at the function level - value is '$myvar'"

  "within the function - can use scope prefix to see global variable `$global:myvar - is
    $global:myvar"

  "within the function - can use scope prefix to see script variable `$script:myvar - is
    $script:myvar"
```

```
    "within the function - local scope is function - `$myvar is $myvar"

}

Invoke-UdfSomething # Show variable scope in function

"Out of the function now..."
# Can we still access the global scope?
'We can still see the global scope...'
get-variable myvar -scope global
"`r`nAnd we can still see the script scope..."
get-variable myvar -scope script    # Local scope is script
```

Let's discuss Listing 10-1 and its output. The script creates a variable with the same name at different scopes. First, the variable $myvar is created at the global scope and assigned a value of 'global', which it then displays. Then, the script attempts to modify $myvar by assigning it a value of 'script'. This creates a new variable of the same name with a script scope. It displays the value of the variable, which we expect to be 'script'. Then, the globally scoped $myvar is displayed to prove we can still access it. Next, a function is called that displays the value of the script variable $myvar, i.e., 'script'. The function attempts to assign a value 'function' to the $myvar, thereby creating a new variable named $myvar scoped to the function. The script then displays $myvar, which should show a value of 'function'. The function variable hides the script variable. Note: We can still access it if we use the scope prefix. Then, the function attempts to display the globally scoped $myvar using the global prefix, which we expect to display 'global'. It then attempts to display the script-scoped $myvar using the script prefix, which should display 'script'. Once again, it displays the locally scoped $myvar by omitting the scope prefix, which should be 'function'. After we exit the function, the script attempts to display the globally scoped $myvar, which should display 'global', and the script-scoped $myvar variable, which should display 'script'. Let's look at the output of this script:

```
$myvar is at the global scope - value is 'global'
Creating a new variable $myvar
By default $myvar is at the script scope - value is 'script'
We can still access the global variable using the scope prefix $global:myvar - value is 'global'
Now in the function...
$myvar in the function sees the script scope - value is 'script'
We assign a value to $myvar creating a function-scoped variable
The default scope for $myvar is now at the function level - value is 'function'
within the function - can use scope prefix to see global variable $global:myvar - is global
within the function - can use scope prefix to see script variable $script:myvar - is script
within the function - local scope is function - $myvar is function
Out of the function now...
We can still see the global scope...

Name                    Value
----                    -----
myvar                   global

And we can still see the script scope...
myvar                   script
```

To review, the globally scoped variable, $myvar, is created and displays the assigned value. When the script assigns a value to $myvar, a script-scoped version of $myvar is created and assigned the value 'script', which is written to the console. Then, the globally scoped variable is displayed. Within the function, we can see that initially $myvar is the script-scoped variable, because its value is displayed. When the function assigns the value 'function' to $myvar, a function-scoped version of $myvar is created and displayed to the console. Then, the function displays the globally scoped $myvar by using the global scope prefix. Then, the script-scoped variable is displayed using the script-scope prefix. The function-scoped variable is displayed again, confirming it is visible as the default local scope. Once we exit the function, the script displays the globally scoped $myvar. Then, it displays the script-scoped variable. The purpose of this exercise is to provide a sense of how scoping is applied in PowerShell.

We intentionally held off on covering scope until this chapter. We need to understand scope if we use PowerShell variables to support application configuration settings. However, I believe it is better to avoid depending on PowerShell scoping in our applications. It is critical to make our applications as transparent as possible—i.e., make it easy to read our code and understand what it is doing. By explicitly defining what each script and function will share with another script or function in the form of parameters, we avoid confusion over what values are being passed and what the state of our variables are at a given point in code execution. We also avoid creating dependencies in our code that make reusability and deployment more complex. For example, if a function depends on getting a value from a variable in the calling script, it cannot be easily reused by other scripts unless they are aware of these internal dependencies. It is possible that a function may have a variable of the same name defined in its parent, but since the function's scope will override the parent's scope, this has no effect on the function.

A Simple Configuration Approach

Even in a small enterprise with few servers, a flexible configuration architecture is needed. The best solution minimizes the number of changes required when deploying the application to an environment. It also must be able to easily accommodate changes in the environment, such a drive remapping, database server name changes, and the like. In a small enterprise where only one or two developers maintain the code, a simple configuration approach is to use PowerShell globally scoped variables. We assign these variable values in the profile so that when our scripts run they will always have values. Note: Variables created in the profile are automatically globally scoped.

Assuming we want this configuration to be used by all users and PowerShell hosts, enter the command that follows to edit the PowerShell profile for all users and all hosts. Note: Start PowerShell as Administrator to be able to save to $profile.AllUsersAllHosts.

```
Notepad.exe $profile.AllUsersAllHosts
```

Then, enter the lines shown in Listing 10-2.

Listing 10-2. Configuration settings

```
$emailserver='smtp.live.com'
$emailaccount='someacct@msn.com'
$emailfrom='someemail@msn.com'
$emailpw='somepassword'
$edwteamemail='edwteam@msn.com'
$emailport='587'
$ftpinpath='\\ftp\inbound\'
$ftpoutpath='\\ftp\outbound\'
$edwserver='(local)'
```

The profile script in Listing 10-2 creates and assigns values to the variables we will use in our PowerShell application. The assumption is that there are not a lot of different resources for a given environment; i.e., there is one data warehouse server for development. When the PowerShell application is deployed to each environment, the values in the profile would be modified as required for that environment. Assuming the profile script in Listing 10-2 has executed, an example of how we would use it in our code is shown in Listing 10-3. It is a call to the function Send-UdfMail from the umd_etl_functions module we discussed in Chapter 8.

Listing 10-3. Calling a function using configuration variables

```
Import-Module -Name umd_etl_functions

$Params = @{
    smtpServer = $global:emailserver
    from = $global:emailfrom
    to = $global:edwteamemail
    subject = 'Important Message'
    body = 'ETL Job executed'
    port = $global:emailport
    usecredential = $false
    emailaccount = $global:emailaccount
    password = $global:emailpw
}
Send-UdfMail @Params
```

The code in Listing 10-3 assigns the list of parameters to $Params and then passes that to the function. This avoids having to use the line-continuation character. This technique is called *splatting*. The code in Listing 10-3 calls the function Send-UdfMail from the umd_etl_functions module in order to send an email using the configuration variables created in the profile. This approach can be effective for simple implementations. For large environments or complex applications, it may not meet the needs. Also, because any PowerShell code can create variables with the same names as the configuration variables, there is the risk that the global variable values will be overridden accidentally, causing problems that are difficult to debug. In the next section, we'll discuss a configuration approach that supports namespaces for our configuration variables.

A More Advanced Configuration Approach

A somewhat more robust approach to the one just discussed is to create a *machine-level environment variable* that holds the path to a file that stores the values of configurable parameters appropriate to the environment as name/value pairs. A machine-level environment variable is a variable that all users can see and that persists when we exit PowerShell. The name/value pairs can easily be loaded into a globally scope hash table variable that PowerShell code can reference. We could just create a globally scoped PowerShell variable that points to configuration file, but that could be removed or modified by a PowerShell user or unrelated script or function. Machine-level environment variables can only be changed by users with Administrator privileges.

The first step is to create the machine-level environment variable. To do this, we must start the PowerShell ISE as Administrator. Since the PowerShell cmdlets cannot create environment variables that persist after we exit PowerShell, we need to use the .NET framework, as shown here:

```
# Create new machine-level environment variable.
# You need to start PowerShell as Admin to do this.
# Types are Machine, Process or User level.
[Environment]::SetEnvironmentVariable("psappconfigpath", `
"c:\psappconfig\psappconfig.txt", "Machine")
Get-Process explorer | Stop-Process #  Line to address Windows bug
```

This statement will create a machine-level environment variable named psappconfigpath with a value of c:\psappconfig\psappconfig.txt. To create a process-level variable, i.e., one that only exists until the PowerShell session ends, we would replace Machine with Process. To create a user-level variable, we would replace Machine with User.

The new variable's value will not be accessible when we use the cmdlet Get-Item until we exit and restart PowerShell. Instead, we can use the .NET method GetEnvironmentVariable, which will display the variable's value without requiring us to restart PowerShell. An example of this is shown here:

```
# Until we exit and restart PowerShell, the new variable may not show up.
[Environment]::GetEnvironmentVariable("psappconfigpath","Machine")
```

We are passing the variable name as the first parameter and the level as the second. We should see the variable's value displayed to the console.

Once we have the environment variable ready, we need to create the file that will hold the configuration values, which we do by entering the following command:

```
Notepad.exe $env:psappconfigpath
```

Then, enter the lines in Listing 10-4 and save the file to c:\psappconfig\psappconfig.txt.

Listing 10-4. Configuration file

```
emailserver=smtp.live.com
emailaccount=someacct@msn.com
emailfrom=someemail@msn.com
emailpw=somepassword
edwteamemail=edwteam@msn.com
emailport=587
ftpinpath=\\\\ftp\\inbound\\
ftpoutpath=\\\\ftp\\outbound\\
edwserver=(local)
```

These lines assign name/value pairs that we can load into a hash table. Notice the use of double backslashes. The backslash is interpreted as an escape character, so we need two of them to tell PowerShell we really want the backslash character. Assuming we want this configuration to be used by all users and PowerShell hosts, enter the command that follows to edit the PowerShell profile for all users and all hosts. Note: You must have started PowerShell as Administrator to be able to save to $profile.AllUsersAllHosts. Consider carefully which profile to use, and limit the scope to what is needed. If there is a risk that other users will modify or reuse the configuration variables, create them in the user-specific profile.

```
Notepad.exe $profile.AllUsersAllHosts
```

Then, enter the following statements into the profile script, save the script, and exit:

```
$global:psappconfig = Get-Content -Path $env:psappconfigpath | ConvertFrom-StringData
(Get-Variable –Scope global -Name psappconfig).Options = "ReadOnly"
```

The first statement will load the name/value pairs from the file pointed to by the environment variable psappconfigpath into the PowerShell globally scoped variable $global:psappconfig. Globally scoped variables are visible to all code executing in the current session. The second statement sets the variable to ReadOnly, which means developers cannot accidently modify it. Technically, they could use the Force parameter, but that requires a conscious knowledge that they are overriding the variable. Since we added the line to the AllUsersAllHosts profile script, everyone will see it for any PowerShell host. To prove this, restart PowerShell and enter the statements seen here:

```
$global:psappconfig            # Lists all the name/value pairs to the console.
$global:psappconfig.edwserver  # Uses the name edwserver to lookup the value
```

If we did everything correctly, these statements should display entries from the text file to the console.

One way to make use of configuration values is to use the $PSDefaultParamterValues, which was covered in Chapter 8. However, that makes it less obvious what values are being used by our functions. Instead, we pass the $psappconfig hash table values as parameters. The code in Listing 10-5 calls the Send-UdfMail function we saw in Chapter 9, passing hash table values from the $psappconfig variable.

Listing 10-5. Calling Send-UdfMail using global configuration variables

```
Import-Module –Name umd_etl_functions

$Params = @{
    smtpServer = $global:psappconfig.emailserver
    from = $global:psappconfig.emailfrom
    to = $global:psappconfig.edwteamemail
    subject = 'Important Message'
    body = 'ETL Job executed'
    port = $global:psappconfig.emailport
    usecredential = $true
    emailaccount = $global:psappconfig.emailaccount
    password = $global:psappconfig.emailpw
}

Send-UdfMail @Params
```

The first line in Listing 10-5 imports the module umd_etl_functions, which includes the function Send-UdfMail. Then, we call that function, passing the appropriate values from $psappconfig. Notice that we use the hash table's key, which automatically gets translated to the associated value, thus making our code self-documenting. We include the global-scope designation when we get the variable values so as to avoid the possibility that a more locally scoped variable with the same name gets used for the value.

This call is just an example. The idea is to write all function calls using the configuration variable's hash table values for any configurable parameters. The nice thing about using this approach to define parameter values is that to deploy the code to another machine, we just need to copy the code and configuration file to the new machine. Then we edit the configuration values to what is appropriate for that environment. However, this configuration design may still be inadequate. For example, if there were different sources of data that arrived on different FTP servers, it may get unwieldy to have to create distinct names for each folder. The ability to support namespaces for each application or source might be needed. Methods to include namespaces will be covered next.

Taking Configuration a Step Further

For larger and more complex environments, the previous configuration design may be insufficient. Consider an instance where there are many different applications that do not all share the same configuration values, even for the same type of item. For example, in an insurance company, claim files may arrive on a different FTP server than account receivable files do. Email settings may also differ. In such cases, it may be useful to be able to group configuration settings by project. To support this, we create a separate CSV file to hold the configuration data; that data is shown in Listing 10-6. These must be saved in a file named c:\pasappconfig\psappconfig.csv.

Listing 10-6. Configuration settings CSV file

```
project,name,value
general,edwserver,(local)
general,emailserver,smtp.live.com
general,ftppath,\\ftpserver\ftp\
edw,teamemail,edwteamdist
edw,stagingdb,staging
finance,ftppath,\\financeftpserver\ftp\
finance,dbserver,financesqlsvr
finance,outfolder,\\somepath\outdata\
```

The first row in Listing 10-6 supplies the column names. The name and value are the configuration properties like edwservername. The project column groups the configurations, which allows us to have the same configuration name more than once. This is needed when different parts of the application need different values. In the listing we can see that the team email is under both the EDW project and the finance project, with different values. At the general level, which might be for global settings, there is an ftppath with a different value than the ftppath seen under the finance project.

To load the configuration values, we've added a function named Set-UdfConfiguration to the umd_etl_functions module. Let's look at the function's code in Listing 10-7.

Listing 10-7. Set configuations function

```
function Set-UdfConfiguration {
 [CmdletBinding()]
       param (
                [string]      $configpath
              )
    [psobject] $config = New-Object psobject

    $projects   = Import-CSV -Path $configpath | Select-Object -Property Project -Unique
    $configvals = Import-CSV -Path $configpath

    foreach ($project in $projects)
    {
        $configlist = @{}

        foreach ($item in $configvals)
        {
            if ($item.project -eq $project.project )
               { $configlist.Add($item.name, $item.value)  }
        }
```

```
    #  Add the noteproperty with the configuration hash table as the value.
    $config |
    Add-Member -MemberType NoteProperty -Name $project.project -Value $configlist
}

Return $config

}
```

The function Set-UdfConfiguration takes one parameter, which is the path to a CSV file with the configuration settings. The file has three columns: project, name, and value. Project is used to group names and values. This allows the same configuration name to be used more than once with different values. The function creates a psobject and adds a property for each project name. The line in the function that does this is copied here:

```
$projects   = Import-CSV -Path $configpath | Select-Object -Property Project |
Get-unique -AsString
```

The file is imported, piped into the Select-Object cmdlet, which extracts the Project property and pipes this into the Get-Unique cmdlet, which returns a list of distinct values that is stored in $projects.

Then, we need to load the list of configuration name/value pairs for each project and create a property on the psobject that contains a hash table of the related name/value pairs. Let's look at the code that does this:

```
foreach ($project in $projects)
    {
        $configlist = @{}

        foreach ($item in $configvals)
        {
            if ($item.project -eq $project.project )
                { $configlist.Add($item.name, $item.value)  }
        }

        #  Add the noteproperty with the configuration hash table as the value.
        $config |
        Add-Member -MemberType NoteProperty -Name $project.project -Value $configlist
    }
```

The outer foreach loop iterates over the list of projects. For each project, a hash table named $configlist is created. Then, an inner foreach loop iterates over the name/value pairs. If the inner loop's project has the same value as the outer loop, the name/value pair is added to the $configlist hash table. When the inner loop is finished, the hash table will contain all the name/value pairs for the project in the outer loop. It is then added as a property, with the current project's name, to the $config object using the Add-Member cmdlet. The outer loop will repeat until it has processed all the projects in the file. At that point, the outer loop is exited and the $config object is returned to the caller as in the following statement:

```
Return $config
```

To use the function, we need to store the path to the configuration file in a machine-level environment variable. To create this variable, we must start PowerShell as Administrator and enter the following statement. Note: We are using the same environment variable name as before, but the file has a `csv` extension this time rather than `txt`. It is a different file.

```
[Environment]::SetEnvironmentVariable("psappconfigpath",
"c:\psappconfig\psappconfig.csv", "Machine")
```

Then, we need to edit the `AllUsersAllHosts` profile by entering the following statement:

```
Notepad.exe $profile.AllUsersAllHosts
```

We need to add the lines that follow to the profile:

```
Import-Module umd_etl_functions

$global:psappconfig = Set-UdfConfiguration ($env:psappconfigpath)
```

Save the file and exit. Then, exit and restart PowerShell so the new profile will execute. Once back in PowerShell, enter the statement that follows to see the new configuration object:

```
$global:psappconfig | Format-List
```

You should see the following output:

```
general : {emailserver, ftppath, edwserver}
edw     : {teamemail, stagingdb}
finance : {dbserver, outfolder, ftppath}
```

We can access just the values associated with a project by using the appropriate property name, as shown here:

```
$global:psappconfig.edw
```

You should see just the configuration values that you see here:

```
Name                    Value
----                    -----
teamemail               edwteamdist
stagingdb               staging
```

To access an individual configuration property, just add the configuration name after the project name, separated by a period, as shown here:

```
$global:psappconfig.edw.teamemail
```

We can access the other projects in the same way, i.e., with statements like these:

```
$global:psappconfig.finance
```

```
$global:psappconfig.finance.dbserver
```

```
$global:psappconfig.finance.ftppath
```

Now that the configuration object is created, we can use it in code:

```
Import-Module umd_database -Force
$result = Invoke-UdfSQLQuery -sqlserver $global:psappconfig.finance.dbserver        `
                            -sqldatabase $global:psappconfig.finance.dbname          `
                            -sqlquery "select top 10 * from person.person;"
```

This code calls the function Invoke-UdfSQLQuery from the umd_database module to run a simple query against the finance database. To change the server or database name, we would just need to edit the values in the file pointed to by the environment variable $env:psappconfigpath. Admittedly, the calling syntax is a bit verbose. We could simplify it by assigning the environment variables to local variables in our scripts. If this is to be done, it is best to do so at the top of the script so it is visible to developers who read the code.

Storing Configuration Values in a SQL Server Table

A nice option in SQL Server Integration Services (SSIS) configurations is the ability to store configuration settings in a database table. When the package executes, SSIS automatically retrieves the configuration entries and loads the values into the package variables as specified by the developer. The configuration table has to be defined with specific columns and formats. The table includes a tag column that groups configuration settings. Let's discuss how we can do the same thing in PowerShell. This is very similar to the prior approach, except we will be loading the configuration values from a SQL Server table. First, we need to create environment variables that store the connection properties to the configuration table. Start PowerShell as Administrator and execute the statements in Listing 10-8.

Listing 10-8. Configuration pointing to SQL Server

```
#  Create new machine-level environment variables to point to
#  the database configuration table.
[Environment]::SetEnvironmentVariable("psappconfigdbserver", "(local)", "Machine")

[Environment]::SetEnvironmentVariable("psappconfigdbname","Development", "Machine")

[Environment]::SetEnvironmentVariable("psappconfigtablename","dbo.PSAppConfig", "Machine")

Get-Process explorer | Stop-Process #  Line to address Windows bug
```

Here, we create environment variables to store the database server, the database name, and the table where the configuration entries are stored. After running these statements, these machine-level variables will be permanently stored on the machine.

In this listing, we are defining the name of the configuration table, psappconfigtablename, as dbo.PSAppConfig. As with SSIS, we need to define this in a very specific manner. To create the SQL Server table in your environment, you will need a SQL Server client like SQL Server Management Studio (SSMS) so you can execute the required SQL statements. The SQL in Listing 10-9 will create the table for us.

Listing 10-9. The configuration table

```
CREATE TABLE [dbo].PSAppConfig
(
        [Project]      varchar(50),
        [Name]         varchar(100),
        [Value]        varchar(100),
        [CreateDate]   datetime  default(getdate()),
        [UpdateDate]   datetime  default(getdate()),
        Primary Key (Project, Name)
)
```

We really just need the Project, Name, and Value columns. The CreateDate will store the date and time the row was inserted, and the UpdateDate is meant to hold the last date and time the row was updated. The date columns come in handy when there is a need to know when data was created or last modified. Notice the primary key is the Project and Name columns concatenated. This is to prevent the insertion of rows with duplicate Project and Name.

Let's insert some configuration rows with the SQL statements in Listing 10-10.

Listing 10-10. Loading PSAppConfig

```
insert into [dbo].PSAppConfig ([Project], [Name], [Value])
Values ('general','edwserver','(local)');

insert into [dbo].PSAppConfig ([Project], [Name], [Value])
Values ('general','emailserver','smtp.live.com');

insert into [dbo].PSAppConfig ([Project], [Name], [Value])
Values ('general','ftppath','\\ftpserver\ftp\');

insert into [dbo].PSAppConfig ([Project], [Name], [Value])
Values ('edw','teamemail','edwteamdist');

insert into [dbo].PSAppConfig ([Project], [Name], [Value])
Values ('edw','stagingdb','staging');

insert into [dbo].PSAppConfig ([Project], [Name], [Value])
Values ('finance','ftppath','\\financeftpserver\ftp\');

insert into [dbo].PSAppConfig ([Project], [Name], [Value])
Values ('finance','dbserver','financesqlsvr');

insert into [dbo].PSAppConfig ([Project], [Name], [Value])
Values ('finance','outfolder','\\somepath\outdata\');
```

Once we have the SQL Server configuration table populated, we need code that will load it into PowerShell. The function in Listing 10-11 is found in the umd_etl_functions module. The function will load the configuration settings for us. Note the statement above the function definition imports the umd_database module, because the function calls the Invoke-UdfSQLQuery function, which is in that module.

Listing 10-11. Loading configuration settings from a database table

```
Import-Module umd_database

function Set-UdfConfigurationFromDatabase
{
 [CmdletBinding()]
        param (
                  [string] $sqlserver,
                  [string] $sqldb,
                  [string] $sqltable
                )

     [psobject] $config = New-Object psobject

     $projects = Invoke-UdfSQLQuery -sqlserver $sqlserver `
                                    -sqldatabase $sqldb `
                                    -sqlquery "select distinct project from $sqltable;"

     $configrows = Invoke-UdfSQLQuery -sqlserver $sqlserver -sqldatabase $sqldb `
                   -sqlquery "select * from $sqltable order by project, name;"

     foreach ($project in $projects)
     {
         $configlist = @{}

         foreach ($configrow in $configrows)
         {
             if ($configrow.project -eq $project.project )
                   { $configlist.Add($configrow.name, $configrow.value)  }
         }

         #  Add the noteproperty with the configuration hash table as the value.
         $config |
         Add-Member -MemberType NoteProperty -Name $project.project -Value $configlist
     }

      Return $config
}
```

The function in Listing 10-11 takes three parameters, which are the name of the SQL Server, the database name, and the table in which the configuration data is stored. Aside from the source of the data, this function is similar to the function that loads the configuration data from a CSV file. The first statement in the function, copied here, creates a psobject to hold the configuration information:

```
[psobject] $config = New-Object psobject
```

Then, the code gets a list of distinct project values using the function Invoke-UdfSQLQuery and storing the result in $projects:

```
$projects = Invoke-UdfSQLQuery -sqlserver $sqlserver `
                               -sqldatabase $sqldb `
                               -sqlquery "select distinct project from $sqltable;"
```

289

The statement here loads the configuration table rows into $configrows:

```
$configrows = Invoke-UdfSQLQuery -sqlserver $sqlserver -sqldatabase $sqldb `
                          -sqlquery "select * from $sqltable order by project, name;"
```

Then, the code that follows loads the psobject $config with a property for each project containing the related name/value pairs:

```
foreach ($project in $projects)
{
    $configlist = @{}

    foreach ($configrow in $configrows)
    {
        if ($configrow.project -eq $project.project )
            { $configlist.Add($configrow.name, $configrow.value)  }
    }

    #  Add the noteproperty with the configuration hash table as the value.
    $config | Add-Member -MemberType NoteProperty -Name $project.project -Value $configlist
}
```

The outer foreach loop iterates over the list of projects. For each project, a hash table named $configlist is created. Then, an inner foreach loop iterates over the name/value pairs. If the inner loop's project has the same value as the outer loop, the name/value pair is added to the $configlist hash table. When the inner loop is finished, the hash table will contain all the name/value pairs for the project in the outer loop. It is then added as a property with the current project's name to the $config object using the Add-Member cmdlet. The outer loop will repeat until it has processed all the projects in the file. At that point, the outer loop is exited and the $config object returned to the caller via the statement here:

```
Return $config
```

We can execute the function with a statement like the one here:

```
$global:psappconfig = Set-UdfConfigurationFromDatabase '(local)' `
'Development' 'dbo.PSAppConfig'
```

Once we have executed the function, we can verify the configuration object has the configuration data with the statements that follow:

```
$global:psappconfig | Format-List
```

```
$global:psappconfig.edw
```

```
$global:psappconfig.finance
```

To demonstrate how to use the configuration object, let's use the connection object from umd_database, as shown in Listing 10-12.

Listing 10-12. Using configurations from a database table

```
Import-module umd_database

[psobject] $myconnection = New-Object psobject
New-UdfConnection([ref]$myconnection)

$myconnection.ConnectionType = 'ADO'
$myconnection.DatabaseType = 'SqlServer'
$myconnection.Server = $global:psappconfig.finance.dbserver
$myconnection.DatabaseName = $global:psappconfig.finance.dbname
$myconnection.UseCredential = 'N'
$myconnection.SetAuthenticationType('Integrated')
$myconnection.BuildConnectionString()
$myconnection.RunSQL("select top 10 * from [Sales].[SalesTerritory]", $true)
```

We create a `psobject`, which is passed by reference to the `New-UdfConnection` function. The function attaches the methods and properties to support database access. We set the various properties and finally execute a `select` statement on the last line, which should list ten rows from the `Sales.SalesTerritory` table in the `AdventureWorks` database.

Using a Script Module to Support Configuration

There are a couple of criticisms that can be made about the previous configuration solutions. First, although they mitigate the risk of code modifying the configuration variables, they do not eliminate the possibility. Second, application developers may not want to or may not have the access to create environment variables and profile scripts on the server. Another approach that can be modified to incorporate the best features of the previously discussed configuration solutions is to use a script module. The idea is to create a script module with the purpose of returning configuration settings. Let's assume our configuration settings are in a text file, as shown in Listing 10-13.

Listing 10-13. Configuration text file

```
emailserver=smtp.live.com
emailaccount=someacct@msn.com
emailfrom=someemail@msn.com
emailpw=somepassword
edwteamemail=edwteam@msn.com
emailport=587
ftpinpath=\\\\ftp\\inbound\\
ftpoutpath=\\\\ftp\\outbound\\
edwserver=(local)
```

In this listing, notice the file is set up as name/value pairs that are perfect for loading into a hash table. Note: This file is also stored under the name `psappconfig.txt` with the code listings so that the function in Listing 10-14 can find it. Now, let's take a look at the code that will retrieve the configuration values.

Listing 10-14. A script module named umd_appconfig that gets configuration settings

```
$configfile = Join-Path -Path $PSScriptRoot -ChildPath "psappconfig.txt"
$configdata = Get-Content -Path $configfile | ConvertFrom-StringData

function Get-UdfConfiguation ([string] $configkey)
{
    Return $configdata.$configkey
}
```

The first line in Listing 10-14 uses Join-Path to concatenate the PowerShell variable $PSScriptRoot with the name of the configuration text file. We could just do a string concatenation, but many PowerShell developers prefer to use the cmdlets specifically designed for this purpose, i.e., Join-Path to build the path and Split-Path to break the path into parts. When the module gets loaded, $PSScriptRoot will have the path where the function or module is stored. Therefore, we need to place the configuration text file in the folder where the module script file is located. The nice thing about this is that we don't have to tell PowerShell where to find the file. The module will be stored in a script file named umd_appconfig.psm1 in folder named umd_appconfig, which is located in a folder where PowerShell knows to look for modules, such as \Documents\WindowsPowerShell\Modules.

The second line in Listing 10-13 loads the configuration text file into a hash table variable named $configdata. Rather than have developers directly access variables in the module, the function Get-UdfConfiguration will return the value associated with any key passed into the $configkey parameter. An example of using this module is provided in Listing 10-15.

Listing 10-15. Using the configuration script module

```
Import-Module -Name umd_appconfig  # Must call this to load configurations

Import-Module -Name umd_etl_functions

$Params = @{
    smtpServer = (Get-UdfConfiguation 'emailserver')
    from = (Get-UdfConfiguation 'emailfrom')
    to = (Get-UdfConfiguation 'edwteamemail')
    subject = 'Important Message'
    body = 'ETL Job executed'
    port = (Get-UdfConfiguation 'emailport')
    usecredential = ''
    emailaccount = (Get-UdfConfiguation 'emailaccount')
    password = (Get-UdfConfiguation 'emailpw')
}
Send-UdfMail @Params
```

The first line in Listing 10-15 imports the umd_appconfig module, which loads the configuration values and defines the function to retrieve them. Then, the umd_etl_functions module is imported, because we need to use the Send-UdfMail function. As we saw previously, we load the function parameters using a technique called *splatting*. The call to Get-UdfConfiguration must be enclosed in parentheses so that the function will be executed first and the returned value will be assigned to the variable on the left. Although the example shown here uses a text file, it could easily be modified to get the values from a CSV or SQL Server table. This approach is the easiest to deploy and offers the most protection of the configuration values. This makes it well suited to large environments with many servers.

PowerShell Development Best Practices

The best practices for any development language should be similar, because they have the same basic goals. These goals include application stability, ease of maintenance, and simplicity of deployment. This book treats PowerShell as a development platform. It may be unique in that respect, and as such, the best practices here may be different than what is presented elsewhere. Other best practices lists I've seen tend to treat PowerShell as an administrative tool, which sometimes negates the goals of professional application development.

Application stability is greatly affected by the degree of dependencies among the components. For example, if a script shares variables with another script, they have a dependency, which means a change to one of the scripts could break the other. Making applications modular reduces this fragility, because modularity means each component can stand alone.

Ease of maintenance covers a number of different concepts. One is the readability of the code. Undescriptive variable and function names, cramming multiple statements on a single line, and lack of indenture to indicate nesting levels of code all undermine readability. Using white space and descriptive names can help.

Another issue for maintainability is the level of hard-coded values in the application. If file paths, server names, login accounts, and so on are hard coded, then the application needs to be revised when it is deployed to another environment. Even in an existing environment where the application is installed, should one of the values need to be changed, the code will need to be revised and tested. Having support within the application to change such values without changing the code is critical to maintainability and deployment.

Maintainability is also affected by the level of reuse. It is better to have a single, flexible function used by many components to accomplish a task than to have many different identical or slightly different functions to perform the same tasks. Otherwise, a required change in functionality may require modifying and testing many functions instead of just one. For example, if many different versions of a logging function were implemented, a change to add a new piece of data may require making a change to multiple functions.

A reason why developers reinvent the wheel by creating duplicate functions is the lack documentation on existing functions. Developers often feel it is safer to write their own functions. Programmers generally do not like to write documentation. Therefore, documentation needs to be integrated into the development process.

The best practices that follow are meant to address these issues. It is not realistic to expect that all the best practices will be implemented at all times. However, applying them as a standard practice will save enterprises considerable time and money. Not everyone will agree with all the best practices listed. However, I recommend that the reader reflect less on the specifics of the best practice recommendation than on the spirit of it. In that way, you can achieve the benefits while customizing the specifics to fit your preferences.

Function Naming

PowerShell function (also called cmdlet) naming is not arbitrary. Microsoft has established naming standards that are generally adhered to and accepted as a best practice by the PowerShell community. Microsoft recommends naming functions in the format Verb-Noun, where the verb conforms to an approved list and the noun describes what the verb acts upon. The list and description of approved verbs can be found at: https://msdn.microsoft.com/en-us/library/ms714428%28v=vs.85%29.aspx. It is important that the developer choose the verb that most closely matches what the function does so developers can easily grasp its purpose—and so that when it is listed using PowerShell cmdlets like Get-Command, it will be listed with similar functions. The ability to easily find functions by what they do is called *discoverability*. It is important that developers name the function in a way that avoids the risk of duplicating a built-in or third-party function. Otherwise, the wrong function may get called by the application, resulting in a bug that can be difficult to track down. Consider the case where a developer writes a function he calls Get-OData that is used by many parts of the application. OData is an open data-retrieval standard promoted by Microsoft. What happens if Microsoft adds a new cmdlet named Get-OData to PowerShell? PowerShell will use the custom function in place of the built-in cmdlet, but that just happens to be the way it is designed, and that could change. Even so, developers that maintain the code might think that the calls to Get-OData are calling the Microsoft cmdlet. If there is a bug, developers may be trying to understand why the parameters to Get-OData do not match Microsoft's supported parameters. They may even think there is a bug in the Microsoft cmdlet, not realizing there is a custom version. In the support of code maintainability, it is critical to make it clear what code is system delivered and what is custom code. In this book, it is clear what functions are custom versus built-in due to the naming standard used. Unlike the verb, the noun does not have to comply with an approved list. So, we can use a noun that makes it clear that the function is a custom one. In this book, the noun prefix Udf is used for this purpose, i.e., Udf indicates the function is user defined. So, in our example, we could name the function Get-UdfOData. This accomplishes the goal of readability and avoids naming collisions, while adhering to PowerShell naming standards.

File Naming

Unless a function is contained in a script module, a good practice is to store it in a script file of the same name as the function, i.e., Add-UdfConnection.ps1. This makes it easier to locate the function. As much as possible, I try to write code as functions because they maximize reusability. However, when I do create script files, I like to prefix them with scr, an abbreviation for *script*. I like to name script modules in a way that is very dissimilar to what Microsoft and third parties tend to use. This makes it readily clear that it is a custom module. I prefix the module name with umd, which stands for user-defined module, and I separate the words with underscores. I provide examples of each file type name.

For a script containing a function definition:

Invoke-UdfSomtTask.ps1

For a script that loads sales data:

scr_do_sales_load.ps1

For a module containing ETL-related functions:

umd_etl_functions.psm1

Scripts are used to call functions. Although they can call other scripts, I find limiting scripts to fall-through code that just calls reusable functions to be more manageable.

In my development, I have found creating separate folders for each type of code helpful. A typical folder hierarchy is shown here:

Directory: C:\Users\BryanCafferky\Documents\PowerShell

```
OMode            LastWriteTime      Length Name
----            -------------      ------ ----
d----        7/30/2014  11:33 AM           documentation
d----        3/13/2015   7:47 PM           function
d----       12/28/2014  10:18 PM           module
d----        8/24/2014  11:27 AM           script
```

Notice that there is a documentation folder. This is where documentation on the custom scripts and functions and overall applications can be kept. Also, using the Write-Verbose cmdlet within a function can provide additional information to developers about the function.

Make Code Reusable

At the start of development, it is tempting to write quick and dirty scripts that get the job done but are not created in a manner that maximizes reusability. This can lead to many specialized scripts that are all doing a similar task. The problem is that all these scripts have to be maintained, and if a change is needed in one, it is probably needed in the others. I make it a rule to write a function for anything I do that has the potential for reusability. It does not take much longer to add the function header with parameters, and it saves time in the long run. If there are more than a few related functions frequently being called, consider making them into a script module, which makes the functions easier to access and simplifies deployment.

Developers will only use functions that they understand how to call. Like Java, PowerShell supports special documentation tags embedded in the source code. The cmdlets like Get-Help can extract these tags to provide help to developers about functions. A good practice is to use a script and function template that has the basic tags in place so developers can just change the function name, fill in the tags, and add the code for the function. No one likes to go back and edit code that is already written, so it is better to start with these tags from the beginning. Another good practice is to use the CmdletBinding attribute, because it adds support for the common cmdlet parameters, parameter validation, and parameter sets. The sample template in Listing 10-16 provides a good starting point for creating a new function. The idea is to just load the template script into the ISE, save it under the name of the new function, and edit the function name and tag values to fit your needs.

Listing 10-16. An example of a function template

```
function Verb-UdfNoun
{
        <#
        .SYNOPSIS
        Enter a short description of what the function does.

        .DESCRIPTION
        Enter a longer description about the function.

        .PARAMETER Parm1
        Describe the first parameter.

        .PARAMETER Parm2
        Describe the second parameter.

        .INPUTS
        Can data be piped into this function?

        .OUTPUTS
        Describe what this function returns.

        .EXAMPLE
        C:\PS> Verb-UdfNoun -parm1 "parm1" -parm2 "parm2"

        .LINK
        Enter a url to a help topic if available.

        #>
```

```
[CmdletBinding()]
param
(
    [string]      $parm1,
    [string]      $parm2
)

#  Insert code below...

}
```

An alternative to using a script as a template is to create a snippet that can easily be inserted into code in the ISE. Details on this can be found at:

```
https://msdn.microsoft.com/en-us/library/ms714428%28v=vs.85%29.aspx
```

Use Source Code Control

Database development code, such as ETL, stored procedures, functions, SQL Agent Jobs, and queries, is often overlooked when it comes to source code control. Sometimes code by database developers is not seen as critical code requiring source code control. Other times, database backups are relied upon to serve that function. Source code control is a good practice for all professional application development. Bear in mind that PowerShell code is not stored in the database. Even if PowerShell's usage is limited to preparing data to be loaded and archiving files after they have been loaded, it is still critical to the application. There are many great source code control systems available. I had a client who had no source code control in place, and I did not want to add the infrastructure maintenance of installing one. I selected GitHub because it came with a nice GUI client front end and automatically backed the source up to the cloud for a very inexpensive price. Svn is a good open-source option, and Team Foundation Services (TFS) is also good. The goal is to protect the source code and enable an easy retrieval of any historic version, should it be needed.

Build In Configurations from the Start

One of the most important best practices is to avoid hard coding values that are likely to change. Server names, service accounts, passwords, database names, file paths, and things like this are environment specific. Often they are outside the developer's control. Setting these up as configurable values from the start makes it easier to deploy the application to another environment. If we do this, moving the application from development to production is just a matter of copying files and editing the configuration values. The point is this: it is better to think out what the configurable parameters for your application will be before you start coding. That way, you can code your function calls using the configured parameters, as we saw earlier in this chapter, and you will be ready to deploy once your application is tested. It is tempting to jump in and code with the idea that you can add the configurable values later. That means you will have to go back and edit code a second time and risk making a mistake that could introduce bugs. This is the lesson I learned in developing SSIS projects, and it applies equally to PowerShell. Earlier in this chapter, we discussed a number of approaches that can be applied to achieve maximum configurability.

PowerShell Application Deployment

Three things must be considered when deploying a PowerShell application: script modules, script files, and jobs. The next subsections go over these in the order listed. Let's start with deploying script modules.

Deploying Script Modules

Deploying PowerShell applications is eased by the fact that it is an interpreted language. There are no DLLs or assemblies to install unless your application makes calls to such external programs. Deployments consist of copying the PowerShell scripts and configuration files to the target machine and modifying the configuration settings as appropriate. The use of script modules can simplify deployments, since PowerShell will automatically locate the module when called. However, the current requirement that all the functions of the module be contained in one script file violates the best practice of modularity. To make a change to a single function, the script, potentially containing numerous functions, must be modified and deployed. If an error is made, the other functions could be affected. It also makes locating the function more difficult, because the developer must search for the function name within the module script. In Chapter 6, a method of overcoming this problem was discussed. Here, I want to provide another method by which to retain the benefits of using modules while keeping the code modular. The idea is to store each of the module's functions in a separate script file. When the module is imported, the module will automatically find the functions and dot source them into memory. Let's look at code in Listing 10-17 that does this.

Listing 10-17. A module that dot sources the functions

```
<#

.Author
    Bryan Cafferky
.SYNOPSIS
    A simple module that uses dot sourcing to load the functions.
.DESCRIPTION
    When this module is imported, the functions are loaded using dot sourcing.

#>

#  Get the path to the function files...
$functionpath = $PSScriptRoot + "\function\"

# Get a list of all the function file names...
$functionlist = Get-ChildItem -Path $functionpath -Name

#  Loop over alll the files and dot source them into memory..
foreach ($function in $functionlist)
{
    . ($functionpath + $function)
}
```

In Listing 10-17, the first non-comment line assigns $functionpath with the path to where the module script is located concatenated with the subfolder "\function". Recall that $PSScriptRoot is a built-in PowerShell variable that gets set to the path of the currently executing code. When the module is imported, $PSScriptRoot is set to the folder where the module is located. In this case, the module's functions are contained in a subfolder named function. The next line in the script calls the Get-ChildItem cmdlet, passing $functionpath and specifying that only the Name property be returned. This list is assigned to the variable $functionlist. Then a foreach loop iterates over the $functionlist collection and issues a dot-source statement for each script file. Recall the use of parentheses, which tell PowerShell to resolve the expression in parentheses before doing the outer command, i.e., dot sourcing the returned file name.

Using the script module in Listing 10-17, we can place all our functions in separate script files in the function subfolder. If a new script containing a function is added to the folder, it will automatically get loaded when the module is imported. If a script is deleted from the folder, it will no longer get loaded on an import. If any function needs to be modified, only the specific script file for the function needs to be edited. It also means that if one function needs to be modified, the developer only needs to check out the single function. Another developer can work on a different function at the same time without being concerned about merging the other developer's changes in later. This improves maintainability and decreases the risk of introducing bugs.

Let's see how this works. Create a new folder in the \Documents\WindowsPowerShell\Modules\ folder named umd_application. Then, copy the script in Listing 10-17 to that folder as umd_application.psm1. Now, create a folder named function within the umd_application folder. Copy each of the functions that follow in Listings 10-18 to 10-20 into the script file as specified in those listings.

Listing 10-18. File name: Invoke-UdfAddNumber.ps1

```
function Invoke-UdfAddNumber([int]$p_int1, [int]$p_int2)
{
      Return ($p_int1 + $p_int2)
}
```

Listing 10-19. File name: Invoke-UdfSubtractNumber.ps1

```
function Invoke-UdfSubtractNumber([int]$p_int1, [int]$p_int2)
{
      Return ($p_int1 - $p_int2)
}
```

Listing 10-20. File name: Invoke-UdfMultiplyNumber.ps1

```
function Invoke-UdfMultiplyNumber([int]$p_int1, [int]$p_int2)
{
      Return ($p_int1 * $p_int2)
}
```

Now, start PowerShell and enter the following statement:

```
Import-Module umd_application
```

Assuming you did everything correctly, the functions should get loaded. To test this, enter the statements seen here:

```
Invoke-UdfAddNumber 5 6

Invoke-UdfSubtractNumber 5 2

Invoke-UdfMultiplyNumber 5 2
```

If these were executed as a script, the output should be:

```
11
3
10
```

An extra benefit of this approach is that we can just copy the same script module for any module we want to create and then place all the functions we want it to contain into the function subfolder.

Deploying Script Files

Script files can be stored in a folder under an account that will be used to execute the scripts, or in a common location; it depends on how you want to configure the application. I recommend putting as much of the code into modules as possible and limiting script files to calling the module functions to do work. This approach was demonstrated in Chapter 9. However, that example did not use configurations, which we would want to do. Listing 10-21 is the script from Chapter 9 revised to use a configuration approach that loads the configurable values into PowerShell global variables.

Listing 10-21. Using configuration settings from global PowerShell variables

```
Import-Module umd_etl_functions

# Wait for the files...
Wait-UdfFileCreation $global:ftppath  -Verbose

# Notify users the job has started using Outlook...
Send-UdfMail  -Server $global:mailserver -From $global:fromemail -To $global:toemail `
    -Subject "ETL Job: Sales Load has started" -Body "The ETL Job: Sales Load has started." `
    -Port $global:emailport -usecredential $global:emailaccount –Password $global:emailpw

# Copy the files...
Copy-UdfFile $ global:ftppath $global:inbound -overwrite

$filelist = Get-ChildItem $global:zippath

#  Unzip the files...
Foreach ($file in $filelist)
{
    Expand-UdfFile $file.FullName $global:unzippedpath -force
}
```

```
# Add file name to file...
Add-UdfColumnNameToFile $global:unzippedpath  $global:processpath "sales*.csv"

# Load the files...
Invoke-UdfSalesTableLoad $global:processpath "sales*.csv" -Verbose

# Archive files...
Move-UdfFile $global:ftppath $global:archivepath  -overwrite

# Notify users the job has finished...
Send-UdfMail  -Server $global:mailserver -From $global:fromemail -To $global:toemail `
            -Subject "ETL Job: Sales Load has ended" –Body "The ETL Job: Sales Load has
             ended." `
            -Port $global:emailport -usecredential $global:emailaccount –Password
$global:emailpw
```

This script is similar to the one in Chapter 9, but here all parameters that might change are stored in globally scoped PowerShell variables; note the $global prefix. The assumption here is that these variables were assigned values previously, probably in the profile script. Moving this script to another machine involves copying the script, the module it uses, and the PowerShell script that loads the configuration values, and then modifying the configuration values as appropriate for the new environment. Note: If you want to run the script in Listing 10-21, you need to review all the configuration variable settings to make sure they will work in your environment.

Deploying Jobs

SQL Server Agent provides an excellent place to create PowerShell jobs. SQL Server Management Studio (SSMS) even provides a feature that allows us to generate a script that can be used to copy the job to another server.

To script out a SQL Agent job, start SSMS, connect to the database with the job you want to script, and locate the job. Then right mouse click on the job and select Script Job as, Create to, and New Query Editor Window, as shown in Figure 10-2.

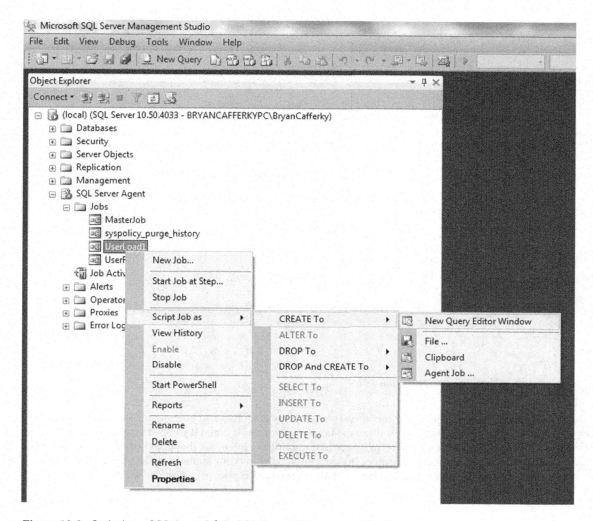

Figure 10-2. *Scripting a SQL Agent Job in SQL Server Management Studio*

The script will be displayed in a new query tab, as shown below in Figure 10-3.

```
SQLQuery2.sql - (Io...BryanCafferky (54))  ×
    USE [msdb]
    GO

    /****** Object:  Job [UserLoad1]     Script Date: 4/4/2015 4:28:27 PM ******/
  ⊟BEGIN TRANSACTION
    DECLARE @ReturnCode INT
    SELECT @ReturnCode = 0
    /****** Object:  JobCategory [[Uncategorized (Local)]]]     Script Date: 4/4/2015 4:28:27 PM ******/
  ⊟IF NOT EXISTS (SELECT name FROM msdb.dbo.syscategories WHERE name=N'[Uncategorized (Local)]' AND category_class=1)
  ⊟BEGIN
    EXEC @ReturnCode = msdb.dbo.sp_add_category @class=N'JOB', @type=N'LOCAL', @name=N'[Uncategorized (Local)]'
    IF (@@ERROR <> 0 OR @ReturnCode <> 0) GOTO QuitWithRollback

    END

    DECLARE @jobId BINARY(16)
  ⊟EXEC @ReturnCode =  msdb.dbo.sp_add_job @job_name=N'UserLoad1',
            @enabled=1,
            @notify_level_eventlog=0,
            @notify_level_email=0,
            @notify_level_netsend=0,
            @notify_level_page=0,
            @delete_level=0,
            @description=N'No description available.',
            @category_name=N'[Uncategorized (Local)]',
            @owner_login_name=N'BRYANCAFFERKYPC\BryanCafferky', @job_id = @jobId OUTPUT
    IF (@@ERROR <> 0 OR @ReturnCode <> 0) GOTO QuitWithRollback
    /****** Object:  Step [WaitForFile]     Script Date: 4/4/2015 4:28:28 PM ******/
  ⊟EXEC @ReturnCode = msdb.dbo.sp_add_jobstep @job_id=@jobId, @step_name=N'WaitForFile',
            @step_id=1,
            @cmdexec_success_code=0,
            @on_success_action=1,
            @on_success_step_id=0,
            @on_fail_action=2,
```

Figure 10-3. A SQL Agent job-creation script

From there, just connect to the server you want to copy the job to and execute the script. Of course, you will need to copy any scripts the job calls to the target server as well. Note: If you just want to clone the job on the same server, change the variable @job_name in the script to a job name that does not exist on the server.

Using SQL Agent as the job scheduler makes it easy to deploy your application. However, PowerShell has its own built-in scheduler, and the Windows Task Scheduler is also an option. We will discuss these in more detail later.

Summary

In this chapter, we discussed configuring PowerShell applications, best practices, and application deployment. We started with how to configure PowerShell applications to maximize flexibility, ease of maintenance, and simplicity of deployment. A nice feature of SSIS is that it has a number of methods to support configuration. We discussed how to achieve comparable functionality in PowerShell, considering several approaches. Then, we discussed the goals of best practices and how to apply them to PowerShell. We closed by discussing PowerShell application deployment and ways to simplify this process.

CHAPTER 11

■ ■ ■

PowerShell Versus SSIS

Introduction

In this chapter we will discuss using PowerShell as an extract, transform, and load (ETL) tool as an alternative to using SQL Server Integration Services (SSIS). We start by comparing PowerShell to SSIS. Then we define the general pattern of an ETL tool—extract from a source, transform the data, and write the data to a destination. In covering the application of these concepts, we employ a fictitious ETL use case that requires a number of files to be loaded into SQL Server tables.

To streamline PowerShell as an ETL tool, we need a reusable framework that makes code easy to develop and maintain while minimizing data-specific coding. We will use the PowerShell pipeline as a data flow. In prior chapters, we built reusable functions to get data, so the challenge here is to create reusable code to support loading data into a database. We'll review a function that builds a mapping collection that defines the source to destination column names. By leveraging the mapping collection together with the pipeline, we will explain how we can load data into database tables with just function calls. The exception to this is when we need column transformations. While these do require data-specific code, we will demonstrate how it can be isolated to a single function that the pipeline passes through. The transformation function can modify or replace the pipeline. Referencing the use case, we demonstrate how to load a number of different file formats into tables. We show how advanced transformations like code/value look-ups and file joins can easily be accomplished. The latter is provided as a function by the Microsoft PowerShell team. We are using the modules umd_database, umd_etl_functions, and umd_northwind_etl in this chapter, so you need to import these in order to run the examples.

Advantages of PowerShell as an ETL Tool

PowerShell has a number of advantages that make it a good choice for ETL work. It's free and pre-installed, and it has features that are missing from SSIS, such as the ability to support user interaction. PowerShell can easily leverage any Windows program, adding functionality that may be difficult to implement in SSIS. The ability to create script modules that encapsulate functions provides a high degree of reusability. SSIS binds its processes to the underlying metadata, thus making packages sensitive to changes, but PowerShell code can be dynamic and adapt automatically to changes. Finally, SSIS upgrades can be time consuming and costly. PowerShell upgrades occur seamlessly with upgrades to the .NET framework.

Pre-Installed and Free

PowerShell is free and is pre-installed on Windows 7 and later. SSIS is part of SQL Server, which requires a paid license. To develop SSIS packages, SQL Server Data Tools must be installed on the client. For organizations that use SSIS to load SQL Server data warehouses, this may not be an issue. But there are times when SSIS is not available. For example, PowerShell could be used by a vendor to load tables to non-Microsoft databases, such as Oracle or MySQL, where the client does not have SQL Server installed. In this way, PowerShell supports database-platform independence, which is needed for multi-platform vendors. There are scenarios in which an end user needs to load database tables but the organization does not want to give the user the SSIS client tools or allow them access to execute packages in the SSIS catalog. PowerShell resolves these issues.

Supports Interaction

There are times when an ETL script may need to get information from the user at run time. Perhaps the script needs to get a filter parameter or must allow the user to select among some options. SSIS is designed to be executed in batch mode, with no support for user interaction. PowerShell supports interactivity, as we have seen. Windows forms can be easily incorporated for a professional interface, or cmdlets such as Read-Host can be used for a simpler implementation.

PowerShell Goes Where SSIS Can't

PowerShell is integrated with the .NET framework, enabling it to programmatically access any Windows resource. In this book, we have seen examples of PowerShell using the Internet Explorer client to navigate the Web, programmatically manipulate office documents, create environment variables, query the event log, and even speak using the speech API (SAPI). But PowerShell can also interface with SharePoint, Exchange Server, Active Directory, and more. The point is that PowerShell was designed to do anything, while SSIS was designed for ETL. There are times when we need those other capabilities. Additionally, Microsoft's cloud environment, Azure, does not have SSIS available. However, PowerShell is available on Azure and is generally promoted as the tool to use to automate work.

Reusability and Extensibility

PowerShell provides the ability to create functions and package them into modules, thus extending PowerShell with new capabilities and a high level of reusability. We can develop a function, deploy it, and never need to write code to do that task again. It can be called anywhere the function is needed. There are many free modules available that add functionality that is not built-in. The great thing is that using modules is a seamless experience. Once imported, the functions are called just like built-in cmdlets. SSIS has little support for reusability. Each package is designed to do a specific task. Other than changing configuration settings, the behavior is static. Even SSIS script tasks and script components cannot be shared. Instead, they need to be copied wherever they are needed, creating code redundancy with related maintenance issues. Note: Technically, functions written in PowerShell script are not considered cmdlets. Only when it is written in a compiled language like C# is it called a cmdlet. However, this distinction is just semantics, and I use the terms *function* and *cmdlet* interchangeably throughout the book.

Dynamic Code

A limitation to SSIS is that packages are tightly coupled to the metadata of the sources and destinations. If a new column is added to a source table, the package may fail because it stores details about the underlying structure. Moreover, there are times when it would be useful to create a dynamic process that could automatically add new tables to the ETL process. An example of this would be a package that loads source tables to a staging area. If a new table is added, it would be nice if the package could just create the table on the destination server and load the data. The database catalog views can provide the metadata needed to do this, but SSIS does not support this level of dynamic processing without getting into some fairly complex scripting. PowerShell is interpreted and therefore is inherently dynamic. Scripts can query the source metadata, create the target tables, and load the data.

Upgrades and Code Dependencies

SSIS is part of SQL Server, and as such gets upgraded with SQL Server releases. Oftentimes, a new release of SSIS is not completely backward compatible and legacy packages must be converted to a new format. This is not a trivial task. For example, to upgrade from SQL Server 2008 R2 to SQL Server 2012, all the packages have to go through the Migration Wizard and be reviewed for any unsupported code. The level of effort depends on how many packages are involved. PowerShell, however, is not affected by SQL Server releases. New versions of PowerShell are released with new versions of the Windows Management Framework, i.e., the .NET library. I have used PowerShell 2.0 through 4.0 and have found no backward compatibility issues. One explanation for this is that PowerShell is so pervasive throughout Windows environments, including Azure, that it must be backward compatible. Microsoft would suffer the most if it were not. Additionally, since PowerShell code is stored in text files, there are no potential file-conversion issues as can be the case with SSIS.

Advantages of SSIS

SSIS has some strengths over PowerShell as an ETL tool. SSIS performs well and can load data very quickly. It provides a sophisticated visual development environment. As part of SQL Server, SSIS integrates extremely well with the SQL Server environment. Over the years, SSIS has developed robust configuration features that simplify ETL maintenance and deployment. SSIS is delivered with a number of useful controls and transformation components designed for ETL work.

Performance

When moving a large volume of data, SSIS can't be beat. It accomplishes this partly by the way it constructs the data-flow buffer. It analyzes the flow from start to finish and allocates enough memory to accommodate the sources, transformations, and derived columns so that the data does not need to be copied more than once. Destination adapters can be adjusted, especially for SQL Server, to optimize batch sizes and use features like fast load. Performance is the forte of SSIS and is often the best reason to choose it for an ETL task.

Visual Development Interface

The Visual Studio development environment for SSIS provides a quick and intuitive interface to develop packages. The ability to drop controls onto the canvas and interactively set properties is appealing to many people. It is ideal for building ETL processes incrementally since the developer can create and test individual components. Unless a script task or script component is needed, no code needs to be written. All work can be done visually. This can be particularly attractive to people without a programming background.

SQL Server Integration and Configuration

With the release of SQL Server 2012, SSIS added tight SQL Server integration. Packages can be grouped into projects that can be deployed directly to the SSIS catalog in SQL Server. SQL Server Management Studio provides a rich visual interface to this catalog, supporting the ability to configure project and package settings. Groups of settings can be saved into a container called an environment, and packages configured to get values from these environments. This makes deployment easy, since the same environment container can exist on each server with different values. SQL Agent jobs running SSIS packages can be configured to use environments as well. A number of built-in reports are available from the SSIS catalog, including reports that provide detailed information about package failures. PowerShell does not inherently support this degree of configurability or integration with SQL Server.

Built-In Components

While PowerShell can do the things that SSIS can do,some coding must be done first. The SSIS built-in data-flow transformations provide fast look up, match, join, and merge functionality. A number of column-transformation functions are available to modify columns in the data flow. For some of these, there is a PowerShell equivalent. For others, it must be written or sought out on the Internet, perhaps in the form of a module.

The PowerShell ETL Framework

ETL (extract, transform, and load), as the name implies, involves three steps. First, extract data from a source. This can be a flat file, an Office document, an XML file, a Web service, or any data source. Usually some level of modification to the data needs to be performed before it is loaded to its destination. Sometimes data needs to be scrubbed of bad values or reformatted to meet reporting requirements. Other times, additional information must be looked up from another source. Often times, the input data needs to be split and sent to multiple destinations. All these tasks are broadly categorized as transforming the data. Once the data transformation is complete, it is loaded to the destination. There are some tasks that don't easily fit into this simple model, such as creating a table in the destination database, unzipping files, or sending email notifications. These additional tasks support the ETL process.

PowerShell is not designed to be an ETL tool. We could just write custom scripts and functions to copy, transform, and load data for each data source. But this would eliminate the benefit of reusability. Instead, let's consider how an ETL framework that supports reusability and maintainability can be created in PowerShell. Let's review a proposed framework in Figure 11-1.

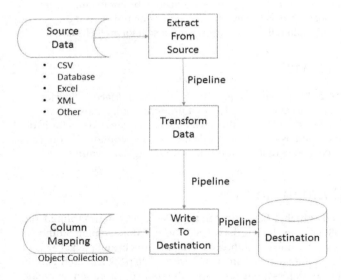

Figure 11-1. *An ETL framework for PowerShell*

SSIS moves data from the source to the destination through something called a data buffer. We don't have this available in PowerShell. However, we do have something analogous, which is the pipeline. In fact, conceptually the SSIS data buffer and the PowerShell pipeline are very similar. So, in our framework we will use the pipeline to move data. This works well, because once data has entered the pipeline, it can be manipulated in a consistent manner. The source becomes irrelevant. In Figure 11-1, we see the first step is for a task to pull data from a source and stream it into the pipeline. From there it flows into a Transform Data step where the pipeline properties are modified, dropped, or added. Once the transformations are complete, the pipeline is passed to the task, which writes it to the destination. The task is not labeled *Load*, because the pipeline data could be used to add, update, or delete the destination data. Note: SSIS destination components only support inserting the data-flow buffer into the destination.

Notice that the "Write to Destination" step has a column-mapping collection as input. To support writing data to the destination, a mapping of source columns to destination columns is needed. Even if no transformations are required, the source and destination column names may be different. We could hard code the mapping in each script, but then our ETL code would be custom developed with no reusability. Instead, we want to create a way to support source-to-destination mapping that can be reused. Note: All the reusable functions we'll look at next that are part of the framework can be found in the module umd_etl_functions.

Mapping

To support the framework in Figure 11-1, we'll create a function that develops a mapping collection of source-to-destination columns. This mapping will be used by the output process to determine where the data should be written. Let's look at the function that follows:

```
function Add-UdfMapping {
 [CmdletBinding()]
      param (
              [string]    $incolumn            , # Column from input pipeline.
              [string]    $outcolumn           , # Output column name.
              [string]    $outcolumndelimiter  , # Character to delimit output column.
              [bool]      $iskey                 # True = Key column, False = Not key column
         )

    $mapping = New-Object –TypeName System.Object
    $mapping | Add-Member -MemberType NoteProperty -Name "InColumn" -Value "$incolumn"
    $mapping | Add-Member -MemberType NoteProperty -Name "OutColumn" -Value $outcolumn
    $mapping | Add-Member -MemberType NoteProperty -Name "OutColumnDelimiter" `
                          -Value "$outcolumndelimiter"
    $mapping | Add-Member -MemberType NoteProperty -Name "IsKey" -Value "$iskey"

    RETURN $mapping

}
```

This function accepts the parameters $incolumn, which is the source column name, $outcolumn, which is the destination column name, $outcolumndelimiter, which will be used when generating a SQL statement to delimit values, and $iskey, which is $true if the column is the key and $false if it is not. This function uses a pattern we have seen before—we use psobject and attach properties to hold values we need to retain. The function in our example creates an object, attaches the properties, and returns the object to the caller. It's a simple function but it provides a nice abstraction to support our ETL framework.

To get our feet wet using the Add-UdfMapping function, we'll start with a simple load. We'll load the state tax rate CSV file to a SQL Server table. Before we create the mapping collection, we can use the SQL script in Listing 11-1 to create the destination table on SQL Server. For the examples, the server instance is (local) and the database is Development. Change these settings to fit your environment.

Listing 11-1. Create the StateSalesTaxRate table

```
CREATE TABLE [dbo].[StateSalesTaxRate](
        [StateProvinceCD] [varchar](255) NULL,
        [StateProvinceSalesTaxRate] [decimal](5, 2) NULL,
        [CreateDate] [datetime] NULL
)
```

The state sales tax file has only two columns, i.e. StateCode and SalesTaxRate. The source column names are different than the target SQL Server column names. We'll create a mapping collection to map the source to target columns using the statements here:

```
Import-Module umd_etl_functions
$mappingset = @()  # Create a collection object.
$mappingset += (Add-UdfMapping "StateCode" "StateProvinceCD" "'" $true)
$mappingset += (Add-UdfMapping "SalesTaxRate" "StateProvinceSalesTaxRate" "" $false)
```

The first line creates an empty collection. Then, Add-UdfMapping is called, passing in the source column name StateCode; the destination column name StateProvinceCD; the character to use as a value delimiter, i.e., '; and $true to the iskey Boolean, indicating this is the key column. The last line adds a mapping for the SalesTaxRate column to the mapping collection. Notice the iskey parameter is $false, because this is not the primary key column. Enter the statement that follows to see the contents of $mappingset:

```
$mappingset
```

This should display the following output to the console:

InColumn	OutColumn	OutColumnDelimiter	IsKey
StateCode	StateProvinceCD	'	True
SalesTaxRate	StateProvinceSalesTaxRate		False

The purpose of the mapping collection is to help our code generate the required SQL statements to load the data. We iterate over the collection to build our statements. Building a string that contains a SQL statement can get a little messy. For a given SQL statement, there is a fixed set of words, the input column names, input column values, and the output column names. Consider the Insert statement for the state sales tax file:

```
Insert into [dbo].[StateSalesTaxRate]
([StateProvinceCD],
 [StateProvinceSalesTaxRate])
Values
('MA',
.06)
```

We would need a statement like this one for each row in the file. The words "Insert into" are static; i.e., they will always be the same. This is followed by the target table name and column name, so those must be variables, but once assigned they will stay the same for all inserts into the table. Then, the characters "Values (" appear, which are static. The source column values separated by commas must be updated for each insert; i.e., we will need to iterate over the source collection, generate the insert statement, and execute it for each set of values. We want to be able to generate Merge, Update, and Delete statements. To provide for maximum flexibility, let's create two helper functions. What follows is a function that takes a mapping collection as a parameter and returns the list of the input column names as a string separated by commas. See here:

```
function Get-UdfInColumnList
{
[CmdletBinding()]
      param (
              [psobject]  $mapping
              )

  $inlist = ""                          # Just intializing
  foreach ($map in $mapping)
  {
    $inlist += $map.InColumn + ", "
  }

  $inlist = $inlist.Substring(0,$inlist.Length - 2)
  Return $inlist

}
```

This function takes the mapping collection as a parameter. The code iterates over the collection, extracting the source column name, i.e., the InColumn property, and appending it and a trailing comma to the variable $inlist. When the loop ends, $inlist contains the list of columns separated by commas. However, there is one extra comma at the end that we remove in the statement just before the Return statement. Finally, $inlist is returned to the caller.

Assuming the umd_etl_functions module has been imported, we can call the function Get-UdfInColumnList with the mapping set we created, as shown here:

```
Get-UdfInColumnList $mappingset
```

We should see the following output:

```
StateCode, SalesTaxRate
```

For the Insert statement, we'll need a list of the output column names separated by commas. The function here will do that:

```
function Get-UdfOutColumnList
{
[CmdletBinding()]
      param (
                [psobject] $mapping
          )
```

```
$outlist = ""                          # Just initializing
foreach ($map in $mapping)
{
  $outlist += $map.OutColumn + ", "
}

$outlist = $outlist.Substring(0,$outlist.Length - 2)
Return $outlist

}
```

Get-UdfOutColumnList takes a mapping collection as a parameter. The code iterates over the collection, extracting the destination column name, i.e., the OutColumn property, and appending it and a trailing comma to the variable $outlist. When the loop ends, $outlist contains the list of columns separated by commas. However, there is one extra comma at the end that we remove in the statement just before the Return statement. Finally, $outlist is returned to the caller.

Assuming the umd_etl_functions module has been imported, we can call the function with the mapping set we created, as shown here:

```
Get-UdfOutColumnList $mappingset
```

We should see the following line written to the console:

```
StateProvinceCD, StateProvinceSalesTaxRate
```

The helper functions are great, but what we really need is a function that will build the SQL statement for us. The function that follows uses the helper functions to generate an Insert, Merge, or Delete statement based on what is requested. See here:

```
function Get-UdfSQLDML {
 [CmdletBinding()]
      param (
                [psobject] $mapping,
                [parameter(mandatory=$true,
                       HelpMessage="Enter the DML operation.")]
                       [ValidateSet("Insert","Merge", "Delete")]
                [string]    $dmloperation,
                [string]    $destinationtablename
             )
 [string] $sqldml = ""
 Switch ($dmloperation)
 {
 Insert
   {
     $sqldml = "insert into $destinationtablename (" + (Get-UdfOutColumn $mapping) + ") `
             values (`$valuelist);" ; break
   }
```

```
   Merge
     {
        $key = $mapping | Where-Object { $_.IsKey -eq $true }
        $sourcekey = $key.Incolumn
        $targetkey = $key.OutColumn
        $sourcecollist = (Get-UdfInColumnList $mapping);
        $insertstatement = `
        "insert (" + (Get-UdfOutColumn $mapping) + ") values (`$valuelist)";

        $sqldml = "
                Merge into $destinationtablename as Target USING (VALUES ( `$valuelist )) as `
                Source ( $sourcecollist `
          ) ON Target.$targetkey = Source.$sourcekey `
          WHEN MATCHED THEN                        `
                UPDATE SET `$updatestatement
          WHEN NOT MATCHED BY TARGET THEN $insertstatement;"; break;
     }
   Delete
     {
        $key = $mapping | Where-Object { $_.IsKey -eq $true }
        $targetkey = $key.OutColumn
        $sqldml = "Delete from $destinationtablename where $targetkey = `$sourcekeyvalue;"
        break
     }
   }

   Return $sqldml
}
```

The function Get-UdfSQLDML is doing a lot. Its purpose is to return the requested SQL statement to the caller using the mapping-set collection. Let's review the code step by step, starting with the function header, copied here:

```
function Get-UdfSQLDML {
 [CmdletBinding()]
      param (
              [psobject] $mapping,
              [parameter(mandatory=$true,
                      HelpMessage="Enter the DML operation.")]
                      [ValidateSet("Insert","Merge", "Delete")]
              [string]   $dmloperation,
              [string]   $destinationtablename
            )
```

In the function header, we can see the function accepts $mapping, i.e., the mapping-set collection, as the first parameter, followed by $dmloperation, which is the type of SQL statement desired, and $destinationtablename, which is the name of the target table. Note: The ValidationSet attribute on the $dmloperation parameter limits accepted values to Insert, Merge, or Delete.

The next part of the function evaluates the $dmloperation parameter to determine the code to execute. Let's look at the code now:

```
[string] $sqldml = ""
Switch ($dmloperation)
{
Insert
  {
    $sqldml = "insert into $destinationtablename (" + (Get-UdfOutColumn $mapping) + ") `
          values (`$valuelist);" ; break
  }
```

The Switch command provides a concise way to test a condition and execute code based on the result. Based on the value of $dmloperation, the related code is executed. If $dmloperation is Insert, then the variable $sqldml is assigned a value to generate an insert statement. Notice the call to Get-UdfOutColumn. It is enclosed in parentheses, so the function will be executed before being added to the string; i.e., it appends the list of destination columns extracted from $mapping. Another interesting feature is the use of the ` character before the variable $valuelist. The reason for this is that we want the variable name, not its value, to be in the string for now. The break statement tells PowerShell to exit without performing the other comparisons. Later, when we are iterating through the source values, we will expand the string to fill in the values.

If the caller passed Merge as the $dmloperation parameter, the code here would execute:

```
Merge
  {
    $key = $mapping | Where-Object { $_.IsKey -eq $true }
    $sourcekey = $key.Incolumn
    $targetkey = $key.OutColumn
    $sourcecollist = (Get-UdfInColumnList $mapping);
    $insertstatement =          `
    "insert (" + (Get-UdfOutColumn $mapping) + ") values (`$valuelist)";

    $sqldml = "
    Merge into $destinationtablename as Target USING (VALUES ( `$valuelist )) as `
    Source ( $sourcecollist `
     ) ON Target.$targetkey = Source.$sourcekey `
      WHEN MATCHED THEN                             `
          UPDATE SET `$updatestatement
      WHEN NOT MATCHED BY TARGET THEN $insertstatement;"; break;
  }
```

The Merge statement is more complex than the Insert statement, and more powerful. The Merge statement will match the source data to the target data based on a key column, and then will execute any number of operations depending on whether there is a match or not. In our case, if there is a match, we want to do an update. If there is no match, we want to do an insert. The first statement in the Merge block locates the key column by piping the mapping set through a Where-Object cmdlet, which returns the row where the IsKey attribute is $true. For simplicity, this is limited to one key column. Then, the source key column name is stored in $sourcekey, and the target key column name is stored in $targetkey. The function Get-UdfInColumnList is called, passing $mapping, with the result stored in $sourcecollist. The Insert portion of the Merge statement is assigned to $insertstatement. The rest of the code, up until the break command, is actually one statement broken up over multiple lines using the continuation character. Since the destination table name will be the same for all the generated Merge statements, it is expanded immediately. However, the value list, $valuelist, will need to be changed for each source row. Therefore, $valuelist is preceded by the escape character ` so it will not be expanded yet. The source column list, target key, and source key will be the same for all generated statements, so they are expanded immediately, i.e., in the variables $sourcecollist, $targetkey, and $sourcekey. The update part of the Merge statement needs to use each set of row values, so we don't expand it yet—in other words, $updatestatement is preceded with the escape character ` so it will not be expanded yet. The last line of the Merge statement includes the variable $insertstatement we built earlier, and it is immediately expanded, except for the embedded $valuelist variable, because that is preceded with the escape character. The break statement is needed to break out of the Switch statement code block.

The third type of SQL statement is a Delete statement. The code that generates this statement type is seen here:

```
Delete
  {
     $key = $mapping | Where-Object { $_.IsKey -eq $true }
     $targetkey = $key.OutColumn
     $sqldml = "Delete from $destinationtablename where $targetkey = `$sourcekeyvalue;"
     break
  }
```

The first line in the Delete code block pipes the mapping collection, $mapping, into the Where-Object cmdlet, which returns just the row flagged as the key. The statement after that stores the target table key column name in $targetkey. The last statement builds the delete statement using the variables $destinationtablename and $targetkey, which are expanded immediately, and $sourcekeyvalue, which is not expanded, i.e., is prefixed with the escape character.

The function Get-UdfSQLDML is a building block that will be used to generate the statements to load data to a database table. Assuming the umd_etl_functions module has been imported, here are some examples of calling those statements:

```
Get-UdfSQLDML $mappingset -dmloperation Insert "dbo.Products"
Get-UdfSQLDML $mappingset -dmloperation Merge "dbo.Products"
Get-UdfSQLDML $mappingset -dmloperation Delete "dbo.Products"
```

This produces the following output to the console. Blank lines are added between statements for readability:

```
insert into dbo.Products (StateProvinceCD, StateProvinceSalesTaxRate) values ($valuelist);

Merge into dbo.Products as Target USING (VALUES ( $valuelist )) as Source ( StateCode,
SalesTaxRate
        ) ON Target.StateProvinceCD = Source.StateCode
        WHEN MATCHED THEN
            UPDATE SET $updatestatement
        WHEN NOT MATCHED BY TARGET THEN insert (StateProvinceCD,
        StateProvinceSalesTaxRate)
        values ($valuelist);

Delete from dbo.Products where StateProvinceCD = $sourcekeyvalue;
```

In these generated statements, notice that there are unexpanded variables. They will be expanded after we have loaded them with values from the source.

We could look to the umd_database module and use the custom connection object created using the function New-UdfConnection, as discussed in chapter 7, to write to the database. However, that object's SQL methods open and close the connection for every execution, which would add a lot of unnecessary overhead. Instead, we will create a simple function that will create and open a database connection and pass it back to us. So we don't have to pass as many parameters, we will still use the connection object created by New-UdfConnection. Let's look at the function:

```
function Get-UdfADOConnection
{
 [CmdletBinding()]
        param (
                [psobject]$connection
            )

if ($connection.UseCredential -eq 'Y')
  {
     $pw =  $sqlpw
     $pw.MakeReadOnly()

     $SqlCredential = `
     new-object System.Data.SqlClient.SqlCredential($connection.UserID, $connection.Password)
     $conn = new-object System.Data.SqlClient.SqlConnection($connection.ConnectionString, `
     $SqlCredential)
  }
  else
  {
     $conn = new-object System.Data.SqlClient.SqlConnection($connection.ConnectionString);
  }

  $conn.Open()

  Return $conn
}
```

Get-UdfADOConnection creates and opens an ADO connection object and passes it back to the caller. It takes the custom database object created by the function New-UdfConnection from the umd_database module. Although we won't use the returned object to load the data, it provides a convenient way to define the required connection properties. The function checks to see if the UseCredential property is set to 'Y' for yes. If so, it opens the connection using credentials. Otherwise, it just opens the connection using the object's connection string property.

The next function, Invoke-UdfSQLDML, uses these functions to do the work of writing to the database. We stream the data into the function via the pipeline. Let's look at the code:

```
function Invoke-UdfSQLDML
{
[CmdletBinding()]
        param (
                [Parameter(ValueFromPipeline=$True)]$mypipe = "default",
                [Parameter(ValueFromPipeline=$False,Mandatory=$True,Position=1)]
                [psobject] $mapping,
                [parameter(ValueFromPipeline=$False,mandatory=$true,Position=2,
                        HelpMessage="Enter the DML operation.")]
                        [ValidateSet("Insert","Update","Merge","Delete")]
```

```
                [string]    $dmloperation,
                [Parameter(ValueFromPipeline=$False,Mandatory=$True,Position=3)]
                [string]    $destinationtablename,
                [psobject] $connection

            )

begin
{
 $sqldml = Get-UdfSQLDML $mapping -dmloperation $dmloperation "$destinationtablename"
 $dbconn = Get-UdfADOConnection $connection
 $command = New-Object system.data.sqlclient.Sqlcommand($dbconn)
}

process
{
    $values = ""
    $updatestatement = ""

     foreach($map in $mapping)
     {
        $prop = $map.InColumn.Replace("[", "")
        $prop = $prop.Replace("]", "")
        $delimiter = $map.OutColumnDelimiter
        $values = $values + $delimiter + $_.$prop + $delimiter + ","
        $updatestatement += $map.OutColumn + " = Source." + $map.InColumn + ","
        #  Get the key column value...
        if ($map.IsKey -eq $true)
        {
            $sourcekeyvalue = $_.$prop
        }
     }

    # Strip off the last comma.
    $updatestatement = $updatestatement.Substring(0,$updatestatement.Length - 1)
    $valuelist = $values.Substring(0,$values.Length - 1)  # Strip off the last comma.
    $sqlstatement = $ExecutionContext.InvokeCommand.ExpandString($sqldml)
    $sqlstatement = $sqlstatement.Replace(",,", ",null,")
    Write-Verbose $sqlstatement

    # Write to database...
    $command.Connection = $dbconn
    $command.CommandText = $sqlstatement
    $command.ExecuteNonQuery()

}
end
{
    $dbconn.Close()
}

}
```

Let's step through this function to see how it works. We'll start with the function header copied here:

```
function Invoke-UdfSQLDML
{
 [CmdletBinding()]
       param (
                [Parameter(ValueFromPipeline=$True)]$mypipe = "default",
                [Parameter(ValueFromPipeline=$False,Mandatory=$True,Position=1)]
                [psobject] $mapping,
                [parameter(ValueFromPipeline=$False,mandatory=$true,Position=2,
                         HelpMessage="Enter the DML operation.")]
                         [ValidateSet("Insert","Merge", "Delete")]
                [string]    $dmloperation,
                [Parameter(ValueFromPipeline=$False,Mandatory=$True,Position=3)]
                [string]    $destinationtablename,
                [psobject] $connection

           )
```

We can see that the first parameter, $mypipe, will come in via the pipeline, because the attribute ValueFromPipeline is true. The second parameter, $mapping, is the mapping collection. The third parameter, $dmloperation, is the type of SQL statement we want the function to use. The ValidateSet attribute limits the allowed values and will be visible to the developer via Intellisense. The fourth parameter, $destinationtablename, is the target table to which we want the data written. The last parameter, $connection, is a psobject created by New-UdfConnection. We use the function New-UdfConnection, which is part of the umd_database module, to create the object to be passed into the last parameter.

Invoke-UdfSQLDML is going to process the pipeline, thus it has three parts, which are begin, process, and end. Let's look at the begin block:

```
begin
    {
     $sqldml = Get-UdfSQLDML $mapping -dmloperation $dmloperation "$destinationtablename"
     $dbconn = Get-UdfADOConnection $connection
     $command = new-object system.data.sqlclient.Sqlcommand($dbconn)
    }
```

The begin block will execute only once, and it does so before the pipeline is received. It's a good place to do setup work. The first statement calls the function Get-UdfSQLDML, passing in the mapping collection, the SQL statement type, and destination table name as parameters. The SQL statement will be returned and stored in the variable $sqldml. The SQL statement will then be complete except for the parts requiring data values. The second statement calls Get-UdfADOConnection, which will open a database connection and return the reference to $dbconn. We don't want to use the SQL methods attached to the connection object passed in as a parameter, because they open and close the connection for each row, which would add a lot of overhead. We want to open the connection once, process all the source rows, and then close the connection. The last line in the begin block creates a command object named $command. The command object is the object that submits SQL statements to the database. After the begin block executes, the function is ready to send commands to the database. Let's look at the process block that actually writes to the database:

```
process
    {
        $values = ""
        $updatestatement = ""
```

```
    foreach($map in $mapping)
    {
        $prop = $map.InColumn.Replace("[", "")
        $prop = $prop.Replace("]", "")
        $delimiter = $map.OutColumnDelimiter
        $values = $values + $delimiter + $_.$prop + $delimiter + ","
        $updatestatement += $map.OutColumn + " = Source." + $map.InColumn + ","
        #  Get the key column value...
        if ($map.IsKey -eq $true)
        {
            $sourcekeyvalue = $_.$prop
        }
    }


    # Strip off the last comma.
    $updatestatement = $updatestatement.Substring(0,$updatestatement.Length - 1
    $valuelist = $values.Substring(0,$values.Length - 1)  # Strip off the last comma.
    $sqlstatement = $ExecutionContext.InvokeCommand.ExpandString($sqldml)
    $sqlstatement = $sqlstatement.Replace(",,", ",null,")
    Write-Verbose $sqlstatement

    # Write to database...
    $command.Connection = $dbconn
    $command.CommandText = $sqlstatement
    $command.ExecuteNonQuery()


}
```

Recall that the begin block prepared the SQL statement, except for supplying the column values. The process block needs to fill in the Values section of the SQL statement and execute the statement. For the State Tax table load, we want to do an Insert. When the process block begins executing, the SQL statement will look like the one that follows. We just need to fill $valuelist with the list of values to be inserted and then tell PowerShell to expand the statement, replacing $valuelist with the variable's contents. Let's look at that statement now:

```
insert into dbo.Products (StateProvinceCD, StateProvinceSalesTaxRate) values ($valuelist);
```

The first two statements in the process block just initialize the variables $values and $updatestatement. Then a ForEach loop iterates over the mapping-set collection so that we can use the mapping to build the values part of the SQL statement. In testing, I discovered that if the source columns have spaces in the names, you need to enclose them in brackets. However, when the data is moved into the pipeline, the brackets are dropped. To generate the SQL statement, we need to remove the bracket characters if present, which is what the first two lines of the ForEach block are doing. Values in a SQL statement require different enclosing delimiters depending on the data type, i.e., single quote for a string and nothing for numbers. The line "$delimiter = $map.OutColumnDelimiter" is getting the value delimiter from the mapping set and storing it in $delimiter. The line after this creates the values part of the SQL statement. The variable name, $values, is critical here, because it must be the same name as the variable embedded in the SQL statement we generated earlier.

After this, the statement $updatestatement += $map.OutColumn + " = Source." + $map.InColumn + "," uses the mapping set to build the input-to-output column assignment needed for an Update statement. In the case of the State Tax table, this will not be used, because we're doing an insert. If we were doing an update, the variable $updatestatement would match the variable name in the generated SQL statement. Next, we see an If block that checks for the IsKey value of true and, if found, loads the value of the column into $sourcekeyvalue.

This variable is needed to create the SQL Merge and Delete statements, i.e. where key = somevalue. By the time the ForEach loop is finished, we will have iterated over the entire set of columns, building required parts of the SQL statement. Column names and values in a SQL statement are separated by commas, which the function added to the end of each as the statement was being built. However, this leaves an extra comma at the end of the list. The first two statements after the ForEach loop just strip off the trailing comma.

The statement after this leverages the ability to force PowerShell to expand variables in a string on demand. For example, '$sqlstatement = $ExecutionContext.InvokeCommand.ExpandString($sqldml)' returns the string $sqldml, with all the embedded variables replaced with the variable contents to $sqlstatement. The statement is now almost ready to be executed, but we need to do one more thing first. Missing values may cause the statement to fail. They can easily be identified because the string will have two commas together, which SQL Server will reject. The statement '$sqlstatement = $sqlstatement. Replace(",,", ",null,")' will replace the double commas with ",null," which tells SQL Server this is a null value.

The Write-Verbose statement after this is a handy feature that allows us to output the SQL statement to the console. With all this string manipulation, it is easy to get something wrong so it's a good idea to be able to see the statement. The nice thing is that it will only display when the Verbose parameter is used. The final three statements in the process block attach the connection to the command object, load the SQL statement into the command object, and execute the statement.

The last block in this function is the End block, which is copied here:

```
end
    {
        $dbconn.Close()
    }
```

The end block just closes the database connection. The End block is only executed after the entire pipeline has been processed, so it's the perfect place to do clean up.

We've created the state tax file columns to destination column mapping collection so we are ready to use the example function to actually load the table. The statements in Listing 11-2 will do this. Note: Listing 11-2 is also coded as a function in the module umd_northwind_etl that is named Invoke-UdfStateSalesTaxLoad.

Listing 11-2. Script to load the state sales tax table

```
Import-Module umd_database -Force
Import-Module umd_etl_functions -Force

# State Code List
$global:referencepath = $env:HomeDrive + $env:HOMEPATH + "\Documents\"

$salestax = Import-CSV ($global:referencepath + "StateSalesTaxRates.csv")

<# Define the mapping... #>
$mappingset = @()  # Create a collection object.
$mappingset += (Add-UdfMapping "StateCode" "StateProvinceCD" "'" $true)
$mappingset += (Add-UdfMapping "SalesTaxRate" "StateProvinceSalesTaxRate" "" $false)

Import-Module umd_database

<# Define the SQL Server Target #>
[psobject] $SqlServer1 = New-Object psobject
New-UdfConnection ([ref]$SqlServer1)
```

```
$SqlServer1.ConnectionType = 'ADO'
$SqlServer1.DatabaseType = 'SqlServer'
$SqlServer1.Server = '(local)'
$SqlServer1.DatabaseName = 'Development'
$SqlServer1.UseCredential = 'N'
$SqlServer1.SetAuthenticationType('Integrated')
$SqlServer1.BuildConnectionString()

# Load the table...
$SqlServer1.RunSQL("truncate table [dbo].[StateSalesTaxRate]", $false)
$salestax |
Invoke-UdfSQLDML -Mapping $mappingset -DmlOperation "Insert" –Destinationtablename `
"dbo.StateSalesTaxRate" -Connection $SqlServer1 -Verbose
```

The first two statements import the umd_etl_functions and umd_database modules. The next line, after the comment, assigns the path to the user's Documents folder, where the state tax rate file should be, to variable $global:referencepath. Note: Make sure you copy the file there. Then, we load the file into $salestax. The code in parentheses forces the path value to be assigned before importing the file. The three lines after that create the mapping set. Since our functions depend on the umd_database, it is imported. The lines between '<# Define the SQL Server Target #>' and '# Load the table...' create a database connection object, which is the custom psobject returned by New-UdfConnection. As mentioned before, we are not going to use this object's built-in SQL methods, because they open and close the connection on each iteration. However, it still provides handy functionality for our needs. The second-to-last line uses the custom database object to truncate the table. The last line pipes the loaded $salestax object into the Invoke-UdfSQLDML function, which loads it into the SQL Server table. The call passes the parameters $mappingset, "Insert" as the DMLOperation, dbo.StateSalesTaxRate as the Destinationtablename, and the custom connection object $SqlServer1 as the Connection parameter. Bear in mind, the functions are reusable, so the actual ETL for this table load would be just the script we just looked at. Other table loads would have the same structure.

After running the script, we should get messages to the console like the ones here:

```
VERBOSE: insert into dbo.StateSalesTaxRate (StateProvinceCD, StateProvinceSalesTaxRate)
values ('WA',0.07);
1
VERBOSE: insert into dbo.StateSalesTaxRate (StateProvinceCD, StateProvinceSalesTaxRate)
values ('WV',0.06);
1
VERBOSE: insert into dbo.StateSalesTaxRate (StateProvinceCD, StateProvinceSalesTaxRate)
values ('WI',0.05);
1
VERBOSE: insert into dbo.StateSalesTaxRate (StateProvinceCD, StateProvinceSalesTaxRate)
values ('WY',0.04);
1
VERBOSE: insert into dbo.StateSalesTaxRate (StateProvinceCD, StateProvinceSalesTaxRate)
values ('DC',0.06);
1
```

The output here just shows the last few lines. We can see that the function Invoke-UdfSQLDML generated and submitted an Insert statement for each row in the input file. A nice feature is that once a data source is loaded into the pipeline, whether it be from another database table, an Excel spreadsheet, XML file, or whatever, we can load it using the function Invoke-UdfSQLDML.

Transformations

What happens when we need to change values in the pipeline or add new columns? We can do both of these tasks by processing the pipeline before we send it to the function that will write to the table. I considered trying to abstract this process as I did with the SQL statement generation. For example, we could extend the mapping collection to include a list of the transformations we want performed. However, this would add a great deal of complexity, and it would be difficult to cover all possible transformations. Instead, we'll look at using a source-specific approach.

As a use case, let's assume that we know one of the rows in the sales tax file is wrong. We'll assume that the tax rate for Massachusetts should be .08, and we want to replace the tax rate for just that state. Also, we were told that management wants to consolidate the United States tax rates with the state/province tax rates in other countries. To support this, we want to add a new column named Country and hard code the value 'US' so we will be able to filter out the United Sates tax rates from other countries after it has been loaded into a consolidated table. Let's look at the function to transform the state sales tax data:

```
function Invoke-UdfStateTaxFileTransformation
{
 [CmdletBinding()]
      param (
                [Parameter(ValueFromPipeline=$True)]$mypipe = "default"
               )
    process
    {

      $mypipe | Add-Member -MemberType NoteProperty -Name "Country" -Value "US"

      if ($mypipe.StateCode -eq "MA" ) { $mypipe.SalesTaxRate = .08 }

      Return $mypipe
    }
}
```

Invoke-UdfStateTaxFileTransformation takes the pipeline as input via parameter $mypipe. Since our goal is just to process the pipeline, we only need the process block. The first line in the process block just adds a NoteProperty to the pipeline called Country with a value of 'US'. Notice that the Add-Member cmdlet call does not include the Passthru parameter because we only want to return the modified pipe. Note also that if you find you are getting duplicate rows in the pipeline when you do a transformation, you should check to see if the Passthru parameter is being passed on any of the Add-Member calls. The second line in the process block tests for a StateCode equal to 'MA' for Massachusetts and, if found, sets the SalesTaxRate property to .08. The last statement returns the modified pipe to the caller.

Let's use Listing 11-3 to test the function `Invoke-UdfStateTaxFileTransformation`.

Listing 11-3. Sales tax transformation

```
Import-Module umd_etl_functions

$salestax = Import-CSV ($env:HomeDrive + $env:HOMEPATH + "\Documents\StateSalesTaxRates.csv")
$salestax | Invoke-UdfStateTaxFileTransformation
```

The first line in Listing 11-3 loads `$salestax` from the sales tax file. The second line pipes this into the transformation function `Invoke-UdfStateTaxFileTransformation`. A portion of the console output is shown to confirm the Massachusetts tax rate was updated:

```
StateCode     SalesTaxRate     Country
---------     ------------     -------
MD            0.06             US
MA            0.08             US
MI            0.06             US
```

We can also see the new `Country` attribute was added. This approach makes transforming data easy. We have all the methods, properties, and cmdlets of PowerShell to use. Although we do not have the transformation GUI that SSIS has, PowerShell provides a much richer set of transformations in the form of cmdlets, including support for regular expressions.

The Northwind Company Use Case

To provide a comprehensive explanation on how to use PowerShell to do ETL work, we will use a fairly extensive use case, which is documented in Figure 11-2.

The Northwind ETL

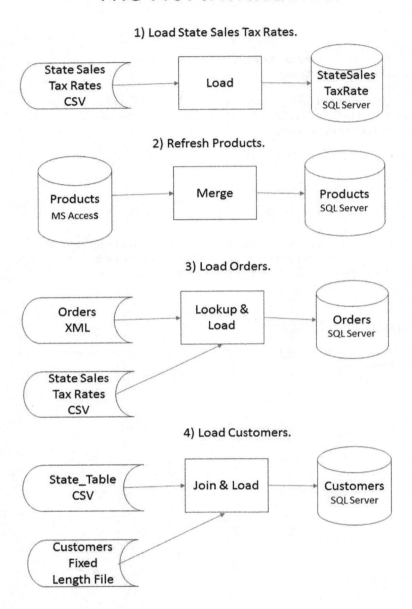

1) Load State Sales Tax Rates.

2) Refresh Products.

3) Load Orders.

4) Load Customers.

Figure 11-2. *Northwind ETL use case*

Northwind wants to load data into their new data warehouse for reporting. They are starting small and only requested the tables in Figure 11-2 be loaded. We already did Step 1, the state sales tax table load. For Step 2, we need to update the products table in SQL Server. The products data is maintained in a Microsoft

Access database table. We will load the data to the SQL Server table using a Merge statement to update existing rows and insert products not on the existing table. Step 3 loads orders data, which is stored in XML format. Unfortunately, the sales tax rate on the orders file is wrong, so we need to look up the correct tax rate in the state sales tax file. In Step 4, we need to load a customer fixed-length flat file, i.e., a file where the columns are padded with spaces so they are always the same length. We will need to join the customer data to the state table in order to get the state name and region. For convenience, the ETL scripts have been packaged into the module umd_northwind_etl, which you can reference.

The Products Table Load

Now that we've walked through how the framework helps us load data into tables using the state sales tax file, let's move on to the next step in our ETL process, the product table load. As before, we'll use the mapping collection to generate the SQL statements, but there are a couple of differences. First, the source data will be a Microsoft Access table. Second, we will use the SQL Merge statement to process the load. When a key match is found, the columns in the target table will be updated. If no match is found, the row is inserted. The source for this data is the Northwind sample database, which is available in the Access 2013 templates. To run the code in Listing 11-4, you must be in the 32-bit version of PowerShell, i.e., the one that has (x86) in the name. This is because the driver used is a 32-bit driver.

We need to create the target table in SQL Server, which we can do with the script in Listing 11-4.

Listing 11-4. Create the products table

```
CREATE TABLE [dbo].[Products](
        [SupplierIDs] [nvarchar](max) NULL,
        [ID] [int] NOT NULL,
        [ProductCode] [nvarchar](25) NULL,
        [ProductName] [nvarchar](50) NULL,
        [Description] [nvarchar](max) NULL,
        [StandardCost] [money] NULL,
        [ListPrice] [money] NOT NULL,
        [ReorderLevel] [smallint] NULL,
        [TargetLevel] [int] NULL,
        [QuantityPerUnit] [nvarchar](50) NULL,
        [Discontinued] [varchar](5) NOT NULL,
        [MinimumReorderQuantity] [smallint] NULL,
        [Category] [nvarchar](50) NULL,
        [Attachments] [nvarchar](max) NULL
)
```

The only transformation we need is to replace a null Minimum Reorder Quantity with a zero. The function to do this is seen here:

```
function  Invoke-UdfProductsTransformation
{
 [CmdletBinding()]
        param (
                [Parameter(ValueFromPipeline=$True)]$mypipe = "default"
                )
```

```
    process
    {
        if ($mypipe."Minimum Reorder Quantity" -eq [DBNull]::Value)
        { $mypipe."Minimum Reorder Quantity" = 0 }

        Return $mypipe
    }
}
```

This function is simple. However, I want to call your attention to where the value of the column "Minimum Reorder Quantity" is compared to [DBNull]::Value. That comparison will test for a database null value. Recall that $null is not really a null, but rather a default value based on the data type, so it will not work if we use it.

Now that we have the destination table defined and have reviewed the transformation function, let's look at the function that will load the products table, Invoke-UdfProductLoad, available in module umd_northwind_etl. We'll start by looking at the entire products table load function and then we'll review it in detail:

```
Import-Module umd_etl_functions -Force # uses this module
Import-Module umd_database -Force

function Invoke-UdfProductLoad
{
<#  Define the mapping... #>
$mappingset = @()  # Create a collection object.
$mappingset += (Add-UdfMapping "[Supplier IDs]" "SupplierIDs" "'" $false)
$mappingset += (Add-UdfMapping "[ID]" "ID" "" $true)
$mappingset += (Add-UdfMapping "[Product Code]" "ProductCode" "'" $false)
$mappingset += (Add-UdfMapping "[Product Name]" "ProductName" "'" $false)
$mappingset += (Add-UdfMapping "[Description]" "Description" "'" $false)
$mappingset += (Add-UdfMapping "[Standard Cost]" "StandardCost" "" $false)
$mappingset += (Add-UdfMapping "[Reorder Level]" "ReorderLevel" "" $false)
$mappingset += (Add-UdfMapping "[Target Level]" "TargetLevel" "" $false)
$mappingset += (Add-UdfMapping "[List Price]" "ListPrice" "" $false)
$mappingset += (Add-UdfMapping "[Quantity Per Unit]" "QuantityPerUnit" "'" $false)
$mappingset += (Add-UdfMapping "[Discontinued]" "Discontinued" "'" $false)
$mappingset += (Add-UdfMapping `
            "[Minimum Reorder Quantity]" "MinimumReorderQuantity" "" $false)
$mappingset += (Add-UdfMapping "[Category]" "Category" "'" $false)
$mappingset += (Add-UdfMapping "[Attachments]" "Attachments" "'" $false)

$global:referencepath = $env:HomeDrive + $env:HOMEPATH + "\Documents\"

<# Create the Access database connection object #>
[psobject] $access1 = New-Object psobject
New-UdfConnection ([ref]$access1)
$access1.ConnectionType = 'ODBC'
$access1.DatabaseType = 'Access'
$access1.DatabaseName = ($global:referencepath + 'DesktopNorthwind2007.accdb')
$access1.UseCredential = 'N'
$access1.SetAuthenticationType('DSNLess')
$access1.Driver = "Microsoft Access Driver (*.mdb, *.accdb)"
$access1.BuildConnectionString()
```

```
<# Create the SQL Server connection object #>
[psobject] $SqlServer1 = New-Object psobject
New-UdfConnection ([ref]$SqlServer1)

$SqlServer1.ConnectionType = 'ADO'
$SqlServer1.DatabaseType = 'SqlServer'
$SqlServer1.Server = '(local)'
$SqlServer1.DatabaseName = 'Development'
$SqlServer1.UseCredential = 'N'
$SqlServer1.SetAuthenticationType('Integrated')
$SqlServer1.BuildConnectionString()

$access1.RunSQL("select * from Products order by id", $true) |
Invoke-UdfProductsTransformation     `
| Invoke-UdfSQLDML -Mapping $mappingset  -DmlOperation "Merge" -Destinationtablename "[dbo].
Products" -connection $SqlServer1 –Verbose

}
```

The first step is to define the mapping as shown here:

```
function Invoke-UdfProductLoad
{
<#  Define the mapping... #>
$mappingset = @()  # Create a collection object.
$mappingset += (Add-UdfMapping "[Supplier IDs]" "SupplierIDs" "'" $false)
$mappingset += (Add-UdfMapping "[ID]" "ID" "" $true)
$mappingset += (Add-UdfMapping "[Product Code]" "ProductCode" "'" $false)
$mappingset += (Add-UdfMapping "[Product Name]" "ProductName" "'" $false)
$mappingset += (Add-UdfMapping "[Description]" "Description" "'" $false)
$mappingset += (Add-UdfMapping "[Standard Cost]" "StandardCost" "" $false)
$mappingset += (Add-UdfMapping "[Reorder Level]" "ReorderLevel" "" $false)
$mappingset += (Add-UdfMapping "[Target Level]" "TargetLevel" "" $false)
$mappingset += (Add-UdfMapping "[List Price]" "ListPrice" "" $false)
$mappingset += (Add-UdfMapping "[Quantity Per Unit]" "QuantityPerUnit" "'" $false)
$mappingset += (Add-UdfMapping "[Discontinued]" "Discontinued" "'" $false)
$mappingset += (Add-UdfMapping `
            "[Minimum Reorder Quantity]" "MinimumReorderQuantity" "" $false)
$mappingset += (Add-UdfMapping "[Category]" "Category" "'" $false)
$mappingset += (Add-UdfMapping "[Attachments]" "Attachments" "'" $false)
```

Notice that the source columns are enclosed in brackets. This is necessary when querying the columns because the column names have spaces in them. As we saw earlier, when we want to access the columns in the pipeline, we need to take out the brackets. My preference is to never include spaces in object names. It just makes it more difficult to work with them. Note: If you select the lines above in the ISE and execute them, $mappingset will be loaded; you can use the following statement to see it:

```
$mappingset
```

We would see the following output:

InColumn	OutColumn	OutColumnDelimiter	IsKey
[Supplier IDs	SupplierIDs	'	False
[ID]	ID		True
[Product Code]	ProductCode	'	False
[Product Name]	ProductName	'	False
[Description]	Description	'	False
[Standard Cost]	StandardCost		False
[Reorder Level]	ReorderLevel		False
[Target Level]	TargetLevel		False
[List Price]	ListPrice		False
[Quantity Per Unit]	QuantityPerUni	'	False
[Discontinued]	Discontinued	'	False
[Minimum Reorder Quantity]	MinimumReorderQuantity		False
[Category]	Category	'	False
[Attachments]	Attachments	'	False

We can see the values for the properties source column name (InColumn), target column name (OutColumn), SQL statement value delimiter (OutColumnDelimiter), and IsKey.

To extract the data from the Access table, we'll need to create a connection object which the statements below, copied from the load function, do. You will need to have Microsoft Access and the Access driver for your version of Access installed to run the code. Adjustments to the Driver property below may also be needed.

```
$global:referencepath = $env:HomeDrive + $env:HOMEPATH + "\Documents\"

[psobject] $access1 = New-Object psobject
New-UdfConnection ([ref]$access1)
$access1.ConnectionType = 'ODBC'
$access1.DatabaseType = 'Access'
$access1.DatabaseName = ($global:referencepath + 'DesktopNorthwind2007.accdb')
$access1.UseCredential = 'N'
$access1.SetAuthenticationType('DSNLess')
$access1.Driver = "Microsoft Access Driver (*.mdb, *.accdb)"
$access1.BuildConnectionString()
```

The first line assigns the path to the Access database file to the global variable $global:referencepath. In a real implementation, configuration variables like this would be better to assign values in the PowerShell profile script, as we covered in Chapter 10. The rest of the lines just assign the connection properties needed for the code to build the connection string.

Next, the function needs to create the destination connection object:

```
<# Create the SQL Server connection object #>
[psobject] $SqlServer1 = New-Object psobject
New-UdfConnection ([ref]$SqlServer1)

$SqlServer1.ConnectionType = 'ADO'
$SqlServer1.DatabaseType = 'SqlServer'
$SqlServer1.Server = '(local)'
$SqlServer1.DatabaseName = 'Development'
```

```
$SqlServer1.UseCredential = 'N'
$SqlServer1.SetAuthenticationType('Integrated')
$SqlServer1.BuildConnectionString()
```

A psobject variable named $SqlServer1 is created and passed into New-UdfConnection, where our custom methods and properties are added. Then, the connection properties are assigned and the method BuildConnectionString is called to generate the connection string.

Now the function is ready to load the data, which it does with the statements here:

```
$access1.RunSQL("select * from Products order by id", $true) | Invoke-
UdfProductsTransformation    `
| Invoke-UdfSQLDML -Mapping $mappingset  -DmlOperation "Merge" -Destinationtablename "[dbo].
Products" -connection $SqlServer1 -Verbose
```

The first statement uses the $access1 custom connection object to get the source data from the Access Products table. Note that the second parameter, $true, indicates that the query does return data. The results are piped into the transformation function Invoke-UdfProductsTransformation, which in turn pipes the data into Invoke-UdfSQLDML; this creates a SQL Merge statement for each row in the source and executes the statement. You should see merge statements generated and displayed to the console that are similar to the ones below, i.e. because we used the Verbose parameter:

```
VERBOSE:
    Merge into [dbo].Products as Target USING (VALUES ( '6',99,'NWTSO-99','Northwind Traders
Chicken Soup','',1
.0000,100,200,1.9500,'','False',0,'Soups','' )) as Source ( [Supplier IDs], [ID], [Product
Code], [Product Name], [Descrip
tion], [Standard Cost], [Reorder Level], [Target Level], [List Price], [Quantity Per Unit],
[Discontinued], [Minimum Reord
er Quantity], [Category], [Attachments]
        ) ON Target.ID = Source.[ID]
            WHEN MATCHED THEN
                UPDATE SET SupplierIDs = Source.[Supplier IDs],ID = Source.[ID],ProductCode
= Source.[Product Code],Produc
tName = Source.[Product Name],Description = Source.[Description],StandardCost = Source.
[Standard Cost],ReorderLevel = Sour
ce.[Reorder Level],TargetLevel = Source.[Target Level],ListPrice = Source.[List
Price],QuantityPerUnit = Source.[Quantity
Per Unit],Discontinued = Source.[Discontinued],MinimumReorderQuantity = Source.[Minimum
Reorder Quantity],Category = Sourc
e.[Category],Attachments = Source.[Attachments]
            WHEN NOT MATCHED BY TARGET THEN insert (SupplierIDs, ID, ProductCode,
ProductName, Description, StandardCost, R
eorderLevel, TargetLevel, ListPrice, QuantityPerUnit, Discontinued, MinimumReorderQuantity,
Category, Attachments) values
('6',99,'NWTSO-99','Northwind Traders Chicken Soup','',1.0000,100,200,1.9500,'','False',0,'
Soups','');
```

The pattern used to load products is the same as for any other load. Define the mappings. Create the source connection. Create the target connection. Pipe the source data through the transformation function and into the function that writes the data to the destination. Now, let's look at the order table load.

The Order Table Load

The next table we want to load is the orders table. The SQL script in Listing 11-5 will create the table on SQL Server so we can load it. Note: The function name of the final load in umd_northwind_etl is Invoke-UdfOrderLoad.

Listing 11-5. Create the orders table

```
Create table dbo.Orders
(
Order_ID        integer primary key,
Employee_ID     integer,
Order_Date      datetime,
Ship_City       varchar(150),
Ship_State      varchar(100),
Status_ID       integer,
Customer_ID     integer,
Sales_Tax_Rate  decimal(8,2)
)
```

The table in Listing 11-5 is a reduced column set from the source that provides an opportunity to discuss some more transformation techniques. For this transformation, instead of modifying the incoming pipeline, we're going to replace it with a new custom pipeline. The Northwind Orders table has a tax rate column, but it is not populated, so we're going to look it up in the transformation and load it to the destination table.

To demonstrate how to load an XML file, the orders table was exported as XML. The statement that follows will load the XML file into the *$orders* object:

```
[xml]$orders = Get-Content ("$global:referencepath" + "Orders.XML" )
```

Notice the cast operator [xml] before $orders. When Get-Content loads the file, this tells PowerShell to format it as an XML document. We can easily access the properties by using the dataroot property, as shown here:

```
$orders.dataroot.orders
```

This statement should list the orders data to the console, as shown here:

```
Order_x0020_ID                            : 81
Employee_x0020_ID                         : 2
Customer_x0020_ID                         : 3
Order_x0020_Date                          : 2006-04-25T17:26:53
Ship_x0020_Name                           : Thomas Axen
Ship_x0020_Address                        : 123 3rd Street
Ship_x0020_City                           : Los Angelas
Ship_x0020_State_x002F_Province           : CA
Ship_x0020_ZIP_x002F_Postal_x0020_Code    : 99999
Ship_x0020_Country_x002F_Region           : USA
Shipping_x0020_Fee                        : 0
Taxes                                     : 0
Tax_x0020_Rate                            : 0
Status_x0020_ID                           : 0
```

Notice the characters 'x0020' interspersed into the column names. This is because the source table has spaces in the column names, which get replaced with 'x0020' when the table is exported. We could just do a quick global replace to fix this, but it provides a good opportunity to discuss how to rename pipeline properties. In fact, what we will do is use the order file pipeline as input to build a custom pipeline that will be loaded into SQL Server. Let's look at the transformation function next:

```
function Invoke-UdfOrdersTransformation
{
 [CmdletBinding()]
        param (
                  [Parameter(ValueFromPipeline=$True)]$pipein = "default",
                  [Parameter(ValueFromPipeline=$false)]$filepath
                )
    process
    {

      $statetaxcsv = Import-CSV ("$filepath" + "StateSalesTaxRates.csv" )
      [hashtable] $statetaxht = @{}
      foreach ($item in $statetaxcsv)
      {
          $statetaxht.Add($item.StateCode, $item.SalesTaxRate)
      }

      [psobject] $pipeout = New-Object psobject

      $pipeout | Add-Member -MemberType NoteProperty -Name "Employee_ID"        `
                          -Value $pipein.Employee_x0020_ID
      $pipeout | Add-Member -MemberType NoteProperty -Name "Order_Date"         `
                          -Value $pipein.Order_x0020_Date
      $pipeout | Add-Member -MemberType NoteProperty -Name "Ship_City"          `
                          -Value $pipein.Ship_x0020_City
      $pipeout | Add-Member -MemberType NoteProperty -Name "Ship_State"         `
                          -Value $pipein.Ship_x0020_State_x0020_Province
      $pipeout | Add-Member -MemberType NoteProperty -Name "Status_ID"          `
                          -Value $pipein.Status_x0020_ID
      $pipeout | Add-Member -MemberType NoteProperty -Name "Order_ID"           `
                          -Value $pipein.Order_x0020_ID
      $pipeout | Add-Member -MemberType NoteProperty -Name "Customer_ID"        `
                          -Value $pipein.Customer_x0020_ID

      $pipeout | Add-Member -MemberType NoteProperty -Name "Sales_Tax_Rate"     `
                          -Value 0

      $pipeout.Sales_Tax_Rate = $statetaxht[$pipein.Ship_x0020_State_x002F_Province]

      Return $pipeout
    }
}
```

This function takes the pipeline, and a file path as input. The file path is the location of the state sales tax file. Notice that we take the pipeline in as $pipein, but the last line returns $pipeout. The original pipeline is replaced with a custom one we will create. To support the look-up of the state sales tax rate, we will load the state sales tax file into a hash table, as shown:

```
$statetaxcsv = Import-CSV ("$filepath" + "StateSalesTaxRates.csv")

[hashtable] $statetaxht = @{}

foreach ($item in $statetaxcsv)
    {
        $statetaxht.Add($item.StateCode, $item.SalesTaxRate)
    }
```

The first line loads the file into variable $statetaxcsv. The statement after that creates an empty hash table named $statetaxht. Then, the ForEach loop loads the key/value pairs using the hash table Add method.

Next, the line copied here creates a new psobject to hold the new pipeline:

```
[psobject] $pipeout = New-Object psobject
```

Once $pipeout is created, the function uses the Add-Member cmdlet to add note properties to $pipeout and assigns them values from the incoming pipeline. The last NoteProperty, Sales_Tax_Rate, is initialized to zero because we are required to provide a value. However, this value is replaced by the statement that follows:

```
$pipeout.Sales_Tax_Rate = $statetaxht[$pipein.Ship_x0020_State_x002F_Province]
```

Recall that hash tables return the value associated with the key when you request the key, so this line is getting the sales tax rate from the $pipeout note property Sales_Tax_Rate. The last line simply returns the new pipeline to the caller.

The statements that follow will test this transformation:

```
[xml]$orders = Get-Content ("$global:referencepath" + "Orders.XML" )
$orders.dataroot.orders | Invoke-UdfOrdersTransformation -filepath $global:referencepath
```

The first line loads the sales tax file into $orders. The second line pipes this into the transformation function Invoke-UdfOrdersTransformation, passing the path to the state tax rate table as a parameter. A sample of the output to the console is shown here:

```
Employee_ID    : 2
Order_Date     : 2006-04-25T17:26:53
Ship_City      : Los Angelas
Ship_State     :
Status_ID      : 0
Order_ID       : 81
Customer_ID    : 3
Sales_Tax_Rate : 0.08
```

In this output, we can see the custom properties we created, including the new Sales_Tax_Rate property. For more ideas about ways pipeline properties can be renamed, consult this interesting blog by Don Jones:

```
https://technet.microsoft.com/en-us/magazine/ff394367.aspx
```

Now, let's look at the function with which to load the order table:

```
function Invoke-UdfOrderLoad
{
<# Define the MS Access Connection - Caution:  32 bit ISE only  #>
$global:referencepath = $env:HomeDrive + $env:HOMEPATH + "\Documents\"

<# Load orders #>
[xml]$orders = Get-Content ("$global:referencepath" + "Orders.XML" )

<# Define the mapping... #>
$mappingset = @()  # Create a collection object.
$mappingset += (Add-UdfMapping "Order_ID" "Order_ID" "" $true)
$mappingset += (Add-UdfMapping "Employee_ID" "Employee_ID" "" $false)
$mappingset += (Add-UdfMapping "Order_Date" "Order_Date" "'" $false)
$mappingset += (Add-UdfMapping "Ship_City" "Ship_City" "'" $false)
$mappingset += (Add-UdfMapping "Ship_State" "Ship_State" "'" $false)
$mappingset += (Add-UdfMapping "Status_ID" "Status_ID" "" $false)
$mappingset += (Add-UdfMapping "Customer_ID" "Customer_ID" "" $false)
$mappingset += (Add-UdfMapping "Sales_Tax_Rate" "Sales_Tax_Rate" "" $false)

<# Define the SQL Server Target  #>
[psobject] $SqlServer1 = New-Object psobject
New-UdfConnection ([ref]$SqlServer1)

$SqlServer1.ConnectionType = 'ADO'
$SqlServer1.DatabaseType = 'SqlServer'
$SqlServer1.Server = '(local)'
$SqlServer1.DatabaseName = 'Development'
$SqlServer1.UseCredential = 'N'
$SqlServer1.SetAuthenticationType('Integrated')
$SqlServer1.BuildConnectionString()

$orders.dataroot.orders | Invoke-UdfOrdersTransformation -filepath $global:referencepath
| Invoke-UdfSQLDML -Mapping $mappingset  -DmlOperation "Merge" -Destinationtablename
"dbo.Orders" -connection $SqlServer1 -Verbose

}
```

The following line defines the path to the orders XML file:

```
$global:referencepath = $env:HomeDrive + $env:HOMEPATH + "\Documents\"
```

Then, we load the orders file into a variable named $orders. Notice that we cast the variable as [xml], which makes PowerShell load the file into a XML object. See here:

```
[xml]$orders = Get-Content ("$global:referencepath" + "Orders.XML" )
```

Since we want to use a custom pipe to load the table, we'll create the mapping and use it as the source, as shown here:

```
$mappingset = @()  # Create a collection object.
$mappingset += (Add-UdfMapping "Order_ID" "Order_ID" "" $true)
$mappingset += (Add-UdfMapping "Employee_ID" "Employee_ID" "'" $false)
$mappingset += (Add-UdfMapping "Order_Date" "Order_Date" "" $false)
$mappingset += (Add-UdfMapping "Ship_City" "Ship_City" "" $false)
$mappingset += (Add-UdfMapping "Ship_State" "Ship_State" "" $false)
$mappingset += (Add-UdfMapping "Status_ID" "Status_ID" "" $false)
$mappingset += (Add-UdfMapping "Customer_ID" "Customer_ID" "" $false)
$mappingset += (Add-UdfMapping "Sales_Tax_Rate" " Sales_Tax_Rate" "" $false)
```

Since we created a custom pipeline, it makes sense that we make the source column names match the destination table column names. Notice we flag the `Order_ID` as the key column. The lines that follow create a database connection object using the `New-UdfConnection` function in umd_database:

```
[psobject] $SqlServer1 = New-Object psobject
New-UdfConnection ([ref]$SqlServer1)
```

Now, we just set the target database connection attributes:

```
$SqlServer1.ConnectionType = 'ADO'
$SqlServer1.DatabaseType = 'SqlServer'
$SqlServer1.Server = '(local)'
$SqlServer1.DatabaseName = 'Development'
$SqlServer1.UseCredential = 'N'
$SqlServer1.SetAuthenticationType('Integrated')
$SqlServer1.BuildConnectionString()
```

Finally, the table is loaded with the statements that follow:

```
$orders.dataroot.orders |
Invoke-UdfOrdersTransformation -filepath $global:referencepath |
Invoke-UdfSQLDML -Mapping $mappingset -DmlOperation "Merge" `
-Destinationtablename "dbo.Orders" -connection $SqlServer1 –Verbose
```

This code is actually one line formatted for readability using the line continuation character. It starts by piping the XML-formatted data in `$orders.dataroot.orders` to the transformation function `Invoke-UdfOrdersTransformation`, which does the transformations on the pipeline. It passes the path to the state tax rate file, because the transformation needs to load that file to get the sales tax rates. The transformation pipes the data to the function `Invoke-UdfSQLDML`, which loads the data. The call to `Invoke-UdfSQLDML` includes the mapping collection, the type of SQL statement to generate, the destination table name, and the custom connection object.

We see the same pattern to load orders as we do for any other load. The mappings are defined. The source connection, in this case an XML file, is created. The target connection is created. The source data is piped through the transformation function and into the function that writes the data to the destination.

The Customers Table

The last step is to load the customers table. This is sourced as an extract from the DestopNorthwind2007 sample database. Use the script in Listing 11-6 to create the table on SQL Server. Note: The function name of the final load in umd_northwind_etl is Invoke-UdfCustomerLoad.

Listing 11-6. Create customers table

```
CREATE TABLE [dbo].[Customers](
        [Customer_ID] [int] NOT NULL,
        [Company_Name] [varchar](50) NULL,
        [First_Name] [varchar](50) NULL,
        [Last_Name] [varchar](50) NULL,
        [Title] [varchar](50) NULL,
        [City] [varchar](50) NULL,
        [State] [varchar](50) NULL,
        [Zip] [varchar](15) NULL,
        [Country] [varchar](50) NULL,
        [State_Name] varchar(255) null,
        [State_Region] varchar(255) null
PRIMARY KEY CLUSTERED
(
        [Customer_ID] ASC
) )
```

This load has a couple of twists that will demonstrate the extensibility of PowerShell. First, the main input file, customers, is a fixed-length flat file. Second, we're going to join the input customer file with the State_Table.csv file we used earlier in the book to translate the state code into the state name and retrieve the region name. We'll begin by putting the fixed-length flat file though a transformation function that extracts the columns and puts them into pipeline properties. There are several ways to do this, and some are less verbose than the method we use here. I like this method because it is very easy to understand and therefore to maintain. It uses the substring method to parse out the columns. Let's look at the code:

```
function Invoke-UdfCustomersTransformation
{
 [CmdletBinding()]
        param (
                [Parameter(ValueFromPipeline=$True)]$pipein = "default"
                )
    process
    {

    [psobject] $pipeout = New-Object psobject

    $pipeout | Add-Member -MemberType NoteProperty -Name "Customer_ID"  `
                        -Value $pipein.substring(0,10).trim()

    $pipeout | Add-Member -MemberType NoteProperty -Name "Company_Name"  `
                        -Value $pipein.substring(11,50).trim()

    $pipeout | Add-Member -MemberType NoteProperty -Name "Last_Name"  `
                        -Value $pipein.substring(61,50).trim()
```

```
        $pipeout | Add-Member -MemberType NoteProperty -Name "First_Name"      `
                            -Value $pipein.substring(111,50).trim()

        $pipeout | Add-Member -MemberType NoteProperty -Name "Title"      `
                            -Value $pipein.substring(211,50).trim()

        $pipeout | Add-Member -MemberType NoteProperty -Name "City"      `
                            -Value $pipein.substring(873,50).trim()

        $pipeout | Add-Member -MemberType NoteProperty -Name "State"      `
                            -Value $pipein.substring(923,50).trim()

        $pipeout | Add-Member -MemberType NoteProperty -Name "Zip"      `
                            -Value $pipein.substring(973,15).trim()

        $pipeout | Add-Member -MemberType NoteProperty -Name "Country"      `
                            -Value $pipein.substring(988,50).trim()
        Return $pipeout

    }
}
```

As we've seen in the other examples, the function Invoke-UdfCustomersTransformation takes the pipeline as a parameter. The first statement in the function creates a new instance of a psobject, which is to be used to create a custom pipeline that will be passed back to the caller. Then, there are a series of Add-Member statements that create a property to hold each column. Each column is extracted using the substring function. Remember, since this is a fixed-length file, the pipeline has just one property, which contains a row from the file. We use the substring method to extract the column based on where it occurs in the line. Admittedly, writing substring method calls can be a bit tedious, but once it has been done, the columns will be defined into separate properties in the pipeline that is returned. Then, it can be used in the same way as any other data source.

Now that we have reviewed the transformation function, let's look at the function that uses it to load the Customers table:

```
function Invoke-UdfCustomerLoad
{
    <#  Define the MS Access Connection - Caution:  32 bit ISE only  #>
    $global:referencepath = $env:HomeDrive + $env:HOMEPATH + "\Documents\"

    #  Load the tables into variables...
    $customer = Get-Content ("$global:referencepath" + "customers.txt" ) |
    Invoke-UdfCustomersTransformation | `
            Sort-Object -Property State

    $states = Import-CSV ("$global:referencepath" + "state_table.csv" ) |
    Sort-Object -Property abbreviation

    <#  Define the mapping and include the columns coming from the joined table... #>
    $mappingset = @()  # Create a collection object.
    $mappingset += (Add-UdfMapping "Customer_ID" "Customer_ID" "" $true)
    $mappingset += (Add-UdfMapping "Company_Name" "Company_Name" "'" $false)
```

```
$mappingset += (Add-UdfMapping "Last_Name" "Last_Name" "'" $false)
$mappingset += (Add-UdfMapping "First_Name" "First_Name" "'" $false)
$mappingset += (Add-UdfMapping "Title" "Title" "'" $false)
$mappingset += (Add-UdfMapping "City" "City" "'" $false)
$mappingset += (Add-UdfMapping "State" "State" "'" $false)
$mappingset += (Add-UdfMapping "Zip" "Zip" "" $false)
$mappingset += (Add-UdfMapping "Country" "Country" "'" $false)
$mappingset += (Add-UdfMapping "name" "State_Name" "'" $false)
$mappingset += `
(Add-UdfMapping "census_region_name" "State_Region" "'" $false)

<# Define the SQL Server Target #>
[psobject] $SqlServer1 = New-Object psobject
New-UdfConnection ([ref]$SqlServer1)

$SqlServer1.ConnectionType = 'ADO'
$SqlServer1.DatabaseType = 'SqlServer'
$SqlServer1.Server = '(local)'
$SqlServer1.DatabaseName = 'Development'
$SqlServer1.UseCredential = 'N'
$SqlServer1.SetAuthenticationType('Integrated')
$SqlServer1.BuildConnectionString()

<# Load the data. #>
$SqlServer1.RunSQL("truncate table [dbo].[Customers]", $false)

Join-Object -Left $customer -Right $states `
            -Where {$args[0].State -eq $args[1].abbreviation} -LeftProperties "*" `
            -RightProperties "name","census_region_name" -Type AllInLeft  |
Invoke-UdfSQLDML -Mapping $mappingset  -DmlOperation `
"Insert" -Destinationtablename "dbo.Customers" -connection $SqlServer1 -Verbose

}
```

The first thing the function does is set the reference to the file folder:

```
function Invoke-UdfCustomerLoad
{
<# Define the data path global variable. #>
$global:referencepath = $env:HomeDrive + $env:HOMEPATH + "\Documents\"
```

The file is loaded using Get-Content piped into Invoke-UdfCustomersTransformation and then sorted by the State with Sort-Object:

```
# Load the tables into variables...
$customer = Get-Content ("$global:referencepath" + "customers.txt" ) | `
Invoke-UdfCustomersTransformation | `
        Sort-Object -Property State
```

The final result is loaded into the variable $customer. We need to sort the object in the order of the key we want to join on, i.e., State. Next, we load the state_table.csv file into a variable, as shown here:

```
$states = Import-CSV ("$global:referencepath" + "state_table.csv" ) |
Sort-Object -Property abbreviation
```

Notice we use Import-CSV to load the state_table.csv file into the pipeline. The first row of the file defines the pipeline property names. This is piped into the Sort-Object cmdlet to sort the pipeline by the state code, which is named abbreviation. The final result is stored in $states. Now, let's look at the mapping-set creation statements:

```
<# Define the mapping and include the columns coming from the joined table... #>
$mappingset = @()  # Create a collection object.
$mappingset += (Add-UdfMapping "Customer_ID" "Customer_ID" "" $true)
$mappingset += (Add-UdfMapping "Company_Name" "Company_Name" "'" $false)
$mappingset += (Add-UdfMapping "Last_Name" "Last_Name" "'" $false)
$mappingset += (Add-UdfMapping "First_Name" "First_Name" "'" $false)
$mappingset += (Add-UdfMapping "Title" "Title" "'" $false)
$mappingset += (Add-UdfMapping "City" "City" "'" $false)
$mappingset += (Add-UdfMapping "State" "State" "'" $false)
$mappingset += (Add-UdfMapping "Zip" "Zip" "" $false)
$mappingset += (Add-UdfMapping "Country" "Country" "'" $false)
$mappingset += (Add-UdfMapping "name" "State_Name" "'" $false)
$mappingset += (Add-UdfMapping "census_region_name" "State_Region" "'" $false)
```

Because we use Add-UdfMapping to create a mapping collection, we have a consistent, repeatable way to define the column mappings regardless of the source or destination of the data. As we've seen previously, these statements create and load the mapping-set collection. Caution: Make sure you carefully review the value delimiter, i.e., the third parameter. This is what is used to generate the SQL statements and, if any are wrong, the SQL statement will fail. We create the target database connection object as shown here:

```
<# Define the SQL Server Target #>
[psobject] $SqlServer1 = New-Object psobject
New-UdfConnection ([ref]$SqlServer1)

$SqlServer1.ConnectionType = 'ADO'
$SqlServer1.DatabaseType = 'SqlServer'
$SqlServer1.Server = '(local)'
$SqlServer1.DatabaseName = 'Development'
$SqlServer1.UseCredential = 'N'
$SqlServer1.SetAuthenticationType('Integrated')
$SqlServer1.BuildConnectionString()
```

Since we are loading the data into a staging table, we need to clear it out before loading it:

```
<# Load the data. #>
   $SqlServer1.RunSQL("truncate table [dbo].[Customers]", $false)
```

Now we come to joining the data. I found a great Join-Object function that was developed by the Microsoft PowerShell team that supports inner and outer joins. It provides excellent functionality. Full details about it are available at the link here:

http://blogs.msdn.com/b/powershell/archive/2012/07/13/join-object.aspx

There is mention on the blog entry about this function possibly being added as a standard PowerShell cmdlet. For the time being, a good way to make it easy to use is to save it as a module so we can import it when needed. I named the module umd_join_object, keeping with my naming convention, but I will leave the function name as it was defined by Microsoft. However, if the function is ever added to PowerShell as a built-in cmdlet, the import of the custom module umd_join_object should be removed wherever it is used and replaced with the new cmdlet. Let's look at the code that joins the data and pipes the output to the function Invoke-UdfSQLDML in order to be written to the SQL Server table:

```
Join-Object -Left $customer -Right $states `
            -Where {$args[0].State -eq $args[1].abbreviation} -LeftProperties "*"   `
            -RightProperties "name","census_region_name" -Type AllInLeft |
Invoke-UdfSQLDML -Mapping $mappingset  -DmlOperation "Insert" -Destinationtablename
"dbo.Customers" -connection $SqlServer1 -Verbose
```

We call the Join-Object function, passing the Left parameter, i.e., the data that will be the left side of the join as $customer, and the Right parameter, i.e., the right side of the join as $states. The Where parameter provides the join criteria, which is to join the State property on $customer with the abbreviation property on $states. The –eq operand tests for a match. The LeftProperties is where we provide a list of what properties from the left-side source we want included in the output. The asterisk signals to include all the left-side properties. The RightProperties is where we provide a list of what properties from the right-side source we want included in the output. Here, we just want the state name, i.e., name, and census_region_name. If we did an inner join, rows where no match was found will be dropped. Since we want all customers returned, we use a left join, which is what the Type parameter, AllInLeft, is requesting. The result is piped into Invoke-UdfSQLDML, which loads the data into the Customers table. Notice we included mappings for the retrieved columns from $state. The name column gets mapped to State_Name, and the census_region_name gets mapped to State_Region. Note: We created the $SqlServer1 connection earlier in the chapter.

The pattern to load customers is almost the same as that for the other loads, even though we have the added complexity of a join. The only difference is that we had to define two sources and join them before piping the results to the destination. So, the steps in this pattern are: define the mappings, create the source connections, create the target connection, and pipe the joined source data through the transformation function and into the function that writes the data to the destination. An option in any load is to load the source data into a variable and then pipe the variable into the destination, versus piping the data directly from the source to the destination.

Packaging Up the ETL Job

We packaged up the ETL scripts into simple functions and put them into the umd_northwind_etl module, which you can copy to your modules folder under a subdirectory of the same name. Once that has been done, you can execute the entire ETL process with the statements in Listing 11-7. Note: This is assuming you have modified all relevant configuration settings to match your environment.

Listing 11-7. The Northwind ETL script

```
Import-Module umd_northwind_etl

Invoke-UdfStateSalesTaxLoad

Invoke-UdfOrderLoad

Invoke-UdfProductLoad

Invoke-UdfCustomerLoad
```

Summary

In this chapter, we discussed using PowerShell as an ETL tool versus using SSIS. We started by comparing the merits of PowerShell and SSIS. Then, we considered the general pattern of an ETL tool—extract from a source, transform the data, and write the data to a destination. To help us cover a range of sources and destinations, we used a fictitious ETL use case that required a number of files to be loaded into SQL Server tables. To get the most value out of PowerShell as an ETL tool, we created a reusable framework that makes it easy to write the code and minimizes data-specific coding. We discussed how the PowerShell pipeline can be used as a data flow. At the center of our PowerShell ETL framework is a mapping collection. In prior chapters we built reusable functions to retrieve data, so the challenge here is getting that data loaded into the destination. The mapping collection will tell the destination function what source columns map to which destination columns. By leveraging the mapping collection together with the pipeline, we explained how a reusable function could load the data into a database table with no custom coding required, i.e. just function calls. The exception to this is when we need column transformations, because these do require data-specific code. However, we showed how transformations can be isolated into a single function and coded in a manner that is easy to read and maintain. Leveraging the use case, we demonstrated how to load a number of different file formats into tables. We even showed how transformations can easily include advanced features like key/value look-ups and file joins based on keys. The latter is a function provided by the Microsoft PowerShell team and is an excellent example of how easily PowerShell can be extended.

CHAPTER 12

■ ■ ■

PowerShell Jobs

In this chapter, we will discuss PowerShell's batch-job execution features, which are implemented in the form of cmdlets. At its simplest, we have the ability to run a script as a background job. However, this requires that the PowerShell session that submitted the job remains active. To avoid this constraint, we can create a scheduled job. PowerShell has a number of cmdlets to support job scheduling. As we will see, these cmdlets are really an interface to the Windows Task Scheduler. We will discuss the cmdlets that support the three components of a scheduled job: the job definition, triggers, and options. The job definition defines what code will be executed. The triggers define when the job should be executed–i.e., the schedule. The options define *how* the job should be executed. We will wrap up the section on job cmdlets by reviewing a script that provides a simple console with which to access our PowerShell jobs. Then, we will discuss why SQL Server Agent is a better solution for job scheduling. We will step through how to create a SQL Server Agent job that executes a PowerShell script. Then, we will discuss how we can easily manipulate SQL Server Agent jobs with PowerShell. Although PowerShell's job scheduling may not be the best solution for production, there are two good reasons we need to understand it. First, PowerShell's job-execution and scheduling features can be very useful in development. Second, PowerShell's remote execution and workflows use batch-execution features, so we need to understand these in order to discuss remote execution and workflows, which will be covered in the next chapter.

PowerShell Jobs

PowerShell has built-in support to run jobs. A job can be run as an immediate background process or be scheduled. Oddly, the internals are different for each method. Jobs executed immediately execute as a background child PowerShell session. To support scheduled jobs, Microsoft decided to leverage the Windows Task Scheduler rather than add native support. To create and maintain scheduled jobs, we use a set of cmdlets from the module PSScheduledJob that interfaces with the Windows Task Scheduler. One benefit of this design is that we can use the Task Scheduler to view, modify, and execute PowerShell scheduled jobs. Note: There is also a ScheduledTasks module that is available only for Windows Server 2012, Windows 8, and Windows 8.1. This module provides cmdlets to create non-PowerShell scheduled jobs in the Windows Task Scheduler, and it will not be covered here. See Table 12-1 for a list of the cmdlets that support unscheduled and scheduled jobs, and a description of what they do. Note: PowerShell calls a schedule a *trigger*, so the cmdlets ending with *JobTrigger* refer to job scheduling.

Table 12-1. *PowerShell Job cmdlets*

CmdLet	Description	Example
Add-JobTrigger	Create a new job schedule	Add-JobTrigger -Trigger (New-JobTrigger -AtStartup) -Name Bryan1PSJob
Disable-JobTrigger	Disable a job schedule	Get-ScheduledJob -Name MyDailyJob | Get-JobTrigger | Disable-JobTrigger
Disable-ScheduledJob	Disable a scheduled job	Disable-ScheduledJob -ID 5
Enable-JobTrigger	Enable a job schedule	Get-ScheduledJob -Name MyDailyJob | Get-JobTrigger | Enable-JobTrigger
Enable-ScheduledJob	Enable a scheduled job	Enable-ScheduledJob -ID 5
Get-Job	Retrieve job information	Get-Job -Name MyDailyJob
Get-JobTrigger	Retrieve job schedule information	Get-JobTrigger -Id 5
Get-ScheduledJob	Get information on scheduled jobs on the computer	Get-ScheduledJob -Name T*
Get-ScheduledJobOption	Get job option information for scheduled jobs on the computer	Get-ScheduledJobOption -Name MyDailyJob
New-JobTrigger	Create a new job schedule	New-JobTrigger -Daily -At 5PM
New-ScheduledJobOption	Create a new scheduled job option	New-ScheduledJobOption -RequireNetwork
Receive-Job	Retrieve the output from a job	Receive-Job -Name MyDailyJob -Keep
Register-ScheduledJob	Create a scheduled job	Register-ScheduledJob –Name TestJob -ScriptBlock { dir $home }
Remove-Job	Delete a job	Remove-Job -Id 2
Remove-JobTrigger	Delete a job schedule	Remove-JobTrigger -Name MyDailyJob
Resume-Job	Resume execution of a previously suspended job	Resume-Job –Id 4
Set-JobTrigger	Modify a job trigger of a scheduled job	Get-JobTrigger -Name MyDailyJob | Set-JobTrigger -At "12:00 AM"
Set-ScheduledJob	Modify a scheduled job	Get-ScheduledJob | Set-ScheduledJob -ClearExecutionHistory
Set-ScheduledJobOption	Modify a job option of a scheduled job	Get-ScheduledJobOption -Name MyDailyJob | Set-ScheduledJobOption -WakeToRun
Start-Job	Begin execution of a PowerShell background job	Start-Job -scriptblock { Get-Date }
Stop-Job	Terminate execution of a job	Stop-Job -Name Job22
Suspend-Job	Suspend execution of a job	Suspend-Job –Name Job25
Unregister-ScheduledJob	Remove the scheduled job from the local computer	Unregister-ScheduledJob –Name TestJob
Wait-Job	Wait for the background job to complete before returning to the command prompt	Start-Job -scriptblock { Get-Date } | Wait-Job

Running Background Jobs
Start-Job

We can use the Start-Job cmdlet to submit a PowerShell script to run in the background immediately. As mentioned previously, the job executes as a child PowerShell session. There are a number of parameters to support how the job is submitted. To simply run a script block as a job, we would enter a command like the one here:

```
Start-Job -ScriptBlock { Import-Module umd_northwind_etl; Invoke-UdfCustomerLoad }
```

We run the Start-Job cmdlet, using the ScriptBlock parameter to pass a short script to execute. Notice that because we packaged up the Northwind customer load into a module's function, we can just import the module and call the function. This provides a concise way to call programs. When we execute the statement, we should see the output that follows, which confirms the job was submitted.

The following message is sent back to the console:

```
Id     Name      PSJobTypeName    State    HasMoreData    Location    Command
--     ----      -------------    -----    -----------    --------    -------
15     Job15     BackgroundJob    Running  True           localhost   Import-Module umd_nor...
```

With names like Job15, it may be hard to remember what the job does. We can use the Name parameter to give a meaningful name to the job. Recall that the product load job reads from a Microsoft Access source, which requires that we run the 32-bit version of PowerShell; we can do this by using the RunAs32 parameter. The statement that follows executes the product load as a background job and gives it a custom Name. Note: According to Microsoft PowerShell Help, on Windows 7 and Server 2008 R2, the RunAs32 parameter cannot be used when the Credential parameter is used. Let's look at the following code:

```
Start-Job  -Name ProductLoad  `
           -ScriptBlock { Import-Module umd_northwind_etl; Invoke-UdfProductLoad }  -RunAs32
```

This will generate the following messages to the console. Notice the name is now ProductLoad, as we specified:

```
Id     Name         PSJobTypeName    State    HasMoreData    Location    Command
--     ----         -------------    -----    -----------    --------    -------
17     ProductLoad  BackgroundJob    Running  True           localhost   Import-Module umd_nor...
```

Another interesting variation is to pass an object into the job using the InputObject parameter, as shown here:

```
Start-Job -Name Test1 -ScriptBlock {"The input object is:"; $input }  -InputObject 1,2,3,4
```

We submitted the script block as a job named Test1 and passed the array of values 1,2,3,4 as the InputObject parameter of Start-Job. Anything passed in using the InputObject parameter can be accessed in the script block using the variable $input. So, this job will write the values of the array. We can view the job output as shown here:

```
Receive-Job -Name InputObj -Keep
```

The cmdlet, Receive-Job, displays the messages written out by the job. The Name parameter identifies the name of the job. We could use the ID parameter to identify the job by its ID. The Keep parameter tells PowerShell to retain the job's output. Without this parameter, the job output is automatically erased. We should see the following job output:

```
The input object is:
1
2
3
4
```

There are a number of optional parameters to use with Start-Job. Some are documented in Table 12-2.

Table 12-2. *Start-Job Parameters*

Parameter	Description
FilePath	Used to specify the path to a script file to be executed. This is an alternative to using the ScriptBlock parameter.
Credential	Used to specify a credential under which to execute the job.
InitializationScript	Specifies a script to run before the job starts, so a good place for set-up work.
PSVersion	If there are multiple PowerShell versions on the machine, use this parameter for 2.0. or 3.0.

Receive-Job

To view the output of a job, we use the Receive-Job cmdlet much the same way as we did for Start-Job. Let's review some of the variations on how we can view job output. Note: To see a list of jobs, just enter Get-Job.

To get a job's output by job ID, we can use the ID parameter, as shown here:

```
Receive-Job -ID 19
```

We can get a reference to the job by assigning the output of the Start-Job cmdlet to a variable. Then, we can use the variable to get the job results, as shown:

```
$myjob = Start-Job -Name InputObj -ScriptBlock { $input }  -InputObject 1,2,3,4
Receive-Job -Job $myjob
```

A nice thing about this approach is that we don't have to remember job names or IDs. It can also be a handy way for a script to retain a job reference for later use.

Since Start-Job is a cmdlet, it can be called at any time, even from within a script contained in a job. When this happens, a child job is created under the parent. Let's look at an example:

```
Start-Job -Name ParentChild -ScriptBlock { "Parent Job" ; Start-Job -ScriptBlock { "Child
Job" } }

Receive-Job -Name ParentChild -Keep
```

Start-Job submits a job named ParentChild, which contains a script block that executes another Start-Job command. To make this easy to follow, the outer job outputs the message "Parent Job" and the child job outputs the message "Child Job". The Receive-Job cmdlet displays the output of the job to the console, as shown here:

```
Parent Job

Id      Name      PSJobTypeName      State      HasMoreData      Location      Command
--      ----      -------------      -----      -----------      --------      -----------
1       Job1      BackgroundJob      Running    True             localhost     "Child Job"
```

Notice that the first line is the message Parent Job, output by the parent job. This is followed by information about the child job; in other words, Receive-Job retrieves the output of the parent job and shows the child job's information.

If we don't want the output of the child job, we should be able to use the NoRecurse parameter, as shown here:

```
Receive-Job -Name ParentChild –Keep -NoRecurse
```

However, in testing the Receive-Job statement, I discovered a bug. NoRecurse is supposed to suppress showing output of child jobs. When I tried it, I got no results back at all. According to the blog link that follows, all output goes to the child job, which renders the NoRecurse parameter useless.

https://connect.microsoft.com/PowerShell/feedback/details/771705/receive-job-with-norecurse-returns-null

Get-Job

Get-Job lists active and completed background PowerShell jobs of the current session. To view scheduled jobs, use the Get-ScheduledJob cmdlet. Let's try Get-Job with no parameters, as shown:

```
Get-Job
```

If there are any jobs in the queue, we should see output similar to what is here:

```
Id      Name      PSJobTypeName      State        HasMoreData   Location    Command
--      ----      -------------      -----        -----------   --------    ------------------------
9       Job9      BackgroundJob      Completed    True          localhost   Dir
13      Job13     BackgroundJob      Completed    True          localhost   Import-Module umd_nor...
15      Job15     BackgroundJob      Completed    False         localhost   Import-Module umd_nor...
```

Get-Job displays entries in the job queue. Although some of the columns are fairly intuitive, let's review what the columns mean; see Table 12-3.

Table 12-3. *Column Descriptions for the Output of Get-Job*

Column	Description
Id	Unique identifying number of the job that can be used with the other job control cmdlets to specify the intended target job
Name	Textual name for the job, which, if not specified by the user when the job is created, is automatically generated by PowerShell as *Jobxx*, where xx is the Job ID.
PSJobTypeName	This will have a value of BackgroundJob for jobs submitted by Start-Job locally. A value of RemoteJob means that the job was started using the AsJob parameter of a cmdlet such as Invoke-Command, i.e., the job is running on another machine. A value of PSWorkFlowJob means the job is a workflow started using the AsJob parameter of the workflows cmdlet.
State	The current state of the job. Valid values are NotStarted, Running, Completed, Failed, Stopped, Blocked, Suspended, Disconnected, Suspending, Stopping
HasMoreData	Indicates if the job output has been retrieved yet. True means it has and False means it has not.
Location	Indicates where the job is running or was run. Localhost means on the local machine. Remote jobs will show the host's machine name.
Command	The PowerShell commands in the job

Not only does Get-Job provide so many job details, it also supports a number of filter parameters so as to limit the list to jobs we are interested in. A listing of these with descriptions and examples is provided in Table 12-4.

Table 12-4. *Get-Job Parameters and Examples*

Parameter	Description	Example
Command	Filters based on a command included in the job	Get-Job -Command "*Get-ChildItem*"
ID	Filters based on the job ID unique to the session	Get-Job –ID 10
IncludeChildJob	Includes child jobs with parents	Get-Job –IncludeChildJob
Name	Filters based on the job name	Get-Job –Name MyJob
State	Filters based on the job state	Get-Job -State Completed
After	Filters out jobs that ran before the specified date/time	Get-Job -After '2015-05-01'
Before	Filters out jobs that ran after the specified date/time	Get-Job -Before '2015-05-01'
ChildJobState	Shows only the child jobs in the specified state	Get-Job -ChildJobState Completed
HasMoreData	Filters based on the HasMoreData column. To see only jobs with more data, use HasMoreData:$true. To see only jobs that do not have more data, use HasMoreData:$false.	Get-Job -HasMoreData:$true
Newest	Specified number of more recent jobs to list	Get-Job –Newest 5

Wait-Job

The `Wait-Job` cmdlet tells PowerShell to wait until one or more background jobs have completed before continuing.

To wait for a specific job, we can use the job ID or job name, as shown here:

```
Wait-Job –ID 5,6
Wait-Job –Name Job10 –Timeout 10
```

The first statement will wait until the jobs with IDs 5 and 6 complete. The second line will wait for the job named Job10 to complete, but limits the wait to ten seconds. Note: For both ID and Name, a list can be specified. We can also pipe a list of jobs into the `Wait-Job` cmdlet as shown here:

```
Get-Job | Wait-Job
```

This statement pipes all jobs into the `Wait-Job` cmdlet, which means the command will stop until all jobs complete. We can wait until any job in a list of jobs completes, as shown here:

```
Wait-Job -id 1,6,10,12 –Any
```

This statement will wait until any one of the listed jobs completes. `Wait-Job` is useful in scripts when a certain job needs to complete before the script continues.

Remove-Job

By default, job output is deleted when we use the `Receive-Job` cmdlet, but this behavior can be overridden with the Keep parameter. We can then use the `Remove-Job` cmdlet to clean up the job queue of unwanted jobs. Bear in mind, background jobs are automatically deleted when the session ends. We can use `Get-Job` to pipe the list of jobs to remove into the `Remove-Job` cmdlet. Here are some examples of this:

```
Get-Job –Name Job* | Remove-Job           # Removes all jobs that start with the letters
                                            Job.
Get-Job –HasMoreData:$false | Remove-Job   # Removes all jobs where output has been
                                            received.
Get-Job –Before '2015-05-01' | Remove-Job  # Removes all jobs completed before the date
```

By using `Get-Job`, we can get more flexibility in what jobs we remove. However, `Remove-Job` has some parameters we can use. Let's see some examples:

```
Remove-Job –ID 12                  # Removes job with ID 12
Remove-Job –Name MyJob –Force      # Removes job named MyJob even if it is running.
Remove-Job –State Completed –Confirm # Prompt for confirmation to remove all completed
jobs.
Remove-Job –Name * -WhatIf         # Writes messages about what jobs would be removed.
```

Stop-Job

To stop a running job, we use the Stop-Job cmdlet. Similar to other job cmdlets we've seen, Stop-Job supports parameters for the job ID and name. Some examples of using Stop-Job are as follows:

```
Stop-Job -ID 15              #  Stops job ID 15
Stop-Job -Name MyJob         #  Stops job named MyJob
Get-Job | Stop-Job           #  Stops all jobs
Stop-Job -Name j* -WhatIf    #  Displays messages about what jobs would be deleted
Stop-Job -Name j* -Confirm   #  Prompts the user to confirm before stopping the jobs
```

Another way to end all background jobs is to exit the session.

Scheduled Jobs

PowerShell's scheduled jobs have all the characteristics of unscheduled jobs. In fact, the job commands we discussed earlier work with scheduled jobs as well. However, scheduled jobs have some things that make them different from temporary jobs.

- The job definition, including the script block or script file path, needs to be stored to disk so it can persist indefinitely and survive system reboots.

- The creation and maintenance of job schedules need needs to be supported.

- Job execution must be independent of any active PowerShell sessions, unlike with temporary jobs, which are lost when the session ends.

- A mechanism is needed to reload job definitions and schedules after a machine reboot.

As mentioned previously, Microsoft's answer to these requirements was to use the Windows Task Scheduler.

Creating a Scheduled Job

With so many cmdlets and options for scheduled jobs, it might be useful to start with a quick overview of creating and executing a simple scheduled job step by step. Let's walk through the process.

1. Create the job schedule, which is called a *trigger*, as shown next. The trigger will execute every day at 10 AM:

   ```
   $jobtrigger = New-JobTrigger -Daily -At '10:00 AM'
   ```

2. Create the job options with a statement like the one that follows, with which we are creating a Verbose job option:

   ```
   $joboptions = New-ScheduledJobOption -Verbose
   ```

3.   Create the scheduled job using the `Register-ScheduledJob` cmdlet. The
     statement in this example will create a new scheduled job using the Verbose
     job option; it will run daily at 10 AM. The trigger and `ScheduledJobOption` are
     defined using the variables we created in steps 1 and 2.

```
Register-ScheduledJob   -Name MyDailyJob -ScriptBlock { Get-Date } `
                        -Trigger $jobtrigger -ScheduledJobOption $joboptions
```

When you run the `Register-ScheduledJob` statement to register the job, a new task is added to the
Windows Task Scheduler. To view it, start the Task Scheduler by clicking on the Start menu, select All
Programs, and then Administrative Tools. The Task Scheduler will be visible in the program list, as shown
in Figure 12-1.

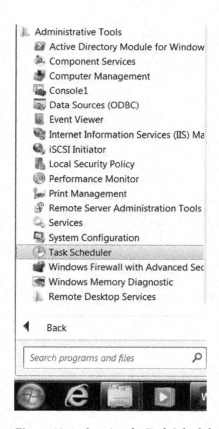

Figure 12-1. *Starting the Task Scheduler*

Click on the Task Scheduler to start it. You will then see the Task Scheduler's main screen, as shown in
Figure 12-2.

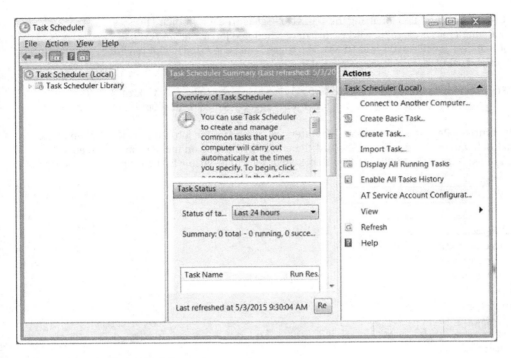

Figure 12-2. *The Task Scheduler main screen*

The Task Scheduler is used by many applications to automate tasks, such as periodically checking for and installing program updates. PowerShell uses it to store and execute scheduled jobs. We can see the PowerShell scheduled jobs by expanding the Task Scheduler Library folder, followed by expanding Windows, and PowerShell. Then, click on ScheduledJobs, and you should see the PowerShell job we just created, as shown in Figure 12-3.

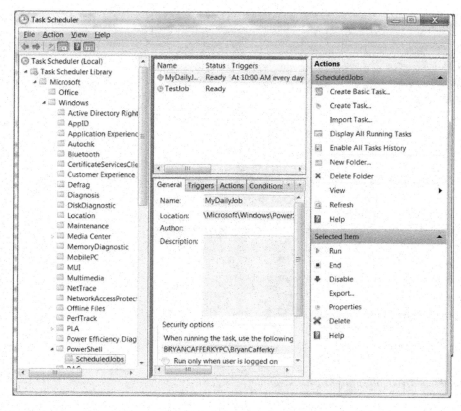

Figure 12-3. *PowerShell scheduled job in the Task Scheduler*

The fact that PowerShell scheduled jobs are persisted in the Task Scheduler confirms that the scheduled jobs cmdlets are really just interfaces to the Task Scheduler. If you created a job named MyDailyJob, you could double-click on the job to see the details, as shown in Figure 12-4.

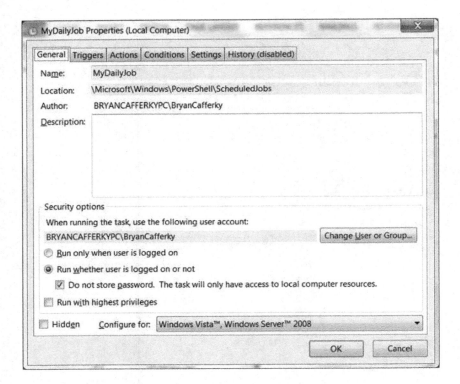

Figure 12-4. *PowerShell scheduled job fetails in Task Scheduler*

Figure 12-4 shows that we can view and edit the PowerShell scheduled job details in the Task Scheduler. At first, it may seem odd that Microsoft simply used the Task Scheduler for PowerShell scheduled jobs instead of creating something specific for PowerShell. However, upon consideration, this has some advantages. One, we get a nice graphical interface with which to view, maintain, and execute jobs. Second, PowerShell scheduled jobs integrate into the Windows architecture as other applications do. Third, features like the recovery of scheduled jobs after a system reboot are built into the Task Scheduler already.

Maintaining Scheduled Jobs

Scheduled jobs, as we have seen, consist of three objects: triggers, job options, and the job definition, which includes the PowerShell code to be executed. There are several cmdlets to help us view, create, and delete job triggers as well as attach them to scheduled jobs. These are Get-JobTrigger, New-JobTrigger, Set-JobTrigger, Remove-JobTrigger, and Add-JobTrigger. Let's review these in detail.

New-JobTrigger

Schedules, called *triggers*, define the parameters of when a job should be executed. In some scheduling systems, SQL Agent, for example, schedules can be defined once, saved under a schedule name, and used by multiple jobs. This is not the case with PowerShell scheduled jobs. A trigger is specific to a job, which is why the New-JobTrigger cmdlet does not support a Name parameter. The same is true of job options. To create a new trigger, we use the New-JobTrigger cmdlet, which would be followed by one or more cmdlets that add the trigger to a scheduled job. Let's look at some examples of using the New-JobTrigger cmdlet.

Note: The examples show the result being assigned to the variable $jobtrigger, because storing the trigger and options in variables provides better readability and reusability, and shorter job definition statements. However, they can be included inline enclosed in parentheses as well. The statement that follows creates a trigger to run a job once:

```
$jobtrigger = New-JobTrigger -Once -At '2105-10-22 10:00 AM'  # Run once at date/time.
```

The previous statement will create a trigger that fires only once, at 10 AM. The following statement uses the AtStartup parameter to trigger an execution whenever Windows starts:

```
$jobtrigger = New-JobTrigger -AtStartup    # Run when Windows starts, i.e., after a reboot.
```

The next trigger will run weekly on Monday and Tuesday at noon:

```
$jobtrigger = New-JobTrigger -Weekly –DaysOfWeek Monday, Tuesday –At "12:00 PM"
```

The trigger that follows will execute at 1:00 AM for two days.

```
$jobtrigger = New-JobTrigger –Daily –At "1:00 AM" -DaysInterval 2
$jobtrigger = New-JobTrigger -Once -At "05/01/2015 1:00:00" `
                        -RepetitionInterval (New-TimeSpan -Hours 2) `
                        -RepetitionDuration (New-Timespan -Days 5)
```

The trigger definition syntax is odd, because although it specified the Once parameter, it is creating a custom schedule that will start on May 1, 2015, and repeat every two hours for a period of five days. Remember, to create a custom schedule, use the Once parameter. To have the schedule continue with no end, use the RepeatIndefinitely parameter, which can only be used when Once is specified.

Add-JobTrigger

We can use the Add-JobTrigger cmdlet to attach a trigger to a scheduled job. Some examples of using this cmdlet are provided here:

```
Add-JobTrigger -Trigger $jobtrigger -Name MyDailyJob
```

This statement assumes we created a job trigger using New-JobTrigger and stored it in $jobtrigger. The statement attaches the trigger to the job MyJob.

The statement that follows creates the trigger using the New-JobTrigger statement enclosed in parentheses, which means it will be executed before attaching to MyDailyJob:

```
Add-JobTrigger -Trigger (New-JobTrigger –AtStartup) -Name MyDailyJob
```

The next statement uses Get-ScheduledJob to get the job definition for MyJob, which is piped into the Add-JobTrigger cmdlet, which adds a trigger for daily execution at 1:00 AM.

```
Get-ScheduledJob MyDailyJob | Add-JobTrigger -Trigger (New-JobTrigger –Daily –At "1:00 AM")
```

The statement that follows copies the trigger from the job SomeOtherJob and copies it to MyJob1 and MyJob2.:

```
Add-JobTrigger -Name MyJob1, MyJob2 -Trigger (Get-JobTrigger -Name SomeOtherJob)
```

The cmdlet `Add-JobTrigger` uses the ID parameter to specify the job by ID, or the `Name` parameter, as shown, to specify the job by name. The job definition can also be piped in, as shown, or passed in using the `InputObject` parameter.

Get-JobTrigger

The `Get-JobTrigger` cmdlet retrieves job trigger definitions from scheduled jobs. The following statement will get the triggers attached to the job `MyDailyJob`:

```
Get-JobTrigger -Name MyDailyJob
```

Multiple triggers can be attached to a single job. We can see the triggers using `Get-JobTrigger` as shown here:

```
Get-JobTrigger -Name MyWeeklyJob
```

Assuming we have multiple triggers attached to the job, the output would look similar to the output shown here:

```
Id         Frequency   Time                     DaysOfWeek           Enabled
--         ---------   --------------------     ------------------   -------
1          Weekly      5/3/2015 12:00:00 PM     {Monday, Tuesday}    True
2          Once        10/22/2105 10:00:00 AM                        True
3          Weekly      5/3/2015 12:00:00 PM     {Monday, Tuesday}    True
```

There are some interesting things to note. First, triggers have a unique ID within a job. Second, we can attach duplicate triggers, as the job in our example has–i.e., two triggers so as to run the job weekly on Monday and Tuesday. Be careful of this. Third, since there is an enabled flag, there must be a way to correspondingly disable the trigger, which we will discuss shortly. Note: The Microsoft online documentation shows the cmdlet `Get-ScheduledJob` as listing all the triggers associated with a job. However, in my testing, only one trigger was shown.

When there are multiple triggers for a job, the trigger ID gives us a way to specify the trigger:

```
Get-JobTrigger -ID 12 -TriggerId 2
```

In this statement, we specify both the job and trigger by their IDs. We should see the trigger details displayed to the console, similar to the output here:

```
Id         Frequency   Time                     DaysOfWeek    Enabled
--         ---------   --------------------     ----------    -------
2          Once        10/22/2105 10:00:00 AM                 True
```

We can also pipe the results of `Get-ScheduledJob` into `Get-JobTrigger`, as shown:

```
Get-ScheduledJob -Name *j* | Get-JobTrigger
```

This statement will display all the triggers associated with any jobs that have the letter j in the job name. As we will see, `Get-JobTrigger` is useful, because we can pipe its results into other cmdlets like `Set-JobTrigger` to apply actions to multiple triggers.

Set-JobTrigger

The Set-JobTrigger cmdlet makes changes to a trigger on a scheduled job. Some examples of using Set-JobTrigger are seen next. Note: To create or change scheduled jobs, you must start PowerShell as administrator. The statement that follows will set MyJob to run when Windows starts:

```
Get-JobTrigger -Name MyJob | Set-JobTrigger -AtStartup –Passthru
```

The statement that follows pipes Trigger ID 2 from MyWeeklyJob into the Set-JobTrigger cmdlet, which sets the trigger to run the job on Tuesdays at 8 AM.

```
Get-JobTrigger -Name MyWeeklyJob -TriggerId 2 |
Set-JobTrigger –DaysOfWeek Tuesday at "8:00 AM"
```

The first statement that follows stores the trigger from MyJob in variable $trigger, which is used with the InputObject parameter on the next line to set the AtLogOn value to the user Domain01\user1, i.e., the job will run whenever the user logs on to the machine. See the following:

```
$trigger = Get-JobTrigger -Name MyJob
Set-JobTrigger –InputObject $trigger -AtLogOn -User Domain01\user1
```

Set-JobTrigger and New-JobTrigger share the same parameters. These are documented in Table 12-5.

Table 12-5. *Set-JobTrigger and New-JobTrigger Parameters*

Parameter	Description
At	Starts the job at a specified time
AtLogon	Starts the job when the specified user logs on
AtStartUp	Runs the job when Windows starts
Daily	Run the job daily
DaysInterval	The number of days between executions for a daily schedule
DaysOfWeek	For a weekly schedule, the days of the week on which the job should run
InputObject	A ScheduledJobTrigger object that will be modified
Once	Runs the job one time only or defines a custom schedule
Passthru	Displays the resulting job trigger details to the console
RandomDelay	Runs the job using a random amount of time delay with an initial start date/time and constrained by a maximum delay value. This parameter takes a timespan object or string value
RepeatIndefintely	Specifies that the job continue running per schedule with no end
RepetitionDuration	Sets a limit on how long the job schedule will execute
RepetitionInterval	Time spacing between job executions. For example, if the value is four hours, the job will run every four hours
User	Specifies that the job be run when the user specified by this parameter logs on
Weekly	Sets a weekly schedule
WeeklyInterval	Sets the number of weeks between executions for a weekly schedule

Getting and Setting Job Options

There are a number of options that can be set so as to control how a scheduled job executes. The cmdlet Get-ScheduledJobOption will display the option name and value for a job. Let's use it to list the settings for MyDailyJob, as shown here:

```
Get-ScheduledJobOption -Name MyDailyJob
```

When we enter this statement, we should see the following output:

```
StartIfOnBatteries     : False
StopIfGoingOnBatteries : True
WakeToRun              : False
StartIfNotIdle         : True
StopIfGoingOffIdle     : False
RestartOnIdleResume    : False
IdleDuration           : 00:10:00
IdleTimeout            : 01:00:00
ShowInTaskScheduler    : True
RunElevated            : False
RunWithoutNetwork      : True
DoNotAllowDemandStart  : False
MultipleInstancePolicy : IgnoreNew
JobDefinition          : Microsoft.PowerShell.ScheduledJob.ScheduledJobDefinition
```

As the list shows, there are quite a few options. However, defaults are provided for most of them that are usually acceptable.

As shown, Get-ScheduledJobOption is the way we retrieve information about job options. There are four ways to call Get-ScheduledJobOption. First, we can pass the job name as shown. Second, we can pass the job ID with the ID parameter. Third, we can pipe scheduled job objects into the cmdlet. Fourth, we can pass the job definition via the InputObject parameter. Examples of these are shown next. The following statement retrieves job option details using the job ID:

```
Get-ScheduledJobOption -ID 10
```

The next statement pipes the output of Get-ScheduledJob into Get-ScheduledJobOption, which will retrieve the job option details.

```
Get-ScheduledJob -Name MyDailyJob | Get-ScheduledJobOption
```

Next, we see the Get-ScheduledJobOption cmdlet's InputObject parameter being used to pass the job definition that was obtained as the result of the Get-ScheduledJob cmdlet that is enclosed in parentheses.

```
Get-ScheduledJobOption -InputObject (Get-ScheduledJob -Name MyDailyJob)
```

We can change job options using the Set-ScheduledJobOption or New-ScheduledJobOption cmdlets. Table 12-6 lists the parameters to these cmdlets and what they do.

Table 12-6. *Scheduled Job Options and What They Do*

Parameter	Description
ContinueIfGoingOnBattery	When True, the job will continue to run even if the computer loses AC power. The default is False.
DoNotAllowDemandStart	When True, users cannot start the job manually. Only the trigger will run the job. The default is False.
HideInTaskScheduler	When True, the job will not be visible in the Task Scheduler on the computer where the job runs. The default is False.
MultipleInstancePolicy	Defines what the Task Manager should do if the job if the job is running when another request to run the job is raised. The default, IgnoreNew, does not create another instance of the job. Parallel causes a new job instance to start immediately. Queue will have the second-run request processed only after the current job instance has finished. StopExisting causes the current job to be cancelled and a new instance to be started.
RequiredNetwork	True means that the job will not start if network services are not available. The default is False. Setting this parameter to True will automatically set RunWithoutNetwork to False.
RestartOnIdleResume	True means that a suspended job will resume when the machine becomes idle and meets any IdleDuration value if set.
RunElevated	True means to run the job elevated to the Administrators permissions. The scheduled job should be registered with the Credential parameter.
StartIfIdle/IdleDuration	This IdleDuration parameter is used with SetIfIdle to define the amount of time the computer must be idle before the job can run. If the idle timeout condition is not met, the job execution is skipped until the next scheduled time. The default is ten minutes.
StartIfIdle/IdleTimeout	These parameters work in tandem with the StartIfIdle/IdleDuration parameters to define how long to wait for the required idle state to occur. If the timeout expires before the idle duration is met, the job will not run until the next scheduled time.
StartIfOnBattery	When True, the job will start even if there is no AC power to the machine.
StopIfGoingOffIdle	True means that if the machine becomes active while the job is running, the job will be suspended. False means to keep running the job. True is the default.
WakeToRun	True means the machine will wake from hibernate or sleep modes to run the job per the schedule. False means do not wake the machine. The default is False.

For some of the options, such as StartIfOnBattery, it seems unlikely we would want to override the default, i.e., risk a system shutdown in the middle of a job execution. However, it may be useful to change some of the other options to meet requirements. Let's review using some of these options and see how they work:

```
New-ScheduledJobOption -RequireNetwork –MultipleInstancePolicy Queue
```

This statement creates a scheduled job option that uses `RequiredNetwork` to tell the Task Scheduler to test and confirm that the network services are running before starting the job. It also sets `MultipleInstancePolicy` to Queue, which requires that in the instance where multiple instances of the job are requested, they should be added to the queue to be executed sequentially.

The statement that follows stores a job option in a variable, which it then uses to apply to a scheduled job:

```
$RunAsAdmin = New-ScheduledJobOption –RunElevated
Register-ScheduledJob -Name MyJob -FilePath C:\PowerShell\Scripts\installpatches.ps1 `
        -Trigger (New-JobTrigger –Daily –At "8:00 AM") -ScheduledJobOption $RunAsAdmin
```

The first statement stores a job option into variable $RunAsAdmin to run the job as administrator. Then, the statement that follows registers a new scheduled job named `MyJob` that runs a script stored on disk daily at 8 AM using the job option in variable $RunAsAdmin; i.e., it will run as administrator. To run these statements, you will need to start PowerShell as administrator. This example references a script file, but the problem with that approach is that the path is hard coded, which means the job will fail if the script is moved. A less fragile approach is to encapsulate the script as a function and add the function to a module so it can automatically be loaded for us using `Import-Module`. Let's look at an example of this:

```
Register-ScheduledJob –Name MyOtherJobAdmin -Trigger (New-JobTrigger -Daily -At "10 AM") `
                -InitializationScript {Import-Module umd_northwind_etl} `
                -ScriptBlock { Invoke-UdfStateSalesTaxLoad } `
                -ScheduledJobOption (New-ScheduledJobOption –RunElevated) `
                -Credential BryanCafferky
```

This statement will register a new scheduled job named `MyOtherJobAdmin` to run daily at 10 AM with administrative permissions. Because the parameter `Credential` is specified, we are prompted for the password when we run the statement. Notice we use the `InitializationScript` parameter to get the umd_northwind_etl loaded before the script block executes. We could also just have included the import-module statement in the script block, i.e., `Import-Module umd_northwind_etl; Invoke-UdfStateSalesTaxLoad`. However, I think using the `InitializationScript` parameter makes the job definition easier to read. We can execute the job immediately despite the trigger by using the `Start-Job` cmdlet, as shown here:

```
Start-Job -DefinitionName MyOtherJobAdmin -Verbose
```

The `Start-Job` cmdlet starts the job named `MyOtherJobAdmin` immediately. An oddity of this cmdlet is that instead of using the parameter `Name` as the other job cmdlets do, it calls the parameter `DefinitionName`. We could also use the `Set-ScheduledJob` cmdlet with the `RunNow` parameter. When we run the statement, we should see output similar to the following:

```
Id  Name            PSJobTypeName   State   HasMoreData  Location  Command
--  ----            -------------   -----   -----------  --------  -------
24  MyOtherJobAdmin PSScheduledJob  Running True         localhost Import-Module umd_nor...
```

To view the job status, use the `Get-Job` cmdlet, and to see the output, use `Receive-Job` output with the Keep parameter if you do not want the output deleted.

Next, we use the `Receive-Job` cmdlet to view the job output. You should see messages showing connection details followed by the insert statements. See the code here:

```
Receive-Job -Name MyOtherJobAdmin –Keep
```

To change an option on a registered job, we can use the Set-ScheduledJobOption cmdlet, as shown here:

```
Get-ScheduledJobOption -Name MyOtherJob4 | Set-ScheduledJobOption -WakeToRun –Passthru
```

The Set-ScheduledJobOption does not take a job name as a parameter. Instead, as shown, we need to get a job option object, which we do by piping the output of Get-ScheduledJobOption into the Set-ScheduledJobOption cmdlet. An alternative to this is to store the scheduled job option in a variable and pass this to Set-ScheduledJobOption as the InputObject parameter. The PassThru parameter causes the option settings to be returned, as shown here:

```
StartIfOnBatteries      : False
StopIfGoingOnBatteries  : True
WakeToRun               : True
StartIfNotIdle          : True
StopIfGoingOffIdle      : False
RestartOnIdleResume     : False
IdleDuration            : 00:10:00
IdleTimeout             : 01:00:00
ShowInTaskScheduler     : True
RunElevated             : False
RunWithoutNetwork       : True
DoNotAllowDemandStart   : False
MultipleInstancePolicy  : IgnoreNew
JobDefinition           : Microsoft.PowerShell.ScheduledJob.ScheduledJobDefinition
```

Notice that JobDefinition is listed. However, this is not something we can change via job option cmdlets.

We have seen that a scheduled job consists of three parts, which are the job definition, one or more triggers, and job options. The job definition defines what PowerShell code will be executed. Triggers define the schedule of when the job should be executed. Job options define special job execution features such as requiring network services be available or that it be run with administrator privileges. There are defaults, so it is not a requirement to set these options.

Scripting with the Job Cmdlets

The PowerShell job cmdlets are useful, but it can get pretty tedious having to type so many commands with all the various parameters. Well, this is PowerShell, right? So, why don't we make this easier for ourselves by using PowerShell scripts? The function in Listing 12-1 uses Out-GridView to display the job queue. The list includes both scheduled and unscheduled jobs. The user can select one or more jobs from the list and then take an action on the selected jobs, such as removing them.

Listing 12-1. A simple PowerShell job console

```
function Show-UdfJobConsole
{
[CmdletBinding()]
        param (
                [string]$jobnamefilter
            )
```

```
function ufn_ShowMessageBox
{
    [CmdletBinding()]
    param (
    [Parameter(Mandatory=$true,ValueFromPipeline=$false)]
    [string] $message,
    [Parameter(Mandatory=$true,ValueFromPipeline=$false)]
    [string] $title,
    [Parameter(Mandatory=$true,ValueFromPipeline=$false)]
    [ValidateRange(0,5)]
    [int] $type
    )

 RETURN [System.Windows.Forms.MessageBox]::Show($message , $title, $type)

}

  $actions = "Show Output", "Stop", "Remove", "Resume", "Clear History"

  while ($true)
  {
  $joblist = Get-Job -Name $jobnamefilter |
            Out-GridView -Title "PowerShell Job Console" -OutputMode Multiple

  if ($joblist.count -gt 0)
  {
      $selection = $actions | Out-GridView -Title "Select Action" -OutputMode Single
      foreach ($job in $joblist)
      {
          switch ($selection)
          {
            "Show Output"
            {
              $joboutput = Receive-Job -ID $job.ID -Keep -Verbose 4>&1
              If ($joboutput -eq $null)
              {
                  ufn_ShowMessageBox -message "No output to display" -title 'Error' -type 0
              }
              $joboutput |
              Out-GridView -Title 'Job Output - Close window to return to the job list' -Wait
            }
            "Cancel"
            {
              $job | Stop-Job
            }
```

```
        "Remove"
        {
            $job | Remove-Job
        }
        "Resume"
        {
            $job | Resume-Job
        }
      }
    }
  }
  else
  {
      Break;
  }
 }
}
```

The function in Listing 12-1 supports one parameter, which is a job name filter used to list jobs that match a given name pattern. A job filter of * will cause all jobs to display. The function contains a nested function, ufn_ShowMessageBox, which is just a wrapper to call the Windows message box method, i.e., [System.Windows.Forms.MessageBox]::Show(). It's a simple call, but is not easy to remember, so we just include it as a subfunction to be used as needed to display messages to the user. Then, the function stores a list of actions that can be taken on the jobs listed in the gridview. It stores this list as an array in the variable $actions. Then, an infinite loop starts, i.e., While ($true). The loop is exited via a break statement. Using the Get-Job cmdlet, the job list is piped into Out-GridView in order to display the list of jobs. Note the use of the OutputMode parameter with the value Multiple. This allows the user to select one or more rows from the grid. When the user clicks the OK button, the selected rows will be stored in the variable $joblist. Before we try to take any actions on the selected jobs, we check to make sure something was selected by testing if $joblist.count is greater than 0.

Now the function pipes the $action array into a gridview. The idea is to use the gridview as an action menu. Notice that the Out-GridView statement has the parameter OutputMode set to Single, which means the user can only select one item. A foreach loop iterates over the selected jobs to execute the selected action.

The rest of the function is pretty simple. A Switch statement is used to check the action selected and execute the related code. $job is the current job in the foreach iteration. One line deserves special attention: $joboutput = Receive-Job -ID $job.ID -Keep -Verbose 4>&1. Verbose messages cannot be captured by default, so they will not get displayed in the output view. By using redirection, we are capturing the verbose message stream, which is identified by Channel 4. Note: The function will let us try to perform actions that are not valid for the job status or type so as to keep the example simple. For example, we can attempt to cancel a completed job, but that would fail, and only workflows can be suspended.

Note: For more information about capturing different types of message streams, see the following link: https://technet.microsoft.com/en-us/library/hh847746.aspx. Now that we understand how the function works, let's try it with the statement that follows:

```
Show-UdfJobConsole *
```

The function Show-UdfJobConsole is called with an asterisk as the jobnamefilter parameter, which means all jobs will be displayed. At the time of writing this, on my machine, I get the gridview shown in Figure 12-5. You should see something similar if you have any job output. If there are no jobs, the script just ends.

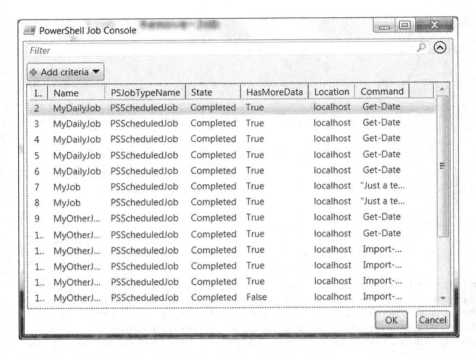

Figure 12-5. *Our custom PowerShell job console*

The point of this function is to show how easy it is to customize PowerShell to fit your needs. If something seems a bit awkward to use or difficult to remember, we can create custom functions to simplify it and increase our productivity. For the function in this example, we would probably want to create an alias to make it even easier to use, as shown here:

```
New-Alias spsj Show-UdfJobConsole
```

We are creating the alias spsj, which stands for *Show the PowerShell Job Console*. If we add this to our profile, it will automatically be created whenever we start a session.

Using PowerShell with SQL Server Agent

Although we can use the scheduled jobs features of PowerShell, SQL Server Agent offers a better solution. Since SQL Server Agent can run virtually anything—including SSIS packages (even from the SSIS Catalog), T-SQL code, PowerShell scripts, Analysis Services packages, and Command Exec scripts—it provides flexible integration of application components. Unlike the Task Scheduler, SQL Server Agent jobs can have multiple steps and be configured to send out job notifications when events such as a job failure occur. It also has many more security features than the Task Scheduler does. All these features are provided with a rich visual interface via SQL Server Management Studio.

As mentioned earlier, SQL Server Agent has built-in support to run PowerShell scripts. Let's walk through creating a simple SQL Agent job to execute a PowerShell script. First, start SQL Server Management Studio. Then, connect to the server on which you want to create the job, such as localhost. Expand the SQL Server Agent folder, right mouse click on the Jobs folder, and select New Job... as shown in Figure 12-6.

Figure 12-6. *Creating a job in SQL Agent*

After you select New Job..., you will see the New Job dialog box, with which you can create a new SQL Agent Job. Enter a name and a description for the job, as shown in Figure 12-7.

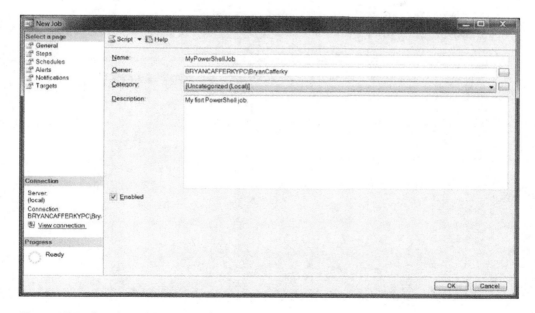

Figure 12-7. *Creating a SQL Agent job—general properties*

Then click on Steps in the Select a Page navigation panel on the left. This will bring up the Job Step listing, as shown in Figure 12-8.

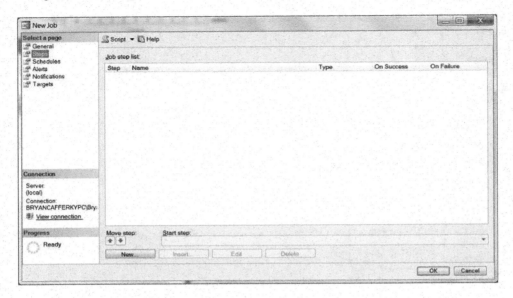

Figure 12-8. *Creating a SQL Agent job step*

On the Job Step screen, click on the New button to create a new job step, which will bring up the Job Step edit screen shown in Figure 12-9.

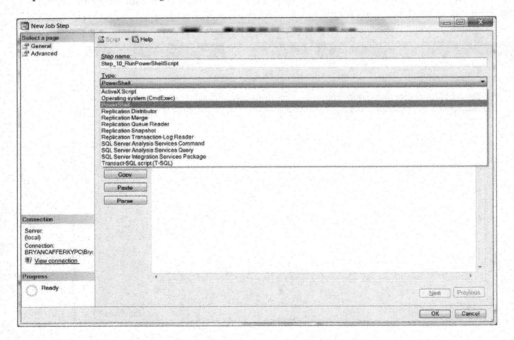

Figure 12-9. *Select PowerShell from the Type drop-down menu*

On the Job Step editor screen, enter a step name and select PowerShell from the Type drop-down list. Then, enter the PowerShell code in the text window, as shown in Figure 12-10.

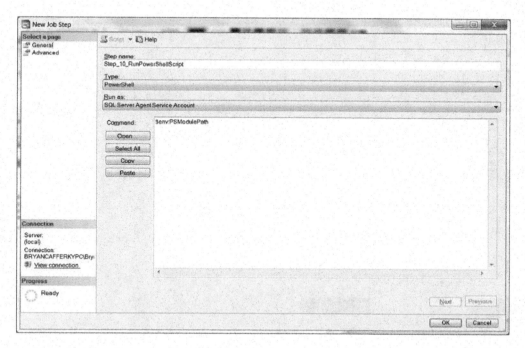

Figure 12-10. *Entering the PowerShell code*

Enter $env:PSModulePath in the text window, which will display the module-path environment variable (as defined) to the logon that is associated with the SQL Agent service. We need to know this in order to know where to place any modules we need to access from our SQL Server Agent jobs. Click on the OK button to save the job and then close the window. Now we can run the job, as shown in Figure 12-11.

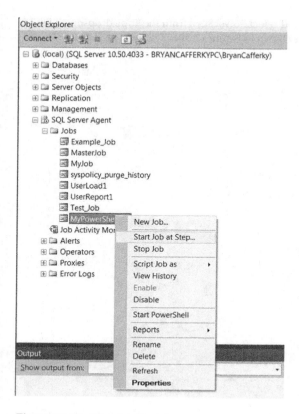

Figure 12-11. *Running the job*

To run the job, right mouse click on the job name and select Start Job. You should see the Start Jobs status window pop up, as shown in Figure 12-12. If there were multiple job steps, we would need to select the one we want to start execution from, but since there is only one step, it just runs the job.

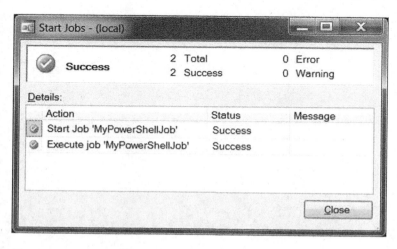

Figure 12-12. *The job-execution dialog box*

If SQL Agent is set up correctly, and the logon associated with the SQL Agent service has permissions to run PowerShell scripts, you should see the status *Success* displayed in the Status column next to the "Execute job 'MyPowerShellJob'" action, as shown in Figure 12-12. To see the job output, right mouse click on the job name and select View History, as shown in Figure 12-13.

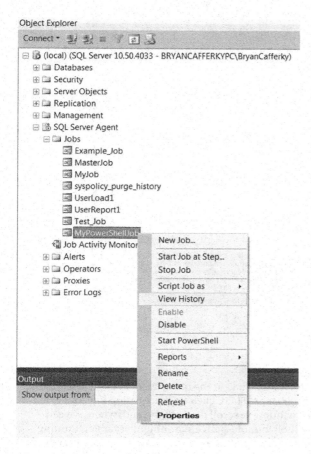

Figure 12-13. *View job history*

This will bring up the Log Viewer, where you can see job's messages, as shown in Figure 12-14.

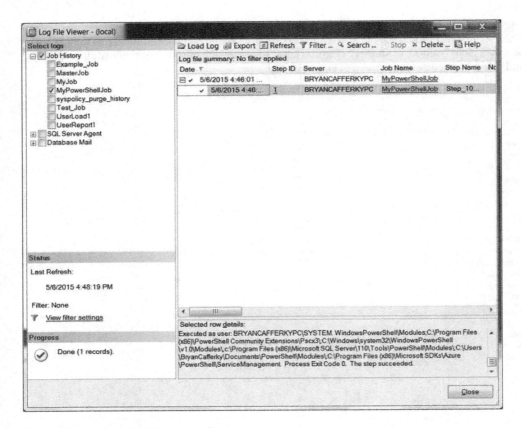

Figure 12-14. *View the job-step results*

In the Log File Summary window of the Log File Viewer, click on the plus sign next to the date in the Date column to expand the folder so we can see the job steps. Then, click on the job-step line and use the scroll bar in the text window at the bottom of the window to scroll down to the end, where we can see the output message—i.e., the value of the PowerShell module-path environment variable. Running PowerShell code from modules allows us to avoid hard coding paths to scripts or pasting code into the job-step text window. However, you need to place the modules in one of the folders displayed in the job output we just viewed.

If your SQL Server Agent is configured to use a proxy account, you will need to give permission to the account to run PowerShell scripts. To do that, expand the SQL Server Agent folder, expand Proxies folder, and right click on the PowerShell folder, as shown in Figure 12-15.

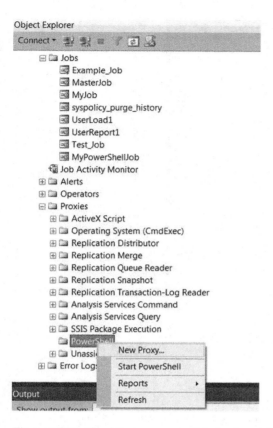

Figure 12-15. *Granting a proxy permission to run PowerShell scripts*

If you see any names listed under the PowerShell folder, these are proxies that have permission to run PowerShell, so you may be able to use one of these. If you do not see any existing proxies, select New Proxy, as shown in Figure 12-15, which will bring up the window to add a new proxy account, as shown in Figure 12-16.

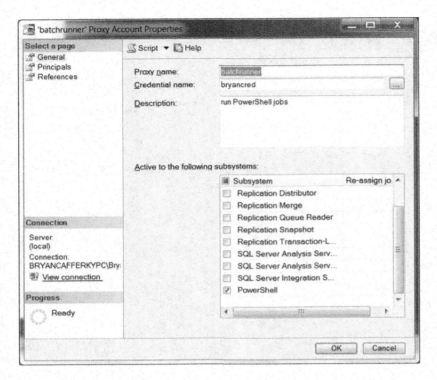

Figure 12-16. *Adding a proxy account to PowerShell*

Enter the proxy name, as shown in Figure 12-16. If you know the credential name that you want to grant PowerShell permissions to, enter that as well. The credential must already exist in order to assign it to the proxy. Use the scroll bars to scroll down to PowerShell in the list and check it so it will be added to the proxy permissions. Note: Other permissions the proxy has will be checked. You can grant additional permissions by checking the related checkboxes. If you don't know the credential name, you can click on the button next to the credential name text box to get some help, as shown in Figure 12-17.

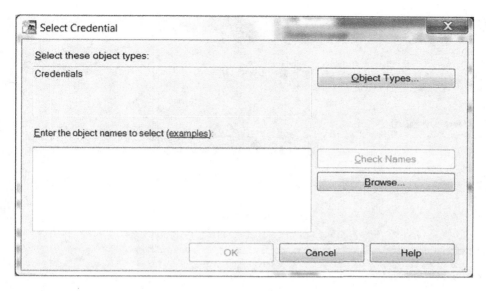

Figure 12-17. Creating SQL Server Agent proxy—selecting a credential

To get a list of credentials available, click the Browse button, which will bring up a list as shown in Figure 12-18.

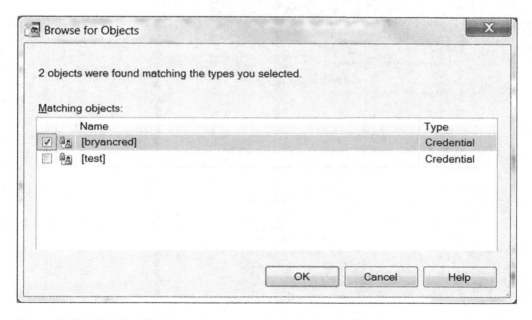

Figure 12-18. Creating SQL Server Agent proxy—browsing credentials

Select the credential from the list using the checkbox. Then, click OK; you will return to the Select Credential window with the selected credential in the text box, as shown in Figure 12-19.

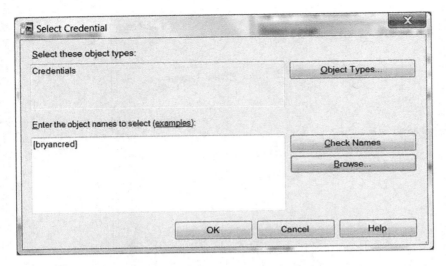

Figure 12-19. *Creating SQL Server Agent proxy—credential selected*

Now, just click the OK button to get back to the Proxy Properties window, with the credential field filled in with your selection, as shown in Figure 12-20.

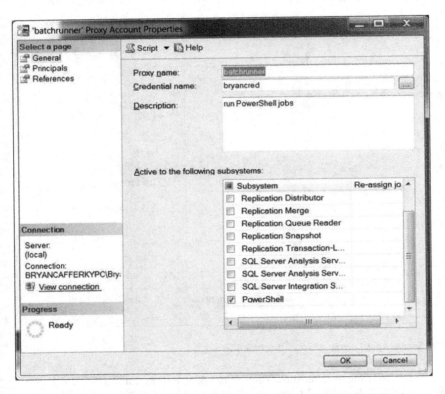

Figure 12-20. *Creating SQL Server Agent proxy—selecting the PowerShell subsystem*

Once SQL Server Agent is configured to run PowerShell code, you have an excellent job-scheduling platform with a rich visual interface—one that can work with SSIS packages, T-SQL code, Analysis Services packages, and Command Exec scripts, thereby providing the flexible integration of application components. The benefits of being able to create multi-step jobs cannot be overemphasized. Many database jobs become complex and require a long sequence of steps to complete them. The visual interface provided in SQL Server Management Studio not only provides easy job maintenance, but also the ability to view job history. As the topic of this book is focused on database development, I should emphasize that SQL Server Agent provides a high level of SQL Server integration.

Accessing SQL Server Agent Jobs from PowerShell

Throughout this book, there is an emphasis on the reach of PowerShell and how easily it can programmatically interface with Windows resources. So, it should come as no surprise that it is also easy to connect to SQL Server Agent and manipulate jobs. We could do this by directly accessing SQL Server Management Objects (SMO), but why not take advantage of the provider interface in the SQLPS module? Let's look at the function in Listing 12-2, which displays a list of SQL Server Agent jobs and will execute the jobs we select.

Listing 12-2. Invoking a SQL Agent job

```
function Invoke-UdfSQLAgentJob
{

[CmdletBinding()]
      param (
                 [string]$sqlserverpath,
                 [string]$jobfilter     = '*'
             )
 #  Import the SQL Server module
 if(-not(Get-Module -name "sqlps"))
 {
    Import-Module "sqlps" -DisableNameChecking
 }

 # Set where you are in SQL Server...
 set-location $sqlserverpath

 while ($true)
 {

  $jobname = $null

  $jobname = Get-ChildItem |
             Select-Object -Property Name, Description, LastRunDate, LastRunOutcome |
             Where-Object {$_.name -like "$jobfilter*"} |
             Out-GridView -Title "Select a Job to Run" -OutputMode Single

  If (!$jobname) { Break }
```

```
    $jobobject = Get-ChildItem | where-object {$_.name -eq $jobname.Name}

    $jobobject.start()

  }

}
```

Notice that the function in Listing 12-2 accepts two parameters: the location of the SQL Server Agent jobs in file-system format, i.e., provider format; and a job-name filter that is used to display only the jobs that match the $jobfilter name pattern. Since this function depends on the SQL Server provider, the first thing it does is load the SQLPS module if it is not already loaded. Then, it uses the Set-Location cmdlet to point to the SQL Agent Jobs folder on the specified SQL Server. From here, it starts an infinite loop that iterates over the job list and runs the selected job. The job name will be stored in the variable $jobname, so we initialize the variable to $null at the start of each iteration.

Now, we have a stack of commands. Get-ChildItem pipes a list of jobs to the Select-Object cmdlet, which extracts specific properties and passes them through the pipeline into the Where-Object cmdlet, which filters out job names that do not match the name pattern specified in $jobfilter. This is passed into Out-GridView, which displays the job properties and replaces the default window title with "Select a Job to Run." The parameter OutputMode Single means that only one selection will be allowed. The function will pause until the user either clicks Cancel or OK or hits Escape. At that point, if the OK button was pressed, the selected job is stored in $jobname. Then, Get-ChildItem is used to load the job object into $jobobject. Finally, the job is submitted using the object's Start method, and we go back to the top of the loop; i.e., we see the list of jobs again. If Cancel was clicked or the Escape key was pressed, the $jobname gets no value and the function exits via the Break statement. Let's try the function out:

```
Invoke-UdfSQLAgentJob -sqlserverpath 'SQLSERVER:\SQL\MyPC\DEFAULT\JobServer\Jobs\' `
                      -jobfilter 'User*'
```

We run the function, passing the SQL Server instance and a job filter of User*, meaning only jobs that start with the string User will be displayed. You will need to change the SQL Server instance to a server available in your environment. On my machine, I have two such jobs, so the Out-GridView displayed appears as shown in Figure 12-21.

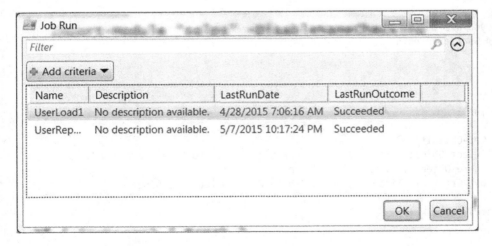

Figure 12-21. *The Out-GridView list of jobs displayed by function Invoke-UdfSQLAgentJob*

Using the gridview display shown in Figure 12-21, click on a job and click OK; the job will be executed. This type of function may come in handy when we are working with PowerShell interactively. However, the function name is not easy to remember or type. Let's make it easier by creating an alias for it, as shown here:

```
New-Alias ssaj Invoke-UdfSQLAgentJob  # ssaj stands for SQL Server Agent Jobs
```

Now, we can run the function just by entering `ssaj`, as shown:

```
ssaj -jobfilter 'User*'
```

Not only is this a lot shorter, but we can also still pass parameters, such as the job filter. Of course, we don't want to enter the `New-Alias` command to define this alias every time we start a session. Instead, we can add the new alias to our profile so it will always be available to us.

We can see how easy it is to interface with SQL Server Agent from PowerShell; not only can SQL Server Agent jobs execute PowerShell scripts, but PowerShell scripts can also execute SQL Server Agent jobs. Using the same techniques, we could even create, modify, or delete SQL Server Agent jobs.

Summary

This chapter explained PowerShell's unattended job-execution features. At its simplest, this is the ability to run a script as a background task. However, this requires that the PowerShell session that submitted the job remains active. PowerShell provides a number of cmdlets to support scheduling jobs. As we saw, these cmdlets are really an interface to the Windows Task Scheduler, and, once created, the jobs can be maintained there. We reviewed the cmdlets that support the three components of a scheduled job: the job definition, the trigger(s), and options. The job definition defines *what* we want executed. The triggers define *when* the job should be executed. The options define *how* the job should be executed. We wrapped up the section on job cmdlets by demonstrating how we can write PowerShell code to make it easier to work with PowerShell jobs. Then, we considered why SQL Server Agent is a better avenue for a job-scheduling solution because of its advanced features, SQL Server Integration, and visual interface. We discussed how to create a job that executes a PowerShell script using SQL Server Agent's built-in PowerShell integration. Then, we reviewed how easily we can manipulate SQL Server Agent jobs with PowerShell. If SQL Server Agent is so much better than PowerShell's job-scheduling features, you may be wondering why we even covered it in such detail. The answer is twofold. First, PowerShell's job-execution and scheduling features can be very useful for development. Second, PowerShell's remote execution and workflows leverage the batch-execution features, so we need to understand this before we can delve into remote execution and workflows in the next chapter.

■ ■ ■

## CHAPTER 13

PowerShell Workflows

In this chapter, we will discuss creating and executing workflows in PowerShell. Workflow Foundation is a .NET framework for defining complex processes that can span a long period of time, can be stopped and restarted where they left off, support the parallel execution of tasks, and can be packaged into reusable components. Until PowerShell 3.0, workflows could only be created in Visual Studio using C# or VB.Net. PowerShell 3.0 added support for the creation and execution of workflows. Since workflows can be executed either locally or on remote machines, we'll start by discussing PowerShell remote execution. Workflows are suspended and restarted using PowerShell job cmdlets, which were covered in the previous chapter. Here, we'll see how they apply to workflows. We will discuss using the commands parallel, foreach -parallel, sequence, and inlinescript to control workflow execution. Then, we will delve into using the cmdlets Checkpoint-Workflow, Suspend-Workflow, and Resume-Job to pause and resume workflow execution. Workflows can work on a single object at a time or on a collection. For example, John Doe applies for insurance coverage, and a series of steps occur until he is either insured or rejected. This pattern of usage is common to ASP.Net applications. A workflow could be used to load a series of external files into staging tables, validate the data, and, finally, load them into a data warehouse. We will cover two data-centric use cases for workflows. One is a typical data-warehouse load scenario. The other uses a workflow to speed up the extraction of data from flat files using parallel processing, similar to Hadoop.

PowerShell Remote Execution

PowerShell can execute commands on other computers either immediately or as a background job. It can even create new PowerShell sessions on other computers. If remoting is not enabled on the target machine, you must enable it. Then, you will be able to send commands to the machine across the network. You can enable remoting via a group policy or by logging into the machine and configuring it for remote execution. See the link that follows for information on handling this via a group policy:

http://www.grouppolicy.biz/2014/05/enable-winrm-via-group-policy/

Let's discuss manually setting up remote execution.

Configuring Remote Execution

To enable a single machine for PowerShell remoting, perform the following steps:

1. Log on to the target machine.

2. Start PowerShell as Administrator, i.e., right mouse click on the PowerShell program in Windows Accessories and select '*Run as Administrator*' as shown in Figure 13-1.

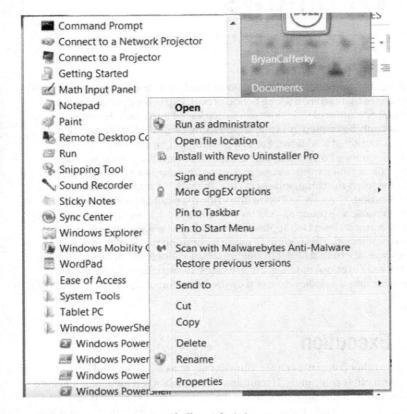

Figure 13-1. *Starting PowerShell as Administrator*

3. Enable remoting by entering the statement seen here:

```
Enable-PSRemoting -Force
```

4. The messages that follow will be seen if remoting is already enabled. Otherwise it will be enabled.

```
WinRM is already set up to receive requests on this computer.
WinRM is already set up for remote management on this computer
```

5. Test the connection by entering the statement that follows, replacing ComputerName with the name of the computer:

```
Test-WsMan ComputerName
```

Messages should be seen displayed to the console like the ones here:

```
wsmid           : http://schemas.dmtf.org/wbem/wsman/identity/1/wsmanidentity.xsd
ProtocolVersion : http://schemas.dmtf.org/wbem/wsman/1/wsman.xsd
ProductVendor   : Microsoft Corporation
ProductVersion  : OS: 0.0.0 SP: 0.0 Stack: 3.0
```

That's all there is to it. You can now execute PowerShell commands to the machine you just configured from other machines. Let's give it a try. From a different machine than the one you just configured, enter the statement that follows, replacing *ComputerName* with the computer you just configured and *UserName* with your network user name:

```
Invoke-Command -ComputerName ComputerName -ScriptBlock { Get-Process } -credential UserName
```

You should see the list of processes running on the remote machine displayed on your console. We'll review what Invoke-Command is in full detail a bit later. The point here was to get remoting set up.

Using Remote Execution with Invoke-Command

The cmdlet Invoke-Command executes a script file or script block either locally or on remote computers. Let's look at a simple example:

```
Invoke-Command –ScriptBlock { Get-Culture }
```

This statement just runs whatever code is in the script block, so the local culture setting should display. If we want to run the code on a remote machine, we can use the ComputerName parameter, as shown here:

```
Invoke-Command –ScriptBlock { Get-Process} –ComputerName machine1, machine2
```

This statement will get a list of running processes on machine1 and machine2. The code executes on those machines but sends the results back to the local session. The AsJob parameter, which can only be used with remote execution, submits the code as a background job, as shown next. The job will show in the local job queue, but will run on the remote machines.

```
Invoke-Command –ScriptBlock { Get-Process } –ComputerName machine1 –AsJob –JobName MyJob
```

The job information displays to the console, as shown here:

Id	Name	PSJobTypeName	State	HasMoreData	Location	Command
5	MyJob	RemoteJob	Running	True	machine1	Get-Culture

Notice the job name is MyJob, because we used the JobName parameter.

In these statements, PowerShell uses the credential of the current session to authenticate the permissions. However, we can use the Credential parameter to specify the user ID and password to be used for authentication, as shown here:

```
Invoke-Command –ScriptBlock { Get-Process } –ComputerName machine1 –Credential myuserid
```

In this statement, we are running the Get-Process cmdlet on machine1 using the logon myuserid. Using the credential parameter and passing just the user ID causes PowerShell to prompt you to enter the password. If we wanted to run this from within a scheduled job, we would need to include the password, which the Credential parameter does not support directly. We can include the password if we create a credential object first and pass that as the Credential parameter. However, storing clear-text passwords is not a best practice, so let's encrypt and store the password in a file from which we can retrieve it when needed. Recall that we have a function in the umd_database module to help us do this, which we can execute as shown here:

```
Import-Module umd_database
```

```
Save-UdfEncryptedCredential
```

When we run these statements, we are prompted to enter the password with the dialog box shown in Figure 13-2.

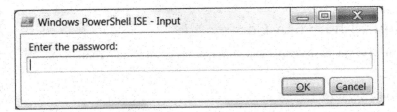

Figure 13-2. *Password prompt from function Save-UdfEncryptedCredentials*

We enter the password and click OK. Now, we are asked to specify where we want the file written, seen in the dialog box shown in Figure 13-3.

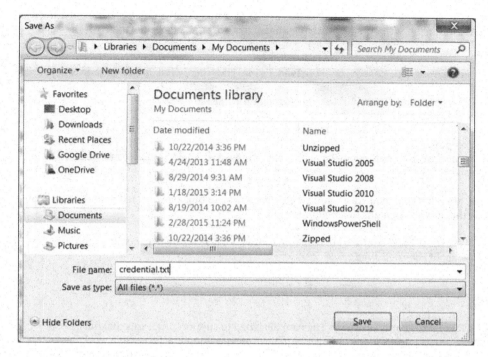

Figure 13-3. Encrypt credential Save As dialog box

Since the Save As dialog box defaults to the Documents folder of the current user, just enter the name of the file and click the Save button. In Figure 13-3, the file is being saved as credential.txt. To see the code for Save-UdfEncryptedCredentials with a full explanation, refer back to Chapter 7, "Accessing SQL Server," under the heading "Encrypting and Saving the Password to a File."

Now that we have the password saved to a file, let's try the Invoke-Command cmdlet using the Credential object, as shown in the code in Listing 13-1.

Listing 13-1. Using a Credential object

```
$password = Get-Content ($env:HOMEDRIVE + $env:HOMEPATH + "\Documents\credential.txt" ) |
        Convertto-Securestring -AsPlainText –Force

$credential = New-Object System.Management.Automation.PSCredential ("someuser", $password )

Invoke-Command -ScriptBlock { Get-Culture } -Credential $credential
```

The first line in Listing 13-1 loads the encrypted password, using Get-Content, from the file we created. The path with file name is dynamically created using the environment variables $env:HOMEDRIVE and $env:HOMEPATH concatenated with the string "\Documents\credential.txt". The result is piped into the Convertto-Securestring cmdlet, passing the parameters AsPlainText so it is a readable string and Force to tell PowerShell we accept the risk of outputting the string in plain text. Although there may be some risk to converting the string to text, because it is a securestring, we cannot see its contents. The credential object requires this type of format for a password. The second statement creates a .NET credential object with the user ID and password. The credential object is stored in variable $credential. Finally, the last line calls Invoke-Command, passing a scriptblock and the credential object we just created. Be aware that there is a limitation with Invoke-Command. It will not accept a credential object unless PowerShell remoting has been enabled, even when running the script on the local machine. If it is not enabled, we get the error message seen here:

```
Invoke-Command : Parameter set cannot be resolved using the specified named parameters.
At line:2 char:1
+ Invoke-Command -ScriptBlock { Get-Culture } -Credential $cred
+ ~~~~~~~~~~~~~~~~~~~~~~~~~~~~~~~~~~~~~~~~~~~~~~~~~~~~~~~~~~~~~~~~
    + CategoryInfo          : InvalidArgument: (:) [Invoke-Command],
ParameterBindingException
    + FullyQualifiedErrorId : AmbiguousParameterSet,Microsoft.PowerShell.Commands.
InvokeCommandCommand
```

Even though we are not trying to make a remote call, the credential object is rejected with the message just shown. The link that follows explains this in more detail:

https://connect.microsoft.com/PowerShell/feedback/details/676872/invoke-command-parameter-bug-parameter-set-cannot-be-resolved

Workflows

Workflows provide a lot of power and flexibility. They are designed to support processes that have a common starting point, go through a series of stages, and have an end point. Each step in a workflow is often associated with a status. For example, an insurance claim may start with the claim submission and a status of 'Initiated'. This is followed by an insurance representative assigning the claim to an adjuster and changing the status to 'Assigned'. The adjuster reviews the claim and approves or rejects it. If approved, an award amount is assigned and a check is issued to the insured. Whether approved or rejected, the insured is notified. At the end of the process the status of the claim is either 'Rejected' or 'Paid'.

Features of workflows that make them attractive to use in development include:

- Can run processes that span long periods of time, even if the machine is rebooted
- Can be stopped and started where they left off
- Can run tasks in parallel on the local machine or across multiple machines
- Can accept parameters
- Can be nested

PowerShell makes implementing workflows easy, but it can be confusing. The workflow keyword is used to define a workflow in a way similar to defining a function, but a workflow is actually quite different. This is because the cmdlets in a workflow are translated into the Workflow Foundation language before being submitted for processing. PowerShell is not running the code—the Workflow Foundation is. Consider the code in Listing 13-2, which creates and then executes a workflow called simple.

Listing 13-2. A simple workflow example

```
workflow simple ([string] $myparm)
{
    "Parameter is $myparm"

    Get-Date
```

```
   "Some activity"

   "Third activity"
}

simple "test"
```

We should see the following output:

```
Parameter is test

Sunday, May 17, 2015 4:03:07 PM
Some activity
Third activity
```

Judging from the code in Listing 13-2, it appears that replacing the word function with workflow is the only difference between writing a workflow versus a function. However, this is not true. In an effort to make it easy for PowerShell developers to migrate to workflows, Microsoft added a cmdlet translator to PowerShell that is invoked via the workflow keyword. Anything contained in the workflow code block is submitted to a translator, which converts the code into workflow code and submits it to the workflow engine to be processed. Let's try the code in Listing 13-3, which breaks the workflow engine, to see the limitations.

Listing 13-3. A simple workflow with a bug

```
workflow simplebroken ([string] $myparm)
{
   Write-Host "Parameter is $myparm"

   $object = New-Object PSObject

   $object | Add-Member -MemberType NoteProperty -Name MyProperty -Value 'something'

   $object.MyProperty
}

simplebroken 'test'
```

The code in Listing 13-3 does not work. In fact, we can't even get the workflow definition to be accepted without errors. The first problem is that Write-Host is not one of the cmdlets supported by the workflow translator, because workflows are not supposed to be interactive. Also, cmdlets that create and change objects—i.e., New-Object and Add-Member—are not supported by workflows. Just to prove the code is valid for a function, let's try the same code but change the workflow keyword to function, as shown in Listing 13-4.

Listing 13-4. A simple workflow with the bug fixed

```
function simplefunction ([string] $myparm)
{
   Write-Host "Parameter is $myparm"

   $object = New-Object PSObject
```

```
    $object | Add-Member -MemberType NoteProperty -Name MyProperty -Value 'something'

    $object.MyProperty

}

simplefunction 'test'
```

We should get the output seen here:

```
Parameter is test
Something
```

The point of Listing 13-4 is that we are limited to the cmdlets supported by the workflow translator. There *is* a way to get around these issues, and that is to use the `inlinescript` command, which will run a series of PowerShell statements together in one activity. Let's look at the code in Listing 13-5.

Listing 13-5. A simple workflow using inlinescript

```
workflow simpleinline ([string] $myparm)
{
  inlinescript
  {
    Write-Verbose "Parameter is $Using:myparm"

    $object = New-Object PSObject

    $object | Add-Member -MemberType NoteProperty -Name MyProperty -Value 'something'

    $object.MyProperty
  }
}

simpleinline 'test' –Verbose
```

Using the `inlinescript` command solved most of the problem. However, `Write-Host` is considered by PowerShell to be an interactive cmdlet, and workflows are supposed to be non-interactive processes. `Write-Verbose` is supported, though, so we use that instead. However, using `inlinescript` raised another issue. The code in the `inlinescript` block runs in separate memory from the workflow, so it cannot see the workflow parameter $myparm. By prefixing the variable with $using, as shown in Listing 13-5, the script can see the workflow parameter. We should get the output seen here:

```
VERBOSE: [localhost]:Parameter is test
Something
```

In addition to the workflow command `inlinescript`, three other workflow commands are supported in executing code, which are `parallel`, `sequence`, and `foreach –parallel`. Let's look at these now.

Parallel Execution

Parallel execution means that multiple processes run at the same time. To run activities in parallel, we use the Parallel command. Since each statement is a separate activity, each will run independent of each other simultaneously. Let's look at a simple example of this in Listing 13-6.

Listing 13-6. A workflow with parallel execution

```
workflow paralleltest {

parallel
{

for($i=1; $i -le 10000; $i++){ "a" }

for($i=1; $i -le 10000; $i++){ "b" }

for($i=1; $i -le 10000; $i++){ "c" }

for($i=1; $i -le 10000; $i++){ "d" }

for($i=1; $i -le 10000; $i++){ "e" }

}
}

paralleltest
```

A sample of the output is seen here:

```
e
a
b
d
c
e
a
b
```

In Listing 13-6, each for loop is run as a separate, parallel activity. Based on the output, we can see that the activities are running concurrently.

Recall that in Chapter 11, we developed a set of ETL scripts for Northwind. Since there are no dependencies among any of the files getting loaded, we could use a workflow to load them in parallel. Let's look at the code to do this in Listing 13-7. Note: As with cmdlet names, Microsoft recommends naming workflows using the verb-noun format, with the verb being from the approved list. The noun can be whatever the developer likes. We will use the noun prefix udw, which stands for user-defined workflow, so an example of a workflow name would be Invoke-UdwMyProcess. Remember, you need to change the configurable settings in the scripts that follow to what is available in your environment in order for the code to work.

Listing 13-7. Running the Northwind ETL as a workflow

```
Import-Module umd_northwind_etl -Force

Clear-Host

workflow Invoke-UdwNorthwindETL
{

 parallel

 {

    Invoke-UdfStateSalesTaxLoad

    Invoke-UdfOrderLoad

    Invoke-udfCustomerLoad

 }

}

Invoke-UdwNorthwindETL
```

When we run the code in Listing 13-7, we can see that the various SQL statements being executed for each load are scrambled in the console, indicating that they are running concurrently. Since these are small loads, using a workflow to load the files in parallel on the local machine actually takes longer than it would when running the loads sequentially without a workflow. Part of the reason for this is that there is some overhead created by PowerShell when it generates the workflow code to send to the workflow engine. Another reason is that we are using the same machine. If our goal is to improve performance, testing is required to determine if workflows help. To maximize performance, processes can be executed on different machines. In the case of the workflow in question, we could rewrite it to run each ETL process on a different computer. The code in Listing 13-8 does this.

Listing 13-8. Running the Northwind ETL as a workflow with parallel activities

```
Import-Module umd_northwind_etl

workflow Invoke-UdwNorthwindETL
{

 parallel

 {

    workflow Invoke-UdwStateSalesTaxLoad
    {
     Invoke-UdfStateSalesTaxLoad
    }
    Invoke-UdwStateSalesTaxLoad -PSComputerName remotepc1
```

```
workflow Invoke-UfwOrderLoad
{
  Invoke-UdfOrderLoad
}
Invoke-UfwOrderLoad   -PSComputerName remotepc2
}

}
```

Invoke-UdwNorthwindETL

By using the PSComputerName parameter when we execute a workflow, the workflow runs on the specified machine. In Listing 13-8, we define the state sales tax load and order load as sub workflows. Then we just call them, specifying the computer on which they should run. For this to work, remote execution must be set up on the target machines, as explained at the beginning of this chapter. In an ETL case like this, although we are spreading the work out, the target of all three ETL processes is the same SQL Server instance, so actual performance improvements may depend on the database server workload. Also, to actually run the code on other machines, we would need to copy the files and functions to those machines as well.

Sequence

To run activities in a specific order we use the Sequence command. This instructs the workflow engine to complete each activity before starting the next one. Let's look at a simple example of this in Listing 13-9.

Listing 13-9. A simple workflow using sequence

```
workflow Invoke-UdwSimpleSequence ([string] $myparm)
{
  sequence
  {
    "First"
    "Second"
    "Third"
  }
}
```

Invoke-UdwSimpleSequence

We should see the following output on the console:

```
First
Second
Third
```

In Listing 13-9, each activity will be executed and completed before the subsequent activity begins. In the code, we just write to the console. Note: For some reason, when we write to the console without explicitly stating the Write-Host cmdlet, it works.

Foreach –Parallel

Sometimes it is useful to start an activity by iterating over a collection. An example of this is shown in Listing 13-10.

Listing 13-10. A simple workflow using ForEach -Parallel

```
workflow Invoke-UdwForeachparallel
{

$collection = "one","two","three"

  foreach -parallel ($item in $collection)
  {
    "Length is: " + $item.Length
  }
}

Invoke-UdwForeachparallel
```

We should see the following output:

```
Length is: 5
Length is: 3
Length is: 3
```

In the workflow in Listing 13-10, the foreach -parallel command iterates over the array $collection. For each item in the array, an activity is executed in parallel. Interestingly, if we want to run activities across multiple computers, we don't need to use the foreach -parallel command. PowerShell automatically runs tasks in parallel on any computers passed via the workflow parameter PSComputerName. Let's look at the code that follows:

```
workflow Invoke-UdwRunRemote ($computerlist)
{
      Get-Process -PSComputerName $computerlist
}

Invoke-UdwRunRemote -computerlist ("remote1", "remote2")
```

In this workflow, we have the parameter defined as $computerlist, which is meant to receive a list of computer names. The cmdlet Get-Process uses the PSComputerName to run the cmdlet on the specified remote machines in parallel. Note: We could just as easily define an inlinescript containing complex tasks so as to run on each machine. The point here is that using workflows with remote parallel execution provides a powerful means to improve performance by scaling out.

Of course, the idea is to use these workflow commands together to meet our requirements. We can nest them or arrange them to fit our needs. Consider Listing 13-11, which uses all three code-execution commands.

Listing 13-11. Putting it all together; using all three workflow commands

```
workflow Invoke-UdwWorkflowCommand {

  sequence
  {
   "1"
   "2"
   "3"
  }

  parallel
  {

    for($i=1; $i -le 100; $i++){ "a" }

    for($i=1; $i -le 100; $i++){ "b" }

    for($i=1; $i -le 100; $i++){ "c" }

  }

  $collection = "one","two","three"

  foreach -parallel ($item in $collection)
  {
   "Length is: " + $item.Length
  }

}

Invoke-UdwWorkflowCommand
```

In Listing 13-11, a sequence command first runs three activities sequentially. Then, three for loops are executed in parallel. Finally, an array of three strings is created and used by a foreach –parallel command to run a separate activity for each array element. The ability to execute code in parallel or sequentially as needed provides good control and allows us to adapt as requirements change.

ETL Workflow

PowerShell workflows offer a lot of uses, but they also pose some challenges. In particular, the automated stopping and resuming of workflows requires special handling. When a workflow is submitted as a job, it runs in the background. If it suspends itself, the only way to restart it is to restart the job. Even if the workflow is submitted using foreground execution, suspending the workflow automatically creates a PowerShell job in the queue. To resume the workflow, we need to know which job to resume. This means we will need to store details about the suspended job.

Let's consider a potential use case. Northwind loads orders and employees to staging tables independent of each other. However, the data warehouse has an Order dimension that uses both order data and related sales employee data. Sometimes the employee data from the human resources system lags behind the arrival of related orders. We need to create a workflow that will load the order data, check the employee staging table for the related employee data, and only load the Order dimension after the employee data has been loaded. We will use file-system events to start and resume the workflow. The overall flow chart is shown in Figure 13-4.

- Order file created event starts the workflow.
- Load the Order file.
- Are all employees on orders on the Employee table?
- If yes, load the Order dimension.
- If no, notify business and suspend the workflow.
- Employee file created event restarts the workflow.
- Load Employees and load the Order dimension.

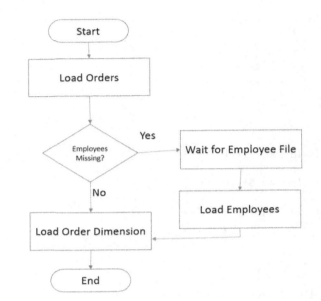

Figure 13-4. *Order load ETL workflow*

In Figure 13-4, we can see that the workflow starts when a file-created event for the Order file is fired. The workflow loads the Order file to a SQL Server staging table. Then, we match the Order rows to the staging Employees table. If there are no unmatched rows, the Order dimension is loaded. If there are orders with no matching employee, we need to suspend the workflow until the Employee file arrives, which we do by registering for a file-created event that waits for the employee data. When the employee data arrives, the event is fired that runs the code to resume the workflow. Note: When we suspend a workflow, we need to persist the data that contains the state of the workflow. This is done with the Checkpoint-Workflow command. Then, to suspend the workflow, we use the Suspend-Workflow command. To restart a workflow, we do not reference the workflow. When the workflow is suspended, a job is created and stored in the PowerShell job queue. To resume the workflow, we need to use the Resume-Job cmdlet.

The Workflow Code

This section has a lot of code, but fear not! We will walk through it step by step. As has been emphasized throughout this book, a good practice is to write encapsulated, reusable functions as much as possible. The code in this section does this extensively. This allows us to read the code at a high level and be able to grasp what it does. However, it also means we will delay covering the underlying functions a bit. The code is layered, so we need to review it by rolling the layers back, starting at the highest level. The functions in this section can be found in the module umd_workflow. You will need to modify configurable settings, such as the SQL Server instance name, to match your environment. The module umd_workflow contains all the code for all workflows that follow.

Let's look at the workflow code:

```
Import-module umd_northwind_etl
Import-Module umd_etl_functions

[psobject] $global:SqlServer1 = New-Object psobject
New-UdfConnection ([ref]$SqlServer1)

$global:SqlServer1.ConnectionType = 'ADO'
$global:SqlServer1.DatabaseType = 'SqlServer'
$global:SqlServer1.Server = '(local)'
$global:SqlServer1.DatabaseName = 'Development'
$global:SqlServer1.UseCredential = 'N'
$global:SqlServer1.SetAuthenticationType('Integrated')
$global:SqlServer1.BuildConnectionString()

Workflow Invoke-UdwOrderLoad
{
 param([string] $sourceidentifier, [string] $sqlserver, [string] $databasename )

 sequence
 {
    Write-Verbose $sourceidentifier
    Invoke-UdfOrderLoad

    $missing_emps = Get-UdfMissingEmployee | Where-Object -Property Employee_ID -ne $null

    if ($missing_emps.Count -gt 0)
    {
     Write-Verbose "Workflow Being Suspended."

    Send-UdfOrderLoadEmail -subject "ETL Job Order Load - Suspended"  '
    -body "The ETL Job: Order Load has been suspended because the employee
     file has not been loaded. Please send the employee file as soon
     as possible."

      Checkpoint-Workflow
      Suspend-Workflow
      Write-Verbose "Workflow Resumed."
      Invoke-UdfEmployeeLoad
      Send-UdfOrderLoadEmail -subject "ETL Job Order Load"  '
                            -body "The ETL Job: Order Load has ended."
}
 Else
 {
  Write-Verbose "finish"

  Invoke-UdfSQLQuery -sqlserver '(local)' -sqldatabase 'development' '
  -sqlquery "update [dbo].[WorkFlowLog] set Status = 'complete' '
  where WorkflowName = 'OrderLoad' and Status = 'suspended';"
```

```
    Send-UdfOrderLoadEmail -subject "ETL Job Order Load"  `
                            -body "The ETL Job: Order Load has ended."
  }
}
}
```

In this code, we start by importing the ETL modules needed, which we discussed in prior chapters, using the statements copied here:

```
Import-module umd_northwind_etl
Import-Module umd_etl_functions
```

Then, we need to create a connection object, which the code copied here does:

```
[psobject] $global:SqlServer1 = New-Object psobject
New-UdfConnection ([ref]$SqlServer1)

$global:SqlServer1.ConnectionType = 'ADO'
$global:SqlServer1.DatabaseType = 'SqlServer'
$global:SqlServer1.Server = '(local)'
$global:SqlServer1.DatabaseName = 'Development'
$global:SqlServer1.UseCredential = 'N'
$global:SqlServer1.SetAuthenticationType('Integrated')
$global:SqlServer1.BuildConnectionString()
```

In this code, we are using the New-UdfConnection function we created in Chapter 7. To do this, the first line creates an empty PSObject variable. This is passed into the New-UdfConnection function, which attaches the methods and function we'll need in order to connect to a data source. The lines after this just assign the SQL Server database connection properties and finally call the BuildConnectionString method so as to generate the connection string. Notice that we are using the $global prefix, which defines the variable scope as global so that all code in the session can access it. We are assigning these values directly to make the code simpler to read, but in practice, we would want to use the configuration approach discussed in Chapter 10 to define these values.

Then, we start the workflow definition as shown here:

```
Workflow Invoke-UfwOrderLoad
{
 param([string] $sourceidentifier, [string] $sqlserver, [string] $databasename )
```

In the workflow definition we can see three parameters. $sourceidentifier is going to be obtained from the code that gets fired by the create file event, which we will discuss later. $sqlserver is the SQL Server instance, and $databasename is the database name. Now, let's look at the first few lines of the workflow, copied here:

```
Sequence
{
Write-Verbose $sourceidentifier
Invoke-UdfOrderLoad
```

The first line tells the workflow engine to sequentially run the activities defined in the braces. Due to the dependencies, the statements must be executed in order. The Write-Verbose statement simply displays the parameter $sourceidentifier. Recall that Write-Host is not supported, so we use Write-Verbose instead. Then the function Invoke-UdfOrderLoad is called. We saw this function in Chapter 11. It will load the orders file into the SQL Server table dbo.Orders. It displays a lot of Write-Verbose messages that show the SQL statements used to load the data.

The line copied here will test whether there are any orders without a matching employee:

```
$missing_emps = Get-UdfMissingEmployee | Where-Object -Property Employee_ID -ne $null
```

The function Get-UdfMissingEmployee will return a record set of any orders with no matching employee row. We will look at the function in detail later. The function results are piped into the Where-Object cmdlet. The function Get-UdfMissingEmployee displays some informational messages that get returned in the pipe, so we use the Where-Object cmdlet to filter the pipe down to the missing employee result set. By filtering on Employee_ID, only pipe rows with that property are returned. Now, let's look at the code that will suspend the workflow if necessary:

```
if ($missing_emps.Count -gt 0)
{
    Write-Verbose "Workflow Being Suspended."

    Send-UdfOrderLoadEmail -subject "ETL Job Order Load - Suspended" '
    -body "The ETL Job: Order Load has been suspended because the employee
     file has not been loaded. Please send the employee file as soon as possible."

    Checkpoint-Workflow
    Suspend-Workflow
    Write-Verbose "Workflow Resumed."
    Invoke-UdfEmployeeLoad
    Send-UdfOrderLoadEmail -subject "ETL Job Order Load" '
                           -body "The ETL Job: Order Load has ended."
}
```

In this code, the first line tests whether there are any missing employee rows. To be honest, I did not think the workflow engine would let me retain an object from one activity to the next like $missing_emps, but for some reason it did. The interaction between PowerShell and the workflow engine can be a bit mysterious. I am guessing this is because Microsoft tried to make the PowerShell interface to workflows work as expected wherever possible. The best way to find out if something will work is to try it. So in this case, if there are missing employees, i.e., if $missing_emps.Count is greater than zero, a message that the workflow is being suspended is displayed, an email is sent notifying an interested party, the workflow state is saved using the Checkpoint-Workflow statement, and the workflow is suspended with the Suspend-Workflow statement. The statements after that are not executed. Rather, the workflow is created as a job in suspended state. The statements after that will not be executed until the job is resumed with the Resume-Job cmdlet. When that happens, the workflow will resume at the line Write-Verbose "Workflow Resumed."

That's all there is to the workflow. The challenge is knowing which job to resume when the Employee file comes in. Let's look at the code that calls the workflow.

Calling the Workflow

The workflow is surprisingly simple. There's just one problem—when the workflow suspends itself, how do we know which job to resume? The same workflow can be submitted more than once, and the workflow engine tracks the instances separately. However, these instances are not readily visible to PowerShell. Instead, we need to capture the job information when the job is suspended. If we run the workflow in the foreground, there is no way to capture the job information when the workflow suspends itself. The Suspend-Workflow statement does not send anything to the pipeline. Instead, we'll submit the workflow as a job at the beginning and capture the job information, as shown in the following code:

```
function Invoke-UdfWorkflow ()
{
<#  Define the mapping... #>
   $mappingset = @()  # Create a collection object.
   $mappingset += (Add-UdfMapping "WorkflowName" "WorkflowName" "'" $false)
   $mappingset += (Add-UdfMapping "ID" "JobID" "" $false)
   $mappingset += (Add-UdfMapping "Name" "JobName" "'" $false)
   $mappingset += (Add-UdfMapping "Location" "Location" "'" $false)
   $mappingset += (Add-UdfMapping "Command" "Command" "'" $false)


   Try
     {
      Invoke-UfwOrderLoad   -sourceidentifier 'Order' -sqlserver $global:SqlServer1.Server '
                            -databasename $global:SqlServer1.Databasename '
                            -AsJob -JobName OrderLoad | Invoke-UdfWorkflowLogTransformation |
                            Select-Object -Property WorkflowName, ID, Name, Location, Command |
                            Invoke-UdfSQLDML -Mapping $mappingset  -DmlOperation "Insert" '
                            -Destinationtablename "dbo.WorkFlowLog" '
                            -Connection $global:SqlServer1 -Verbose
     }
    Catch
     {
     "Error:  $error"
     }
}
```

The first set of lines creates a mapping set. In Chapter 11, we defined an ETL framework that included the use of mapping sets. This will be used to write the workflow job information to a SQL Server table. We are mapping the workflow name, the job ID, the job name, the job location (i.e., the machine), and the Workflow command (i.e., code). Then a Try block is executed. At first glance, it may look like there are multiple statements in the Try block, but notice the tick mark at the end of each line. Recall that the ' character continues a statement onto the next line. So, the code in the Try block is one long statement. This is because we need to keep the pipeline all the way through a number of cmdlets and functions.

The first statement is running the workflow Invoke-UfwOrderLoad, passing the values 'Order' as sourceidentifier, the global object property $global:SqlServer1.Server as sqlserver, and the global object property $global:SqlServer1.Databasename as databasename. The AsJob parameter tells PowerShell to run the workflow as a background job, and the JobName assigns the name OrderLoad to the job. Since this is our only chance to capture the job information, we pipe the output into a custom function Invoke-UdfWorkflowLogTransformation, which transforms the pipeline as needed to write it to the SQL Server table. This is piped into the Select-Object cmdlet, which extracts just the properties we need and pipes them into the custom function Invoke-UdfSQLDML. This writes the pipeline to the SQL Server table dbo.WorkFlowLog. Recall that in Chapter 11, we used Invoke-UdfSQLDML to write pipeline data to a SQL Server destination. We are leveraging our previously created functions for ETL so as to capture the workflow job information. If this chain of statements encounters a terminating error, the Catch block is executed.

In this example, we see the function Invoke-UdfWorkflowLogTransformation being called. The function just adds a single, hard-coded property to the pipeline, i.e., OrderLoad, which is the name for the workflow we want stored in the SQL Server table. Let's look at the code now:

```
function  Invoke-UdfWorkflowLogTransformation
{
 [CmdletBinding()]
      param (
                  [Parameter(ValueFromPipeline=$True)]$pipein = "default"
                )
    process
    {

      $pipein | Add-Member -MemberType NoteProperty -Name "WorkflowName"     '
                          -Value "OrderLoad"
      Return $pipein
    }
}
```

As we've seen previously, this function defines the pipeline as a parameter named $pipein with the parameter attribute ValueFromPipeline=$True. Then, we just add a property to it using the Add-Member cmdlet. The Return statement returns the pipeline variable to the caller. Note: Do not use the Passthru parameter with the Add-Member cmdlet or you will get duplicate pipelines.

Starting the workflow is easy. Restarting it is a bit more challenging. However, since we have a log that stored the job details of the job that started the workflow, we can use that to resume the job. Let's look at the code that does this:

```
function Resume-UdfWorkflow ()
{
    Try
    {
      $job = Invoke-UdfSQLQuery -sqlserver $global:SqlServer1.Server '
            -sqldatabase 'development' '
            -sqlquery "select JobID from [dbo].[WorkFlowLog] where WorkflowName = 'OrderLoad'
             and Status = 'suspended';" '

      Resume-Job -id $job.JobID -Wait

      Invoke-UdfSQLQuery -sqlserver $global:SqlServer1.Server '
                      -sqldatabase$global:SqlServer1.DatabaseName '
        -sqlquery "update [dbo].[WorkFlowLog] set Status = 'complete' where WorkflowName =
         'OrderLoad' and Status = 'suspended';" '

    }
    Catch
    {
      "Error:  $error"
    }
}
```

In this function, the first statement in the Try block calls the function `Invoke-UdfSQLQuery` to execute a SQL query that will retrieve the job information of the suspended job. The results are stored in `$job`. We'll look at the code for that function a bit later. We use the `JobID` property of `$job` to resume the workflow, i.e., `Resume-Job -id $job.JobID -Wait`. The `Wait` parameter tells PowerShell to stop and wait for the job to finish before proceeding to the next line. After this, we call `Invoke-UdfSQLQuery` to update the status of the row in the workflow log table with a status of `'complete'`.

We've seen the code that starts the workflow, and we've seen the code that resumes the workflow. But how will these be called? We want it to be completely automated, so we'll use the .NET `FileSystemWatcher` to trap when the Order file is created in the expected folder. When this happens, the workflow will be started. We'll use another `FileSystemWatcher` to trap when an Employee file is created in the expected folder in order to resume the workflow.

Let's look at the function to register a trap to the order file-create event:

```
function Register-UdfOrderFileCreateEvent(
[string] $source, [string] $filter, [string]$sourceidentifier)
{
    try
    {
      $filesystemwatcher = New-Object IO.FileSystemWatcher $source, $filter -Property
      @{IncludeSubdirectories = $false; NotifyFilter = [IO.NotifyFilters]'FileName, LastWrite'}
      Register-ObjectEvent $filesystemwatcher Created -SourceIdentifier $sourceidentifier '
                     -Action { Invoke-UdfWorkflow }

    }
    catch
    {
       "Error registering file create event."
    }
}
```

The function takes the parameters `$source`, which is the path to the folder we want to monitor, `$filter`, which is the file-name filter to watch for, and `$sourceidentifier`, which is just a name for the event. The first line in the `try` block creates an instance of the `FileSystemWatcher`, with `$source` as the folder to watch and `$filter`, along with the file name to watch for. The statement after this registers the event, which means it assigns an action to be taken when the event fires. The `Action` parameter specifies the function `Invoke-UdfWorkflow` to start the workflow. What this all means is that when an `Order` file is created in the target folder, the function `Invoke-UdfWorkflow` will execute.

The function to register an event trap for the employee file creation is as follows:

```
function Register-UdfEmployeeFileCreateEvent([string] $source, [string] $filter,
$sourceidentifier)
{
    try
    {
      $filesystemwatcher = New-Object IO.FileSystemWatcher $source, $filter -Property
      @{IncludeSubdirectories = $false; NotifyFilter = [IO.NotifyFilters]'FileName, LastWrite'}

      Register-ObjectEvent $filesystemwatcher Created -SourceIdentifier $sourceidentifier '
                     -Action { Resume-UdfWorkflow }

    }
```

```
catch
{
  "Error registring file create event."
}
}
```

This function takes the parameters $source, which is the path to the folder we want to monitor, $filter, which is the file-name filter to watch for, and $sourceidentifier, which is just a name for the event. One thing to bear in mind about using the File System Watcher to trap events is that the event registration is lost when the PowerShell session ends. The first line in the try block creates an instance of the FileSystemWatcher, with $source as the folder to watch and $filter, along with the file name to watch for. The statement after this registers the event, which means it assigns the action to be taken when the event fires. The Action parameter specifies the function Resume-UdfWorkflow, which will resume the job with the suspended workflow. If the code in the try block fails, the catch block will display the error message.

Register the Events

Using the functions just reviewed, we register to trap the file-creation events with the code in Listing 13-12.

Listing 13-12. Register the file-create events

```
Import-Module umd_workflow

$global:rootfilepath = $env:HOMEDRIVE + $env:HOMEPATH + '\documents\'

Register-UdfOrderFileCreateEvent $global:rootfilepath "Orders.xml"  -sourceidentifier 'orders'

Register-UdfEmployeeFileCreateEvent $global:rootfilepath "Employees.txt" '
                          -sourceidentifier 'employees'
```

The first statement in Listing 13-12 defines the path where the files will be created as a global variable named $global:rootfilepath. This will be the Documents folder for the current user. Then, the event trap is registered for the creation of the orders.xml file. This is followed by the event-trap registration for the Employee file.

Once the code in Listing 13-12 is executed, the function Invoke-UdfWorkflow will start when the Orders.xml file is created in the user's Documents folder. This starts the workflow, and if the Employee file has not already been loaded, i.e., if there are orders with employee IDs that are not on the Employees table, the workflow will suspend itself. When the Employees.txt file is created in the Documents folder, the function Resume-UdfWorkflow will be called, which looks up the job ID of the suspended workflow and resumes it right after the point where the workflow was suspended.

Sending Mail

It's often useful to send email notifications to relevant employees telling them when jobs have started, finished, or failed. The function that follows is used to send an email as needed during the order-load process:

```
function Send-UdfOrderLoadEmail ([string]$subject, [string]$body)
{
    $credin = Get-Content ($global:rootfilepath + 'bryan256') | convertto-securestring
    $credential = New-Object System.Management.Automation.PSCredential '
                ("bryan@msn.com",  $credin)
```

395

```
    Send-MailMessage -smtpServer smtp.live.com -Credential $credential '
    -from 'bryan@msn.com'  -to 'bryan@msn.com' -subject "$subject" '
    -Body "$body" -Usessl -Port 587
}
```

The first line in the function's body retrieves a previously encrypted password from a file. The line after this uses the retrieved password with the email account to create a credential object. Then, the Send-MailMessage cmdlet is executed with parameters for the SMTP server, the credential object, the from email address, the to email address, the subject, and body text. The Usessl parameter secures the email, and Port specifies what port address is to be used.

Workflow Creation Steps

When we put all the previous code together, we have a complete workflow to support the order load. The workflow steps for creating a new order are as follows:

Workflow Start: An Order file arrives in the Documents folder.

1. The FileSystemWatcher Created File event fires, executing the workflow Invoke-UdwOrderLoad.

2. Invoke-UdwOrderLoad loads the Orders file into the SQL Server Orders table.

3. The workflow runs a query to find any employees on the orders that are missing on the Employees table.

4. If there are any missing employees:

    •   The workflow is suspended.

    •   Send email notification.

5. If there are no missing employees:

    •   Load the table DimOrderEmployee.

    •   Send email notification.

Workflow Resumes: An employee file arrives in the Documents folder.

1. Load the file into the Employees table.

2. Load the table DimOrderEmployee.

3. Send email notification.

In the module, the Send Email steps are commented out because they will fail until you enter valid configuration and credentials for them. Once you have done this, just remove the comment tags. Assuming you have all the modules loaded and the file-creation events have been registered, you can test the workflow. Copy the Orders.xml to your Documents folder, which should fire the workflow to load it. Then, copy Employees.txt to your Documents folder, which should resume the workflow loading the Employee file and the DimOrderEmployee dimension table.

A Poor Man's Hadoop

When I first studied the capabilities of workflows, it occurred to me that they provide much of the functionality that the open source, big-data tool, Hadoop, provides. I thought it would be interesting to see if we could create a Hadoop-like function using PowerShell workflows. Hadoop's most impressive feature is the speed at which it can extract data from large files. Hadoop does this by splitting up the work among multiple machines, called nodes. The data is duplicated across the nodes by something called the Hadoop File System. If we had a number of large files that we needed to extract data from, we could copy one or more files to a number of machines and use remote workflows to have the files processed in parallel, just like Hadoop does. Best of all, it is a lot less work to set up, and everything can be done in PowerShell. The functions in this section can be found in the module umd_workflow. You will need to modify configurable settings like email smtp server name to match your environment.

Setting Up the Poor Man's Hadoop Workflow

Imagine we have a number of large text files, such as web logs. We want to search for rows that have a specified string and extract them to another file, which we could load into SQL Server for querying. We will have a workflow run that executes each search for each file in parallel. To try this out, we need some text files to work with. Let's use the code in Listing 13-13 to generate these files.

Listing 13-13. Script to generate test data

```
$filepath = $env:HOMEDRIVE + $env:HOMEPATH + "\Documents\"

function New-UdfFile ([string]$fullfilepath)
{
  for ($i=1; $i -le 1000; $i++)
  {
    Get-ChildItem | Out-File ($fullfilepath) -Append
  }
}
```

The function in Listing 13-13 takes the full path with file name as the parameter $fullfilepath. To generate data, a for loop iteratively calls Get-ChildItem to get a file list, which is piped into Out-File, where it is written to the filepath parameter. Now, let's call the function twice to create two files to test with, as shown here:

```
New-UdfFile ($filepath + "logfile1.txt")
New-UdfFile ($filepath + "logfile2.txt")
```

These function calls are to run the function New-UdfFile so as to create some test files for us. The first call will create a file named logfile1.txt and the second call will create a file called logfile2.txt. Admittedly, these files are not real log files, but they generate text files well enough to test our search workflow.

To run multiple searches in parallel, we need to use a workflow. The workflow that follows will call our function to search the files:

```
workflow Search-UdwFile ([string]$filepath, $filelist, $searchstring)
{
    foreach -parallel ($file in $filelist)
    {
      Write-Verbose 'Processing searches...'
```

```
  inlinescript
    {
      function Search-UdfSingleFile ([string]$searchstring,[string] $outfilepath)
        {
          begin
          {
            "" > $outfilepath  # Clear out file contents
          }
          process
          {
            if ($_ -like "*$searchstring*")
            {
             $_ >> $outfilepath
            }
          }
        }

      $sourcefile = $using:filepath + $using:file ;
      $outfile = $using:filepath + "out_" + $using:file ;
      Get-Content $sourcefile  |
      Search-UdfSingleFile -searchstring  $using:searchstring -outfilepath $outfile
    }
  }
}
```

The workflow keyword tells PowerShell that what follows is a workflow, which means everything will be translated into workflow code and submitted to the workflow engine. Three parameters are supported: $filepath, which is the folder where the files are stored, $filelist, which is an array of file names to be searched, and $searchstring, which is the string to be searched for. We want to run a separate process for each file in the list, i.e., run them in parallel. Therefore, we see the foreach –parallel command, which will spawn a separate activity for each file. Write-Verbose is just there to confirm the workflow is running.

To perform the search, we need to use a lot of PowerShell code not supported by workflows. Therefore, we use the workflow command inlinescript to submit code as an activity. The workflow process is separate from the regular PowerShell process, so we include the search function definition within the inline script. Note: We could also import the function if it were in a module. To maximize speed and minimize memory requirements, the function takes the source file as pipeline input, i.e., we will pipe the source file into the function.

The function takes two parameters: $searchstring, which is the string we want to look for, and $outfilepath, which is the path and file name where the matching rows will be written to. Recall that a begin block will execute once, before the pipeline starts to be received. We are clearing out the output file here by piping a zero-length string to the file. The character > means to overwrite the file. The process block will execute for every row in the pipeline. Notice we did not declare the pipeline as a parameter. We don't need to declare the pipeline, but if it is not declared as a parameter, we need to use the system default name, $_, to access each iteration. The statement "if ($_ -like "*$searchstring*")" will test every row as it comes in for a string matching the $searchstring parameter. If a match is found, the row is appended to the output file specified in the $outfilepath parameter. Recall that >> means to append to the file. Note: When we want to search a string for a character pattern, we use the like operator. If we want to search an array to see if it contains something, we use the contains operator.

After the function definition, the script builds the path to the source file using the workflow parameters. For the inlinescript to access the workflow parameters, we need to prefix the parameters with $using. This is because the inlinescript runs in a separate process. Then, the output file path is stored in $outfile. Finally Get-Content is called to pipe the contents of the source file into the Search-UdfSingleFile function. The result file where matches are written is the input file name, prefixed with out_.

Calling the Poor Man's Hadoop Workflow

We've discussed the workflow code and embedded search function. Now, let's review the code in Listing 13-14 that will call the workflow.

Listing 13-14. Calling the workflow

```
Import-Module umd_workflow  # To get the functions we will use  below

$filelist = "logcombined.txt", "logcombined2.txt", "logcombined3.txt", "logcombined4.txt"

Clear-Host  # Just to clear the console.

$starttime = Get-Date
Search-UdwFile -filepath $filepath -filelist $filelist -searchstring "*txt*"
$endtime = get-date
"Execution time: " + ($endtime - $starttime)
```

The first line in Listing 13-14 assigns the list of file names to search to $filelist—this is a string array. Then, Clear-Host clears the console so we can see the output more easily. Since the idea behind using a workflow is to improve performance, there is code to store the start time and end time and then calculate the duration of the run. The cmdlet Get-Date returns the current date/time. So, we are storing the start time before running the workflow. Then, the workflow is called, passing the path to where the files are stored as $filepath, the list of files to be searched as $filelist, and the string to search for as *txt*. Running parallel processes on a single machine may hit a performance limit at some point. Workflows can be executed remotely; i.e., we can submit them to multiple machines to execute in parallel. To run multiple instances of the file-search workflow, we just need to modify the execution code, as shown in Listing 13-15.

Listing 13-15. Calling the workflow to run remotely

```
Import-Module umd_workflow  # To get the functions we will use below

$filelist1 = "logcombined.txt", "logcombined2.txt"
$filelist2 = "logcombined3.txt", "logcombined4.txt"

Search-UdfFile -filepath $filepath -filelist $filelist1 -searchstring "*txt*" '
            -PSComputerName remote1 –AsJob –JobName 'remote1search'

Search-UdfFile -filepath $filepath -filelist $filelist2 -searchstring "*txt*" '
            -PSComputerName remote2 –AsJob –JobName 'remote2search'
```

In order for us to search files on other machines, we need to copy the files we want searched to the remote machines. Once that is done, we can just run the code, and it will submit the workflows to machines remote1 and remote2 to be executed in a background job. Note the special line-continuation character, `, which allows a statement to span multiple lines. The workflow Search-UdfFile is executed, passing the path to the source files as $filepath and the list of files to be searched as $filelist1 in the first execution and $filelist2 in the second. The $searchstring parameter defines the character string to search for. PSComputerName is the workflow parameter that tells PowerShell where to run the workflow. AsJob makes the workflow run as a background job on the remote machine, and JobName names the job. Although the job runs remotely, the local job queue tracks it for us just like a local job.

Summary

In this chapter, we discussed creating and executing PowerShell workflows. Workflows can support complex processes that can span a long period of time, can be stopped and restarted while retaining state, can support parallel execution, and can be packaged into reusable components. PowerShell 3.0 introduced support for creating workflows, which previously could only be created in Visual Studio using C# or VB .NET. We discussed how workflows can be executed either locally or on remote machines. We discussed using the workflow commands `parallel`, `foreach –parallel`, `sequence`, and `inlinescript` to control workflow execution. Then, we covered using the cmdlets `Checkpoint-Workflow`, `Suspend-Workflow`, and `Resume-Job` to pause and resume workflow execution. Workflows can work on a single object at a time or on a collection. In database development, we tend to work with sets of data. We covered two data-centric examples of using workflows. One was in a typical data-warehouse load scenario. The other was using a workflow to speed up the extraction of data from flat files using parallel processing, similar to Hadoop. Workflows should be reserved for solutions that require their capabilities. Often, simpler approaches can be used. However, when you need them, workflows offer amazing power.

Index

Get the eBook for only $5!

Why limit yourself?

Now you can take the weightless companion with you wherever you go and access your content on your PC, phone, tablet, or reader.

Since you've purchased this print book, we're happy to offer you the eBook in all 3 formats for just $5.

Convenient and fully searchable, the PDF version enables you to easily find and copy code—or perform examples by quickly toggling between instructions and applications. The MOBI format is ideal for your Kindle, while the ePUB can be utilized on a variety of mobile devices.

To learn more, go to www.apress.com/companion or contact support@apress.com.

CPSIA information can be obtained at www.ICGtesting.com
Printed in the USA
LVOW03s2235151015

458426LV00004BA/82/P